THE "BELLY-MYTHER" OF ENDOR

Society of Biblical Literature

Writings from the Greco-Roman World

John T. Fitzgerald, General Editor

Editorial Board

Number 16

THE "BELLY-MYTHER" OF ENDOR
Interpretations of 1 Kingdoms 28 in the Early Church

Volume Editor
Abraham J. Malherbe

The "Belly-Myther" of Endor

Interpretations of 1 Kingdoms 28 in the Early Church

Translated with an Introduction and Notes by

Rowan A. Greer

and

Margaret M. Mitchell

Society of Biblical Literature
Atlanta

THE "BELLY-MYTHER" OF ENDOR
Interpretations of 1 Kingdoms 28 in the Early Church

Library of Congress Cataloging-in-Publication Data

The "Belly-Myther" of Endor : interpretations of 1 Kingdoms 28 in the early church / translated with an introduction and notes by Rowan A. Greer and Margaret M. Mitchell.
          p. cm. — (Society of Biblical Literature writings from the Greco-Roman world ; v. 16)
Includes bibliographical references and index.
ISBN-13: 978-1-58983-120-9 (pbk. : alk. paper)
ISBN-10: 1-58983-120-9 (pbk. : alk. paper)
   1. Bible. O.T. Samuel, 1st, XXVIII–Criticism, interpretation, etc.
   2. Bible. O.T. Samuel, 1st, XXVIII–Criticism, interpretation, etc.–History–Early church, ca. 30-600. I. Greer, Rowan A. II. Mitchell, Margaret Mary, 1956-.

BS1325.52.B45 2006
222'.4306–dc22
                                            2006029289

---

07 08 09 10 11 12 13 14 — 5 4 3 2 1

Printed in the United States of America on acid-free, recycled paper conforming to ANSI/NISO Z39.48-1992 (R1997) and ISO 9706:1994 standards for paper permanence.

Table of Contents

Preface

Wretch that I am! Of my own ruin author!
Where are my old supports? The valiant youth
Whose very name was terror to my foes,
My rage has drove away. Of God forsaken
In vain I ask His councel! He vouchsafes
No answer to the sons of disobedience!
Ev'n my own courage fails me!—Can it be?
Is Saul become a coward?—I'll not believe it:
If heav'n denies thee aid, seek it from hell!

George Frederick Handel, *Saul*, 1739

For Handel in his oratorio, Saul, who sings these words, is
a tragic hero, and this reading of Saul's story is probably the one
that first strikes the modern reader. Saul's meeting with the belly-
myther of Endor can seem no more than a final setting of the seal
on Saul's fate. In the early church, however, it was not so much
Saul that occupied center stage in the story of 1 Kgdms 28[1] as the
apparition of Samuel the prophet. William Blake understood the
story this way. Handel's operas and oratorios may have inspired
Blake, but that is not the case here. The Rosenwald Collection of
the National Gallery in Washington includes a pen-and-ink water-
color over graphite that is one of Blake's earliest works, produced
within a year or so of his entrance into the Royal Academy Schools
in August of 1779. The ghost of Samuel is the central figure and
rises starkly in the center of the painting. Samuel stares at Saul,
who half-kneeling on the left reels back and with outstretched
hands appears to be warding off Samuel's judgment. The belly-
myther crouches at the right of the painting, and one of Saul's
servants stands transfixed at the far left.[2] It is the apparition of
Samuel that also engages the imagination of the early church. Was

---

[1] Because the Septuagint is the Bible for the Greek patristic exegetes discussed in this volume, we refer to the book as 1 Kingdoms; in Hebrew and
English it is called 1 Samuel.

[2] See Peter Ackroyd, *Blake: A Biography* (New York: Knopf, 1996), 28,
77–78, 138.

it really Samuel's spirit that came up, or was it no more than a demonic deception?

Thanks to the work of four modern scholars, we now have easy access to some of the significant treatments of 1 Kgdms 28 that survive from the early church. In 1986 Pierre and Marie-Thérèse Nautin published their edition of Origen's homilies on Samuel, including the fifth homily, on 1 Kgdms 28. Three years later Manlio Simonetti published his edition of three works bound together in the manuscript tradition: Origen's homily, Eustathius of Antioch's much longer treatise refuting Origen's interpretation of 1 Kgdms 28, and the short letter of Gregory of Nyssa that gives us his interpretation of the story. In 2002 José H. Declerck published his edition of all the works of Eustathius that survive. These volumes and the notes included in them place the materials in the wider context of early Christian exegesis and theology.

MONACENSIS GRAECUS 331 (M)

This tenth-century manuscript, preserved in Munich, is virtually the sole reliable witness to the three works we have mentioned.[3] The picture is somewhat complicated by the fact that Eustathius's citations of Origen's homily do not always conform exactly to M's text of the homily. Moreover, there is fragmentary evidence for Origen's work in the Tura papyri (dated ca. sixth to seventh century), discovered in 1942. What is fascinating, however, is to speculate concerning how the three writings came to be combined, how they were then included with three other writings, how this collection found its way west and eventually was transcribed as M. It is possible to imagine the story as follows. In about the year 240 Origen was invited to preach in Jerusalem in the presence of Alexander, the bishop. This was obviously a great honor, since we can suppose that, when the bishop was present, he would be the

---

[3] For descriptions of the manuscript, see Pierre and Marie-Thérèse Nautin, *Origène: Homélies sur Samuel* (SC 328; Paris: Cerf, 1986), 11–13; and José H. Declerck, *Eustathii Antiocheni Opera* (CCSG 51; Turnhout: Brepols; Leuven: Leuven University Press, 2002), xxx–xxxii, lxix–xciv. Sometimes the evidence from the Tura papyrus (T) is relevant for establishing the text, but it is possible that Eustathius's citations of Origen's homily are not exact or derive from a different Greek manuscript.

one to preach. As we learn from the opening of Origen's homily, a long lesson was read from the later chapters of 1 Kingdoms. Origen left to the bishop the choice of what part to consider, and in this way the story of Saul and the belly-myther of Endor became Origen's topic. The story was already problematic, and Origen is clearly entering a debate that was already taking place.

The homily itself apparently provoked further debate, or at least that is what Eustathius supposes.[4] Included in his treatise are several passages not found in Origen's homily as we have it. There are several possible explanations, including the guess that Origen made an addendum to his homily or the idea that Eustathius is simply citing Origen's comments as he found them in other of Origen's writings, now lost to us. A third possibility, as the Nautins have suggested and argued for, is that Origen preached a second homily, which was available to Eustathius.[5] Answering this question is rendered all the more difficult by the fact that, as throughout his treatise, Eustathius is fashioning some statements of Origen's by bricolage into his own personification of his provocateur. Whatever the explanation, Eustathius wrote his treatise against Origen's interpretation of 1 Kgdms 28 some eighty years after Origen had preached. In about 320 Eustathius was bishop of Berea, and it is the absence of any reference to the Arian controversy in the treatise that explains the consensus that it was written before he became bishop of Antioch shortly before the council of Nicaea in 325. Eustathius's treatise was written in reply to a letter from Eutropius, who is probably to be identified with the bishop of Hadrianopolis.[6] Since Eutropius received both the treatise and

---

[4] See Eustathius, *On the Belly-Myther* 26.

[5] See the discussion in Nautin and Nautin, *Origène*, 86–89. The Nautins print the "second homily" as homily 6, but this fragmentary text is based entirely upon Eustathius, *On the Belly-Myther* 26. Declerck (*Eustathii Antiocheni Opera*, c) notes: "Today there is a tendency to suppose the first possibility [a second homily]. It is equally possible that the texts of the 'second interpretation' cited by Eustathius come from an 'excursus' made in the context of a homily on a reading that had nothing to do with the story of the necromancer." Declerck also notes Klostermann's suggestion that the difficulty can be resolved by positing a lacuna in M's text of Origen's homily.

[6] This Eutropius was deposed by the intrigues of Julian the Apostate's mother, Basilina (Athanasius, *Fug.* 3 and *H. Ar.* 5). See Michel Spanneut, *Recherches sur les écrits d'Eustathe d'Antioche avec une édition nouvelle des fragments dogmatiques et exégétiques* (Lille: Facultés Catholiques, 1948), 60.

a copy of Origen's homily, the two writings clearly circulated together from early in the fourth century.

Declerck carries the imaginary story still further and suggests that the two writings were preserved in Antioch by Eustathius's followers, that is, the "old Nicene" church that remained faithful to the memory of Eustathius and to the faith of Nicaea but that refused communion with the eventually dominant church of the "new Nicenes" under Meletius, who became bishop of Antioch in 360. Thus, the fate of the two writings became linked to the long-lasting schism in Antioch, and the Eustathians may have added Gregory of Nyssa's letter, written late in the fourth century, in order to prove that an important "new Nicene" endorsed Eustathius's doctrines. In this way we can account for the "three-book" collection that is at the heart of the texts we have translated and that found its way into M. Since the other three-book collection found in M is arguably monophysite in character, the prototype of M may have been made in the East and then taken to southern Italy by refugees in the seventh century. The absence of the collection of writings in Constantinople, together with the southern Italian provenance of M, suggest that it migrated to the West at an early date.[7]

OUR COLLECTION OF SOURCES

The three-book collection of Origen's homily, Eustathius's treatise, and Gregory of Nyssa's letter is, of course, the central part of what follows. Our translation employs the text established by Simonetti for Origen and Eustathius, and that of Hörner in Gregorii Nysseni Opera (GNO) for Gregory's letter.[8] Nevertheless,

----

[7] See Declerck's discussion in *Eustathii Antiocheni Opera*, lvii-lx, especially lx: "There is a risk in a definite statement concerning the provenance of this manuscript and concerning the path it followed before ending up in Italy. But if the manuscript already collected the group of 'dogmatic writings' ... and the 'tribiblos' dedicated to the story of the necromancer, it is possible that the archetype of the existing *monac. gr. 331* had been copied in a monophysite area of the Byzantine empire (Syria, Palestine, Egypt?); its transmission to southern Italy could have been linked in some fashion to the invasions (Sassanid, Arab) of the seventh century."

[8] For full bibliographic information, see "Rights and Permissions," pp. xxi–xxii.

we have occasionally departed from these texts in our translation, after consultation with the Nautins for Origen and Declerck for Eustathius, and we have sometimes departed from Simonetti's text and punctuation. We indicate such instances in the footnotes. The first three texts are selections from Justin Martyr's *Dialogue with Trypho*, Tertullian's *On the Soul*, and the *Martyrdom of Pionius*.[9] These passages supply the chief evidence for the debate concerning 1 Kgdms 28 before the time of Origen. Arranged in chronological order, the last three selections that follow Eustathius's treatise (from Apollinaris, Diodore, and Gregory of Nyssa) show how the debate continued toward the end of the fourth century.

THE "BELLY-MYTHER"

The major translation issue we faced in this corpus of texts was how to render ἐγγαστρίμυθος, the term the Septuagint uses to translate the Hebrew phrase in 1 Sam 28:7 that describes the woman Saul consults, אשת בעלת־אוב. The Hebrew here, as well as the ancient Near Eastern religious or magical practice to which it refers, is somewhat ambiguous but may have meant something like "a woman having mastery over necromancy," or "over ghosts."[10] The Septuagintal word-choice ἐγγαστρίμυθος and the conceptual

---

[9] See "Rights and Permissions," pp. xxi–xxii.

[10] For the lexical evidence, see BDB, 15, under the root אוב ("have a hollow sound"), which lists four glosses for the word אוֹב: 1. "skin bottle" (Job 32:19); 2. "necromancer" (Lev 19:31; 20:6, 27; Deut 18:1; 1 Sam 28:3, 9; 2 Kgs 23:24; Isa 8:19 [with note: "where represented as chirping and muttering, in practice of their art of seeking dead for instruction, prob. ventriloquism, & so Gr versions"]; 2 Chr 33:6 = 2 Kgs 21:6); 3. "ghost" (Isa 29:4); 4. "necromancy" as in אשת בעלת אוב in 1 Sam 28:7 ("a woman who was mistress of necromancy"); 1 Chr 10:13. The whole entry ends with this interesting parenthesis: "In these three exx. אוֹב is usually interpreted as ghost or familiar spirit conceived as dwelling in necromancer; but this apparently not the ancient conception" (BDB, 15). *HALOT* 1:20 notes several cognate possibilities and meanings in Syriac, Arabic, and Hittite and offers the definition "prophesying spirit of the dead." They note explicitly the ambiguity over the identity of the אוב, whether it is "in man or woman (Lev 20:27)" or, in the case of our text, the "woman is." Jastrow (ספר מלים, 21) translates אוב "ghost"; בעל אוב as "necromancer" (*b. Sanh.* 65a). He also quotes *b. Šabb.* 152b on 1 Sam 28:7 as an example of the saying "the necromancer is a liar" (אוב טמיא כדיב). For intertwined lexical and

world of religious practices that it conjures up[11] lie right at the heart of the early Christian disputes over the proper interpretation of 1 Kgdms 28, and the word itself figures importantly in the exposition of the various positions we shall encounter in this volume, all of which are based on the Greek text as authoritative scripture. This general fact—that translation is also an act of re-enculturation—extends to us modern readers, of course, for the terms we choose may clang oddly and misleadingly with our contemporary associations. The terminological problem is particularly acute for this passage, since English speakers are most accustomed to calling this woman "the witch" of Endor, a title that perhaps evokes pointed hats and the perils of Dorothy and Toto more than necromancy, the diviner's arts, or ecstatic prophecy.[12]

history of religions issues, see J. Tropper, *Nekromantie: Totenbefragung im Alten Orient und Alten Testament* (AOAT 223; Neukirchen-Vlyun: Neukirchener, 1986), esp. 191–200; Brian B. Schmidt, *Israel's Beneficent Dead: Ancestor Cult and Necromancy in Ancient Israelite Religion and Tradition* (FAT 11; Tübingen: Mohr Siebeck, 1994), who prefers "the One-who returns" (151); see also idem, "The 'Witch' of En-Dor, 1 Samuel 28, and Ancient Near Eastern Necromancy," in *Ancient Magic and Ritual Power* (ed. Marvin W. Meyer and Paul A. Mirecki; Religions in the Graeco-Roman World 129; Leiden: Brill, 1995), 111–29; and Daniel Ogden, *Greek and Roman Necromancy* (Princeton: Princeton University Press, 2001), with further literature on 134 n. 16.

   [11] See the valuable comments by I. Trencsényi-Waldapfel, "Die Hexe von Endor und die griechisch-römische Welt," *Acta orientalia academiae scientiarum Hungaricae* 11 (1960): 201–22, especially 207, on how translators, like those of the Septuagint, import their own cultural circles into the words they chose for the original terms, sometimes changing the conceptualization significantly.

   [12] Interestingly, despite its contemporary currency in English-speaking culture, the term "witch" actually does not appear within English translations of 1 Sam 28. An electronic search of early English-language Bibles reveals that the editorially supplied *chapter headings* use the term, as in the Bishops' Bible (1568), "Saul consulteth with a witch," or the King James Version (1611); KJV says "Saul seeketh to a witch," even though the actual translation renders the term "a woman that hath a familiar spirit." The Douay-Rheims translation (from the Vulgate) does have "witch" for אוב at 1 Chr 10:13, which is a retrospective of our narrative (although the Vulgate reads here *pythonissa*). The roots of the English term "witch" are in Old English *wicca* (masculine *wizard*); perhaps it was applied to the woman in 1 Sam 28 by the parallel in Exod 22:17 or Deut 18:10 (both rendering a different Hebrew term, מכשף). In English, as well, much depends on definitions. Despite the Disney-fication of the term in modern American culture, the meaning given in the *OED* actually brings it quite close to the phenomenon of our text: "a female magician, sorceress; in later use

But the possibility for confusion does not end there. The translation of ἐγγαστρίμυθος proposed by the standard Greek lexica, "ventriloquist,"[13] while it has the virtue of etymological exactitude, since it is a literally precise rendering of the Greek into Latin cognates ("speaking from the belly"), runs the real risk of evoking images of the parlor-trick verbal comedy of an Edgar Bergen and his Charlie McCarthy.[14] For that reason we have avoided it. Current English Bible translations (made from the Hebrew) include "medium" (RSV/NRSV, NIV), "a woman who consults ghosts" (JPS), "necromancer" (JB), and "a woman who has a familiar spirit" (KJV). "Medium" is vague enough to do the job, but one loses both the compound term and the more specific ancient resonance of how an ἐγγαστρίμυθος is thought to have operated. "Necromancer," "dead-diviner," is a compound word (although not a literal one for our term),[15] but if we used it in translating works of these early Christian authors we would be verbally granting the woman the craft that is precisely what is at dispute among many interpreters: whether she indeed does have the capacity to foretell the future by raising the dead! And both "medium" and "necromancer" may obscure the role of *speech* inherent to the Greek term ἐγγαστρίμυθος and the phenomenon of verbal oracular utterance that it seems to denote. The virtue of "a woman who has a familiar spirit" is the way it captures the sense of possession, but "familiar spirit" is surely ambiguous ("familiar" to whom?), and in any case the phrase is too unwieldy to use consistently. Given all these problems, how to render it?

---

esp. a woman supposed to have dealings with the devil or evil spirits and to be able by their co-optation to perform supernatural acts."

   [13] This is the gloss given in both LSJ, 467, and PGL, 397, for ἐγγαστρίμυθος.

   [14] For a stunning treatment of the larger picture, see the study of Steven Connor, *Dumbstruck: A Cultural History of Ventriloquism* (Oxford: Oxford University Press, 2000), who includes an excellent discussion of Origen and Eustathius on 75–101.

   [15] There is an exact Greek cognate, νεκρόμαντις. It is rarely attested but found, e.g., in a work attributed to the tragedian Lycophron (third or second century B.C.E., depending upon judgment of authenticity), *Alex.* 682 (LSJ, s.v.). Much more common are the cognates νεκυομαντεία and νεκυομαντεῖον (see Ogden, *Greek and Roman Necromancy*, xvii–xx, xxxi–ii, employing the definition, "communication with the dead in order to receive prophecy from them" [xix]).

The term ἐγγαστρίμυθος is a Greek compound word composed of "in the belly" (ἐν + γαστήρ) and "myth/fable/speech" (μῦθος). Because this etymology is central to some of the exegetical arguments made by ancient commentators, we sought a compound word in English. In this we are mirroring the ancient definitions of the term, which rendered the compound periphrastically, such as Aelius Dionysius (second century C.E.), who defines ἐγγαστρίμυθος as ὁ ἐν γαστρὶ μαντευόμενος, "the one divining in the belly."[16] Going in this direction, ἐγγαστρίμυθος can thus be translated into English as either "belly-speaker," "belly-talker," or "belly-myther." We have chosen the latter and employed this neologism consistently throughout.

Our decision to go with a somewhat hyper-literal rendering was made especially in order to capture the cultural resonance the term would, and—as one can see in the texts translated in his volume—did evoke for the early Christian interpreters. Like "belly-myther," it is a *foreign* term and a *negative* term, which for Christian (and Jewish) readers was associated with pagan, and especially *Greek*, divinatory practices. The practices done by ἐγγαστρίμυθοι are expressly forbidden by God elsewhere in the Bible in laws addressed to Israel and appropriated by Christians (Lev 19:31; 20:6, 27; Deut 18:11). With an eye to religious polemic the Septuagintal translator had transferred a somewhat mysterious reference to ancient Mesopotamian-styled mantics[17] into a

---

[16] *Attikai lexeis*, book 2, s.v. ἐγγαστρίμυθος. This association is replicated in LSJ, 467, where ἐγγαστρίμυθος = ἐγγαστρίμαντις. For another literal rendering, see the scholion to Plato, *Soph.* 252c: Εὐρυκλῆς γὰρ ἐδόκει δαίμονά τινα ἐν τῇ γαστρὶ ἔχειν, τὸν ἐγκελευόμενον αὐτῷ περὶ τῶν μελλόντων λέγειν· ὅθεν καὶ ἐγγαστρίμυθος ἐκαλεῖτο ("For Eurycles appeared to have some demon in his belly, which commanded him to speak about the future; it is from this that he was called also *engastrimythos*"). A related term that the *Suda* says Sophocles used (*Aichmalotides*, frg. 59) was στερνόμαντις, "chest-diviner." The literalism associated with the term ἐγγαστρίμυθος is nicely captured in Lucian's satirical send up in *Lexiphanes* 20–21, in which a purgative draught is given to expel— through flatulence—the spirit in the belly that has caused obnoxious, strange speech in the "word-flaunting" title character, who exclaims, "I seem to have imbibed some belly-mything" (ἐγγαστρίμυθόν τινα ἔοικα πεπωκέναι).

[17] Schmidt, *Israel's Beneficent Dead*, 206–20, has argued for a late compositional dating of 1 Sam 28 (post-Deuteronomistic) because necromancy is not attested in Syria-Palestine but well-known in Mesopotamia throughout the first millennium B.C.E.). For the Septuagintal translators, however, it would still reek of antiquity.

stereotypical Greek form of alien prophetic speech. One source
on the ground for this is Plutarch, the priest of Apollo, who recognizes these lower-level oracular types (but repudiates the idea
that Apollo himself worked this way): "For it is entirely simple-
minded and childlike to suppose that the god himself, just like
the *engastrimythoi* (called of old Eurycleis, but now Pythones)
by entering into the bodies of the prophets, speaks, using their
mouths and voices as his instruments."[18] These "belly-mythers,"
who used to bear the name of an eponymous ancestor of oracular
prowess, Eurycles, speak out from their stomachs with a resident-
alien voice that forecasts the future. The synonymy to which
Plutarch attests of ἐγγαστρίμυθος with the "Pythones" connected
with the Delphic cult of Apollo gives them immediate repre-
hensibility for a Christian exegete such as Eustathius, who five
times refers to the ἐγγαστρίμυθος at Endor as a πυθόμαντις, "Pythian
prophetess."[19] The fully negative connotations of this association are clear, for in Scripture itself a πύθων[20] "divining spirit of
Python" makes a single appearance in Acts 16 and is handily ex-
punged by Paul.[21] In Greek and Roman sources on this divinatory
practice there is some confusion about whether the ἐγγαστρίμυθος
itself *is* the divining spirit or whether the divining spirit takes up

---

[18] Plutarch, *De defectu oraculorum* 414E: εὔηθες γάρ ἐστι καὶ παιδικὸν
κομιδῇ τὸ οἴεσθαι τὸν θεὸν αὐτὸν ὥσπερ τοὺς ἐγγαστριμυθοὺς Εὐρυκλέας πάλαι
νυνὶ δὲ Πύθωνας προσαγορευομένους ἐνδυόμενον εἰς τὰ σώματα τῶν προφητῶν
ὑποφθέγγεσθαι τοῖς ἐκείνων στόματι καὶ φωναῖς χρώμενον ὀργάνοις.

[19] 3.7; 5.4; 11.8; 20.1; 26.7. The Vulgate renders the phrase in 1 Sam
28:7 as *mulier habens pythonem*.

[20] Taking its name from the serpent Apollo killed at Delphi.

[21] Acts 16:16–19; cited by Eustathius at *On the Belly-Myther* 11.5–8.

residence *in them*,[22] a confusion mirrored in the Christian texts.[23] But the association of the ἐγγαστρίμυθοι with pagan cult was for Christian interpreters axiomatically a form of trafficking in the realm of the δαίμονες.[24] Even Christian interpreters who disagree

[22] For discussion, bibliography, and a collection of some key sources, see Trencsényi-Waldapfel, "Die Hexe von Endor," esp. 219–22; Ogden, *Greek and Roman Necromancy*, 112–15; and idem, *Magic, Witchcraft and Ghosts in the Greek and Roman Worlds: A Sourcebook* (Oxford: Oxford University Press, 2002), 30–35. Methodological decisions about the proper categorization and analysis of these materials and the behaviors to which they bear witness are exceedingly difficult to make (for instance, is the "ghost-exorcism" in Philostratus, *Vit. Apoll.* 4.20 quite comparable to the ἐγγαστρίμυθος?). See the critical review of Ogden's *Greek and Roman Necromancy* by Sarah Iles Johnson (*BMCR* [2002]: n.p.; online: http://ccat.sas.upenn.edu/bmcr/2002/2002-06-19.html). We can echo still the position articulated fifty years ago by E. R. Dodds: "I should like to know more about these 'belly-talkers'"! (*The Greeks and the Irrational* [Boston: Beacon, 1957], 71).

[23] For instance, Eustathius sometimes represents the woman as herself being a demon (see *On the Belly-Myther* 20.1 and the wordplay there on how demons whom she sees coming up from the ground are "biological kin" of the same mother as she [see note 63 in the translation]), but in other places she is "demon-possessed" (e.g., 3.4, 9; 4.1; 11.4). Eustathius also thinks Saul, who asked for and apparently received the divination from her, was likewise demon-possessed (e.g., 7.3; 9.14; 10.8; 15.1), even as the "Samuel" who fraudulently appeared was the demon itself impersonating the holy man (12.10; 13.3, 5, 6, etc.). Without systematizing the phenomenon, Eustathius brings together all these somewhat logically inconsistent views of demonic identity and activity in the encounter in his rousing conclusion: "Therefore, if the name itself has been rightly assigned to the actual thing, the belly-myther in all likelihood fabricates a myth in her belly. For she does not speak from the natural mind in a sane fashion, but the demon lurking in her inner organs encroaches upon her and disables her thinking, and composing mythic fictions, he makes them resound from her belly. Changing himself into diverse forms, he leads her soul by various hallucinations. And when he transforms himself into all sorts of different shapes, being a creature of many faces, no less does he pretend both to come up from the earth and to call out. Then in both ways, changing his ministrations at the same time as his forms, he seems to present himself coming up as someone different from the one who summons him. Yet though it is one and the same running about here and there, he changes his appearances so that he demonstrates in deeds and words that he is a liar" (30.1–3).

[24] See the keen comments of Connor, *Dumbstruck*, 74, on Christian constructions of the dangerous Delphic oracle: "The pythia is important because she stands on the threshold of the pagan and the Christian worlds. She is meant to stand as the image of an inheritance from or throwback to foul, forgotten, chthonic beginnings: she provides the vent or doorway through which the dark,

completely about what exactly this woman did or did not do for Saul unanimously agree that an ἐγγαστρίμυθος is a demon or a human inhabited by a demon who speaks out of her belly.[25] While the terms δαίμων or δαιμόνιον can and often do have a neutral sense in Greek religion and thought (for a "divinity"),[26] in Christian texts under the force of monotheism they are always and pervasively negative and are especially associated with pagan religious rites, as influentially by Paul already in 1 Cor 10:20. The general collocation of religious assumptions Christian interpreters of 1 Kgdms 28 would bring to the term include: it is something Greeks do; it involves demonic powers working inside of a person that emit utterances; and these are forms of false prophecy meant to trick people.[27] We hope our word "belly-myther,"[28] which comes closest to a literal replica of the problematic Greek term, will convey that range of nuances and will allow the reader

demonic, imperfectly superseded world of magic may creep back."

[25] Origen, who argues that Samuel really was raised by her, recognizes the problem of having a δαιμόνιον raise the soul of a prophet, but he does not for a moment question that she was, or acted under influence of, a demon (2.4–5; in this he agrees with his opponents—see 3.1). This is true of all the authors translated in this volume. See, e.g., the simple equation in *The Martyrdom of Pionius* 14.7: "the wicked belly-myther, herself a demon" (ἡ ἄδικος ἐγγαστρίμυθος, ἡ δαίμων).

[26] See Jonathan Z. Smith, "Towards Interpreting Demonic Powers in Hellenistic and Roman Antiquity," *ANRW* 2.16.1:425–39.

[27] These are nicely illustrated by Theodoret: "What is an *engastrimythos* ['belly-myther']? Some people, acting under the power of some demons, greatly deceive many ignorant folks, as though they were actually prophesying. The Greeks call them *enteromanteis* ['innards-mantics'], since the demon is thought to utter forth from inside them" (τί ἐστιν ἐγγαστρίμυθος; Τινὲς ὑπὸ δαιμόνων τινῶν ἐνεργούμενοι, ἐξηπάτουν πολλοὺς τῶν ἀνοήτων, ὡς δῆθεν προαγορεύοντες· οὓς ἐντερομάντεις οἱ ἕλληνες προσηγόρευον, ὡς ἔνδοθεν δοκοῦντος τοῦ δαίμονος φθέγγεσθαι; *Quaestiones in Leviticum* in N. Fernández Marcos and A. Sáenz-Badillos, eds., *Theodoreti Cyrensis quaestiones in Octateuchum* [Textos y Estudios Cardinal Cisneros 17; Madrid: Poligloti Matritense, 1979], 181, lines 12–15).

[28] The closest alternative we considered was was "belly-talker" (μῦθος can mean both "speech" and "fable" or "myth"), but because for Christian authors from early on the term μῦθος carried troublesome associations (1 Tim 1:4; 4:7; 2 Tim 4:4; 2 Pet 1:16), as is confirmed by Eustathius's play on the fictional associations of the μῦθος part of the compound in 26.10–29.4, we have chosen "belly-myther." If this be taken as too "Eustathian" a rendering, we would invite readers to toggle between "belly-talker" and "belly-myther" as they go through the texts.

to see the ways in which the term itself functions in the arguments.

ANALYSES

Many important and intriguing issues are raised by these early Christian interpretations of 1 Kgdms 28. While we cannot by any means exhaust them here, the first half of this volume seeks to open up some crucial topics by offering analytical treatments of these writings from several different perspectives. The two interpretive essays with which we begin were originally written independently, but we hope that they will complement each other. Greer has examined the theological contexts of the texts we have translated and demonstrates why this collection of works needs to be read together, for they can be seen as vital segments in complex early-church debates about postmortem hopes for Christians. Mitchell has studied the rhetorical character and context of the two major texts and seeks to draw conclusions from them about the character of early Christian exegesis. She has also contributed the two outlines of the rhetorical composition of Origen's homily and Eustathius's treatise that follow, to aid readers in following the logic and disposition of those complex arguments.

TEXTS AND TRANSLATIONS

The second half of the volume presents the Greek and Latin texts, together with the English translations, which represent our collaborative effort. It perhaps bears repeating that this volume does not represent a new critical edition of these texts but reprinted versions of existing published editions (see the comprehensive list on pp. xxi–xxii). Notes on variant manuscript readings have of necessity been limited to what we considered the most significant ones for the general sense of the passages in question. We encourage readers to consult the editions for a full *apparatus criticus*.

    A final note on style: we have decided to conform the scriptural references to the Old Testament to the Septuagint and translated those passages accordingly. Obviously, this means that 1 Samuel is 1 Kingdoms and that the numbering of the psalms differs from the Masoretic Text and modern conventions. The

scriptural references are included in parentheses in the translations. In the case of Eustathius's treatise we have italicized his
citations of Origen in the English, so readers can see the debate
unfold. We have adapted Simonetti's text by placing quotation
marks around these exact citations in the Greek text so they not
be confused with scriptural quotations, which throughout the volume are set in bold italics. Inexact or unidentified quotations are
not so designated in the Greek and are set in quotation marks in
the translation.

It remains our great pleasure to thank our series editor, John
T. Fitzgerald, for tremendous patience and invaluable advice in
midwifing this project and our collaboration. We would also like
to thank our volume editor, Abraham J. Malherbe, for incisive
comments that have improved the whole work. Scott Bowie deserves our thanks for valuable assistance in reading the proofs.
Alas, the errors that remain are due to our own clouded vision.
Above all, despite our limitations, it is our hope that readers will
find the texts and the issues they raise as fascinating as we have.

Rowan A. Greer and Margaret M. Mitchell
April 1, 2006

Rights and Permissions

ANALYSES

2. This essay is a revision of Margaret M. Mitchell, "Patristic Rhetoric on Allegory: Origen and Eustathius Put 1 Samuel 28 on Trial," *JR* 85 (2005): 414–45. Reprinted with permission of The University of Chicago Press.

TEXTS

1. Justin Martyr, *Dialogue with Trypho* 105. Text from Georges Archambault, ed. and trans., *Justin: Dialogue avec Tryphon* (Paris: Picard et fils, 1909), 144, 146, 148, 150.
2. Tertullian, *On the Soul* 54–58. Text from J. H. Waszink, *Tertullian: De anima* (2nd ed.; Amsterdam: Meulenhoff, 1947), 72–80.
3. *The Martyrdom of Pionius* 12–14. Text from Herbert Musurillo, *The Acts of the Christian Martyrs* (Oxford: Clarendon, 1972), 150, 152, 154, 156. Reprinted by permission of the publisher.
4. Origen, *Homily 5 on 1 Kingdoms* (= *De engastrimytho*). Text from Manlio Simonetti, ed., *La maga di Endor: Origene, Eustazio, Gregorio di Nissa* (Florence: Nardini, 1989), 44–74 (even numbers only). Reprinted by permission of the publisher.
5. Eustathius of Antioch, *On the Belly-Myther, Against Origen* (= *De engastrimytho contra Origenem*). Text from Manlio Simonetti, ed., *La maga di Endor: Origene, Eustazio, Gregorio di Nissa* (Florence: Nardini, 1989), 94–206 (even numbers only). Reprinted by permission of the publisher.
6. Apollinaris of Laodicea, Fragment. Text from Robert Devreesse, *Les anciens commentateurs grecs de l'Octateuque et des Rois (fragments tirés des chaînes)* (Vatican City: Biblioteca apostolica vaticana, 1959), 154. Reprinted by permission of the publisher.

7. Diodore of Tarsus, Fragment. Text from Robert Devreesse, *Les anciens commentateurs grecs de l'Octateuque et des Rois (fragments tirés des chaînes)* (Vatican City: Biblioteca apostolica vaticana, 1959), 163–65. Reprinted by permission of the publisher.

8. Gregory of Nyssa, *Letter to Theodosius concerning the Belly-Myther* (*De pythonissa ad Theodosium episcopum*). Text from Hadwiga Hörner in J. Kenneth Downing, Jacobus A. McDonough, and Hadwiga Hörner, eds., *Opera dogmatica minora*, vol. 2 (GNO 3; Leiden: Brill, 1987), 99–108. Reprinted by permission of the publisher.

Abbreviations

Aphthonius

Prog.   *Progymnasmata*

Aristotle

Rhet.   *Rhetorica*

Athanasius

Fug.   *Apologia de fuga sua*
H. Ar.   *Historia Arianorum*

Augustine

Div. quaest. Simpl.   *De diversis quaestionibus ad Simplicianum*

b.   Babylonian Talmud

Cicero

Inv.   *De inventione rhetorica*

Clement of Alexandria

Strom.   *Stromateis*

Gregory of Nyssa

Antirrhet.   *Antirrheticus adversus Apollinarium*
Beat.   *De beatitudinibus*
Benef.   *De beneficentia*
De hom. op.   *De hominis opificio*
De iis qui bapt. diff.   *De iis qui baptismum differunt*
Ep.   *Epistulae*
In Eccles.   *In Ecclesiasten homiliae*
In Flacillam   *Oratio funebris in Flacillam imperatricem*
In inscr. Ps.   *In inscriptiones Psalmorum*

In sextum Ps.	*In sextum Psalmum*
In XL Mart.	*In XL martyres*
Melet.	*Oratio funebris in Meletium episcopum*
Mihi fecistis	*In illud: Quatenus uni ex his fecistis mihi fecistis*
Orat. Cat.	*Oratio catechetica*
Sanc. trin.	*Ad Eustathium de Sancta Trinitate*
Virg.	*De Virginitate*
Vita Moys.	*De vita Moysis*
Vita Macr.	*Vita S. Macrinae*

Hermogenes

Stat.	*De statibus*

Homer

Il.	*Iliad*

Ignatius

Eph.	*Epistula ad Ephesios*

Irenaeus

Haer.	*Adversus haereses*

Jerome

Vir. ill.	*De viris illustribus*

Justin Martyr

1 Apol.	*Apologia 1*
Dial.	*Dialogus cum Tryphone*

Libanius

Prog.	*Progymnasmata*

Lycophron

Alex.	*Alexandra*

Methodius

Res.	*De resurrectione mortuorum*

Nicolaus

Prog.   *Progymnasmata*

Origen

Cels.   *Contra Celsum*
Comm. Jo.   *Commentarii in evangelium Joannis*
Comm. Matt.   *Commentarium in evangelium Matthaei*
Dial.   *Dialogus cum Heraclide*
Hom. Exod.   *Homiliae in Exodum*
Hom. Gen.   *Homiliae in Genesim*
Hom. Jer.   *Homiliae in Jeremiam*
Hom. Luc.   *Homiliae in Lucam*
Hom. Num.   *Homiliae in Numeros*
Princ.   *De principiis*

Ovid

Met.   *Metamorphoses*

Philostratus

Vit. Apoll.   *Vita Apollonii*

Plato

Phaed.   *Phaedo*
Phaedr.   *Phaedrus*
Resp.   *Respublica*
Soph.   *Sophista*
Tim.   *Timaeus*

Plutarch

Def. orac.   *De defectu oraculorum*

Pseudo-Hermogenes

Prog.   *Progymnasmata*

Quintilian

Inst.   *Institutio oratoria*

Rhet. ad Her.   *Rhetorica ad Herennium*

Rhet. Alex.	*Rhetorica ad Alexandrum*
Šabb.	*Šabbat*
Sanh.	*Sanhedrin*
Scholia in Theonem Rhet.	*Scholia in Theonem Rhetorem*

Sextus Empiricus

Math.	*Adversus mathematicos*

Tertullian

An.	*De anima*
Apol.	*Apologeticus*
Idol.	*De idololatria*
Jejun.	*De jejunio adversus psychicos*
Marc.	*Adversus Marcionem*
Prax.	*Adversus Praxean*
Res.	*De resurrectione carnis*

Theon

Prog.	*Progymnasmata*

Vergil

Aen.	*Aeneid*

Xenophon

Cyr.	*Cyropaedia*

SECONDARY SOURCES AND OTHER ABBREVIATIONS

ANRW	*Aufstieg und Niedergang der römischen Welt: Geschichte und Kultur Roms im Spiegel der neueren Forschung.* Edited by H. Temporini and W. Haase. Berlin: de Gruyter, 1972-.
AOAT	Alter Orient und Altes Testament

AThR	*Anglican Theological Review*
BDB	Brown, F., S. R. Driver, and C. A. Briggs. *A Hebrew and English Lexicon of the Old Testament.* Oxford: Clarendon, 1907.
BMCR	*Bryn Mawr Classical Review*
CCSG	Corpus Christianorum: Series graeca. Turnhout. 1977-.
CCSL	Corpus Christianorum: Series latina. Turnhout. 1953-.
CQ	*Classical Quarterly*
CWS	Classics of Western Spirituality. New York, 1978-.
Did	*Didaskalia*
FAT	Forschungen zum Alten Testament
FC	Fathers of the Church
frg.	fragment
GCS	Die griechische christliche Schriftsteller der ersten [drei] Jahrhunderte
GNO	Gregorii Nysseni Opera. Edited by W. Jaeger. Leiden: Brill, 1960-. Works are cited according to the volume and page number of the GNO.
Greg	*Gregorianum*
HALOT	Koehler, L., W. Baumgartner, and J. J. Stamm. *The Hebrew and Aramaic Lexicon of the Old Testament.* Translated and edited under the supervision of M. E. J. Richardson. 4 vols. Leiden: Brill, 1994–99.
HTR	*Harvard Theological Review*
HUT	Hermeneutische Untersuchungen zur Theologie
JB	Jerusalem Bible
JPS	Jewish Publication Society, *Tanakh*
JR	*Journal of Religion*
KJV	King James Version
LCL	Loeb Classical Library
LSJ	Liddell, H. G., R. Scott, H. S. Jones. *A Greek-English Lexicon.* 9th ed. with revised supplement. Oxford: Clarendon, 1996.
LXX	Septuagint
NIV	New International Version
NRSV	New Revised Standard Version
OED	*Oxford English Dictionary*

NPNF	*Nicene and Post-Nicene Fathers*
PG	Patrologia graeca [= Patrologiae cursus completus: Series graeca]. Edited by J.-P. Migne. 162 vols. Paris: Migne, 1857–86.
PGL	*Patristic Greek Lexicon.* Edited by G. W. H. Lampe. Oxford: Clarendon, 1968.
RST	*Recherches de science religieuse*
RSV	Revised Standard Version
SBLTT	Society of Biblical Literature Texts and Translations
SBLWGRW	Society of Biblical Literature Writings from the Greco-Roman World
SC	Sources chrétiennes. Paris: Éditions du Cerf, 1943-.
TU	Texte und Untersuchungen
VC	*Vigiliae christianae*
ZKT	*Zeitschrift für katholische Theologie*

Analyses

Some Observations on the Texts Translated: Theological Perspectives

Rowan A. Greer

The texts that we have translated deal with a number of religious and theological questions that preoccupied the ancient church. How should scripture be understood and its apparent contradictions resolved? What attitudes should Christians have toward pagan culture? Was it possible to despoil the Egyptians and make every thought captive to Christ, while at the same time repudiating pagan religion as demonic? What powers did demons retain after Christ's defeat of Satan? Interpreting the story of how the belly-myther was supposed to have summoned Samuel from hell to confront Saul raised all these questions and others. Foremost among them was how to explain what happens to people after death and what their ultimate fate would be.

It is far too simple to argue that there were two clearly opposed views, but it is helpful to place the question in the context of a polarity between views that emphasized the spiritual and contemplative dimensions of salvation and ones that insisted upon its physical character in the bodily resurrection. This polarity almost certainly involves attempts to reconcile the Platonizing idea of the soul's immortality with Jewish and Christian beliefs in the resurrection of the body. Both extremes, however, were concerned to insist upon the double meaning of human destiny in the age to come, that is, its spiritual *and* its physical character. Thus, the polarity presupposes agreement at a general level and, despite acrimonious debate particularly about Origen's teaching, can be understood as a disagreement regarding where emphasis should be placed.

In what follows I wish to focus first on the issue of the afterlife but then to offer observations tied to each of the texts we have translated. Here my aim will be to set the texts in the larger

contexts of the writers' exegetical and theological work, so far as that is possible. And by doing so I hope to show two things. First, no matter how helpful a framework for examining our texts may be supplied by the polarity I have mentioned, the polarity itself becomes quite complex the more it is considered. Second, the texts do not confine themselves to the question of the afterlife. Eustathius, for example, makes the interpretation of 1 Kgdms 28 his central concern and seems more preoccupied with insisting upon God's sovereignty at the expense of demonic powers than with sorting out a Christian view of the life to come.

THE LIFE TO COME AND THE RESURRECTION

Despite what I have just said, it is possible to discern the polarity of views about human destiny in the contrast between Origen's argument in his homily and the view Eustathius presupposes in his polemical treatise. Origen's concern, of course, is with the fate of the soul, but he elaborates that concern in all his writings not only in terms of themes correlative with the Platonism of his time but also by a commitment to commonplace Christian ideas such as Christ's harrowing of hell. Thus, he supposes that before the incarnation all souls were confined to hell but that now Christians—and perhaps all rational beings—have "something more." That is, once the soul of Christ had harrowed hell, it becomes possible for souls no longer to be imprisoned under the earth but instead to begin their ascent toward the perfect contemplation of God. It is because of this conclusion that he wants to insist that Samuel's soul did in fact come up and speak with Saul. He is not quite so clear and definite that the belly-myther actually succeeded in bringing up Samuel. But Samuel's presence in hell, like that of John the Baptist, can be explained by arguing that the prophets were proclaiming ahead of time to the souls in hell that Christ would come to deliver them.

Diametrically opposed to Origen's view is the one we find held by Eustathius and Gregory. Largely because of their interpretation of the parable of Lazarus and Dives in Luke 16, they suppose that souls must remain in hell until the time of the general resurrection. This view includes the idea that there are two rather different waiting rooms, represented by Abraham's bosom

where Lazarus reposes and by the fiery place where the rich man is tormented. These two "places" are separated from one another by a "great chasm" (Luke 16:26), and Eustathius and Gregory also assume that there is a chasm separating the souls in hell from our world. Consequently, it would be impossible for Samuel to be brought up by the belly-myther for this reason alone, even if it were not clear that Christians should have nothing to do with the demonic divination of belly-mythers. If the chasm separated wicked souls from righteous ones, how much more must it separate evil demons from the righteous. To be sure, the two scenarios are not entirely contradictory. Origen claims to believe in the resurrection, while Eustathius and Gregory clearly accept the idea that Christ harrowed hell. As well, we find a sort of middle view, held by Diodore of Tarsus and possibly entertained by Origen, that attributes the bringing up of Samuel to God rather than to the belly-myther and her demon. More important, however, is the conclusion that the debate reflected in the dispute between Origen and his opponents, including those envisaged in his homily as well as Eustathius, is one that existed before Origen's time.

Both the Nautins and Simonetti place the puzzle that is created in the context of other evidence,[1] and they assume on the whole that one issue involved in the exegetical dispute has to do with the afterlife and, particularly, the resurrection of the body. Origen's concern is with the soul's journey to God, and his opponents worry that this concern might well undermine belief in the general resurrection. Of course, Origen's view of the resurrection of the body is difficult to discern, not only because his writings are often fragmentary and often in Latin translations that are problematic because of the controversies about Origen's teaching, but also because his is a speculative rather than a systematic approach to issues of this kind. Nevertheless, it does seem clear that his teaching about the resurrection body does not represent his primary interest and that it was not without reason that he was accused of denying the resurrection. Moreover, at least from the time of Justin Martyr in the second century much of Christian theology is Platonizing in character, and it is certainly easier from

---

[1] See K. A. D. Smelik, "The Witch of Endor: 1 Samuel 28 in Rabbinic and Christian Exegesis Till 800 A.D.," *VC* 33 (1979): 160–79. He assembles as many texts referring to 1 Kgdms 28 as possible. He, however, omits the fragments from Apollinaris and Diodore that we have translated.

this perspective to insist upon the immortality of the soul than to
affirm a bodily resurrection. In any case, Justin Martyr in *Dial.*
105 appeals to 1 Kgdms 28 in order to show that before Christ the
souls even of the righteous like Samuel were subject to the evil angels. Christ's soul is, of course, free from such servitude, and it
is possible that Justin believes that the same freedom can attach
to the souls that are Christ's. At least the implications of Justin's
discussion resemble the view we find in Origen's homily. And in
a fragment from Apollinaris's writings preserved in a catena we
have the same sort of view appearing in the middle or late fourth
century.

Tracking down the opposing view is more interesting, and
here Simonetti is more cautious than the Nautins. But they all
agree that both Tertullian and the *Martyrdom of Pionius* represent
what must be a reaction against the view I have just described, a
reaction designed to protect the doctrine of the resurrection. Tertullian's treatise *On the Soul* was written in Latin early in the third
century, while the *Martyrdom of Pionius* was composed in Greek
after Pionius's martyrdom in Smyrna during the Decian persecution in 250. Consequently, it is difficult to suppose that the
writer of the martyrdom was acquainted with Tertullian's writings. Nevertheless, the two texts are connected by a similar use
not only of 1 Kgdms 28 but also of the parable of Lazarus and
Dives. As well, both texts cite 2 Cor 11:14–15 to demonstrate that,
since Satan can turn himself into an angel of light, it would not
be difficult for him to turn himself into an apparition of Samuel.
These considerations suggest that there is a common source used
by both Tertullian and the martyrologist. Such a source exists in a
fragment preserved by John Damascene in his *Sacra Parallela* and
bearing the title: "From Josipus's treatise entitled *Against Plato
concerning the Cause of the Universe and against the Greeks.*" Pierre
Nautin identifies this treatise with one of the writings listed on a
statue discovered in 1551 on the Via Tiburtina in Rome: *Against
the Greeks and Plato or Concerning the Universe.* This statue is
usually identified with Hippolytus, and Nautin's argument that
it represents the otherwise unknown Josipus and that the writings listed on the statue are to be attributed to him rather than
to Hippolytus is by no means universally accepted. Nevertheless,
one of the other writings listed on the statue is [Εἰς ἐγ]γαστρίμυθον.
Jerome in *Vir. ill.* 61 attributes to Hippolytus a treatise entitled

De Saul et Pythonissa. The Nautins' argument is, of course, far more complex and involves distinguishing between Hippolytus and Josipus by attributing some of the writings usually thought to be Hippolytus's to the Roman presbyter Josipus.[2]

We do not, of course, possess any fragments from this treatise *On the Belly-Myther*, no matter who wrote it. Nor does it matter what opinion one should have regarding Nautin's hypothesis. The point I should make is that in the fragment attributed to Josipus in the *Sacra Parallela* we do have an account of the topography of hell that is indeed very like what we find in the last section of Tertullian's *On the Soul*, where he addresses the problem of the soul's fate after death.[3] The passage John Damascene preserves has to do with demons, but it is primarily concerned to describe hell (Hades) in terms that build upon the Lukan parable. Hell is a subterranean place, deprived of this world's light. There all the souls of the righteous as well as the wicked are kept in a guard house (φρούριον), where angel warders (φρουροί) administer provisional rewards and punishments. In one part of hell there is a lake of fire,[4] but no one has yet been cast into it. Nevertheless, the wicked are placed near it, where they are tormented both by the sight of their fate and by the great heat of the fiery lake and gehenna. They are also in torment because they are able to see the righteous who repose in Abraham's bosom but remain separated from them by a great chasm. In contrast, the righteous, who enter hell by the same road, are escorted by the angels to the right and to a luminous place where they rejoice in the sight of their future eternal life in heaven, in short, to Abraham's bosom. Both the wicked and the righteous souls remain in hell until the time God has fixed for judgment. All will then partake of the resurrec-

---

[2] The interested reader should consult the whole of Nautin's argument in Pierre Nautin, *Hippolyte et Josipe* (Paris: Cerf, 1947). In their edition of Origen's homilies (SC 328) the Nautins suggest that the source for Origen's opponents' view, which can be identified with that of Tertullian and Pionius, is to be found in Josipus's Εἰς ἐγγαστρίμυθον (78). Simonetti remains agnostic about Nautin's theory about Josipus, but he does admit the common source idea (Manlio Simonetti, *La Maga di Endor: Origene, Eustazio, Gregorio di Nissa* [Biblioteca Patristica 15; Florence: Nardini, 1989], 13 n. 11).

[3] For the text, see Karl Holl, *Fragmente vornicänischer Kirchenväter aus den Sacra Parallela* (TU 20.2; Leipzig: Hinrichs, 1899), 137–43. Nautin's French translation may be found in *Hippolyte et Josipe*, 74–78.

[4] Cf. Rev 19:20; 20:10, 14, 15; 21:6.

tion of the body and will be judged by Christ. The righteous will
recover the same bodies in which they had lived, but wonderfully
transformed, while the wicked will receive their bodies capable of
eternal suffering. But both sorts of bodies will be composed of
the same elements as those once united with the soul in this life.
The passage includes a defense of the resurrection and an appeal to
the Greeks and Platonists to enlarge their understanding. If Plato
taught that the soul is begotten and immortal, surely one can believe that God's power extends to giving life to the body. Let me
note in passing that the fragment says nothing about Christ's descent to hell after his death and before his resurrection.

There can be little doubt that the main outlines of this assessment of the fate of the soul after death agree with Tertullian's
understanding and seem to be reflected in Pionius's speech in the
martyrdom. Moreover, they seem coherent with the view that
Origen opposes in his homily, and they certainly fit Eustathius's
convictions. There are apparently two opposing views, both of
which are oriented toward how we should understand the fate of
the soul after death. Justin, Origen, and Apollinaris assume that
before Christ all souls were sent to hell but remained subject to
the authority of the demons or the evil angels. But after Christ's
descent to hell, souls—at least those of the righteous—need no
longer go to hell. In contrast Tertullian, Pionius, Eustathius, and
Gregory of Nyssa assume that even before Christ souls find their
place in hell either in the repose of Abraham's bosom or in some
kind of fiery torment, that this arrangement remains in place until
the end of the world and the general resurrection, and that demons
could have no power over the souls of the righteous either before
or after the coming of Christ. The first view appears to ignore
the resurrection or at least to treat it as no more than a final seal
of approval for the righteous. The second view insists that there
can be no full salvation until the resurrection. Moreover, the first
view leaves room for the reality of Samuel being brought up by the
belly-myther's demon. The second view, however, refuses to admit that souls can leave hell or that the souls of the righteous can
ever be subject to demonic powers. Consequently, it is obliged to
treat the story in 1 Kgdms 28 as a demonic illusion.

On the whole, this assessment of the evidence seems to me
helpful and convincing. At the same time, there are some obvious
complications. The first view, that of Justin, Origen, and Apol-

linaris, can certainly leave room for the resurrection. And there are hints in Origen's version of the view that he is uncomfortable with the idea that demons could have power over the souls of the righteous. Origen, while he insists that it was really the soul of Samuel that came up, is not entirely clear as to whether it was the belly-myther and her demon that effected this. The second view, as we find it primarily in Tertullian and Eustathius, can certainly include the idea of Christ's harrowing of hell, as well as the notion that souls receive in some fashion preliminary rewards and punishments. These themes have a tendency to obscure the sharp contrast with the first view. Finally, Diodore's interpretation looks like a mediating view. He agrees that Samuel was indeed brought up but argues that God rather than the belly-myther was the one who had power to do this. There are other complications and difficulties, as I shall try to show. In what follows I do not mean to abandon the general interpretive framework suggested by the Nautins and Simonetti. But I do want to argue that a great many considerations qualify that framework. What I hope to do is to examine each of the texts we have translated and to the degree possible place them in the contexts of what can be known of the writers' larger theological structures.

JUSTIN MARTYR

Justin's comments in *Dial.* 105 are part of a longer interpretation of Ps 21 as a prophecy of Christ (97–106). Here his concern is with Christ's soul, a concern that springs from the reference to "soul" in verse 21. He uses 1 Kgdms 28 to support his conviction that souls survive death, and this means that he thinks it was Samuel's soul that came up. He does not seem at all troubled by the fact that this happened by the intervention of demons. Indeed, he makes this explicit in another context (*1 Apol.* 18), where he argues that "even after death souls are in a state of sensation" and adduces as proof necromancy, "the divinations you practice by immaculate children," and other pagan practices. But the important point he wishes to make is that Christ's soul was not subject to the evil angels. In other words, Christ's prayer in Ps 21:21–22 was answered. Moreover, this gives some assurance to the righteous that they too will be freed from the power of demons. We might even infer that

their souls need no longer go to hell. One problem, of course, is that drawing these conclusions is making much of little. But another is that here Justin makes no mention of the resurrection, and yet there can be no doubt that he affirms it. Still more important, however, is that if we turn our attention to the whole of Justin's corpus of writings, we discover grave obstacles to the interpretation just given.[5]

There are several passages in which Justin addresses the question of what happens to the soul after death and before the resurrection. The opening chapters of the *Dialogue* include Justin's account of his conversion. Having made his way through the various philosophical schools, he finds a Platonic teacher and hopes to have what he regards as the aim of Plato's philosophy, the vision of God. Disappointed, however, he walks in a solitary place near the sea, only to be unexpectedly confronted by an old man looking for his lost sheep. The old man is a Christian, and the conversation he has with Justin revolves around the topic of the soul. He argues that the soul is "generate," that it has a beginning, and, we may assume, that it is created. Nonetheless, he does not contend "that all souls die, for that would indeed be some good luck for the bad." The old man continues by saying (*Dial.* 5):[6]

> The souls of the pious dwell in some better place, but the evil and wicked in a worse one, both awaiting the time of judgment. Then the one group, proven to be worthy of God, die no more, the other are punished as long as God's will allows them to exist and to be punished.

There is, of course, no attempt to explain where we are to locate these two places or whether they are not so much places as spiritual conditions. But it is not difficult to discern some resemblance to the view that contrasts Abraham's bosom with the rich man's place of torment.

---

[5] For a summary of Justin's views, see Brian E. Daley, *The Hope of the Early Church: A Handbook of Patristic Eschatology* (Cambridge: Cambridge University Press, 1991), 20–22.

[6] See the discussion in J. C. M. Van Winden, *An Early Christian Philosopher: Justin Martyr's Dialogue with Trypho, Chapters One to Nine* (Leiden: Brill, 1971), 84–100. The idea that there are mortal souls that do not die depends upon Plato, *Tim.* 41ab. *Dial.* 5.5 appears to recognize that the souls of the wicked finally die, but this contradicts what Justin says in *1 Apol.* 8.4. See Van Winden, *Early Christian Philosopher*, 106.

To be sure, it would be possible to argue that Justin does not necessarily share the old man's opinions in every detail. Such a conclusion seems unlikely to me, primarily because there are other hints in Justin's writings of the same distinction between the soul's survival and the general resurrection. Justin's defense of the resurrection appears in *1 Apol.* 18–19, and there he insists upon the survival of souls after death and upon the resurrection, which will take place "in God's appointed time." In *Dial.* 45 Justin raises the question of the salvation of those who were righteous before Christ and claims that they will be saved not because they observed the Jewish law, but because "they did that which is universally, naturally, and eternally good." As a result, they will be saved at Christ's second coming, "when some are sent to be punished unceasingly into judgment and condemnation of fire, but others shall exist in freedom from suffering, from corruption, and from grief, and in immortality." One other passage has at least the possibility of supporting the point I am making. At the beginning of his interpretation of Ps 21 (*Dial.* 99) Justin treats the third verse of the psalm, which speaks of crying to God day and night, as a reference to Christ's prayer in Gethsemane, the agony in the garden. He points out that Matt 26:39 ends the prayer with "yet not what I want but what you want." Justin takes a further step and claims that Christ knew his fate ahead of time, just as we need not suppose God ignorant when he asked Adam where he was or inquired of Cain about Abel. The last part of Ps 21:3 proves his point. The Septuagint translates the half verse: "And it is not for want of understanding in me."[7] Therefore, it is not Christ who was ignorant but rather those who thought they could put him to death "and that he, like some common mortal, would remain in Hades." To be sure, this allusion would not require us to say that common mortals remain in hell after Christ had descended there. But my conclusion is that Justin is quite capable of arguing that souls after death survive but must await the general resurrection.

A further complication has to do with Justin's references to the millennium. In *Dial.* 80–81 he clearly accepts this doctrine but recognizes that there are faithful Christians who do not. At the same time, he warns Trypho that there are some so-called Christians who not only reject the millennium but also say that "there

---

[7] καὶ οὐκ εἰς ἄνοιαν ἐμοί.

is no resurrection of the dead, and that their souls, when they die, are taken to heaven." Justin summarizes his own view by saying:

> But I and others who are right-minded Christians on all points are assured that there will be a resurrection of the dead and a thousand years in Jerusalem, which will then be built, adorned, and enlarged.

But it is not clear that Justin always keeps this opinion in mind. In *Dial.* 113 he gives a typological reading of Joshua's partition of the land of promise. Christ will apportion the good land to each one and, "after the resurrection of the saints, shall give us the eternal possession." It is not entirely clear whether this statement envisages the millennium or not; in any case, if it does, the resurrection takes place after rather than before the millennium. There are also places where Justin appears to speak of the eschatological Jerusalem as the spiritual destiny of the saints quite apart from millennial notions.[8]

In sum, we can find a bewildering array of ideas in Justin's writings. Righteous souls after death have the possibility of going to heaven. All souls after death must await the time of judgment and resurrection. It is possible that the souls of the wicked will perish after they have been sufficiently punished. The second coming of Christ need not be tied to a millennium. There will be a millennium, but it is not clear whether the resurrection precedes or follows it. The only certain conclusion is that it is impossible to put together what Justin says in any coherent framework. The problem seems to me one that can partly be explained by suggesting that Justin both repeats Christian traditions that he has inherited and thinks through for himself some aspects of that teaching. What he repeats is not necessarily anything he has tried to understand in his own way. I think of the preacher who assures his congregation that they are washed in the blood of the lamb but fails to explain what on earth that might mean. It even makes sense

---

[8] See the discussion in Erwin R. Goodenough, *The Theology of Justin Martyr* (Jena: Frommann, 1923; repr., Amsterdam: Philo, 1968), 202–26, esp. 224: "But the few remarks which Justin makes in passing concerning the state of existence of souls after death are so contradictory as to make certainty about his beliefs impossible." See also L. W. Barnard, "Justin Martyr's Eschatology" *VC* 19 (1965): 94: "It is a hopeless task to reconcile this belief in an earthly millennium in Jerusalem with Justin's other opinion that the new Jerusalem will be an immediate, spiritual, eternal land or inheritance."

to me to suggest that Justin as a Platonist is committed to the immortality of the soul but as a Christian is equally committed to the doctrine of the resurrection. But he has not managed to find a way of reconciling the two commitments. The problem, I suspect, is not merely his. The line of thought established by 1 Kgdms 28 that leads from *Dial.* 105 to Origen's homily may still be drawn, but it is obscured by what Justin says elsewhere.

TERTULLIAN

The passage from *On the Soul* that we have translated supplies a reasonably complete view of Tertullian's teaching regarding the fate of the soul after death. His basic conclusion is that with the sole exception of the martyrs, who go to paradise, all souls after death go to hell (55.4–5). Even the Greek philosophers posit an interval between death and the final fate of the soul (54.1). But, as the parable of Lazarus and Dives in Luke 16 shows, there are two places in hell: Abraham's bosom and the place of torment. It would appear that this distinction involves the bestowal of preliminary rewards or punishments (58.1, 5–7), and there is even a hint that some sort of purification may take place for some (58.8). Moreover, Christ's descent to hell not only demonstrates that as human he suffers the same fate as all but also has the purpose of making at least some of the souls in hell his fellow heirs (54.1). Yet neither a preliminary judgment nor the descent of Christ abolishes the requirement that souls remain in hell, awaiting the resurrection (55.2–3; 56.5, 7). Thus, Samuel must remain in hell, and the story told in 1 Kingdoms must be understood as a demonic contrivance and delusion (57.8–9, 11). Tertullian strongly repudiates necromancy and argues that it is a form of idolatry. Just as demons take the form of idols, so they take the form of the dead. They can appear in dreams, and exorcism can give us a clear idea of how the demons operate.

Tertullian has his opponents, but it is no easy task to discover who they are or exactly what they are saying. Tertullian's arguments are as crabbed as his Latin. One thing is clear. His opponents are denying that all souls go to hell. In 55.2–3 they are clearly Christians who say "Christ descended to hell so that we should not go there." Later we learn that they are concerned to ex-

clude from hell the souls of infants, virgins, and the righteous, and Tertullian claims that these opponents also say "all wicked souls are kept away from hell" (56.8). The context in which Tertullian places the supposed view of these people that neither the souls of the righteous nor the souls of the wicked go to hell includes a discussion of the unburied and the untimely dead who the pagans say are doomed to wander about in this world (56.1–57.1). It may be impossible to make sense of Tertullian's argument and to clarify the position he is attacking. Could it be, however, that the opponents are not in fact claiming that wicked souls escape hell? It seems to me possible that they are arguing that beliefs about the unburied and the untimely dead simply prove that not all souls go to hell and that this supports their fundamental conviction that righteous souls do not go to hell. Such a conclusion would explain why they ask whether "every soul" is "under the power of hell" (58.1). What I am suggesting is that Tertullian has seized upon one aspect of the opponents' argument, emphasized its implication, and turned it into a claim that even the wicked do not go to hell.

If my suggestion has merit, the opponents are not denying that the wicked will be punished by being sent to hell. What they are affirming is that their fate and the entrance of the righteous into paradise are definitive punishments and rewards meted out immediately at death. No "preliminary sentence" is necessary. But the opponents immediately go on to say that they deny this "because the restoration of its [the soul's] flesh should be expected as something that shares in its deeds and deserts" (58.2). What does this mean? Tertullian appears to suppose that the expectation is waiting for the general resurrection, and he goes on to argue that the soul's independence and priority with respect to the body makes it reasonable to suppose "that the soul should be first to receive the deserts owed to it" (58.7) and not merely be obliged to wait for the resurrection. I think it possible that he has misunderstood the view he is attacking. Earlier in his argument Tertullian has his opponents affirm that their sleep or rest will be "in paradise, where even now the patriarchs and prophets are clinging to the Lord's resurrection (*appendices dominicae resurrectionis*), having passed out of hell" (55.4). This might imply that entrance into paradise is what matters and that the resurrection of the body is an unimportant afterthought. Christ's harrowing of hell has both

delivered the souls of the patriarchs and prophets and opened the way to paradise for all the righteous. The resurrection will follow but will add nothing to the judgment already made. Tertullian's opponents are primarily concerned to argue that the final destiny of all human beings takes place immediately after death. The righteous enter paradise raised from the dead, while the wicked are consigned to hell. Moreover, the righteous "cling to" the resurrection, which seems to be in some sense present to them. What does seem clear is that there can be no waiting in hell for righteous souls, according to the opposing view, and that this opinion correlates in some measure with Origen's position. But the confusions and difficulties involved in trying to penetrate Tertullian's characterization of the view he wishes to refute, together with the apparent insistence of that view on the resurrection of the body, makes it difficult to argue that it is the same as Origen's.

Whatever we make of the opinion Tertullian wishes to refute, his own opinion is entirely clear.[9] All souls go to hell save those of the martyrs, who go to paradise, but there are two places in hell, as the parable of Lazarus and Dives indicates. Tertullian nowhere else that I can find refers to 1 Kgdms 28, but he does employ the Lukan parable in a number of places.[10] One passage in *Against Marcion* is of interest because Tertullian restricts the term *hell* to the place of torment.[11] He argues that scripture itself:

> in distinction from hell (*inferis*) marks off for the poor man Abraham's bosom. For, I suppose, hell is one thing, Abraham's bosom quite another. For it says that between those regions a great gulf intervenes and prevents passage from either side to the other... Hence it becomes plain to any wise man who has ever heard of the Elysian fields that there is a sort of distinct locality referred to as Abraham's bosom.

[9] See Daley, *Hope of the Early Church*, 34–37.

[10] These include two uses of the parable for homiletical purposes. In *Jejun.* 16 and *Idol.* 13.4 he appeals to the reversal of fortune attaching to the fates of Lazarus and Dives. The rich man who feasted in this life is punished in the life to come, whereas Lazarus who fasted is refreshed.

[11] *Marc.* 4.34 (Ernest Evans, *Tertullian: Adversus Marcionem* [Oxford Early Christian Texts; 2 vols.; Oxford: Clarendon, 1972], 2:453–57). Cf. *Marc.* 3.24 (Evans, 1:247), where Tertullian denies Marcion's view that "your Christ promises the Jews their former estate, after the restitution of their country, and, when life has run its course, refreshment with those beneath the earth in Abraham's bosom." Tertullian's response includes a discussion of the millennium.

Abraham's bosom is "not so deep as hell," and this is why the rich man must lift up his eyes. It gives the souls of the righteous "refreshment . . . until the consummation of all things makes complete the general resurrection with its fullness of reward." This "temporary refuge" is equated with the Elysian fields, which would be familiar to Tertullian's readers because of the sixth book of Vergil's *Aeneid*.[12] What we learn from this by no means contradicts what we discover in the passage from *On the Soul* that we have translated, but it does add some interesting details.

There is, however, one other theme to be found by examining Tertullian's use of the Lukan parable, namely, his insistence upon the corporeal nature of the soul. Since he assumes that Luke 16 refers to the souls of Lazarus and Dives, it is the mention of a tongue, a finger, and a bosom that demonstrates that the soul is corporeal:[13]

> Therefore, if the soul reaps an early amount of torment or refreshment in hell's prison or lodging, in fire or in Abraham's bosom, the corporeality of the soul will be proved. For incorporeality suffers nothing, since it does not have that by which it can suffer—or if it does have it, it will be a body. For insofar as everything corporeal is capable of suffering, so everything capable of suffering is corporeal.

Thus, it is not merely the fact that Lazarus and Dives are described in bodily terms; more than that, their experience of torment and refreshment proves the soul to be corporeal.[14] Tertullian's Stoic orientation is responsible for this doctrine. He even defines God as corporeal in *Prax.* 7. The divine substance, however, is a very special sort of body called *spiritus*, and we must think of the soul's bodily substance in some such way. The idea is of a spiritual body of some sort and is probably not opposed to Platonic presuppositions so absolutely as might first seem the case. Indeed, Irenaeus had already used the parable of Lazarus and Dives to argue for the bodily form of the soul.[15]

---

[12] *Aen.* 6.539–543, 637, 678, 724–751.

[13] *An.* 7. Cf. *An.* 9.8, where Tertullian uses the creation of Adam to argue that the soul that God breathes into the lifeless lump pervades it, conforming itself to the shape of the body. The passage continues by appealing to Luke 16.

[14] See also *Res.* 17 and *Marc.* 5.9–10.

[15] *Haer.* 2.34.1.

I am not sure that I have succeeded in understanding the view against which Tertullian is arguing in the last part of *On the Soul*. But his own view does indeed seem clear and consistent. Moreover, it is also evident that his opposition to any notion that would give the soul complete salvation springs from his concern to retain the central importance of the general resurrection. His view certainly does inform his understanding of 1 Kgdms 28, but it would be difficult to argue that this is its basis. What I think we are beginning to discover is that the parable of Lazarus and Dives is really the most important text and that it lies at the heart of the view we apparently find in the Martyrdom of Pionius, in Origen's opponents, in Eustathius, and in Gregory of Nyssa.

THE MARTYRDOM OF PIONIUS

According to the martyrology, Pionius was a presbyter and teacher of the Catholic church in Smyrna and was put to death during the Decian persecution on March 12, 250. The account that we possess includes lengthy speeches of Pionius, and even if we assume that they are literary creations of the author, they tell us a good deal about what Christians were saying in Asia Minor in the middle of the third century. To be sure, there is room for skepticism regarding what the narrative tells us. But it does not seem to me necessary to discount its evidence. In the passage we have translated Pionius and his companions are in prison. The first group of visitors are pagans, and the narrative as a whole gives the impression that many of the pagans are quite sympathetic to the arrested Christians. It is equally clear that the narrative goes out of its way to attack the Jews. The second group of visitors consists of "many" Christians who had lapsed by being compelled to sacrifice. Pionius addresses these apostates, giving them advice and urging them to repent and return to Christ. The text does pose some puzzles. If it is correct to argue that these Christians who have been "dragged away by force" have sacrificed, then it seems surprising that the sin against the Holy Spirit consists in attending the Jewish synagogue. Presumably this is because they are not compelled to join the Jews. Pionius in his speech is concerned to refute what the Jews say about Christ. In 13.8 their claim is that

"Christ practiced necromancy and divination with the cross."[16] It
is not entirely clear what the Jews are claiming according to Pionius in 14, but it looks as though they are arguing that Christ's
resurrection is really no more than necromancy. We must, I think,
suppose that the Jews are making two different slanders, attacking
Christ as a necromancer and attacking Christian belief in the resurrection as no more than necromancy.

It is in the context of the second Jewish opinion that Pionius
introduces the story of the belly-myther and her bringing up of
Samuel. In interpreting the story, Pionius assumes that a wicked
demon could not have power over a righteous soul like that of
Samuel. He alludes to Luke 16 when he says that Samuel's soul
was resting in Abraham's bosom, and the implication is that no
evil demon could cross the chasm separating the wicked from the
righteous. Moreover, the demonic apparition of Samuel is proved
to have lied when he said to Saul "You too shall be with me today." Pionius has confused 1 Kgdms 28:19 with Christ's words to
the penitent thief in Luke 23:43. Nevertheless, the lie is proved
by the fact that the wicked Saul could not have crossed the chasm
to rest in Abraham's bosom with the soul of Samuel. That Satan
and his ministers could disguise themselves in this way is proved
by 2 Cor 11:14–15. We do indeed have what represents the main
lines of the interpretation of 1 Kgdms 28 to be found in Tertullian, Eustathius, and Gregory of Nyssa, together with the texts
from Luke 16 and 2 Cor 11. This interpretation of 1 Kgdms 28
belongs in the context of Pionius's refutation of the Jewish claim
that Christ's resurrection was a case of necromancy. In 14.5–6
Pionius envisages two possible responses to his interpretation of
Samuel's appearance. If the Jews say the belly-myther brought
Samuel up, they admit that "wickedness has more power than
righteousness." If they agree that necromancy is a demonic fiction, "then they should not assert it of Christ the Lord." It is hard
to see how the second response would settle the question, since
Jews and Christians would simply disagree as to whether Christ's
resurrection was a demonic summoning of the dead. But Pionius's
argument may presuppose differing Jewish views of the possibility
of necromancy. What appears to be an older Jewish understand-

---

[16] See also the alternative translation suggested in n. 2 of the translation
that makes Christ the object of necromancy.

ing implies an exaggerated assessment of demonic power, while a Jewish denial of necromancy would make their slander about Jesus' resurrection nonsense.[17] No matter how we solve the puzzle, Pionius's interpretation of the story supports the conclusion that Tertullian and Pionius reflect the same view of the fate of the soul after death and that they drew upon a common source. There remains, however, the difficult question of the impact of rabbinic interpretations upon Christian writers.

ORIGEN

Origen bases his homily on the narrative meaning of 1 Kgdms 28, that is, the "letter" as opposed to the "spirit" of the possible "elevated" or allegorical meanings. In his theory as he expounds it in *Princ.* 4 he distinguishes the body, soul, and spirit of scripture. The body is the obvious meaning of the text, and I should suggest that it is better to describe this meaning as "narrative" rather than "literal" or "historical." The soul of scripture tends to be its moral meaning, while its spirit has to do either with Christ or with the final character of the *apokatastasis*, the restoration of all things. Origen applies this theory in his homilies to a greater degree than has often been recognized. Moreover, his attitude toward the narrative meaning is by no means as negative as it has often been described. To be sure, there are passages where the narrative meaning does not "touch us" and is not "beneficial" (2.1), but the story of Saul, the belly-myther, and Samuel is not one of them. It is not until the end of the homily that we fully discover what is "beneficial" about the narrative. Origen begins by arguing for his point on the basis of his conviction that the Holy Spirit is the narrator and is by definition a true one.[18] He sees that there are difficulties with his conclusion. In particular, he seems to recognize the problem that it is hard to see why Samuel's soul would be subject to a petty demon (2.4–5). And while he strongly insists that Samuel was really brought up, he asserts the role of the belly-myther only by implication. These things are "written" and "true," even though assuming they are true "furnishes us with a matter for investigation and an occasion for doubt" (2.5).

---

[17] See Smelik, "Witch of Endor," 160, 162–63.

[18] 2.5, but note that he repeats the point at 4.2–4, 7–9; 5.2; 6.2.

Origen supports his basic position by several arguments. One is that the Samuel who is brought up and speaks to Saul cannot be a demon, because demons are unaware of God's dispensations and cannot prophecy (4.9).[19] Another point is that it is by no means unacceptable to think that Samuel was in hell. If Christ went to hell after his death, why should we be surprised to find Samuel and the other prophets and righteous there as well (6.3–6)? Christ descended to hell in order to conquer death and to save, while the prophets went there before him to predict and proclaim his coming to the souls in hell (6.7–10; 8.1; 9.1–6). In 7.4–11 he makes the point with respect to John the Baptist. Like Peter, John was initially unwilling to accept Christ's humiliation and death, but both Peter and John the Baptist learned their lesson.[20] Thus, Samuel and the other righteous are in hell not so much because they are subject to demons or evil angels as because they have the positive function of preparing the souls beneath the earth for the descent of Christ. Two further points elaborate this positive assessment. First, when Samuel does come up to converse with Saul, he is accompanied by other spirits of the prophets and probably by angels (7.2–3). Second, while Samuel is "below" by the facts of the matter, he is "above with respect to ethical purpose"[21] (8.2–3). All these themes revolve around positive reasons for Samuel's being in hell, but another reason emerges towards the end of the homily. Origen appeals to the story of the fall in Genesis and, specifically, to Gen 3:24, which refers to the cherubim and the flaming and turning sword that guard the way to the tree of life. No one could return to paradise before Christ. Instead, all souls were sent to hell to wait until Christ came to reopen the way to the tree of life (9.7–11). Origen even uses the Lukan parable not to argue for two places in hell but to prove that Abraham is there (9.9). By now we begin to see what is "beneficial" about the narrative of 1 Kgdms 28. Its importance has to do with the necessity of discerning "what our condition will be after we depart

---

[19] See also 5.1, 3–4; 8.3; and Nautin and Nautin, *Origène*, 85 n. 2. In addition to the text from Ignatius, *Eph.* 19.1, we can add 1 Cor 2:8.

[20] For John the Baptist as a prophet in hell foretelling Christ's descent, see Origen, *Hom. Luc.* 4.5 and *Comm. Jo.* 2.224. For Peter's unwillingness to accept the lowly Christ, see *Comm. Matt.* 12.20.

[21] The Greek term προαίρεσις literally means "(free) choice" and more broadly refers to the exercise of that free choice in an ethical direction.

from this life" (5.1; cf. 4.10). The concern is not with the resurrection of the body but rather with our "departure (ἔξοδος) from
this life, in other words, with the fate of the soul. In concluding
his homily (10) Origen articulates his triumphant conclusion that
because of Christ we have "something more" than Samuel. Christ
has opened paradise.

Origen is aware that his interpretation is controversial, and
he refers to the opposing view of "some of our brothers" in several places (3; 4.6; 6). They appear to argue that we cannot trust
the belly-myther, since Paul says in 2 Cor 11:14–15 that Satan
and his ministers can disguise themselves as an angel of light and
ministers of righteousness. Thus, the entire story is a demonic
fabrication. Origen, of course, attempts to refute this opinion
not so much by vindicating the belly-myther as by insisting that
Samuel really came up. The other objection made by his opponents is their denial that Samuel could be in hell. If we are to argue
that the opponents' interpretation is fundamentally the same as
that found in Tertullian and Pionius, this denial would be quite
contradictory. Indeed, Origen's insistence that Samuel was in hell
would seem more in accord with what Tertullian and Pionius say.
A possible solution of this puzzle occurs to me. Tertullian, as I
have noted above, can restrict the meaning of "hell" to the place of
torment as opposed to Abraham's bosom. From this perspective,
to deny that Samuel is in "hell" would merely mean that he was
in Abraham's bosom. And on this reading we could construe the
opponents' objection as an argument against the notion that the
belly-myther really brought up Samuel. Perhaps demons do have
access to the souls in hell as the place of torment, but one could
deny that they have any access to souls in the bosom of Abraham.
If there is any merit to this suggestion, then we might conclude
that Origen has shifted attention away from his opponents' argument based on the demonic character of the belly-myther toward
their secondary argument that she would not have had access to
Samuel because he was in Abraham's bosom.

Let me now turn to other passages in Origen's writings and
argue that he is consistent in emphasizing the significance of the
soul's departure and its ascent to God but that he does not always
insist upon the purely narrative meaning of terms such as "the bosom of Abraham," "the place of torment," and "paradise." To be
sure, he can continue to recognize that Samuel was in hell. In one

of his homilies on Jeremiah,[22] he speculates that Samuel was there "not because he was sentenced but he came to be an observer and contemplator of the mysteries of matters below the earth." This new and positive explanation begins to loosen Samuel's ties to hell. And in a passage from the *Commentary on John* Origen comes close to removing Samuel from hell altogether. He is commenting on John 8:52, where the Jews affirm that Abraham and the prophets are dead, and he begins by pointing out that the Jews had no understanding of what Paul says in Rom 5. He continues by saying:

> [The Jews] had an idea of the death of Abraham and the prophets, since they heard that Samuel, though he was beneath the earth because of death, was brought up by the belly-myther, who thought there were gods somewhere beneath the earth and said, "I saw gods coming up from the earth." But they did not understand the life of Abraham and the prophets nor that the God of Abraham, Isaac, and Jacob was the God not of their dead but of the living (Matt 22:32).[23]

It is not necessary to suppose that Origen repudiates the narrative meaning of 1 Kgdms 28, but what he makes of that meaning has primarily to do with an insistence upon the soul's survival after death and upon the "something more" given us by Christ's harrowing of hell. Even in his homily on 1 Kgdms 28 he makes it clear that hell is no longer a waiting room established for the time before the general resurrection.

This conclusion suggests a further question: Does Origen suppose that Christ has abolished or changed the topography of hell? He frequently speaks of Christ's descent to hell after his death.[24] Moreover, he is aware of the difficulty of reconciling Christ's three days and three nights "in the heart of the earth" (Matt 12:40) with his promise that the penitent thief will be with him in paradise "today" (Luke 23:43). The problem arises in his

[22] 18.2 (John Clark Smith, *Origen: Homilies on Jeremiah, Homily on 1 Kings 28* [FC 97; Washington, D.C.: Catholic University of America Press, 1998], 191).

[23] *Comm. Jo.* 20.42 (A. E. Brooke, *The Commentary of Origen on S. John's Gospel* [2 vols.; Cambridge: Cambridge University Press, 1896], 2:101).

[24] For example, *Princ.* 2.5.3; *Cels.* 2.16; 2.43; *Hom. Exod.* 6.6 (where he cites Eph 4:9–10); *Hom. Exod.* 6.8. Several passages speak of Christ's descent and ascent, e.g., *Hom. Num.* 27.3; *Hom. Jer,* 18.2.4; *Cels.* 1.35.

discussion of John 13:33: "You will look for me; and as I said to the Jews so now I say to you, 'Where I am going, you cannot come.'"[25] Origen argues that the text refers to "the departure of Jesus' soul from this life." Since the Jews were going to die (John 8:21) and since Christ was going to descend to hell, it seems puzzling that they cannot go where Christ was to go. The solution is to say that Christ was also going to paradise, "where those who died in their sins were not going to be." The next question is why the disciples cannot follow Christ. Origen's solution is to argue that "now" modifies "come," rather than "say" in the text from John—"you cannot come now." That is, the disciples are to follow only after they have fulfilled their work on earth by receiving the Holy Spirit and walking in the way of the cross. Finally, Origen turns to the problem of reconciling "the heart of the earth" with "paradise." His solution is "that in all likelihood before he departed to what is called the heart of the earth he established in the paradise of God the one who said to him, 'remember me when you come into your kingdom.'" "Today" need not be taken literally but can simply refer to the present time.

It is, however, clear that Origen does not regard Christ's descent to hell as an end in itself. Instead, he thinks of it as the means of enabling souls to ascend with him. For example, in commenting on Gen 46:4 ("I will also bring you up again") he refers to Christ's descent to hell but also to the promise of paradise given to the penitent thief, a promise made not only to him but to all the saints.[26] There is another example of this concern in his rather long discussion of "below," "above," "of this world," and "not of this world" in John 8:31.[27] He adds to his consideration the contrast between heaven and earth found, for example, in John 3:31. A key text in his discussion is Eph 4:10: "He who descended is the same one who ascended far above the heavens, so that he might fill all things." Despite the difficulties attaching to defining terms such as "below," "this world," and "earth," there are three meanings that emerge. First, Christ descended to this world "to seek out and to save the lost" (Luke 19:10). Christ made "those be-

---

[25] *Comm. Jo.* 32.32 (Brooke, *Commentary of Origen*, 2:209). Cf. the discussion in Jean Daniélou, *L'Être et le temps chez Grégoire de Nysse* (Leiden: Brill, 1970), 179.

[26] *Hom. Gen.* 15.5.

[27] *Comm. Jo.* 19.20–22 (Brooke, *Commentary of Origen*, 2:27–29).

low" citizens of the "places above" and by his ascension "far above
the heavens" made a way for them to follow. Second, Christ descended to hell, as Ps 21:30 proves, and he made a way to heaven
also for the souls imprisoned there. Finally, there is "a more mysterious meaning" that is not spatial in character. This meaning
has to do with the ascent of Jesus' soul to God and to the spiritual world (κόσμος νοητός). "See if the one who says 'I am not of
this world' can be the soul of Jesus dwelling in the whole of that
world, encompassing it in every way and leading his disciples to
it." Even though he takes seriously doctrines that have to do with
Christ's actual sojourn on earth and his descent to hell, Origen's
interest lies in the spiritual meaning of what Christ accomplished.
Souls after this life will ascend by stages toward their destiny of
the perfect contemplation of God. The "rational being, growing
at each successive stage ... attains perfection, first that perfection
by which it rises to this condition [the 'face to face' vision], and
secondly that by which it remains therein."[28]

Origen's insistence on the spiritual meaning of redemption
helps explain why he uses terms such as "heaven," "paradise,"
and "Abraham's bosom" in such a confused manner. "Paradise"
usually refers not so much to a place as to the condition of the
rational beings both before their fall and after they have fulfilled
their destiny in the *apokatastasis*.[29] Used this way, "paradise" and
"heaven" have essentially the same spiritual meaning. Moreover,
as Eustathius points out (21.2-3), Origen gives the biblical paradise an allegorical meaning. In one place, however, Origen does
treat paradise as "an abiding place" (John 14:2) for souls on their
way toward perfection:

> I think that the saints as they depart from this life will remain
> in some place situated on the earth, which the divine scrip-
> ture calls "paradise." This will be a place of instruction and,
> so to speak, a lecture room or school for souls, in which they
> may be taught about all that they had seen on earth and may
> also receive some indications of what is to follow in the fu-
> ture, seen indeed 'through a glass darkly," and yet truly seen
> "in part" (1 Cor 13:12), which are revealed more clearly and

[28] *Princ.* 2.11.7 (G. W. Butterworth, *Origen: On First Principles* [Lon-
don: SPCK, 1936; repr., Gloucester, Mass.: Smith, 1973], 153).
[29] See SC 253 (*Traité des principes II*), 250 n. 43, for a list of passages and
a brief discussion.

brightly to the saints in their proper times and places.[30]

This passage may be the one swallow that does not prove the summer. On the whole, paradise refers to the heavenly destiny of the rational beings.

In a similar way, Origen can understand the bosom of Abraham as a way of describing the final destiny of the rational beings. In the *Commentary on John* he discusses the bosom of the Father (John 1:18), the bosom of Jesus (13:23), and the bosom of Abraham. We should not take these expressions literally, nor can we ask how many souls the bosom of Abraham could hold.[31] Elsewhere he says that Abraham's death enlarged his bosom to such a degree that saints coming from the four corners of the earth will be escorted there by the angels.[32] We are obviously not meant to take what he says literally. In at least two passages Origen identifies the bosom of Abraham with paradise.[33] The conclusion I should draw is that Origen's real interest lies in the mystery of the soul's journey toward God. His speculations create a large setting for this journey, and he thinks of it as taking place not only in this life but in what happens after our departure from it, whether we are to think of the further stages as successive world orders or as a passage through various spheres of being. At the same time, as I have tried to suggest, he takes seriously the traditional views of Christians. His interpretation of 1 Kgdms 28 at the narrative level is sufficient proof of this conclusion. Let me then turn to two problems that appear at this narrative level, that of the belly-myther's role and the peculiar fact that the soul of Samuel and the souls of Lazarus and Dives are described in bodily terms.

As I have suggested, Eustathius is correct in faulting Origen for being less than clear as to whether it was really the belly-myther that brought up Samuel. Eustathius's rather garbled account of what appears to be Origen's "second homily" (26.2–3) implies that in it Origen did in fact admit that the belly-myther brought up Samuel. In his other writings Origen rarely alludes to 1 Kgdms 28, but one such reference occurs in his discussion of Caiaphas's prophecy in John 11:49–53: "it is better for you

---

[30] *Princ.* 2.11.6 (Butterworth, *Origen*, 152).
[31] *Comm. Jo.* 32.30 (Brooke, *Commentary of Origen*, 2:189).
[32] *Hom. Gen.* 11.3.
[33] *Dial.* 23; *Hom. Num.* 26.3–4.

to have one man die for the people than to have the whole nation destroyed."[34] Why does John regard what Caiaphas said as
a prophecy? Origen begins his answer by pointing out that not all
who prophesy are prophets any more than all who do something
just are just people. And he supplies an argument for the wickedness of Caiaphas, who nonetheless prophesies. He makes his point
by appealing to scripture. Balaam was no prophet but instead a
soothsayer (μάντις). Nevertheless, an angel guided him, and the
Lord put a word in his mouth (Num 23:5, 12). Does this need to
mean that the Holy Spirit inspired Balaam? Origen's answer is in
the negative, and he points out that even the evil spirits bear witness to Jesus in Mark 1:24. There are a number of other examples,
including the "spirit of divination" (πνεῦμα πύθωνα) of Acts 16:16
and the lying spirit of 3 Kgdms 22:22.[35] Several examples from 1
Kingdoms follow: the evil spirit that tormented Saul (16:14), the
prophesying of Saul's messengers and of Saul himself (19:19–24),
and the divination of the idol priests with respect to the ark (6:9).

The last example Origen gives is 1 Kgdms 28, which he mentions in passing as he turns towards his conclusion:

> In listing these passages we must not omit the one concern-
> ing the belly-myther and Samuel. From them Saul learned
> that he was going to die the next day together with his sons.
> The person able to converse about various spirits, evil and
> good, will discern the accurate meaning of these passages—
> even if there may also exist some spirits in between these two
> extremes.

The broad conclusion Origen wishes to make is clear. Not
only do people who are not prophets prophesy, but it is also the
case that they need not be inspired by the Holy Spirit, so long
as what they prophesy is true. The application of this conclusion to the example from 1 Kgdms 28 seems somewhat cryptic
to me. Samuel is a prophet, and if we assume, as Origen does in
his homily, that he was really brought up, then it is hard to see
that another "power" than the Holy Spirit is associated with him.
Perhaps Origen's idea is that in all the examples he has cited something foreign to the Holy Spirit is occurring. The other power

---

[34] *Comm. Jo.* 28.13–17 (Brooke, *Commentary of Origen,* 2:124–33).

[35] Although I have no explanation for it, the fact is that Eustathius employs these same examples (2.8; 11.5–7; 14.1–3).

would appear to be the belly-myther's familiar spirit. The implication would then be that the belly-myther's agency in bringing
up Samuel does not in any way interfere with Samuel's appearance
and his prophecy. To be sure, Origen falls short of drawing this
conclusion. Had he done so, it might have met the objection that
we shall see Eustathius making.

The other major issue raised by the narrative reading of
1 Kgdms 28 has to do with the bodily and visible appearance of
Samuel. Once more we can appeal to a place where Origen alludes
to 1 Kgdms 28, even though that passage is less important than
the Lukan parable of Lazarus and Dives. In book 3 of his treatise
On the Resurrection Methodius of Olympus cites a passage that apparently comes from Origen's lost treatise on the same topic and
that has been preserved in Greek by Photius. In this passage Origen points out that there is a difficult obstacle to understanding the
parable of Lazarus and Dives because the passage clearly presents
them after their death but in bodily terms.[36] Simpler Christians
understand these references to mean that Lazarus and Dives continue to be and to act just as they did while alive. But those with
a more accurate understanding realize that the characters in the
parable are neither in this life nor in that of the resurrection, and
so they are obliged to seek some explanation of the finger, the
tongue, and the other details that will be suitable to a time after the
soul's departure from the body and before the resurrection. Origen speculates as follows:

> Perhaps the shape (σχῆμα) of the soul at the time of its depar-
> ture from this life, since it has a form similar to (ὁμοιοειδές) a
> passible and earthly body, can be grasped in this way. If any
> one of those who have fallen asleep is at some time recounted
> to have appeared, he is seen similar to his shape when he had
> flesh... Moreover, Samuel when he appears, as is evident...
>
> [This proves to be a difficulty] especially if we are compelled
> by arguments to prove that the essence of the soul is of it-
> self incorporeal, since Samuel is visibly present because he is
> encompassed with a body.[37] Moreover, the rich man who is

[36] Methodius, *Res.* 3.17–18 (Georg Nathanael Bonwetsch, ed., *Methodius Olympius, Werke* [GCS 27; Leipzig: Hinrichs, 1917], 413–16).

[37] My translation is admittedly interpretive. Bonwetsch does not indicate
lacunae in the apparatus but does so in his punctuation. The sense of the passage
appears to reflect a Platonizing attempt to preserve the incorporeality of the soul

being punished and the poor man resting in Abraham's bosom teach that, even now that they have departed from this
life, the soul employs a body. This is because they were there
before the Savior's coming and the end of the age and, consequently, before the resurrection, and because one was said
to be punished in hell and the other to be refreshed in Abraham's bosom.

Samuel, Lazarus, and Dives are all dead, and so we must
suppose that it is their souls that appear. Origen must find some
way of reconciling his belief in the incorporeal nature of the soul
and the scriptural fact that these souls are visible in what seems to
be a bodily way.

Methodius tells us that Origen's solution is to argue that the
"body" of Samuel and the others is "another vehicle (ὄχημα ἄλλο)
similar in form (ὁμοιοειδές) to this perceptible one." Following
Plato, Origen argues that this "vehicle" does not affect his conviction that the soul is in some sense (ὑπό τι) incorporeal. The idea,
while it is not Plato's, does depend upon several passages in the di-
alogues where the word "vehicle" is used as a way of talking about
the bodies employed by the stars and by souls.[38] Consequently, the
notion of an astral body possessed by souls emerges in Platonism
and is designed to explain how the soul can be incorporeal and yet
joined to the body. The "vehicle" is a kind of middle ground.[39]
The term does not occur elsewhere in Origen's writings, but it is
possible to argue that the idea does. One of Origen's longest dis-
cussions of the resurrection is *Cels.* 5.17–24. Here two scriptural
texts occupy a central position in the argument: 1 Cor 15 and 2 Cor
5:1–4. From the first passage Origen deduces a sharp distinction
between the "seed" (the body that is sown) and "the body that shall

but to recognize that aspect of the soul that allies it with the body.

[38] *Tim.* 41e, 44e, 69c; *Phaedr.* 247b.

[39] I am probably over-simplifying. The classical discussion is by E. R.
Dodds, *Proclus: The Elements of Theology* (2nd ed.; Oxford: Clarendon, 1963),
313–21. See Henri Crouzel, "Le thème platonicien du 'véhicule de l'âme' chez
Origène," *Did* 7 (1977): 225–37; and idem, *Origen* (Edinburgh: T&T Clark,
1989), 241–42; Henry Chadwick, "Origen, Celsus, and the Resurrection of the
Body," *HTR* 41 (1948): 83–102; Alan Scott, *Origen and the Life of the Stars: A
History of an Idea* (Oxford: Clarendon, 1991), 77–79, 109, 116, 155–56; Lloyd
G. Patterson, *Methodius of Olympus: Divine Sovereignty, Human Freedom, and
Life in Christ* (Washington, D.C.: Catholic University of America Press, 1997),
144 and the whole of ch. 5.

be." He interprets the second passage in a similar way:

> But though it may need a body in order to pass from one
> place to another, the soul that has studied wisdom ... un-
> derstands the difference between the earthly house which is
> destroyed in which is the tabernacle, and the tabernacle it-
> self in which those who are righteous groan being burdened,
> not because they desire to put off the tabernacle, but because
> they want to be clothed upon, in order that as a result of this
> "mortality may be swallowed up by life" (2 Cor 5:1–4, 1 Cor
> 15:53).[40]

The "seed" and the "tabernacle" in these Pauline passages
represent a principle that underlies both the corruptible body possessed in this life and the incorruptible body of the resurrection, a
principle of continuity that balances Origen's unwillingness to admit that this body is the same as the resurrection body.[41]

In *Cels.* 5.23 Origen speaks of a "seminal principle" (λόγος
σπέρματος), which he elsewhere identifies with the "tabernacle."[42]
We find a similar idea in the passages from Origen's comments
on Ps 1 preserved by Methodius. The soul has a characteristic
form that is bodily (εἶδος σωματικόν) and that represents not an
outward shape but an inner principle of continuity. Even in this
life bodies are in a constant state of flux, and the discontinuity
of infancy, youth, and old age is obvious. Nevertheless, there is
also continuity as the individual passes through these stages. The
characteristic form, then, persists after this life and at the resurrection is clothed with the resurrection body.[43] In another passage
cited by Methodius we find the same idea:

> For it is necessary for the soul that is existing in corporeal
> places to use bodies appropriate to those places. Just as if we

[40] *Cels.* 5.19 (Henry Chadwick, *Origen: Contra Celsum* [Cambridge:
Cambridge University Press, 1953], 279).

[41] See Daley, *Hope of the Early Church,* 52: "Clearly, for Origen the real
conflict is not between a hope in resurrection and a belief in the immortality of
the soul, but between the materialistic popular conception of risen life ... and a
more spiritual one."

[42] *Cels.* 7.32 (Chadwick, *Origen,* 420): "It [the doctrine of the resurrec-
tion] teaches that the tabernacle of the soul, as it is called in the Bible, possesses
a seminal principle. And in this tabernacle those who are righteous groan, being
weighed down, and desiring not to put it off but to be clothed on top of it."

[43] Methodius, *Res.* 3.3–4, 3.7 (Bonwetsch, *Methodius Olympius,* 391–94,
398–400).

became aquatic beings, and had to live in the sea, it would
no doubt be necessary for us to adopt a different state similar to that of the fish, so if we are to inherit the kingdom of
heaven and to exist in superior places, it is essential for us
to use spiritual bodies. This does not mean that the form of
the earlier body disappears, though it may change to a more
glorious condition.[44]

At least two other themes also occur. Origen can distinguish
the underlying material substance of the body from its qualities,
and this implies that what he calls the "form" or the "seminal principle" can change its quality. In the resurrection—and perhaps
under the conditions of the precosmic existence of souls and of
their existence after death and before the resurrection—the quality is "ethereal and divine."[45] In two passages Origen refers to
"apparitions of shadowy souls," particularly near tombs.[46] He is
referring to Plato's *Phaed.* 81bcd. In the first passage these are
the souls of the wicked, while the soul "not weighed down by the
leaden weights of evil, is carried on high to the regions of the purer
and ethereal bodies." But in the second passage the apparitions
round the tombs are explained "by the fact that the soul is sub-
sisting in what is called the luminous body (αὐγοειδεῖ σώματι)."

There are obvious difficulties involved in attempting to put
Origen's various observations in any truly systematic structure.[47]
In particular, I wonder whether we can simply equate the ethereal body of the resurrection, which appears to be similar to or the
same as the body the souls have in their precosmic existence, with
the "bodies" that Samuel, Lazarus, and Dives have in scripture.
It might make more sense to argue that the "characteristic form,"
the "seminal principle," and the "material substance" represent
the continuity of the soul's capacity for incorporation. Understood this way, the ethereal body would clothe the characteristic
form but would not be identical with it. Puzzles remain, but several conclusions can be drawn. First, it is clear, as is increasingly
recognized, that we should not read Origen through the lenses

[44] Ibid. 1.22 (Bonwetsch, *Methodius Olympius*, 246). The translation is
Chadwick, *Origen*, 420 n. 7.
[45] *Cels.* 4.60, cf. 3.41–42. But see Origen's denial of ether in *Princ.* 3.6.6.
[46] Ibid., 7.5, 2.60 (Chadwick, *Origen*, 398, 112).
[47] See SC 253 (*Traité des principes II*), 101–2 n. 30; 102 n. 34; 105 n. 4;
139–41 n. 7; 144 n. 10.

of his opponents in the early church. Second, there can be little doubt that what Origen wants to say is that the soul is incorporeal in its nature but that it always makes use of a form of some kind. There may be a paradox involved, but no Platonist would wish the idea of the soul's form or vehicle to be confused with the Stoic view of the soul's corporeality. Third, the view I have presented, which fundamentally follows that of Crouzel, enables us to take seriously those places where Origen insists that only God is incorporeal in an absolute sense.[48] To sum up my argument, Origen is primarily interested in the spiritual destiny of the soul. But he is also concerned to integrate the body into what is basically a spiritual structure of thought. One may question his success but not his intent. As a result, it is not really surprising that he can read 1 Kgdms 28 at the narrative level. This is true if for no other reason than that the conclusion he reaches on the basis of the letter of scripture is a spiritual one. We have "something more" than Samuel, because our souls can pursue their journey without stopping in hell.

EUSTATHIUS

It is certainly possible to argue that one of Eustathius's aims in refuting Origen's interpretation of 1 Kgdms 28 has to do with his insistence upon the resurrection of the body and his conviction that all souls must wait in hell until that time. He does indeed seek to preserve the picture of two places in hell that is based upon the parable of Lazarus and Dives, and so he agrees with Tertullian (55.2; 57.11) and Pionius (14.7). Samuel's prediction that Saul and Jonathan will be with him "tomorrow" is a demonic blasphemy not only because it is a perversion of Christ's promise to the penitent thief but also because it fails to recognize the barrier that exists between the wicked and the righteous (14.12):

> Therefore, if a sort of chasm (Luke 16:26) is lying between the righteous and the wicked so that those on this side are not able to pass through to there, and those on that side cannot get here, it is established that Saul, being wicked, is not with the prophet Samuel.

[48] E.g., *Princ.* 1.6.4; 2.2.2; 4.3.15; *Hom. Exod.* 6.5.

THE "BELLY-MYTHER" OF ENDOR

"Samuel" must really be a minister of Satan because his prediction is a lie designed to abolish the distinction between good and evil people. Eustathius's point also implies that Samuel could not have left hell. The belly-myther's familiar spirit could not have crossed the chasm to bring Samuel up. This is the chief point, whereas Origen shifts attention to the question whether the Samuel of the story was really Samuel. "What needs to be investigated is not whether it was Samuel, but whether a demon had such authority as to call up the souls of the righteous from hell and send them back again" (17.2).

Eustathius, however, is not clear as to the difference made by Christ's harrowing of hell. He does recognize that, when "the soul of Christ came to the regions of the netherworld, at the same time it also led the soul of the thief on that very day to paradise" and that Christ's "soul ransomed souls of the same kind, at once both by going down to the chaotic subterranean regions and by restoring to the most ancient plot of paradise the thief, who entered it secretly by the might of Christ's unconquerable kingdom" (18.1–2). But we are left to wonder whether Abraham's bosom has become paradise and remains a lodging for those awaiting the resurrection of the just. Despite the puzzles that are raised, Eustathius is concerned with the resurrection. In 22.5–6 he refers to the treatise on the resurrection written by "Methodius, who is worthy of holy memory," and to his refutation of Origen's definition of the resurrection "as one of form but not of the body itself." In sum, there is much to be said for understanding one of Eustathius's motives as related to defending the resurrection of the body, which must be awaited by souls after death and which will take place at the end of the age.

At the same time, Eustathius's basic aim in the treatise is specifically exegetical. He is obviously willing to agree with Origen that the narrative meaning must be explained. Consequently, it is not possible to argue that the issue is one that revolves around the conflict between an Antiochene insistence upon the letter of scripture as opposed to an Alexandrian commitment to allegorism.[49] Instead, the issue is one that opposes two different interpretations of the narrative meaning itself. Eustathius's chief

---

[49] See Frances Young, *The Art of Performance: Towards a Theology of Holy Scripture* (London: Darton, Longman, & Todd, 1990), 94–96.

presupposition appears early in his treatise (3.3):

> For demons do not have authority over spirits and souls, but
> the One who is Lord of all at once—God. As a result, the
> capacity to summon and to call souls up again from hell must
> be granted to the divine nature alone.

This conviction occurs repeatedly in the treatise (10.5–6;
16.10; 20.3), and it represents Eustathius's conclusion (30.6).
One hermeneutical principle involved is a theological one, but
Eustathius must explain how his presupposition can also be his
conclusion. He does this by examining the narrative as carefully as
possible in order to show that what is supposed to have happened
was no more than a demonic fiction. He pays close attention to the
details of the text in order to make his argument.

Eustathius repeatedly points out that both Saul and the
belly-myther are possessed by demons and are, consequently, mad
or demented. In the case of Saul, as 15.1–2 shows, he appeals
to the text in 1 Kgdms 19:9 that tells of the "evil spirit from
the Lord" that possessed Saul. It is presumably this that explains Saul's wickedness: his sparing of Agag and the spoils of
victory "for the sake of shameful gain" (1 Kgdms 15:9), his persecution of David, and his slaughter of the priests of the Lord
(1 Kgdms 22:18). Saul's culminating sin, of course, is to consult
the belly-myther despite the fact that he had "cut off the belly-
mythers and the wizards from the land" (1 Kgdms 28:9). The
biblical text establishes that the belly-myther plies her trade by
means of a familiar spirit (1 Kgdms 28:8), and it follows that (2.7):

> since Saul placed the request to receive divination through
> the belly-myther, someone could say that his words were
> true. But is there anyone who does not know that when Saul
> turned to deadly divination and the diabolic operations of
> myths, he was being driven to savage rages by the demon?

The belly-myther herself is by definition demon-possessed
(26.10; 30.1). Moreover, a careful reading of the text leads to the
conclusion that (3.8–9):

> nowhere at all has the plain sense of the divine text said
> that Samuel was brought up through the agency of the
> belly-myther. Rather, she proleptically declares through the
> agency of the demon raging with frenzy in her that it is nec-
> essary to bring him up. Then, boasting that she saw even

gods coming up, she was deceitfully giving tell-tale signs of
the man to trick him. And Saul, since he was out of his mind,
"knew" from what he had heard that this was Samuel himself (1 Kgdms 28:14).

Like Origen, Eustathius is paying close attention to what the
text says and what it fails to say.

It is somewhat more difficult to demonstrate that the Samuel
who comes up is a demonic apparition, but if Eustathius is to refute Origen he must make this point. He seeks to do so in two
ways. First, there are at least three peculiarities in the narrative
itself that point toward the delusory character of Samuel's appearance. One is that it is not entirely clear from the narrative whether
Samuel is visible or not (5.4–6). The belly-myther claims to see
him, but Saul is obliged to ask her what she sees. He "knows"
from what she tells him that it is Samuel, but nowhere does the
text say that he sees Samuel. Samuel's soul would have been invisible, for if he came up in a bodily form, surely Saul would
have seen him. Another peculiarity is that Saul worships Samuel
(1 Kgdms 28:14). Why would he do so now when he had failed
to worship the prophet when he was the ruler of the people? Why
would Saul not have worshiped the gods who came up? (10.8–11).
Finally, Samuel's words in 1 Kgdms 28:15 ("Why have you disturbed me by bringing me up?") imply that Samuel is unwillingly
subject to the authority of the belly-myther's demon. Eustathius
draws the conclusion that it was the demon impersonating Samuel
that said this in order to establish its authority (11.1–2).

The second way Eustathius argues for the demonic character
of "Samuel" revolves around what Samuel is supposed to have said
in his prophecy (1 Kgdms 28:16–19). Most of this simply repeats
what the real Samuel had already prophesied while he was alive
(12.1–8, 16.2, 23.2). Eustathius demonstrates this by appealing to
the larger narrative in 1 Kingdoms. The demonic Samuel has simply appropriated what he knows from scripture (23.4–8), and his
lie consists in claiming that Samuel's words are his own. To be
sure, the prophecy that "tomorrow you and Jonathan will be with
me" is something that the demon adds on his own. But this is no
more than guessing and contriving "verisimilitudes based on what
was likely to happen" (13.5–7). Eustathius is willing to agree with
Origen that demons have no knowledge of God's dispensations,
but he argues that nothing Samuel says requires such knowledge.

What is true in his prophecy is taken from scripture or from events that have already occurred. His guesses prove to be inaccurate. For example, Saul did not in fact die the next day. Finally, "the devil has prior notice[50] of the evils inflicted upon wicked people, since he is himself the contriver of everything that is most hateful" (14.4–5; cf. 13.9–10). We learn from Christ's words in John 8:44 that the devil is a liar (4.2) and that he tells the truth only when compelled to do so in exorcism (4.4; 11.6). This may be more obvious in the case of the demon-possessed Saul and of the belly-myther with her familiar spirit, but it is also true of the false Samuel (30.2):

> And when he transforms himself into all sorts of different shapes, being a creature of many faces, no less does he pretend both to come up from the earth and to call out. Then in both ways, changing his ministrations at the same time as his forms, he seems to present himself coming up as someone different from the one who summons him. Yet though it is one and the same running about here and there, he changes his appearances so that he demonstrates in deeds and words that he is a liar.

Eustathius finds the idea in 2 Cor 11:14–15 (Satan as an angel of light and his ministers as ministers of righteousness), and the many-formed devil (4.9; 13.10; 15.3) is also the one who summons his "cohort of demons" as the "gods" the belly-myther sees coming up from the ground (10.2; 20.1).

Eustathius argues that all these considerations enable us to understand the character of the narrative. Origen is wrong to suppose that what is written is necessarily meant to be true.[51] "You hide by your silence what the text actually says—that he [Saul] saw absolutely nothing at all" (7.2). Despite the fact that Origen abandons what Eustathius regards as his usual allegorical approach and rightly interprets the text at the narrative level, "he does not pay attention to the body of scripture right-mindedly" (21.1) and is unable to "explicate what is the plain sense (τὸ σαφές; cf. 1.4) on the basis of its logical sequence" (22.7).[52] Part of what

---

[50] προμανθάνειν (but *not* προγιγνώσκειν).

[51] See Eustathius's citations from Origen's homily and his responses, in *On the Belly-Myther* 5.1–2; 6.3; 7.1; 16.5–6.

[52] The Greek is οὐδ' αὖ τὸ σαφὲς ἐξ αὐτῆς ἱστορῆσαι τῆς ἀκολουθίας. For "sequence," see also 16.1.

this means is that the narrative must be placed in its proper context, which includes the totality of scripture. Origen ignores those
passages in scripture that condemn divination and necromancy
(11.12–13; 24.6–7, 11–16; 25.8–9); he "pretends not to know these
testimonies" (26.1). In principle, there are no contradictions in
scripture, and even if there are, we must accept the majority view,
which prohibits divination (25.3–12). The story of Saul and the
belly-myther is in scripture (16.10),

> but the author by no means foretells in his own persona that
> what is written took place. For the book would in that case
> not have been read in the church, if it cried out things that
> stand in direct opposition to the prophetic voices.

We must make a distinction between the narrator and the
speeches he puts into the mouths of those whose story he is telling
(25.7). Origen is wrong to suppose that the belly-myther's words
are those of the Holy Spirit (3.4–5).[53] Eustathius must admit that
at least at one point the narration itself drives against the view for
which he is arguing. When we read "the woman saw Samuel," we
are obliged to press beyond the distinction between the narrative
and the speeches included in it to the character of the narrative itself.

In section 8 Eustathius argues that we can discern the character of a narrative by paying attention to what it fails to say and
by the way it introduces its characters. In the story of Elijah and
the priests of Baal (3 Kgdms 18:19–40), "the text of scripture did
not define precisely whether they [the priests of Baal] prophesied
things that were true or false" (8.4). Obviously, however, no one
could have the impression that they were true prophets (8.7):

> in exactly the same way in 1 Kgdms 28, by first setting forth
> the personae possessed by demons and the acts of unlaw-
> ful divination, he indicated precisely by deliberate omission
> (κατὰ ἀποσιώπησιν)[54] what people in their right minds ought
> to think about those who are out of their minds.

Eustathius refers here to one of the common figures of
speech defined in the handbooks known as "preliminary exercises"

---

[53] Eustathius nowhere affirms or denies the inspiration of the Holy
Spirit. Reading between the lines one could argue that his view of inspiration
leaves room for the human aspect of scriptural authors and narrators.

[54] See n. 27 in the translation on the rhetorical figure by this name.

(*progymnasmata*), which were designed as elementary instruction
in the rhetorical schools of his time.[55] In his work concerning
figures of speech, Alexander, who was Numenius's son and a
second-century rhetorician, defines *aposiopesis* as "holding back
what is passed over in silence, either omitting it because it is
known or keeping silent about it because it is shameful."[56] It is for
the first reason that the narratives in 3 Kingdoms and 1 Kingdoms
do not explicitly treat the priests of Baal and the belly-myther
as false and demonic. The very way they are introduced into
the narrative makes them obvious for what they are. Eustathius
makes the same argument concerning the magicians of Egypt in
the opening chapters of Exodus. When they turn their staffs into
serpents (Exod 7:11–12), their "lie convicts itself by its sheer unreality," since Aaron's staff swallowed theirs up (9.4). Moreover,
when the magicians turn the waters to blood and produce more
frogs, the deceptive character of what they accomplish is proved
by the fact that they would not have deliberately compounded
their sufferings by realities (9.6–10).

   That scripture fails to make clear judgments about the demonic character of the belly-myther's divination need cause no
surprise, since such a judgment is possible for anyone who reads
the narrative carefully (16.11–13):

> the author has characterized the words as belonging to the
> "belly-myther," and the insane "knowledge" of the ruler
> demarcated as full of ignorance. For if it will be fitting to
> examine the holy scriptures this way, then is it the case that
> when they say that the devil openly proclaims himself even
> to be God, we will because of this be obliged to believe him
> because we attribute everything to the narrative sense of

---

[55] See Ronald F. Hock and Edward H. O'Neill, *The Chreia in Ancient
Rhetoric*, vol. 1: *The Progymnasmata* (SBLTT 27; Atlanta: Scholars Press,
1986); and George A. Kennedy, *Progymnasmata: Greek Textbooks of Prose Composition and Rhetoric* (SBLWGRW 10; Atlanta: Society of Biblical Literature,
2003). See Frances Young, "The Rhetorical Schools and Their Influence on
Patristic Exegesis," in *The Making of Orthodoxy: Essays in Honour of Henry
Chadwick* (ed. R. Williams; Cambridge: Cambridge University Press, 1989),
182–99. She argues persuasively that Antiochene exegesis must be explained by
the influence of Greek rhetoric. Of course, Origen also employs these conventions.

[56] Alexander, *Peri schematon* 16 (Leonard Spengel, *Rhetores Graeci* [3
vols.; Leipzig: Teubner, 1854–56], 3:22).

the text, as Origen proposes? ... For in truth the "narrative voice" has characterized his boastings [the devil's in Matt 4:8–9] and declares them not true.

We may suppose that Eustathius is using the rhetorical method of "disproving" to make his point,[57] even though he does not emphasize the technical terms. Perhaps this is because of the view we find in Pseudo-Hermogenes that "what is altogether false can neither be proved (κατασκεύειν) nor disproved (ἀνασκεύειν), as myths."[58]

What is clear is that Eustathius understands the narrative of 1 Kgdms 28, especially the words of the woman, to be a myth and articulates that understanding by appealing to the commonplaces of the rhetorical handbooks (27.2):

> For the rhetorical handbooks clearly show that "a myth is a fabrication composed with persuasive attraction with an eye to some matter of vital importance and utility."

Both Theon and Aphthonius define myth as "a false account imitating the truth," and Nicolaus adds the words "by a persuasive composition."[59] Part of what Eustathius says suggests to me that he is in some degree conflating "mythical" and "fictional" narratives. Pseudo-Hermogenes distinguishes a narrative (διήγημα) from a narration (διήγησις), primarily in terms of length. There are four kinds of narratives: mythic; fictional, which they also call dramatic, such as the tragedies; historical; and political.[60] In the rest of section 27 Eustathius may be employing the method of "disproving," but he is certainly including in his definition of myth themes that reflect the "fictional." Theon, in fact, can make a simple distinction between a narrative "about things that happened" and a narrative that treats things "as though they had happened."[61] There are six elements in a narrative: the person,

---

[57] See pp. xci–xcvii, below, on ἀνασκευή and κατασκευή.

[58] Spengel, *Rhetores Graeci*, 2:8–9. Theon (second century c.e.), however, recognizes that when the narrative makes it clear that it is a myth, the technique can be used: "For when the mythmaker himself confesses he has written both false and impossible things, but that they are persuasive and useful, he can be proved wrong because he says what is unpersuasive and useless" (Spengel, *Rhetores Graeci*, 2:76).

[59] Spengel, *Rhetores Graeci*, 2:72; 2:21; 3:453.

[60] Ibid., 2:4.

[61] Ibid., 2:78–79.

what is done by the person, the place where it takes place, the time, the manner of doing, and the reason. Fictional imitation of the truth will include these factors, and we can think not only of myths in the strict sense but also of other narratives.

One obvious element in a narrative is "personification" (προσωποποιία). Theon defines this figure of speech as "the introduction of a person who recites words appropriate both for himself and for the underlying facts (ὑποκειμένοις πράγμασιν) in an indisputable way."[62] Alexander defines it as "the fashioning of the person either of someone who never existed to begin with or of someone existing or of someone no longer existing."[63] In at least three places Eustathius refers to personification. In 12.8 he describes the demon that appeared as Samuel as "engaging in deceitful impersonation (προσωποποιῶν)." In 27.6 he makes the more general comment that myth "by like personification describes in detail deeds that were actually not done." Finally, in 27.4 he says that a myth "dramatizes its setting (προσωποποιεῖ ὑπόθεσιν) with a careful eye for each part." Of particular interest is Eustathius's use of the word I have translated "setting." I should suggest we can understand what he means by what he says immediately before the phrase I have cited. A myth "gives form to deeds without any substance, when there is no possible underlying ground for confirmation" (27.3). The term "setting" (ὑπόθεσις) also occurs in 21.6 and 22.2. The word can mean a great many different things, including "theme." But Eustathius is using it to refer to the true setting and circumstances of the person in a true narrative. It is possible to correlate this usage with an observation Theodore of Mopsuestia makes in the preface to his comments on Ps 36. Each of the psalms usually reflects a particular "persona," and the "setting" is the context in which that persona speaks. But Ps 36 is an example of a psalm without such a setting. David in the Psalms sometimes provides a general exhortation without a setting (ἐκτὸς ὑποθέσεως).[64] There is the possibility of allying Eustathius's

---

[62] Ibid., 2:115. We could, of course, translate "supposed" facts.

[63] *Peri schematon* 12 (Spengel, *Rhetores Graeci*, 3:19).

[64] Robert Devreesse, *Le Commentaire de Théodore de Mopsueste sur les Psaumes* (Studi e Testi 92; Vatican City: Biblioteca apostolica vaticana, 1939), 206. For a translation of Theodore's commentary on the Psalter, see now Robert Charles Hill, trans., *Theodore of Mopsuestia: Commentary on Psalms 1–81* (SBLWGRW 5; Atlanta: Society of Biblical Literature, 2006). See the discus-

exegetical methods and conventions to what we find in the later Antiochenes.

The point of my discussion is to suggest that Eustathius is using the commonplaces of Greek rhetorical education and to underline the importance of Prof. Mitchell's essay in this volume. One final observation occurs to me. The definitions of myth he finds include some positive themes. Myths can be persuasive and useful (27.2), though, of course, Eustathius finds nothing persuasive or useful in 1 Kgdms 28. Does this explain his appeal to Plato in sections 28 and 29? To be sure, Plato also has some positive things to say about myths. They have a charm and a kind of truth (28.1). They can teach eloquence (29.1). But if Plato excludes the poems of Homer and Hesiod as false myths, how much more must we exclude the myth concocted in the belly-myther's belly. Aesop's fables must also be excluded, and this idea reflects the fact that in the rhetorical handbooks they are often listed as examples of myths.[65] Perhaps the appeal to Plato is meant to undermine whatever positive the handbooks have to say about myths, while the appeal to the use made of Aesop's fables represents an empirical argument to the same effect. And since Homer, Hesiod, and Aesop were part of the normal school curriculum, we can suppose that Eustathius's comments represent some caution regarding the education of his time.

Although it represents something of a digression, I should like to make one other set of observations about Eustathius's trea-

---

sion of *hypothesis* in Young, "Rhetorical Schools," 190–91. She understands *hypothesis* more broadly than I am suggesting and may well be correct. "Summary and paraphrase is a persistent Antiochene technique for bringing out the gist of the argument, and the *hupothesis* usually includes this, together with historical or circumstantial introductory material." Young continues by relating *hypothesis* to *skopos*. Cf. Young, *Art of Performance*, 98. See also Christoph Schäublin, *Untersuchungen zu Methode und Herkunft der antiochenischen Exegese* (Theophania 23; Cologne-Bonn: Hanstein, 1974). He discusses *hypothesis* in the context of Theodore's exegesis (84–94) and underlines the "historical" dimension of the term. See 93–94: "This already means that Theodore's 'hypotheseis' are to be assessed as more than 'simple indications of content.' After all, they include what agrees with the results of his own linguistic and, especially, historical investigation." He alludes to Theodore's introduction to Ps 36 in his notes (69, 161–62) but fails to comment on ἐκτὸς ὑποθέσεως.

[65] See Spengel, *Rhetores Graeci*, 2:73 (Theon); 2:21 (Aphthonius); 3:452 (Nicolaus).

tise. There are a number of passages that reflect his theological commitments, and they are of considerable interest because they are up to a point congruent with later Antiochene views. For example, Eustathius takes Origen to task for suggesting that Christ's soul is "above" by ethical purpose (17.3–10). Of course, he does not disagree with Origen that Christ's soul went to hell. What bothers him is that Origen seems to have forgotten that Christ's soul was "strengthened by divine power because of the constant association (συνουσίαν) of God the Word so he, too, had authority that extended everywhere" (17.10). It is not his ethical purpose so much as "the excellence of his divinity" (17.8) that enables him to be above as well as below. Eustathius is not being fair to Origen, since Origen would not deny the union of Christ's soul with the Word. What Eustathius says is more interesting, however, for its evidence for his own views. His reference to the "excellence of divinity" here and in 19.2, together with his use of the expression "the working of divinity" (19.4), could imply that he thinks of the second person of the Trinity as no more than a divine "energy." This would leave him open to the charge of Sabellianism, and it was almost certainly that charge that resulted in his deposition by the "Arians" shortly after the council of Nicaea.[66] This charge is almost certainly untrue, and yet it sticks to some extent for the simple reason that even after Nicaea the "old Nicenes" had no formula for the three persons of the Trinity. It was only when "three persons" was added to the formula "one essence," thanks largely to the Cappadocians, that any acceptable definition of the Christian God emerged. We cannot fault Eustathius for failing to have language that was hammered out half a century later.

More interesting is what Eustathius says about the incarnate Lord. His insistence upon the importance of Christ's human soul is worth noting, since his later arguments against the Arians will revolve in part upon their denial of a human soul in Christ. As well, to posit a human soul is part of a recognition of the full humanity of Christ. Eustathius tends to make a clear distinction between the Word as the "God within" and the "pure man" who appears outwardly (10.14). Their union can be described by employing the metaphors of clothing and the temple. These themes

[66] For a full account of Eustathius's career and fate see R. P. C. Hanson, *The Search for the Christian Doctrine of God* (Edinburgh: T&T Clark, 1988).

have a tendency to suggest a "two sons" Christology, and they certainly resemble what we find in the later Antiochenes: Diodore, Theodore, and Theodoret. To be sure, Eustathius is concerned to argue that Christ's soul or "the human form which God the Word bore" (18.5) owes its special powers to its union with God the Word, but I am not convinced that this represents any real contrast to the later Antiochenes. Another consideration has to do with the fourth-century schism in Antioch. When Eustathius was deposed and disappeared from the pages of history, his followers remained loyal to his memory and constituted themselves as a small confessing church in Antioch. In 360 Meletius became the bishop and turned out, surprisingly, to be a "new Nicene." Despite attempts to reconcile the "old Nicene" Eustathians with Meletius's church, the schism persisted for much of the century. Diodore and those after him, of course, were not Eustathians but belonged to the church over which Meletius and later Flavian presided. Yet even this consideration does not seem to me to exclude the possibility that in Eustathius's writings we find the roots of the later Antiochene theology.[67] If this is so and if, as seems likely, we date his treatise *On the Belly-Myther* before Nicaea, we can argue that the Antiochene Christology is by no means merely a reaction to Arianism and Apollinarianism.

To return from my digression, let me conclude this discussion of Eustathius's treatise. It seems to me quite possible to argue that one basic motive underlying his argument does have to do with protecting the doctrine of the resurrection. This conclusion would endorse the general picture drawn by the Nautins and Simonetti. At the same time, it is clear that his basic aim is exegetical. That is, he wishes to correct Origen's understanding of the narrative meaning of 1 Kgdms 28. Moreover, his method in doing so depends in an unusually obvious way upon the conventions of Greek rhetorical education. One final complication remains. At several points Eustathius claims that, however inadvertently, Origen by his interpretation is introducing into the

---

[67] It would take me too far from my basic purpose to say more. The reader can consult Michel Spanneut, *Recherches sur les écrits d'Eustathe d'Antioche avec une édition nouvelle des fragments dogmatiques et exégétiques* (Lille: Facultés Catholiques, 1948); J. N. D. Kelly, *Early Christian Doctrines* (New York: Harper, 1958); Aloys Grillmeier, *Christ in Christian Tradition: From the Apostolic Age to Chalcedon (451)* (trans. J. Bowden; London: Mowbray, 1965).

church the impiety of pagan divination.[68] If we underline these passages, then the issue of the resurrection would appear to take second place to that of opening the door of the church to pagan, and hence demonic, religious practices.

APOLLINARIS

In general terms the fragment from Apollinaris repeats Origen's conviction that because of Christ's harrowing of hell we have "something more." That is, the gates of hell have been broken open, and Christ has opened "through his own ascent a way up for the souls that were held fast." Indeed, hell seems almost to have been abolished. Moreover, Apollinaris thinks of the harrowing of hell in terms of Christ's victory rather than merely in terms of his preaching to the souls imprisoned in hell. There is, however, one significant point to make. Apollinaris makes no mention of Christ's soul, and this is exactly what we should expect. He understands the incarnation as the appropriation of a human body—or of a human body and its animating soul—by the Word of God. There is no real difference between passages where he defines Christ in a dichotomous way and those where he employs a trichotomous understanding. The point is that the Word of God takes the place of the rational soul in the incarnate Lord. Thus, his general agreement with Origen must be qualified by his failure to retain Origen's view of Christ's soul.[69]

DIODORE

Diodore begins by agreeing with Eustathius that the belly-myther did not in fact bring up Samuel, and he adds to the arguments we have already observed one that springs from the fact that "the woman cried out with a loud voice" (1 Kgdms 28:12). He explains this by pointing out that she saw many "gods" instead of

---

[68] 3.4; 7.3; 21.1; 25.1; 27.1.

[69] See Richard A. Norris Jr., *Manhood and Christ: A Study in the Christology of Theodore of Mopsuestia* (Oxford: Clarendon, 1963), 81–121. For the question whether Apollinaris was a millenarian, see Daley, *Hope of the Early Church*, 80.

the one prophet and that when she did see Samuel, he was standing. Necromancers bring up souls either feet first or laid out flat,
like corpses in the grave. The argument, however, is not meant
to deny that it was really Samuel that came up. Consequently,
Diodore must refute some of the arguments that are used by Tertullian, Pionius, and Eustathius. Even the prooftext from 2 Cor
11 is inadmissible because God's "regard for Israel ... would not
have permitted a demon in the form of Samuel to be present."
That Samuel really was brought up—but by God rather than by
the belly-myther—has a parallel in Pseudo-Philo and in later Jewish exegesis.[70] Having established this mediating interpretation,
Diodore must explain why God brought up Samuel. Of course,
it was to glorify Samuel, but the true purpose was to explain to
Samuel why the prayers for Saul he offered to God while he was
still alive went unanswered. The significance of the fragment from
Diodore lies primarily in the fact that Gregory of Nyssa knows
some such interpretation and feels obliged to reject it.

GREGORY OF NYSSA

Only the first four sections of Gregory's letter address the
interpretation of 1 Kgdms 28.[71] He apparently knows of an interpretation similar to that of Diodore in that it argues that Samuel
was brought up so that he could learn why his prayers for Saul
had been vain and could see for himself Saul's wickedness in
consulting the belly-myther. Unlike Diodore, however, Gregory
characterizes this view not as arguing that God himself brought
up Samuel but as claiming only that "God permitted the prophet's
soul to be brought up by magical arts of this kind" (102).[72] Gre-

---

[70] Smelik, "Witch of Endor," 161–64.

[71] We cannot know the identity of the Theodosius to whom he writes,
even though there are several bishops of that name who could be candidates for
the role.

[72] It is worth noting that Augustine in *Div. quaest. Simpl.* 2.3 enter-
tains this possibility on the grounds that God permitted Satan to tempt Job and
Christ and even to take Christ up to the pinnacle of the temple. But he also considers it possible that "Samuel" is a demonic delusion. See the introduction in
Almut Mutzenbecher, ed., *Sancti Aurelii Augustini De diversis quaestionibus ad
Simplicianum* (CCSL 44; Turnholt: Brepols, 1970), xxvi–xxvii: "So it appears
to us that his [Augustine's] answer to the question concerning the appearance of

gory rejects such an interpretation primarily because he supposes there to be a "chasm"—the one referred to in the parable of Lazarus and Dives (Luke 16:26)—separating the righteous from the wicked (102–103). Neither willingly nor unwillingly could Samuel have crossed this chasm. The rest of Gregory's discussion is designed to demonstrate the demonic character of the story. Careful readers will not be deceived by what merely imitates prophecy, just as they will realize that when "God" first speaks to Balaam, it was only the one he supposed to be God. Similarly, in 1 Kgdms 28 "Samuel" is not the true Samuel. In consulting Gregory's other writings I have been able to find only one other reference to 1 Kgdms 28.[73] Nevertheless, the parable of Lazarus and Dives is crucial to his interpretation of the narrative about Saul and the belly-myther, and it occupies a significant place in his other writings.[74] In several places Gregory uses the passage from Luke as a basis for his exhortations to care for those who are poor like Lazarus and to avoid the fate of Dives, who represents a cautionary example.[75] He can also treat the "chasm" as one dividing the righteous from the wicked, himself from the ideal of virginity and, positively, from the temptation of wealth, and Meletius from those who mourn his death.[76] Let me confine my attention to his use of the parable in passages dealing with the fate of the soul after death, with Christ's work during the three days between his death and his resurrection, and with the general resurrection.

Samuel is entirely dependent upon sources. . . Augustine takes account of both possibilities, but finally leaves the question open. . . There remain, therefore, as possible sources only Origen for the meaning *iuxta historiam* and above all Tertullian and Ambrosiaster for the thesis of an illusion."

[73] *Sanc. trin.* (GNO 3.1:9). Gregory refers to the "gods" seen by the belly-myther and explains them as demons on the basis of Ps 95:5. He also explains the "god" who speaks to Balaam in Num 22:8 the same way. Both points, of course, occur in his letter to Theodosius.

[74] See Monique Alexandre, "L'interprétation de Luc 16. 19–31, chez Grégoire de Nysse," in *Epektasis: Mélanges patristiques offerts au Cardinal Jean Daniélou* (ed. Jacques Fontaine and Charles Kannengiesser; Paris: Beauchesne, 1972), 425–41.

[75] *Benef.* (GNO 9:106); *Mihi fecistis* (GNO 9:123); *Beat.* 3, 4, 5 (GNO 7.2:108, 113, 130); *In Eccles.* 6 (GNO 5:389).

[76] *In sextum Ps.* (GNO 5:193); *Virg.* 3.1 (GNO 8.1:256); *Ep.* 25.16 (GNO 8.2:82–83; *Melet.* (GNO 9:451–52).

The "bosom of Abraham" represents one biblical metaphor by which to describe the fate of the soul after death, and in a number of places Gregory, like Origen, treats the expression as the equivalent of others. In the *Life of Moses* Gregory allegorically identifies the hole or cleft in the rock on which Moses stands (Exod 33:22) with the "heavenly house not made with hands" (2 Cor 5:1) and the prize of "the crown of righteousness" (2 Tim 4:8), both of which represent the Christian's ultimate destiny. Gregory continues by identifying eighteen other biblical expressions with the cleft in the rock and this destiny, among which we find "bosom of the patriarch."[77] Still more interesting is Macrina's prayer immediately before her death in the *Life of Macrina*:

> You have released us, O Lord, from the fear of death. You have made the end of life here on earth a beginning of true life for us. You let our bodies rest in sleep in due season and you awaken them again at the sound of the last trumpet. You entrust to the earth our bodies of earth which you fashioned with your own hands and you restore again what you have given, transforming with incorruptibility and grace what is mortal and deformed in us. . . You have opened up for us a path to the resurrection, having broken down the gates of hell and reduced to impotence the one who had power over death. . . Put down beside me a shining angel to lead me by the hand to the place of refreshment where is the water of repose near the lap of the holy fathers, You who have cut through the flame of the fiery sword and brought to paradise the man who was crucified with you, who entreated your pity, remember me also in your kingdom. . . Let not the dreadful abyss separate me from your chosen ones.[78]

The prayer is a liturgical pastiche of biblical citations and allusions, and it binds together a number of the themes we have already encountered. There is a clear reference to Christ's harrow-

---

[77] *Vita Moys.* 245–247 (GNO 7.1:119; Abraham J. Malherbe and Everett Ferguson, trans., *Gregory of Nyssa: The Life of Moses* [CWS; New York: Paulist, 1978], 118). The biblical texts include "pleasure of paradise," "Jerusalem which is above," "kingdom of heaven," and "prize of calling." See also the allusion to Dives in *Vita Moys.* 286 (GNO 7.1:131; Malherbe and Ferguson, *Gregory of Nyssa*, 127).

[78] *Vita Macr.* 24 (GNO 8.1:397–98). English translation by Kevin Corrigan, *The Life of Saint Macrina by Gregory, Bishop of Nyssa* (Peregrina Tranlations Series 10; Toronto: Peregrina, 1987).

ing of hell, and the waters of paradise are "near" if not the same as
the lap or bosom of the patriarchs.[79] Macrina's prayer, however,
does distinguish "the place of refreshment" from the final desti-
nation of the Christian at the general resurrection.[80]

A problem emerges: while it seems reasonably clear that
Gregory supposes that paradise and the bosom of Abraham are
two different ways of describing not so much a place as the condition of the righteous after death, he can sometimes think of that
condition as preliminary and sometimes give the impression that
it is their final destiny.[81] The ambiguity correlates with similar
problems found in what he says about the resurrection of the body
and, I should argue, with a fault line that runs through all his
writings. If the destiny of the soul is what matters, then the resurrection becomes something of an afterthought, and the soul need
not wait for its fulfillment. On the other hand, when he insists
upon the resurrection, Gregory must regard the soul's destiny as
incomplete until the general resurrection. This, at least, is one
way of construing my perplexity. One thing, however, is clear.
There is a sharp distinction between the souls of the righteous
and those of the wicked. In one of his homilies on the forty martyrs of Sebaste, Gregory speaks of the flaming and turning sword
that barred the way to paradise after Adam and Eve were expelled.
As Christ's promise to the thief proves, the "turning" sword now
distinguishes the unworthy from the worthy. The sword's point
is directed to the unworthy, but it turns away for the worthy and
gives them "an unhindered way to life."[82] Unworthy souls may
well include those who have deferred baptism, and Gregory is by
no means certain that those "not adorned with the grace of re-
birth" will find a welcome for their souls. Such souls will in all
likelihood wander about, carried around in the air.[83] They remain

---

[79] Cf. *In Flacillam* (GNO 9:489–90), where Flacilla's right faith after her
death has taken her to the bosom of Abraham (the father of faith), which is beside
the spring of paradise and under the shade of the tree of life.

[80] See Daniélou, *L'Être et le temps*, 208–9.

[81] See ibid., 182–83, where he argues that Gregory abolishes traditional
distinctions between paradise, the hands of the Father (Luke 23:46), and the
heavenly Jerusalem.

[82] *In XL Mart.* 16 (GNO 10.1:156).

[83] *De iis qui bapt. diff.* (GNO 10.2:364). See Daniélou, *L'Être et le temps*,
207. Gregory is probably alluding to Plato's *Phaed.* 81bcd.

far too attached to this life to be freed from it even after they have left the body.[84] These souls require further purification, but Gregory apparently believes that they, too, will be perfected.[85]

The second theme that a study of Gregory's use of the parable of Lazarus and Dives introduces is the complex issue of how Christ after his death could be in paradise with the penitent thief, in hell with the souls of the departed, and in the "hands of the Father." Gregory addresses this problem in a number of places, and since Daniélou has given a persuasive treatment of it, let me simply try to summarize his argument.[86] In his Easter sermon *De tridui spatio* Gregory distinguishes the heart of the earth, paradise, and the hands of the Father. This triple distinction at first resembles the distinction between Christ's spirit, soul, and body found in the paschal homily attributed to Hippolytus and in Origen's writings. But Hippolytus says that Christ's spirit went to heaven, his soul to paradise, and his body to the earth. In contrast, Origen places his spirit in the hands of the Father, his soul in hell, and his body in the tomb. Origen, then, reflects the view also held by Eustathius, that it was Christ's soul that went to hell.[87] We can reconstruct Origen's view of what happened after Christ's crucifixion as follows: he deposited his spirit into the hands of the Father, while his soul briefly sojourned in paradise to escort the soul of the penitent thief there; his soul then went to hell and returned to paradise; his body was raised and appeared to Mary Magdalene; finally, he recovered his spirit, ascending to the Father. Origen says nothing, however, about the role of the Word. Gregory is indebted to Origen for some aspects of his own view, but the understanding that dominated the church in the fourth

---

[84] Cf. the following passages, where Dives proves to be such an unworthy soul: *Beat.* 3, 4 (GNO 7.2:108, 113); *In inscr. Ps.* 2.6 and 2.16 (GNO 5:87 and 173); *In Eccles.* 6 (GNO 5:389).

[85] *Orat. Cat.* 26 and 35 (GNO 3.4:66–67 and 91–92).

[86] Daniélou, *L'Être et le temps*, 174–85. See also H. Drobner, "Three Days and Three Nights in the Heart of the Earth: The Calculation of the Triduum Mortis according to Gregory of Nyssa," and A. Spira, "Der Descensus ad Inferos in der Osterpredigt Gregors von Nyssa *De Tridui Spatio*," both in *The Easter Sermons of Gregory of Nyssa* (ed. A. Spira and C. Klock; Patristic Monograph Series 9; Cambridge, Mass.: Philadelphia Patristic Foundation, 1981), 263–78 and 195–261, respectively.

[87] Ibid., 177–78. Daniélou adduces *Dial.* 8 and three passages from *Comm. Jo.*

century was that Christ's death was simply the separation of his soul and his body and that the Word remained united to the soul but not to the body. This understanding became problematic once Apollinaris's teaching began to circulate. That is, for him Christ did not possess a human, rational soul; consequently, Christ's death was the separation of the Word from the human body and his resurrection their reunion.

Therefore, Gregory's solution to the problem of what happened to Christ after his death is elaborated in opposition to Apollinaris's teaching.[88] That is, the Word remained present both to Christ's soul and to his body. As well, he reduces Origen's triple distinction to a double one in two ways. Christ's spirit and soul are the same, and we must equate "the hands of the Father" and "paradise." Thus, Christ's soul went to paradise, while his body went to hell or to the tomb, but the Word remained present with both. Perhaps Gregory's clearest statement of this solution is to be found in the sermon he preached at Easter in 382, shortly before his treatise against Apollinaris:

> How is the Lord simultaneously both in Hades and in Paradise? One solution to the problem is that nothing is beyond God, in whom all things are constituted. Another, to which the present discussion points, is that, since God had transformed the whole man into the divine nature through combination (ἀνάκρασις) with himself, at the time of the dispensation of the passion what had once been combined did not withdraw from either part ... but the godhead voluntarily unyoked the soul from the body, and showed itself remaining in both.[89]

Thus, the Word "annihilated him who had control of death" through the body that was preserved without corruption and through the soul that "prepared for the robber the road that leads to paradise." Gregory continues by justifying the equation of paradise with the hands of the Father by appealing to Isa 49:16 and by assuming that Isaiah's reference to Jerusalem is also a reference to

---

[88] See *Antirrhet.* (GNO 3.1:153) and *Ep.* 3.22 (GNO 8.2:25). Daniélou cites both these passages. Two others can be added, both of which argue on the basis of Dives's attachment to earthly things that Christ's body is not bereft of the Word's presence: *Antirrhet.* (GNO 3.1:178 and 211).

[89] Spira and Klock, *The Easter Sermons*, 42–43. The text of the sermon *De tridui spatio* is in GNO 9:273–306.

paradise. It is important to note that Gregory by no means wants to think in terms of specific locations. Rather, the biblical references denote various conditions in which the soul and the body are to be found.

Daniélou concludes his argument by pointing out that Gregory immediately before the passage I have cited says that he has "discovered" (μαθών) this explanation.[90] Gregory was apparently acquainted with Pseudo-Athanasius's *Against Apollinaris*, probably written by a follower of Athanasius sometime between 373 and 381. What he learned was the idea that the Word remained united to Christ's body after the crucifixion. But Gregory does not follow the treatise in all respects, since it locates Christ's soul in hell rather than in paradise. There is one other passage that Daniélou does not mention but that is interesting because it explains the meaning of Luke 16. In his sermon *On the Holy Pascha* Gregory is concerned to prove the resurrection from scripture:

> If there is no resurrection, then Lazarus and the rich man, the horrifying gulf, the unchecked blaze of fire, the burning tongue, the craving for a drop of water and the finger of the poor are myth; for it is clear that all these things depict the future state of the resurrection. Tongue and finger are not counted as constituents of the soul, but parts of the body. And let no one think that these things have already happened. In fact they are a prior announcement of the future.[91]

While Gregory wants to affirm the truth of the passage, that truth has to do with its prophecy of the resurrection. Since Lazarus and Dives are souls, the bodily references cannot be understood literally. As we shall see, Gregory does not follow Origen by supposing that the soul retains its bodily form after death.

Let me turn now to the final issue, the resurrection itself.[92] Both in *On the Making of Man* and in *On the Soul and the Resurrection* Gregory treats the subject partly by interpreting the parable of Lazarus and Dives. Since both these treatises were written about two years before his treatise against Apollinaris, we need not expect them to reflect precisely the view just discussed. *On*

[90] Ibid., 41. Daniélou, *L'Être et le temps*, 183–84.

[91] Spira and Klock, *The Easter Sermons*, 20 (GNO 9:265).

[92] See Daley, *Hope of the Early Church*, 87–89.

the Making of Man 25–27 is a defense of the resurrection of the body and includes a number of traditional arguments from scripture and from nature. Toward the end of his discussion Gregory argues that the soul's affinity for its body does not cease when they are separated at death. There remains "a certain close relationship (φυσικῇ σχέσει καὶ στοργῇ) and power of recognition (ἐπίγνωσις)." It is as though some signs (σημεῖα) remain imprinted on the soul:

> For that some signs of our compound nature remain in the soul even after dissolution, is shown by the dialogue in Hades, where the bodies had been conveyed to the tomb, but some bodily token still remained in the souls by which both Lazarus was recognized and the rich man was not unknown.[93]

Gregory explains these "signs" by employing what at first seems to be Origen's notion of a "bodily form" (εἶδος) as that principle of continuity underlying the flux of the body. This form is like a seal that stamps its mark on the soul. While Gregory's argument is not exactly lucid, he does want to make two changes in Origen's idea. First, what remains in the soul are the signs of the form and not the form itself. In death the form is dissolved into its elements (στοιχεῖα). Second, it will be the same elements that are reunited with the soul at the resurrection. That Lazarus and Dives somehow remain recognizable even though they are souls without bodies and without any bodily form represents, I think, a confusion.

In *On the Soul and the Resurrection* Gregory clarifies his view by abandoning altogether the quasi-Origenist idea of the bodily form and the signs it leaves on the soul. The impact of Methodius's teaching becomes more obvious, since Gregory insists that there is full continuity between the present body and the resurrection body both at the level of its elements and at that of its structure.[94] Now we learn that the form is effaced when its elements are dissolved but that the soul remembers both the elements and the form they composed, just as an artist remembers his colors and the way he has composed them. In some such way "does

---

[93] *De hom. op.* 27.2 (PG 44:225B; *NPNF* 2.5:418).

[94] See T. J. Dennis, "Gregory on the Resurrection of the Body," in Spira and Klock, *The Easter Sermons*, 55–64; Patterson, *Methodius of Olympus*, 186–96.

the soul know the natural peculiarities of those atoms [elements] whose concourse makes the frame of the body in which it has itself grown, even after the scattering of those atoms." By remembering them the soul will be near each of them, embracing what is its own by its power of recognition (γνωστικῇ δυνάμει).[95] Just as the shipwrecked sailor clings to a plank when his vessel has broken apart, so the soul because it is not confined by space clings to all the elements of the body when they are dispersed.[96] Gregory asks Macrina whether "the Lord's narrative about those who are in hell" may not contradict this understanding of what happens after death. Macrina begins her reply by agreeing that the parable certainly is told in a bodily way but that "many hints (ἀφορμάς) are interspersed in it to rouse the skilled inquirer to a more discriminating study (λεπτοτέραν θεωρίαν) of it." A truthful understanding of the narrative is impossible on the basis of the obvious meaning, and it is necessary to transfer each detail to a spiritual meaning (νοητὴν θεωρίαν).[97] She continues by giving three spiritual interpretations of the parable of Lazarus and Dives. The second of these repeats the understanding she has already given of the soul's memory of its bodily elements and their structure. We are to understand the references in the narrative to a tongue, a finger, and the rest as to what exists for the soul only potentially after the dissolution of the body. Moreover, we should not think of hell as a place but as "a certain unseen and incorporeal condition in which the soul resides."[98]

The first and the third of the spiritual interpretations of the parable Macrina gives are related to one another. Once humanity "deserted the lot that was unmixed with evil" and so lost paradise, God providentially divided human life into two parts, this world and the age to come. He then gave humans their choice of where to seek their goods. The "chasm" in the parable, then, separates those who choose their goods in this life from those who wisely choose "the hope of the future" rather than "the enjoyment of the present." They find repose in "Abraham's bosom" because "bosom" can mean "bay" or "harbor" and so refer to the "measureless

---

[95] PG 46:73B-76B (*NPNF* 2.5:445).

[96] PG 46:44D-48A (*NPNF* 2.5:437–38).

[97] PG 46:80BC (*NPNF* 2.5:446–47).

[98] PG 46:84D-85B (*NPNF* 2.5:447–48).

blessings" prepared for those who will be "brought to anchor in the waveless harbour of that gulf of blessings."[99] The third and last interpretation of the parable is the Lord's teaching:

> that those still living in the flesh must as much as they ever can separate and free themselves in a way from its attachments by virtuous conduct, in order that after death they may not need a second death to cleanse them from the remnants that are owing to this cement of the flesh, and, when once the bonds are loosed from around the soul, her soaring up to the Good may be swift and unimpeded, with no anguish of the body to distract her.[100]

In contrast, the soul that clings to carnal things will suffer torment because it has been "materialized (ὑλωδεστέρας) by such surroundings." This explanation "harmonizes to a certain extent with the assertion made by some persons that around their graves shadowy phantoms of the departed are often seen."[101] Gregory prefers to think of the contrast between the two kinds of souls as one of disposition or spiritual condition, but he is willing to entertain this pagan view even though its implication drives against his conviction that souls after death are incorporeal, bereft even of the bodily form that will be restored only at the resurrection.

Indeed, Macrina a little later in the dialogue comes quite close to treating the resurrection of the body as a purely secondary concern. She argues that in the long run God will be "all in all" (1 Cor 15:28) and that scripture "teaches the complete annihilation of evil." The soul will continue to enlarge without limit in order to receive the blessings God gives, and in this way Macrina alludes to Gregory's teaching about ἐπέκτασις, perpetual progress in the good. She concludes her speech by saying:

> But if there be in you any clinging to this body, and the being unlocked from this darling thing give you pain, let not this, either, make you despair. You will behold this bodily envelopment, which is now dissolved in death, woven again out of the same elements, not indeed into this organization (κατα-

---

[99] PG 46:81B–84C (*NPNF* 2.5:447). Cf. *Beat.* 3 and 4 (GNO 7.2:108 and 113); *In inscr. Ps.* 2.6 (GNO 5:87).

[100] PG 46:88A (*NPNF* 2.5:448).

[101] PG 46:88B (*NPNF* 2.5:448). The allusion is to Plato's *Phaed.* 81bcd. Cf. *De iis qui bapt. diff.* (GNO 10.2:364) and see Daniélou, *L'Être et le temps*, 207.

σκευήν) with its gross and heavy texture, but with its threads
worked up into something more subtle and ethereal, so that
you will not only have near you that which you love, but it
will be restored to you with a brighter and more entrancing
beauty.[102]

Macrina may be speaking of her own body, and while one
might infer that she regards the perfection of her soul as more
important than the body's resurrection, she obviously is willing
to affirm that the same elements and structure that comprise the
body now will be restored in a wonderfully transfigured condition.

Let me conclude by turning attention back to Gregory's interpretation of 1 Kgdms 28. His conviction that the story is a
demonic fiction and illusion coheres with the way he tends to interpret the parable of Lazarus and Dives. These two characters and
Samuel in the story of the belly-myther are disembodied souls.
Gregory corrects Origen by insisting upon this point and by denying, at least in principle, that they could be visible. The elements
that make up the earthly body as well as the structure they form
are dissolved and scattered at death. Nonetheless, the soul by
its memory of the body or by the signs the body has stamped
on it has the power at the resurrection to restore both the bodily
elements and the bodily structure, but in a transfigured condition in which the body will no longer be corruptible and passible.
Although he differs from Origen in crucial respects and accepts
important features from Methodius's account of the resurrection,
Gregory certainly takes the resurrection seriously. At the same
time, I should argue that his more obvious concern in the passages
examined is with the spiritual meaning of the biblical texts and
with the soul's destiny. There would be other ways of approaching Gregory's thought that would drive in a different direction.
His traducianist view of the soul's origin and his conviction that
the human body allies us with the beasts and the lower orders of
creation and that this alliance is crucial for a transfigured creation
suggest a different assessment of the body.

[102] PG 46:108A (*NPNF* 2.5:453). Her speech begins in PG 46:101B
(*NPNF* 2.5:452).

AN INCONCLUSIVE CONCLUSION

In a general way it seems to me that the framework constructed by the Nautins and Simonetti provides a helpful way of examining the texts we have assembled and translated. The polarity of views concerning what happens after death enables us to see an ongoing debate in the early church that has partly to do with reconciling the spiritual and the physical dimensions of a Christian understanding of human destiny and that correlates with the difficulty of fitting together the immortality of the soul and the resurrection of the body. It also helps to explain why 1 Kgdms 28 was so important. At the same time, I confess to a fascination with the ways in which the details of the texts and the larger exegetical and theological concerns of the writers muddy the waters. It is difficult to suppose that the early church ever fully came to terms with the meaning of the resurrection of the body and the life everlasting. Nor need we think that the significance of 1 Kgdms 28 is entirely restricted to this issue. Perhaps the best conclusion is to suggest that the texts introduce us to a number of debates that were as inconclusive in their own times as they are in ours. We probably cannot claim to have found the final solution as to how we should interpret scripture, and we certainly have not come to firm conclusions either about human destiny or about the evil forces at work in our world.

Patristic Rhetoric on Allegory: Origen and Eustathius Put 1 Kingdoms 28 on Trial

Margaret M. Mitchell

Margaret M. Mitchell

THE CHANGING MAP OF PATRISTIC EXEGESIS

The standard textbook diagram of early Christian exegesis as characterized by a basic dichotomy between Alexandrine allegory and Antiochene literalism has eroded considerably in the past decades. Earlier scholars were not unaware that there were problems with an absolutely neat polarization of exegetical camps,[1] but now even a guarded reaffirmation of the older consensus model (i.e., one that acknowledged such "border concepts" mediating between the two, such as Antiochene typology or θεωρία) would find far fewer adherents than two decades ago.[2] Recent research

[1] See, e.g., Robert M. Grant, *The Letter and the Spirit* (London: SPCK, 1957), 105: "the difference between Alexandria and Antioch can be exaggerated... In practice, as contrasted with theory, the two kinds of exegesis come together."

[2] Important voices in this conversation include Frances M. Young, *Biblical Exegesis and the Formation of Christian Culture* (Peabody, Mass.: Hendrickson, 2002); Elizabeth A. Clark, *Reading Renunciation: Asceticism and Scripture in Early Christianity* (Princeton, N.J.: Princeton University Press, 1999); David Dawson, *Allegorical Readers and Cultural Revision in Ancient Alexandria* (Berkeley and Los Angeles: University of California Press, 1992); John David Dawson, *Christian Figural Reading and the Fashioning of Identity* (Berkeley and Los Angeles: University of California Press, 2002). Instead of two neat categories, Young proposes five kinds of literal reading, eight types of allegory (rhetorical, parabolic, prophetic, moral, natural/psychological, philosophical, theological, and figurative), and four subsets of types; Clark identifies eleven "modes of reading" used by an array of patristic exegetes to support their own readings either promoting or denigrating Christian monasticism. I have argued that a further complication of the literal/allegorical dichotomy may be found in the Antiochene Chrysostom's personification and characterization

has significantly altered the map of patristic exegesis by emphasizing the broad array of reading strategies employed by early
Christian biblical interpreters and has shifted the approach from a
systematic investigation of biblical interpretation as solely rooted
in philosophical or theological hermeneutics to concentrated attention on the extent to which exegetical work was a tool for
enacting particular ecclesiastical, theological, and social agendas.
A key underpinning of these advances has been an appreciation of
the thorough immersion of early Christian writers (despite their
own disclaimers) in Greco-Roman rhetorical arts, which requires
the reconsideration of many earlier historical certainties.[3]

THE SOURCE OF THE LITERAL/ALLEGORICAL DICHOTOMY

I suggest that this is a good moment to look at, not simply past,
the traditional view, for it did not arise from nowhere. I seek
to demonstrate here, through an examination of the rhetorical
techniques at work in the remarkable exegetical debate between
Origen and Eustathius of Antioch on the "belly-myther of Endor" passage in 1 Kgdms 28, that the firm dichotomy between
"literal" and "allegorical" interpretation so valuably problema-
tized by recent scholarship was not simply a modern scholarly
construct stemming from our need for neat categories.[4] Rather,
it was, less consciously than realized, perhaps, a reinstantia-
tion of the antithetical cast in which such interpretations were
themselves presented by patristic authors, even as these same au-

of the apostle Paul, who functions as both historical personage and figural
representation of contemporary religious ideals, by metonymy, metaphor, and
synecdoche; see *The Heavenly Trumpet: John Chrysostom and the Art of Pauline
Interpretation* (HUT 40; Tübingen: Mohr Siebeck, 2000; Louisville: Westminster John Knox, 2001).

[3] See, e.g., Averil Cameron, *Christianity and the Rhetoric of Empire: The
Development of Christian Discourse* (Sather Classical Lectures 55; Berkeley and
Los Angeles: University of California Press, 1991); Peter Brown, *Power and Per-
suasion in Late Antiquity: Towards a Christian Empire* (Madison: University of
Wisconsin Press, 1992), and further literature in n. 6 below.

[4] References to the text of Origen, *Hom. 5 on 1 Kingdoms*, and to
Eustathius, *On the Belly-Myther*, are given following the paragraphing of Simonetti, *La Maga di Endor*, reproduced in this volume, as checked against the
more recent critical edition edited by Declerck, *Eustathii Antiocheni Opera*. The
translations are those of Greer and Mitchell, as found below, pages 33–157.

thors' exegetical practice in many ways contradicts or violates
the methodological exclusivity that they vehemently defend in
any single case.[5] And, I hope to demonstrate, they inherited
that rhetorical move—of dichotomizing the treatment of written
sources in such a way—from the *paideia* of the rhetorical schools,[6]
which, it is important to emphasize, was designed not to create schools of readers (either literal or allegorical) but to train
rhetoricians who could argue for the meaning of a text that a given
situation required, by means of a set of standard *topoi* for either
case.[7] Hence the construction of a hard and fast distinction between a literal and a figurative reading of a text is itself a rhetorical
act moored in rhetorical training,[8] which generates the paradox

[5] A precise analogy may be found in the old view that early Christian
authors stood apart from the larger "pagan" rhetorical culture, based on Christian authors' apologetic disavowal of rhetorical skill for themselves or their
scriptures. That this rhetorical *topos* (one found abundantly in the rhetorical tradition being ostensibly attacked) cannot be accepted as historical fact has been
convincingly demonstrated by Cameron, *Christianity and the Rhetoric of Empire*;
Brown, *Power and Persuasion*; and a host of studies on individual authors. On
John Chrysostom, e.g., see Robert L. Wilken, *John Chrysostom and the Jews:
Rhetoric and Reality in the Late Fourth Century* (The Transformation of the
Classical Heritage 4; Berkeley and Los Angeles: University of California Press,
1983); Margaret M. Mitchell, "Reading Rhetoric with Patristic Exegetes: John
Chrysostom on Galatians," in *Antiquity and Humanity: Essays on Ancient Re-
ligion and Philosophy Presented to Hans Dieter Betz on His Seventieth Birthday*
(ed. Adela Yarbro Collins and Margaret M. Mitchell; Tübingen: Mohr Siebeck,
2001), 333–56; idem, *Heavenly Trumpet*, 241–45, 278–91.

[6] For the broad influence of rhetorical education on early Christian practice, see Robert M. Grant, *The Earliest Lives of Jesus* (New York: Harper, 1961);
Christoph Schäublin, *Untersuchungen zu Methode und Herkunft der antiochenischen Exegese* (Theophania 23; Cologne-Bonn: Hanstein, 1974); Bernhard
Neuschäfer, *Origenes als Philologe* (Schweizerische Beiträge zur Altertumswissenschaft 18/1–2; Basel: Reinhardt, 1987); and Young, "Rhetorical Schools,"
182–99. One should not, however, overstate the distinctiveness or complete separation between rhetorical and philosophical schools; see Young's own caution
on this point (169) and her inclusion of Origen among those who "were the heirs
of both traditions."

[7] See, e.g., Cicero, *Inv.* 2.41.121.

[8] It may be useful at this point to recall the well-known debate going back
at least to the influential articles of Tate in the 1920s and 1930s over whether
Stoic allegorists of the Homeric epics did so "defensively" or "offensively";
see J. Tate, "The Beginnings of Greek Allegory," *Classical Review* 41 (1927):
214–15; idem, "Cornutus and the Poets," *CQ* 23 (1929): 41–45, and idem, "On
the History of Allegorism," *CQ* 24 (1930): 1–10; see more recent discussion

that the appeal for a single, clear meaning from either direction be-
lies the textual ambiguity that gave rise to the exegetical disputes
in the first place.[9]

In the rhetorical τέχναι ("handbooks") the treatment of textual hermeneutics comes under forensic cases, where documents
are among "inartificial proofs" (ἄτεχνοι versus ἔντεχνοι πίστεις)
serving as evidence, alongside witnesses.[10] Aristotle in the *Rhetorica* supplied a concise list of *topoi* to be used, depending upon
whether ὁ γεγραμμένος ("what stands written"), normally in regard to νόμοι ("laws"), is ἐναντίος ... τῷ πράγματι ("contrary to the
case at hand"), ἀμφίβολος ("ambiguous") or πρὸς τὸ πρᾶγμα ("for
our case").[11] The set of basic commonplaces recommended by
Aristotle would equip an orator with arguments to use in any of
these three situations to bring forward written evidence of whatever sort appeared best to support his particular suit. Hence, if
the literal sense of the text seems contrary to one's case, then one

in, e.g., A. A. Long, "Stoic Readings of Homer," in *Homer's Ancient Readers: The Hermeneutics of Greek Epic's Earliest Exegetes* (ed. Robert Lamberton
and John J. Keaney; Princeton, N.J.: Princeton University Press, 1992), 41–66.
Whatever the merits of either option (surely a chicken or egg case!), this formu-
lation clearly assumes that ancient moments of allegorical interpretation were
based in a rhetorical purpose and enscripted in rhetorical forms. The reason
the dichotomy does not work there, either, is that rhetorical training of course
included both strategies, to be used when the occasion warranted.

9 Aphthonius, a fourth-century teacher of rhetoric, said that both arguments of refutation and of confirmation are to be constructed only for matters
that are "not very clear" (*Prog.* 5 [H. Rabe, ed., *Aphthonius, Progymnasmata*
(Leipzig, Teubner, 1926), 10, lines 11–12]). Pseudo-Hermogenes says it is impossible to do either for "things which are utterly false" (*Prog.* 5 [H. Rabe, ed.,
Hermogenes, Opera (Leipzig: Teubner, 1913), 11, line 4]). Quintilian remarks
that philosophers recognize the ambiguity in all texts (*nullum videatur esse ver-
bum quod non plura significet* [*Inst.* 7.9.1]); the rhetorician will, however, insist
that his interpretation (whether literal or figurative) is self-evidently true (see
the wry comments of Sextus Empiricus, *Math.* 2.63–71).

10 The direct relevance of this background in rhetorical theory to our
text is shown in the way in which Eustathius chides Origen for making his case
against his opponents ἀτεχνίᾳ δὲ μᾶλλον ἢ τέχνῃ δοκῶν ἀνασκευάζειν αὐτὸ
("supposing he would refute it artlessly rather than by the *ars rhetorica*"; 4.10).
Furthermore, Eustathius himself quotes the traditions of the rhetorical handbooks (αἱ ῥητορικαὶ τεχνογραφίαι) in his treatment of μῦθος ("myth") in 27.2; see
below, and Margaret M. Mitchell, "Rhetorical Handbooks in Service of Biblical
Exegesis."

11 Aristotle, *Rhet.* 1.15.1–12.

should argue either that the judge's role is to uphold the law in a
more general way in the promotion of justice rather than remaining strictly bound by the wording of a single law, or one should
seek to demonstrate that the problematic law either contradicts another law that has been approved or even contradicts itself.[12] In
the opposite instance, where an orator finds that the precise wording of the text actually supports his case, then he should insist that
it is not the judge's role to alter what is written but to abide by it,
for "to seek to be wiser than the laws is what is expressly forbidden
in the most esteemed laws."[13]

The tradition of grammatical and rhetorical education was
remarkably stable from the Hellenistic down into the Roman im-
perial period and through late antiquity.[14] A fuller treatment of
the same types of commonplaces seen in Aristotle is found in the
rhetorical handbook of the young Cicero, who discusses the subject of *controversiae quae in scripto versantur* ("controversies which
turn on texts").[15] Cicero's long discussion of the various ways
a rhetorician was trained to deal with written evidence—under
the categories of ambiguity, letter and meaning/intent, contrary
laws, analogy, and definition—provides more than ample demonstration that literary criticism in the rhetorical schools was not
intended to inculcate any single brand of philosophical hermeneutics but rather to equip one to argue for or against "the letter" as
required in a given case.[16] The *topoi* given for each side (those

[12] Ibid. 1.15.9.

[13] Ibid. 1.15.12.

[14] Robert A. Kaster, *Guardians of Language: The Grammarian and Society in Late Antiquity* (Berkeley and Los Angeles: University of California Press,
1988); George A. Kennedy, *Classical Rhetoric and Its Christian and Secular Tradition from Ancient to Modern Times* (Chapel Hill: University of North Carolina
Press, 1980), esp. 86–107; evidence for late antiquity is especially to be found in
the *Progymnasmata*, some of which were recently translated by Kennedy, *Progymnasmata;* the Greek texts may be found in Spengel, *Rhetores Graeci*, and
other individual Teubner volumes (cited above).

[15] Cicero, *Inv.* 2.39.115–154.

[16] Sextus Empiricus makes just this point in arguing against the rhetoricians: "That rhetoric is against the laws is manifestly clear even in the things
proposed in their mal-artful 'arts of rhetoric' handbooks (ἐν ταῖς κακοτέχνοις
τέχναις). For at one time they advise one to attend to the text and the statements
of the lawgiver (τῷ ῥητῷ καὶ ταῖς φωναῖς τοῦ νομοθέτου)—as clear and in need
of no interpretation (ὡς σαφέσι καὶ μηδεμιᾶς ἐξηγήσεως δεομέναις)—and at an-

arguing for or against the literal meaning, whom Cicero characterizes as *qui scriptum defendet*[17] versus *contra scriptum qui dicet*[18])
include also stock ways of characterizing the flaws of the opposing
argument. For instance, if a text is ambiguous, one should show
how the text should have been written if our opponent's reading
of it were true,[19] just as one should argue for one's own reading on
the basis of what the same writer has stated both in the full extent
of the document in question and in any of his other writings.[20] A
good sense of this forensic approach to written documents may be
attained from the following extended passage from Cicero's handbook:

> An advocate who will defend the letter (*qui scriptum defendet*)
> will be able to use all of the following topics (*loci*) most of the
> time, and the greater part of them on every occasion; first,
> high praise of the writer, and a common topic (*locus com-
> munis*) that the judges should regard nothing except what is
> written; and this may be made more emphatic if some statu-
> tory document is offered, i.e., either a whole law or some part
> of it; after that one may use the most effective argument, a
> comparison of the action and purpose of the opponents with
> the letter of the law (*facti aut intentionis adversariorum cum
> ipso scripto contentione*), showing what was written, what was
> done, what the judge has sworn to do. And it will be well to
> vary this topic in many ways, first expressing wonder in his
> own mind as to what can possibly be said on the other side,
> then turning to the judge's duty and asking what more he
> can think it necessary to hear or expect. Then one may bring
> in the opponent himself like a witness (*tum ipsum adversar-
> ium quasi in testis loco producendo*), that is ask him whether
> he denies that the law is so written, or denies that he has
> acted contrary to it or endeavored so to do (*hoc est interrogan-
> dum utrum scriptum neget esse eo modo, an ab se contra factum
> esse aut contra contendi neget*), and offer to stop speaking if
> he dares deny either. But if he denies neither statement and
> still continues to dispute, say that there is no reason why any-

other time they turn around and advise one not to follow either the text or the
statements (προσέχειν μήτε τῷ ῥητῷ μήτε ταῖς φωναῖς) but the intention of the
lawgiver (ἀλλὰ τῇ διανοίᾳ κατακολουθεῖν)"; *Math.* 2.36–37 (my translation).

[17] Or *qui pro scripto dicet; Inv.* 2.46.135.
[18] *Inv.* 2.47.138.
[19] Ibid. 2.41.120.
[20] Ibid., 2.40.117.

one should think that he will ever see a more shameless man (*nihil esse quo hominem impudentiorem quisquam se visurum arbitretur*).[21]

Cicero's *De inventione* was a compilation of Greek traditions and extant Latin rhetorical training manuals and lecture notes for the use of a Roman elite in the waning years of the Republic. But the distance from Cicero's courtroom techniques to the debate between Origen and Eustathius in the eastern Empire in the third and fourth centuries c.e. is actually not so great. Indeed, the bridge between the two can be pinpointed exactly in the *paideia* of the secondary educational system in the late antique East, in which students were taught to bring just these types of forensic, "cross-examinational" tactics to bear on narratives and their interpreters. In practicing the forms of ἀνασκευή ("refutation") and κατασκευή ("confirmation"),[22] pupils were given a standard assignment of either defending or repudiating the historical veracity of the mythic tale (διήγημα) of Daphne being pursued by

---

[21] Ibid. 2.43.125–26; translation by H. M. Hubbell (LCL 386; Cambridge, Mass.: Harvard University Press, 1949).

[22] Nicolaus of Myra (late fifth century c.e.) says that ἀνασκευή ("refutation") and κατασκευή ("confirmation") are most closely related to τὸ δικανικόν ("forensic/courtroom rhetoric" [J. Felten, *Nicolaus, Progymnasmata* (Leipzig: Teubner, 1913), 33, lines 14–15]). On these as standard rhetorical forms taught in school, see, e.g., Pseudo-Hermogenes, *Prog.* 5 (Rabe, *Hermogenes, Opera,* 11), and throughout the *Progymnasmata* (more references follow in the notes below). Origen speaks of his intent as κατασκευάζειν in 8.1, and Eustathius of his opponent engaging in both ἀνασκευάζειν (4.10) and κατασκευάζειν (21.11), and, even more often, with the synonymous rhetorical term—as demonstrated by the definition given in Pseudo-Hermogenes, *Prog.* 5 (Rabe, *Hermogenes, Opera,* 11, line 3: κατασκευὴ δὲ τοὐναντίον βεβαίωσις)—βεβαιοῦν ("substantiation"; 4.7; 16.7; 21.3; 26.9). He uses it once of his own purpose (7.4). Origen's use of these techniques on Gospel narratives was demonstrated by Grant, *Earliest Lives of Jesus,* 77–79; cf. 38–49.

xcii THE "BELLY-MYTHER" OF ENDOR

Apollo.[23] Like Origen and Eustathius,[24] they concern themselves especially with the topics (κεφάλαια) of what is possible (δυνατόν),[25] clear (σαφές),[26] logical (ἀκόλουθον),[27] and credible (πιθανόν)[28] and make heavy employment of the criterion of self-contradiction (τὸ

[23] There are various versions of the myth, most famously found in Ovid, *Met.* 1.452–567. That it was a standard topic is demonstrated by its place among the *Progymnasmata* of Libanius (among the *narrationes; Prog.* 17 [R. Foerster, ed., *Libanii Opera* (12 vols.; Leipzig: Teubner, 1903–23; repr., Hildesheim: Olms, 1963), 8:44–45]) and especially the testimony of Nicolaus: οἷον ἀνασκευά-ζειν ἡμῖν πρόκειται τὸ περὶ τῆς Δάφνης, εἴτουν διήγημα (*Prog.* [Felten, *Nicolaus, Progymnasmata,* 31, lines 9–11]; translated by Kennedy, *Progymnasmata,* 145, as, "For example, we are assigned to refute the story of Daphne, thus to refute a narrative"). The fullest treatments are found in Aphthonius, *Prog.* 5–6 (Rabe, *Aphthonius, Progymnasmata,* 10–16).

[24] On Origen's employment of these tests, see Neuschäfer, *Origenes als Philologe,* 1:243.

[25] To cite just two examples, Origen argues that the narrative must be true because it would not be possible for a demon (rather than God or the Holy Spirit) to know the future of the Israelite kingdom (5.1–3). In reply, Eustathius argues for the impossibility that the belly-myther could even bring up the soul of a mouse or flea, let alone that of a holy prophet (3.3).

[26] Eustathius complains that Origen is not able to see τὸ σαφές ("what is clearly the case," "the plain sense") in the narrative (7.4). In turn, the Antiochene announced at the outset of his treatise that his own goal was to set the two interpretations side by side and "to make evident the plain sense" (literally, "to clarify the clear sense" [τρανῶσαι τὸ σαφές; 1.4]). See also 12.5; 22.7; 23.4–5.

[27] Literally, "what follows." Origen characterizes his opponents' insistence that Samuel was not really brought up by the woman as founded upon this rhetorical appeal: Ὁρᾶτε τί ἀκολουθεῖ τῷ Σαμουὴλ ἐν ᾅδου ("Look at what follows from Samuel's being in hell"; 3.4). On the other side, see especially the combination of appeals in Eustathius's charge against Origen for failing to meet this standard of proof: οὐδ' αὖ τὸ σαφὲς ἐξ αὐτῆς ἱστορῆσαι τῆς ἀκολουθίας ("Yet even here he did not explicate what is the plain sense on the basis of its logical sequence"; 22.7). Eustathius claims that his own reading meets this criterion; see 8.6: "Therefore, does it not follow that we can see from the very letter of the narrative (ἀκολούθως ἐκ τῆς αὐτῆς τοῦ γράμματος ἱστορίας) that this case is just like the former?"; also 16.1; cf. 10.5; 14.4.

[28] Origen's opponent finds the text "incredible" because the mad-woman is not to be believed: Οὐ πιστεύω τῇ ἐγγαστριμύθῳ (3.2–3). Origen for his part fears that if this passage is found to be false, then it will lead to more general ἀπιστία (2.5). As we shall see below, much of Eustathius's treatise concerns the credibility of the different witnesses. In particular, he also takes up the issue of persuasiveness and trustworthiness of myth as a class of literature (26.10–29.4).

ἐναντίον, τὸ μαχόμενον)²⁹ within the narrative itself and in regard to the opposing interpreter's claims about it.³⁰ Quite likely Eustathius (trained at Antioch, where the garden of Daphne was a local theme park to the myth) would in his earlier education have cut his teeth on this very example, as might have Origen.³¹ Would they have learned something from that assignment that would affect their later debate about the historicity of a biblical narrative that involved similiar dynamics of female agency and the reliability of the divine to play by its own rules?³²

²⁹ Nicolaus says this tactic, τὸ καλούμενον μαχόμενον ("that which is called 'warring with oneself'"), is ἀγωνιστικώτατον ("most worthy of a contest"); it is used when "we prove that our opponent is speaking against himself and talks in a contradictory manner (ὅπου τοῦτον ὥσπερ ἀντιλέγοντα αὐτοῦ ἑαυτῷ καὶ ἐναντίως δείκνυμεν λέγοντα)" (*Prog.* 6 [Felten, *Nicolaus, Progymnasmata,* 32, lines 11–14]).

³⁰ For this list, see Pseudo-Hermogenes, *Prog.* 5 (Rabe, *Hermogenes, Opera,* 11, lines 8–20). The opposite pleas are made in an argument of κατασκευή ("confirmation").

³¹ Origen alludes to this interpretive procedure, employing the appropriate technical vocabulary, in his debates about the Greek myths and the gospels with Celsus and "the Jew." See, e.g., *Cels.* 1.42.1–5: Πρὶν ἀρξώμεθα τῆς ἀπολογίας, λεκτέον ὅτι σχεδὸν πᾶσαν ἱστορίαν, κἂν ἀληθὴς ᾖ, βούλεσθαι κατασκευάζειν ὡς γεγενημένην καὶ καταληπτικὴν ποιῆσαι περὶ αὐτῆς φαντασίαν τῶν σφόδρα ἐστὶ χαλεπωτάτων καὶ ἐν ἐνίοις ἀδύνατον ("Before we begin the defence, we must say that an attempt to substantiate almost any story as historical fact, even if it is true, and to produce complete certainty about it, is one of the most difficult tasks and in some cases is impossible"; trans. Henry Chadwick, *Origen, contra Celsum* [Cambridge: Cambridge University Press, 1953], 39). Grant, *Letter and Spirit,* 102, finds in this passage clear demonstration of "the Greek rhetorical origin of [Origen's] negative method."

³² There are some very telling parallels that I can only name here: like 1 Kgdms 28, the Daphne-Apollo myth involves a woman of questionable provenance who has an illicit encounter with a male figure that results in prophetic activity of debatable source and genuineness. Both narratives involve boundary crossings between earth and the subterranean realm and between the human and the supernatural, and dark hints of improper divine conduct. Perhaps most important, the history of interpretation of both narratives was famously disputatious, focused on whether either incident actually happened as narrated, particularly in view of its implications (one way or another) for the attributes and capacities of the gods, on the one hand, and the hermeneutics of textual appropriation, on the other. Some suggestive points of contact between the MT and the LXX versions of 1 Sam 28 and traditions about the Delphic Pythia (both as instances of necromantic prophesy "in the belly") were noted in the far-ranging study by Trencsényi-Waldapfel, "Die Hexe von Endor," and, most recently and

THE TEXT ON TRIAL—I KINGDOMS 28

This forensic, schoolroom approach to the treatment of written evidence was operative in the highly contentious debate between Origen and Eustathius on 1 Kgdms 28.[33] We shall see that both exegetes employ courtroom language and tactics in their framing of the exegetical debate and use stereotypical characterizations of "literal" and "allegorical" readings that were recommended in rhetorical training as means of substantiating their own case and denigrating that of their opponent.

At the outset we need to contextualize this piece of exegetical drama. In the Masoretic Text of 1 Sam 28, Saul at first punishes and exiles those in his kingdom who engage in mantic practices, but then immediately thereafter, due to the pressures of war and the complete silence with which his deity greeted any attempts by Saul to discern the divine will, the king asks his servants to find him a "woman who has mastery of necromancy," in Hebrew אשת בעלת־אוב (1 Sam 28:7). The crucial step for the history of Christian interpretation of this incident is the LXX translator's decision to render this title as ἡ ἐγγαστρίμυθος (the "belly-myther"), a term used, for example, by Plutarch in reference to the Eurykleis or Pythones.[34] The woman promises to raise up for Saul whomever he asks. He requests Samuel; then the woman says she sees him and describes him as a "straight man with a double-cloak," whereupon Saul declares "it is Samuel." The apparition thus identified groans and speaks to Saul a prophecy that the king-

keenly in the fascinating study by Connor, *Dumbstruck*, 45–102.

[33] The Origen-Eustathius duel had long been taken to represent a clear divide between the two "schools," but more recent scholarly treatments, such as those of Young, *Biblical Exegesis*, 163–64, and "Rhetorical Schools," and Joseph W. Trigg, "Eustathius of Antioch's Attack on Origen: What Is at Issue in an Ancient Controversy?" *JR* 75 (1995): 219–38, have rightly noted that in fact and in substance it complicates the traditional divide between Alexandrine allegory and Antiochene literalism.

[34] "For it is entirely simple-minded and childlike to suppose that the god himself, just like the *engastrimythoi* (called of old Eurykleis, but now Pythones [ἐγγαστριμύθους Εὐρυκλέας πάλαι νυνὶ δὲ Πύθωνας προσαγορευομένους]) by entering into the bodies of the prophets, speaks, using their mouths and voices as his instruments" (*Def. orac.* 414E). See full discussion of the term, and defense of our translation, "belly-myther," in preface, pp. xi–xviii.

dom has been taken from him and given to another (David) and
that he and his sons will die the next day and will be with him (in
Sheol). The passage ends with ἡ ἐγγαστρίμυθος preparing a meal to
revive Saul, after which he goes back to the camp and is killed in
the very next battle; the kingdom does fall into the hands of David.
This biblical text posed many difficulties for both Jewish and
Christian interpreters, chiefly because the woman's action, though
prohibited by Torah itself, uncannily creates a speech-platform
for the highly esteemed prophet Samuel, and consequently the
text raises many larger issues of the nature of inspired or prophetic
speech and its truthfulness.[35] But the story was also considered by
some, as by Justin Martyr in the first known Christian use of the
passage (*Dial.* 105; see text and translation in this volume), to provide useful scriptural proof for life after death and resurrection.

Origen's homily on this passage was delivered as part of a
series of sermons on 1 Samuel (1 Kingdoms in LXX). Already
by that time it had earned the sobriquet ἡ ἱστορία ἡ διαβόητος ἡ
περὶ τῆς ἐγγαστριμύθου ("the [in]famous narrative concerning the
belly-myther"; 1.2). A written rebuttal to Origen's exegesis was
composed by Eustathius of Antioch sometime in the first half of
the fourth century (he died ca. 337, having been a major figure at
the Council of Nicaea), nearly a century after Origen delivered his
homily in Jerusalem ca. 238–42 C.E. Eustathius's treatise was written at the request of one Eutropius, whom he addressed as a "most
distinguished and holy preacher of orthodoxy" (1.1). Eutropius
had asked for Eustathius to give his opinion about the passage because he was "not satisfied with what Origen has published on this
subject" (1.2). With sometimes quite caustic invective, such as
Ὠριγένης ὁ πάσας οἰόμενος εἰδέναι τὰς γραφάς ("Origen, who thinks he
knows all the scriptures"; 21.12; 26.1), and epithets, such as ὁ κομ-
ψός ("the dandyishly clever"; 3.4), ὁ μεγαληγόρος ("the braggart";
20.2), ὁ πολύφημος Ὠριγένης ("the highly acclaimed Origen"; 24.1),
or ὁ πολυΐστωρ Ὠριγένης ("the learned Origen"; 23.2), Eustathius
baldly accuses Origen of bad motives behind his bad exegesis: blasphemy and attempting to smuggle necromantic practices into the

---

[35] See Smelik, "Witch of Endor," 160–79. The text was also a subject of
debate between Jews and Christians, as *Mart. Pionii* 13.3–14 (text and translation in this volume) shows.

church (3.4; 21.1, etc.).[36] Each author, as we shall see, engages in
exegesis as an ἀγών, a "contest" or "trial" about truth, against a
clearly demarcated opponent across the aisle.[37] Both Origen and
Eustathius, in line with the counsel of Cicero quoted above, bring
their opponent into the "courtroom" and put him on the stand to
answer for his faulty interpretation. Both authors claim that their
reading is closer to τὰ γράμματα αὐτά ("the words [or letters] themselves"), but neither interpretation, as we shall see, is precisely as
its author wishes to characterize it.

ORIGEN'S "LITERAL" INTERPRETATION

Origen's homily opens with his summary of the four pericopes
from 1 Samuel (1 Kingdoms) that have just been read aloud
in the liturgy. Then, since he is a visiting preacher, he defers
to the presiding bishop to indicate which of the four he would
wish Origen to "investigate" or "examine" (ἐξετάζειν).[38] The answer comes back: "let the matters concerning the belly-myther
be examined" (Τὰ περὶ τῆς ἐγγαστριμύθου, φησίν, ἐξεταζέσθω; 1.3).
Origen begins with a preamble comparing two hermeneutical
axioms. The first is that some narratives, taken on the historical level, do not "touch us," but others do, since they are
"necessary for our hope" (2.1). The belly-myther narrative is
this kind of text, and as such, ἀναγκαία ἀλήθεια κατὰ τὸν λόγον
("its truth is necessary, in accordance with the word"; 2.3).[39]
This is the case, he argues, even before one gets to the ἀνα-

---

[36] Slandering those who promote the opposing interpretation (εἰπεῖν τὴν
τῶν φησάντων διαβολήν) is recommended by Aphthonius (*Prog.* 5 [Rabe, *Aphthonius, Progymnasmata*, 10, lines 13–14]). Eustathius denies at the outset that
he is engaging in συκοφαντεῖν ("making false accusations"; 1.4).

[37] Although without attention to this forensic setting in particular,
Dawson has well appreciated the combative nature of early Christian exegesis: "Ancient allegorical compositions and interpretations constituted fields
on which struggles between competing proposals for thought and action took
place" (*Allegorical Readers*, 2).

[38] Or, "cross-examine," as we shall see below.

[39] I.e., "literally." Cicero recommends that one who upholds the literal
sense of a text should always say that this is necessary in matters of the highest
importance (*lex aut ad res maximas; Inv.* 2.46.135). For Cicero, these include
utilissima, honestissima, and *religiosissima.*

γωγή ("elevated sense"), Origen's common term for "allegory."[40]

Origen's argument confirming the veracity of the narrative (κατασκευή) is cast primarily as a proof of refutation (ἔλεγχος) of a prevalent contrary interpretation, which he quotes directly at the outset: "Indeed, we know that some of our brothers have faced off against scripture and say, 'I do not believe the belly-myther (οὐ πιστεύω τῇ ἐγγαστριμύθῳ). The belly-myther says she has seen Samuel. She is lying (ψεύδεται). Samuel was not brought up; Samuel does not speak'" (3.1).

Origen sets up the exegetical contest by bringing his opponent into view via προσωποποιία, whereby he impersonates the rhetorically impassioned response the proponent of the ἐναντίος λόγος ("opposing position") gives to the idea that Samuel was literally "brought up" by the woman: "Why was Samuel in hell (ἐν ᾅδου)? Look at what follows from Samuel's being in hell. Samuel in hell? Why not also Abraham, Isaac, and Jacob in hell? Samuel in hell? Why not also Moses, the one joined with Samuel according to what has been said, 'not even if Moses and Samuel take their stand will I listen even to them'? Samuel in hell? Why not also Jeremiah in hell? . . . In hell also Isaiah, in hell also Jeremiah, in hell all the prophets, in hell!" (3.4–5).[41]

Having represented the opposing counsel in this manner, in an extended rhetorical division (2.4–4.1), Origen's first argumentative move is to present his listener with an absolute dichotomy that is worthy of any charge to a jury: "Are these things written?

----

[40] "(S)ince we have not yet arrived at the benefits of the 'elevated sense' for each person who knows how to 'elevate,' or to hear what is 'elevated' by others" (ἐπεὶ οὐδέπω φθάνομεν ἐπὶ τὰ τῆς ἀναγωγῆς παντὶ τῷ εἰδότι ἀνάγειν ἢ ἀκούειν ἀναγομένων χρήσιμα; 2.1). With this threefold paronomasia Origen is supplying a significant hint about his purpose. He is not eschewing the allegorical task altogether in this homily but rather is signaling that it has not yet arrived. Hence I must disagree with the interpretation of the Nautins here, on 174 n. 2: "En réalité, l'homélie s'en tiendra jusqu'à la fin au sens littéral. Ce qui tiendra lieu d'anagogê, ce sont les considérations sur l'utilité de la descente du Christ et des prophètes en enfer, qui suivront la lecture glosée du text." We shall see below that the ἀναγωγή ("elevated sense") is not in fact displaced in this homily.

[41] Origen himself characterizes the rhetorical anaphora in this personified speech as bombastic rhetoric (πιθανῶς καταβομβεῖν; 4.1). Eustathius recognizes the use of personification in Origen's exegesis: τὰς τῶν ἀντιδοξούντων αὐτῷ γνώμας ἐκτιθέμενος ("he continues by setting forth the opinions of those who take the view opposite to his"; 16.7).

Are they true or are they not true?" (2.5). Having posited this pair
of alternatives, he then (as the handbooks recommend) lays alongside each option its interpretive consequence: "[On the one hand,]
to say they are not true leads to unbelief (ἀπιστία), and it will come
down on the heads of those who say it. But [on the other hand] to
say they are true furnishes us with a matter for investigation (ζήτησις) and an occasion for doubt (ἐπαπόρησις)" (2.5).[42]

Origen argues that, since the words are written by the person
(πρόσωπον) of the Holy Spirit, they must be true and therefore worthy of trust.[43] In this regard he conforms to rhetorical theory, in
which the one who seeks to uphold a literal reading is counseled to
begin with praise of the author[44] and to provide a strongly implied
warning against contradicting the divine beings who have inspired
a text.[45] Origen substantiates his appeal to the authority of the divine authorship by what he insists is a literary-critical principle
respected by all who are widely read:

> Whose persona is it that says (τίνος πρόσωπόν ἐστιν τὸ λέγον),
> "the woman said"? Is it, then, the persona of the Holy Spirit
> (τὸ πρόσωπον τοῦ ἁγίου πνεύματος) by whom scripture is be-
> lieved to have been written (ἐξ οὗ πεπίστευται ἀναγεγράφθαι ἡ
> γραφή), or is it the persona of someone else (ἢ πρόσωπον ἄλλου
> τινός)? For, as those who are familiar with all sorts of writ-
> ings know (ὡς ἴσασιν καὶ οἱ περὶ παντοδαποὺς γενόμενοι λόγους),
> the narrative persona throughout is the persona of the au-
> thor (τὸ γὰρ διηγηματικὸν πρόσωπον πανταχοῦ ἐστὶ πρόσωπον
> τοῦ συγγραφέως). And the author responsible for these words
> is believed to be not a human being (συγγραφεὺς δ' ἐπὶ τού-
> των τῶν λόγων πεπίστευται εἶναι οὐκ ἄνθρωπος), but the author

---

[42] Eustathius refers to this as συλλογιστικῇ δεινότητι χρώμενος ("employing syllogistic cleverness"; 16.9).

[43] "Scripture, which it is necessary to believe" (ἡ γραφὴ ᾗ δεῖ πιστεύειν;
4.8). This is an instance of the interpretive strategy of λύσις ἐκ προσώπου ("solution by appeal to the speaker"; see Neuschäfer, Origenes als Philologe, 263–76)
but one that (anomalously) flattens all the dramatis personae into the single voice
of the author.

[44] Aphthonius, Prog. 6 (Rabe, Aphthonius, Progymnasmata, 13–14); cf.
Cicero, Inv. 2.43.125 (scriptoris collaudatio).

[45] "The one who speaks against (ἀντερεῖν) the poets seems to me to be
speaking against the Muses themselves. For if the things poets utter come
through the intention of the Muses, then how could it be that the one who seeks
to reproach the poets is not speaking against the Muses?" (Aphthonius, Prog. 6
[Rabe, Aphthonius, Progymnasmata, 14, lines 9–12]).

is the Holy Spirit who has moved the human beings to write (ἀλλὰ συγγραφεὺς τὸ πνεῦμα τὸ ἅγιον τὸ κινῆσαν τοὺς ἀνθρώπους). (4.2)

Origen here effaces completely other literary approaches to this matter (which he probably did know, such as in Plato's *Republic* book 3),[46] because he wishes to treat the entire text of 1 Kgdms 28 as the words of the author, whom he identifies with the Holy Spirit. In this way he seeks an "all or nothing at all" approach to the "truth" or facticity of the episode, claiming that the entire text is the witness that testifies to the fact that "Samuel is really the one who was brought up." Origen's reading contradicts that of his opponents, who, as we have seen, maintained that the woman lied (ψεύδεται, "perjured herself") or that she did not "see Samuel" but instead a petty demon "pretending to be Samuel." Origen dismisses such claims with what appears to be a call for a strictly literal reading: "Scripture did not say otherwise" (ἡ γραφὴ οὐκ ἄλλως εἶπεν; 4.9). Instead, the text (words of the συγγραφεύς, the Holy Spirit) says that "Saul knew that it was Samuel," so, by an ironic inverse appeal to the possible, Origen clucks, οὐδεὶς ἔγνω τὸ μὴ ὄν ("no one knows that which does not exist"; 4.7). He also argues that a petty demon could not possibly have been responsible for the words of "Samuel," because no *daimonion* would know the divine plan about the fate of the kingdom of Israel that the apparition foretold and that came to pass in the demise of the Saulide kingdom.

After this long major section of ἔλεγχος ("refutation") of the ἐναντίος λόγος ("the opposing interpretation"), Origen engages in an argument to provide the solutions, which he appropriately terms λύσεις,[47] to the difficulties that attend his own proposition that Samuel is the one who was raised up and that the words of

---

[46] The discussion between Socrates and Adeimantus in the *Republic* (3.6, 392C–394B) of the distinction between simple narrative and the creation of dialogue set in characters' mouths, called ἁπλῆ διήγησις ("simple narration") and διήγησις μιμήσεως ("narration by imitation"), respectively.

[47] For this term in rhetorical theory contemporary to Origen, see, e.g., Anonymous Seguerianus 186 (text in Mervin R. Dilts and George A. Kennedy, eds. and trans., *Two Greek Rhetorical Treatises from the Roman Empire* [Mnemosyne Supplements 168; Leiden: Brill, 1997], 52), and later Nicolaus, *Prog.* (Felten, *Nicolaus, Progymnasmata*, 29, lines 12–15).

the scriptural text are true.[48] He presents this as the ἀγών ("trial"), which his opponent flees from engaging but which he will readily and bravely undertake.[49] Origen's method of proof consists in putting his opponent on a fictional witness stand[50] and asking him a series of questions—τίς μείζων, "who is greater?"—that will ultimately force the opponent to admit that the one who is greater than all the prophets and patriarchs is Jesus, who *was* in hell, who went there because the prophets, who predeceased him, were prophesying his advent both during their lives and afterwards, there in hell.[51] That is what Samuel was doing in hell, and he was there because, until the advent of Christ and his postmortem trip to hell to preach the gospel to the saints confined there, no human being had access to heaven, to the paradise that was guarded since the divine verdict in the garden of Eden.

Origen concludes that this text, therefore, is not an "obstacle" (πρόσκομμα) to faith (as the opponent would have it, with his incredulity that Samuel should have been in hell) but is rather the repository of ἅγιοι λόγοι μεγάλοι καὶ ἀπόρρητοι οἱ περὶ τῆς ἐξόδου ("words that are holy, great, and ineffable, words concerning our departure from this world"; 4.10).[52] Rather than falsifying the faith or the scripture, this text actually points believers to τὸ περισσόν, "the something more," the special advantage that believ-

---

[48] Ταῦτα μὲν οὖν (δηλοῖ) ὅτι οὐκ ἔστιν ψευδῆ τὰ ἀναγεγραμμένα καὶ ὅτι Σαμουήλ ἐστιν ὁ ἀναβεβηκώς ("All this demonstrates that the things written are not false and that it is Samuel who has come up"; 6.1).

[49] Eustathius returns the *topos* when charging Origen with cowardice and trying to flee the trap he has fallen into (26.5).

[50] We have noted that this tactic is recommended by Cicero (*Inv.* 2.43.125). The forensic setting of this approach to the interpretive enterprise, even if adopted as a kind of literary fiction, means that we must take with seriousness Origen's term ἀγών, here and in 4.10 and 6.2, as referring to more than a vague "struggle" or "difficulté" (Trigg, "Eustathius of Antioch's Attack on Origen," 226; Nautin and Nautin, *Origène*, 185), but, rather, a case requiring proof and adjudication. Such conventional adversarial tactics would seem to argue against Trigg's contention that it is only Eustathius who embarks on the exegetical work with "hostility" (235), in contrast to Origen's open-mindedness and equanimity. Both are using the vigorous rhetoric customary in arguments of direct refutation of an opponent's position.

[51] Origen emphasizes that this is the point he is seeking κατασκευάσαι ("to establish" or "to confirm"; 8.1).

[52] Cf. *Princ.* 4.2.9, in reference to texts that cannot be taken literally but rather hold deliberate clues from the Holy Spirit to look for a deeper meaning.

ers now possess over the prophets and saints who died before the advent of Christ, namely, access to heaven. The "truth" of the passage becomes a proof of the "truth" of the Christian hope for the resurrection of the believer.

Origen's exegesis of 1 Kgdms 28 presents the listener with many immediate trappings of a "literal" reading of the text: he insists that one pay attention to the exact wording (κατὰ τὸν λόγον) and emphasizes that he is reading it initially according to ἱστορία ("the historical or narrative sense"), not yet according to the ἀναγωγή (the "elevated" or "spiritual meaning"), and his major point is that it really happened—that is, Samuel *was* raised—because the text says so. Yet Eustathius, although he grants that Origen's reading of this passage stands out as an exception to his more usual "allegorical" or "tropological" interpretations, does not consider Origen's a truly "literal" reading either. He complains that, "though he took it in hand to allegorize (ἀλληγορῆσαι) all the scriptures, he does not blush to understand this passage alone according to the letter, declaring his interpretation hypocritically, even though he does not pay attention to the body (σῶμα) of scripture right-mindedly" (21.1). Playing on the courtroom *topos* of rhetorical inconsistency in the treatment of texts, Eustathius not only charges his opponent with such serial crimes as "tropologizing," "tautologizing" and "allegorizing," but moreover submits that, even when he tries to read a narrative right, Origen manages to obscure τὸ σαφές ("the clear sense"; 22.7). Hence Eustathius does not take Origen's claim to be giving a "literal interpretation" (κατὰ τὸν λόγον) at face value.

Perhaps we would not, either, though for different reasons. Much depends on what one means by the "literal," but Origen's reading seems to exceed the bounds of the exact wording of the text, which never mentions heaven, or Christ, or contains any promise of afterlife for believer or anyone else. Obviously, Origen's eyes as he reads are fixed not just on the text. His eye is equally set (as we have noted) on an alternative reading of the text that has him bothered: an interpretation that denies the event happened as described—that the "belly-myther" actually "brought Samuel up" (ἀνήγαγεν)—maintaining instead that she lied to deceive demented Saul. And Origen has his gaze above all securely fastened on what is "necessary for our hope," that is, the eschato-

logical fate of all believers.[53] Out of this triangle of concerns (the text, the "opposing interpretation," and "the ultimate concern" of "our hope" and that "faith" not be endangered), Origen argues strenuously that what the text describes actually did happen: Samuel was raised up. But his argument in defense of what seems to be a literal meaning actually seeks to instantiate a spiritual meaning on the highest mystery of the faith: the postincarnational promise of postmortem life for all believers who live morally good lives. Hence, the very insistence upon ἡ ἱστορία ("the narrative sense"), on the meaning κατὰ τὸν λόγον ("the literal sense"), on ἡ γραφὴ αὐτή ("the text itself"), on ἡ διηγηματικὴ φωνὴ τῆς γραφῆς ("the narrative voice of the text") heard by "hearers able to listen to words that are holy, great, and ineffable, words concerning our departure from this world" (4.10) paradoxically creates the conditions for a supreme ἀναγωγή ("elevated sense") of the text, as the site of revelation of the secure eschatological hopes of each Christian.

Seen in this light, and considering the likelihood that the end of the discourse has been its σκοπός ("rhetorical goal") all along, it appears that the whole is structured around a deliberate paronomasia between the ἀναγωγὴ τῆς ψυχῆς τοῦ δικαίου ("the bringing up of the righteous man's soul") Samuel (6.1) and the ἀναγωγή ("the elevated sense," Origen's favored term for spiritual or allegorical interpretation)[54] made available by this exegesis for the hearer of Origen's homily.[55] It certainly seems clear that Origen's whole de-

---

[53] Despite many fine observations in his essay, Trigg's assertion that "it is Origen who does not allow doctrinal and moral concerns to predetermine an interpretation which the narrative, by itself, does not suggest" ("Eustathius of Antioch's Attack on Origen," 234), seems quite hard to defend in the face of Origen's clear intent to demonstrate that the passage does not provide an obstacle to Christian hope for postmortem survival.

[54] Grant, *Letter and Spirit*, 124. For the conjunction of terms elsewhere in Origen's writings see, e.g., *Comm. Jo.* 1.26.180: ἀνάγειν δὲ καὶ ἀλληγορεῖν ("to elevate and to allegorize"); discussion in Grant, *Letter and Spirit*, esp. 98–104.

[55] See n. 40 above for a contrary view. The end of the homily itself points to a more deliberate intention, for it appears to be on the basis of logical inference from the earlier propositions and conclusions that Origen turns back to the wordplay at the beginning, which implicitly promised an eventual turn to the "elevated sense," at least for those who know "how to 'elevate' or to hear what is 'elevated' by others" (2.1). Notice that the capacity to hear and understand lofty things is precisely what is called forth from the reader who joins the ἀγών

fense of Samuel's having actually "been brought up" (ἀναχθῆναι, or "elevated") from hell is in service of a grand-scheme "other meaning" than the simple narrative intends—becoming a tale about the fate of all postmortem souls—both before and after the arrival of Christ. Origen's emphasis on the groundedness of this meaning in the history depicted in the text itself is part of the persuasiveness of the mysterious message he discerns through his reading and investigation of the text by the critical praxis of subjecting ἱστορία ("narrative account") to ἐξέτασις ("cross-examination"). Origen's interpretation is a "spiritual reading" wrapped up in a "literal procedure," which is completely determined by the presupposition that a text in which are things "necessary for our hope" (i.e., in the resurrection) must be "true" in a literal sense (ἀναγκαία ἀλήθεια κατὰ τὸν λόγον; 2.3). The appeal to the literal, in other words, is itself a rhetorical move that, in the way presented, greatly constricts the interpretive options for his hearers and funnels them toward his particular spiritual interpretation.[56] And that is its intention. By facing up to the ἀγών ("trial") he depicted his opponents as seeking to evade, Origen seeks to turn this text from hostile witness to favorable testimony for his chosen thesis and his ultimate catechetical goal. But was Eustathius's reading, an "opposing interpretation" that also claims to be "literal" (i.e., focused on αὐτὸ τὸ τῆς ἱστορίας γράμμα, "the very letter of the narrative"), any closer to actualizing that claim?

in 4.10, who is promised both a refutation of the first interpretation and a clarification of Origen's own, and that the ἐπίλογος states the hermeneutical axiom that full understanding of this text (νενόηται) rests upon divine revelation given to some, which is the basis of the ἀναγωγή, according to 2.2. Eustathius himself replicates a version of this wordplay in his repudiation of Origen's allegorical treatment of Lazarus in John 11 (21.8; cf. also 22.4).

[56] Differently, Trigg: "Origen is at ease with indeterminacy. . . . For Origen biblical interpretation is an ongoing struggle in which there may, indeed, be definitive progress . . . but there is no final, definitive outcome" ("Eustathius of Antioch's Attack on Origen," 235). But the entire discourse points to the security of a single, indisputable outcome about the things "necessary for our hope." The term ἀναγκαία ("necessary") would seem to be the opposite of the hermeneutical freedom Trigg celebrates in Origen here (235).

EUSTATHIUS'S "BRIEF" AGAINST ORIGEN

As introduced above, Eustathius writes at the bidding of Eutropius to give his judgment about Origen's exegesis of the passage
that is said to have swayed many, owing to that scholar's reputation.[57] This leads Eustathius immediately to a comparative
method, based on the disjunctive syllogistic reasoning that, if
there are two opposite interpretations of a passage, the refutation
of one constitutes definitive proof for the other.

> Therefore, lest I should appear to be introducing a forensic
> suit on my own behalf (ἵν' οὖν μὴ δόξαιμι κατ' ἐμαυτὸν ἀγῶνα
> δικανικὸν εἰσάγειν), I consider it not unsuitable to yoke to-
> gether his entire interpretation with my explanation of the
> text (συζεῦξαι τὴν ἐξήγησιν αὐτοῦ τῇδε τοῦ γράμματος ὑπαγορίᾳ),
> and through each to make evident the plain sense. This may
> keep some from supposing that we are making false accusa-
> tions (συκοφαντεῖν) against people anywhere who have been
> persuaded to hold Origen's opinions; nor will they suppose
> that the opinions of each side are equally contestable (ἀμφή-
> ριστοι). For it is possible to carry out the investigation by a
> side-by-side comparison (ἐκ τῆς παραλλήλου συγκρίσεως ἀν-
> τεξετάζειν) of how both sides stand in their opinions and for
> scholars to choose the better opinion from the two. Indeed,
> no competitive race horse is judged approved, however well-
> gaited, when it runs by itself—not even if it is exceptionally
> nimble and displays its moves as though on wings. This is
> also true of any athlete who can run swiftest in the stadium
> and of anyone else—the supple wrestler and the pancrati-
> ast or "all-in" contestant who fights the roughest, or the one
> who "beats the air" with vain motions. But on the contrary,
> the contests unite them in close quarters to stand against
> their opponents (ἀλλὰ συσταδὸν ἁρμόττει τὰ μαχόμενα τοῖς
> ἐναντίοις ἀντιστατεῖν) so that the superior of the two may be
> determined. (1.4–7)

---

[57] Aphthonius, *Prog.* 6.13.25 (Rabe, *Aphthonius, Progymnasmata*, 13, line
25) gives advice for how when one is refuting an argument confirmed by an opponent the first step is to praise his fame. Eustathius mocks Origen's reputation
elsewhere in the treatise, too (as at 23.3 and 24.1; see also 25.1; 26.8, and the
epithets quoted in the text above, p. xcv).

This *prooimion* shows how much Eustathius and Origen hold in common. They both agree on the fundamental, agonistic terms of debate. Exegesis is, or at least involves, an ἀγών.[58] The text is to be subject to a cross-examination (ἐξέτασις). The word ἀγών is used for athletic contests, of course, but also refers to disputes in rhetorical skill and, perhaps even more often, lawsuits.[59] Later in the treatise Eustathius will characterize Origen's exegesis as styled for the courtroom: "that dogmatician Origen, arguing against his opponents with the skill of a trial lawyer (δικανικῇ δεινότητι διαλεγόμενος), cited this passage too."[60] That early Christians should use such courtroom language to refer to their exegetical practices reflects their indebtedness to the larger oratorical culture of the Greco-Roman world, which was thoroughly competitive and combative.[61] Moreover, along with the term ἀγών ("trial") comes a necessarily dichotomous, antithetical hermeneutic. In a trial texts are treated as witnesses whose testimony either works for one's side or against it. The task of both defenders and prosecutors is to convince the judge or jury that truth is on their side, falsehood on that of their opponent; equivocation is not possible. The readers of these exegetical arguments in each case are asked to "render

---

[58] Indeed, Eustathius even uses the full technical term for a forensic suit: ἀγὼν δικανικός (1.4).

[59] LSJ 19, s.v. ἀγών, III.3. See, e.g., the repeated use of cognates of ἀγών in Nicolaus of Myra's discussion of ἀνασκευή and κατασκευή (*Prog.* 6 [Felten, *Nicolaus, Progymnasmata,* 29–35]).

[60] 4.10. Eustathius's treatise is filled with forensic language. See, e.g., the uses of αἰτία ("charge," "accusation"; 26.5), ἐγκληματικὴ δίκη ("writ of accusation"; 26.6), ἐγκλήματα/ἐγκαλεῖν ("charges/bring charges"; 11.14; 12.1), τὰ τῆς κατηγορίας ὑπομνήματα ("bill of indictment"; 11.17), ἀπολογεῖσθαι ("defend oneself"; 26.3, 8), ἔλεγχος/(δι)ελέγχεσθαι ("refutation/refute," "conviction/convict," "proof, [re]prove"; 7.3; 9.4; 9.10; 24.5; 2.2; 9.14; 10.3; 12.3; 13.3; 14.6; 15.7; 25.8; 26.3; 26.5; 27.3), μάρτυς/μαρτυρία/μαρτυρεῖν ("witness/testimony/testify"; 10.4; 18.3; 18.6; 23.4; 25.11; 2.9; 9.1; 10.6; 11.6; 13.10; 25.8; 26.1; 26.9); (συν)ομολογεῖν ("confess," "admit"; 12.2; 12.3; 14.6), ψηφοφορία/(ἐπι)ψηφίζεσθαι/(κατα) ψηφίζεσθαι ("decree," "verdict/render a verdict," "cast a vote"; 10.4; 26.9; 10.6; 16.3; 25.2; 25.3; 25.8), ἀνθυπενεκτέον ("cross-examine"; 16.10); δικ-cognates in the treatise are too numerous to catalogue. What argues for the forensic cast to these terms (which may be debated in some individual cases) is the way they are used in conjuction with one another (and the overall preponderance of such language is surely striking).

[61] As particularly well articulated by Brown, *Power and Persuasion.*

cvi   THE "BELLY-MYTHER" OF ENDOR

a verdict" (ψηφίζειν) about the options presented, by picking the best one (11.5).[62]

What is essential to the forensic treatment of texts is that they are on a par with witnesses; indeed, in a real sense they are witnesses that are to be scrutinized for their truthfulness or mendacity.[63] Like Origen, Eustathius sets out to "to look at the letter of the narrative" (τὸ τῆς ἱστορίας γράμμα θεωρεῖν; 2.1), but in his hands this quest leads to the clear conclusion that Origen's so-called literal reading actually promotes the exact "opposite" of the words of the text.[64] This turn-about comes back around, then, to precisely the charge Origen himself had laid against his opponents: "despite doing so with the best of intentions he says things that directly contradict what is written" (ἀπὸ ἐνδόξων μὲν ἐπιχειρεῖ, ἐναντία δὲ λέγει τοῖς γεγραμμένοις; 4.1). The rhetorical handbooks gave stock advice for examining witnesses; a comprehensive statement, with characteristic vocabulary, can be found in the *Rhetorica ad Alexandrum*, which is usually attributed to Anaximenes:

> Testimony (μαρτυρία) is the confession (ὁμολογία) of a willing conscience. It is necessary that what the witness says be either convincing (πιθανόν) or unconvincing (ἀπίθανον), or ambiguous (ἀμφίβολον) in credibility (πρὸς πίστιν); likewise also the witness is either credible (πιστός), incredible (ἄπιστος) or ambiguous (ἀμφίδοξος)... When the witness is suspect it is necessary to point out that neither for some favor nor for revenge nor for gain might such a man as this give lies in his testimony (τὰ ψευδῆ μαρτυρεῖν). And it is neces-

[62] The word literally means "to cast one's vote." See, e.g., the stern warning Eustathius gives his readers against the perils of casting a vote that would contradict the divine testimony in 10.6; see also 16.3; 25.3, discussing the side that Scripture "weighs in on" with its vote (ἀντιδοξοῦσιν ἑαυταῖς αἱ θεῖαι γραφαί; ταῖς δὲ πολλαῖς ἡ μία μάχεται ψῆφος;), and other counter-votes in 25.4 (καταψηφίζεσθαι); 25.8.

[63] See Aristotle, *Rhet.* 1.15, who considers both νόμοι ("laws") and μάρτυρες ("witnesses") as forms of πίστεις ἄτεχνοι ("inartificial proofs"). This rhetorical background to assessing the truth of written records is illuminating for our third- and fourth-century exegetical ἀγών ("trial") about the ἐγγαστρίμυθος ("belly-myther"), where what is precisely at stake is the reliability of vocalized words. Quintilian includes under the category *testimonia* both reports in texts and those of live witnesses (*Ea dicuntur aut per tabulas aut a praesentibus*; *Inst.* 5.7.1), the connection being of course that texts are often depositions of oral testimony.

[64] See 4.5, quoted in the text below, p. cviii.

sary to instruct [the jury] that it is not advantageous to offer
a lie when testifying, for the benefits (ὠφέλειαι) are meager,
a harsh penalty accrues if one is convicted, and the laws call
for the one who is found out to have done it to suffer loss, not
only financially, but also in terms of reputation (εἰς δόξαν) and
lack of credibility (εἰς ἀπιστίαν). That is how we shall make
our witnesses credible. But when we are arguing against a
testimony (ἀντιλέγοντες μαρτυρίᾳ), it is necessary to slander
(διαβάλλειν) the character of the witness as a wicked person,
or to cross-examine his testimony (τὸ μαρτυρούμενον ἐξετάζειν) if it happens to be unconvincing (ἀπίθανον), or even to
speak against both at the same time, bringing together the
most damning evidence against our opponents (οἱ ἐναντίοι)
into one presentation. (*Rhet. Alex.* 15 [1431b])

In the main body of Eustathius's treatise he engages in a
vigorous cross-examination of the series of witnesses involved
in the case of the "belly-myther," with the firm purpose of discrediting them thoroughly and exposing any contradictions in or
among their testimonies.[65] The commonplaces recommended by
Anaximenes will all come into play, as we shall see. Eustathius
begins, as even rhetorical handbooks recommend, by calling a surprise witness: his opposing counsel, Origen.[66]

ORIGEN AS WITNESS

Just as Origen had used personification to enter the testimony
of those championing the interpretation of 1 Kgdms 28 that he
sought to overturn, Eustathius summons his opponent as a witness,[67] setting against him the words of Jesus in John 8:44, to
the effect that the devil is a liar: "Now what do you say, Origen

---

[65] As the treatise *Rhetorica ad Herennium* says, those who uphold and
those who denigrate witnesses both focus on the common topics of (1) the
auctoritas and *vita* of the witnesses as crucial to their credibility and (2) the *con-
stantia* or *inconstantia testimoniorum* (2.6.9). These two tactics (together with a
third for demolishing testimony—that what the witness said could not possibly
have happened or, if it did, the witness in question could not have seen it) are to
be used *ad improbationem et ad interrogationem*.

[66] See Cicero, *Inv.* 2.43.126, quoted above, pp. xc–xci.

[67] In the *prooimion* Eustathius had explained the reason for this method:
he would first lay out very clearly Origen's own ἐξήγησις so that he would not
be accused of συκοφαντεῖν ("prosecuting vexatiously," or "bringing false accu-

(τί τοίνυν φῄς, ὦ 'Ωρίγενες)? (For it is necessary to question you [ἀνάγκη γὰρ ἐρέσθαι σε].) Which is it—are these words that the Savior spoke true, or will you contradict (τοὐναντίον) them in your reply?" (4.3).[68]

Without an apparent hint of self-irony (for bringing a witness back from the dead to testify against necromancy!), Eustathius rehearses Origen's claim that the words in the text had to be true because their author was the Holy Spirit, and then he turns to the jury of his readers, wags his head, and says,

> Does he [i.e., Origen] not, then, understand how contradictory to the sense of the narrative (ἐναντία ... τῇ τοῦ διηγήματος ἐκδοχῇ) his view appears? Indeed, those who have spent more time becoming conversant with a wide range of literature (οἱ παντοίοις σχολαιότερον ὁμιλήσαντες λόγοις) know better that the narrative discourse of the author (ἡ διηγηματικὴ τοῦ συγγραφέως ὁμιλία) has put down these things that the belly-myther appeared to do or say to Saul, who seeks a divinatory word. Of course, the author (ὁ συγγραφεύς), because he was telling a story about her and setting out her words in a style appropriate to her (τοὺς λόγους αὐτῆς ἐπὶ λέξεως ἐκτιθέμενος), said, "And the woman said, 'Whom shall I bring up for you?'" Who is so simple-minded as to pretend not to understand that these are not the statements of the author but of the woman who was acting under demonic influence (αὗται μὲν τοῦ συγγραφέως οὐκ εἰσιν αἱ φωναί, τῆς δὲ δαιμονώσης εἰσὶ γυναικός)? Even her name brought this to the forefront (ἧς καὶ τοὔνομα προύταξεν). (4.5–7)

sations"; see LSJ 1671, s.v. συκοφαντεῖν). Hence he plans to let Origen speak for—and hang—himself.

[68] Cicero recommends this strategy: "first expressing wonder in his own mind as to what can possibly be said on the other side (*quidnam contra dici possit*)... Then one may bring in the opponent himself like a witness (*tum ipsum adversarium quasi in testis loco producendo*), that is ask him whether he denies that the law is so written, or denies that he has acted contrary to it or endeavored to do so (*hoc est interrogandum utrum scriptum neget esse eo modo, an ab se contra factum esse aut contra contendi neget*)... But if he denies neither statement and still continues to dispute, say that there is no reason why any one should think that he will ever see a more shameless man (*Si neutrum neget et contra tamen dicat: nihil esse quo hominem impudentiorem quisquam se visurum arbitretur*)" (*Inv.* 2.43.125–126). Compare Eustathius's outrage that Origen is so shameless that "without a blush" (οὐκ ἐρυθριᾷ) he dares to attribute the words of a mad woman to the Holy Spirit (3.5).

The cross-examination of Origen proceeds apace from there, with Eustathius either quoting Origen's actual words from his homily (φησί, "he says") and showing their inconsistency with the text[69] or, by personification, conjuring up what Origen might say to his insistent, searing questions (ἴσως ἐρεῖς, "perhaps you will say"), declaring that he has trapped his opponent (ἁλισκόμενος εὐπετῶς)[70] in his own various statements and their logical implications.[71] There are, consequently, only two possible motives a "jury" can allow: either Origen is prevaricating, deliberately perjuring himself by saying what he knows is not true,[72] or he is sadly deluded, revealing himself to be a man embarrassingly lacking in literary acumen.[73] Eustathius hopes to demolish this legendarily wise witness so utterly as to leave him in the guise of "an old crone,"[74] an ironic doppelgänger for the despicable woman whose

[69] "Therefore, the facts themselves (αὐτὰ τὰ πράγματα) fight against your words, Origen!" (μάχεταί σου τοῖς λόγοις, Ὠρίγενες; 5.5).

[70] 6.1; 22.5, etc. Compare Quintilian, *Inst.* 5.7.11, on how the goal of cross-examination is to lead the witness into a trap (*inducuntur in laqueos*), just as when coaching one's own witness a lawyer is to make sure they do not contradict themselves (*ut . . . constent sibi*).

[71] "Do you see to how great an absurdity (ἀτοπία) the proposition that you teach has led?" (4.4).

[72] "For he seems either to act stupidly, due to poor training (ἀμαθία), or to be trafficking with evil intent" (26.1; cf. 23.8). It is most striking, and surely no coincidence, that Eustathius depicts Origen and the devil (acting through the demon) in precisely the same way. Both "play a part" (ὑποκρίνεσθαι/ὑπόκρισις), acting under pretense and "feigning doubt" (ἐπαπορεῖν) (of Origen, see 4.7; 6.7; 15.6; 16.5; 21.1; 23.3; of the devil, 11.1; 12.1; and esp. 12.8), "lie" ([κατα]ψεύδεσθαι) (of Origen, see, e.g., 21.10; 26.8–9; of the devil, e.g., 14.6), and "blaspheme" (βλασφημεῖν) (of Origen: 3.5; 17.3; of the devil: 14.6).

[73] Quintilian recognizes the same two options: fraud or ignorance (*Inst.* 5.1.2). Not surprisingly, Origen had postulated these same two options for his opponents (4.1).

[74] The lexical play is very clear in the Greek: both the woman of Endor and Origen are "old crones" worthy of ridicule, not credibility (this rhetorical move has been well appreciated also by Connor, *Dumbstruck*, 82, 87). She is αὕτη γραῦς ("this old crone"; 3.3) or ἡ δαιμονῶσα γραῦς ("the demon-colluding old crone"; 29.1), though the biblical text in fact said nothing about her age. Origen ταυτολογεῖ γραωδῶς ("says the same thing over and over like an old crone"; 17.2); when treating the narrative of Job, instead of praising the saint's ethical demeanor and urging imitation, he devotes his attention, like some old crone (γραωδῶς), to silly allegorization of the names of Job's daughters (21.7). At one point Eustathius exclaims, "He seems to me to speak at least no less insanely

word he has dared to ascribe to the Holy Spirit. Eustathius even goes so far as to claim that his exegetical opponent, Origen, is actually serving as "counsel for lawless divination."[75] Having called Origen as his first witness, Eustathius retains him in the courtroom but then turns to the witnesses inside the biblical text that Origen, "their lawyer," had brought forward in support of his "literal" reading.

CROSS EXAMINATION OF THE TEXTUAL WITNESSES

Having demolished Origen's foundational claim that the text speaks with a unified voice representing a single witness, Eustathius differentiates three discrete μάρτυρες ("witnesses") in the pericope, who correspond to the three πρόσωπα, the *dramatis personae* of the text—Saul, the woman, and the apparition "Samuel"—none of whom is to be identified with the Holy Spirit. Indeed, in Eustathius's eyes, to coalesce or confuse such characters with the Holy Spirit is to commit shameless blasphemy. Then he looks carefully at what the text says and, as had Origen before him, what it does not say.[76] Applying a forensic suspicion to the account of the story as narrated, Eustathius points out that the "event" is not directly narrated[77] but rather is mediated

---

than the woman!" (20.4). One other calumny Eustathius heaps on the two in common is κουφολογία ("empty words," "vacuous speech"; see 7.6; 17.6; 22.5, of Origen, and 25.11, of the "belly-myther"). Among the methods Hermogenes recommends for discrediting an opposing witness is to engage in slander (δια-βάλλειν) by saying that "they are not worthy of belief because of age" (διὰ τὸ μὴ εἶναι δι' ἡλικίαν ἀξιοπίστους), presumably because they are too old (or perhaps as well too young; *Stat.* 3 [Rabe, *Hermogenes, Opera,* 45, lines 17–20]).

[75] τῆς ἀθεμίτου μαντείας ὑποθήμων (5.6); cf. the ironic depiction of οἱ ἐγ-γαστρίμυθοι in 25.1 as ἀγαθῶν ὑποθήμονες ἔργων ("counselors of good deeds"). This seems of a piece with Anaximenes' advice, quoted above, to point out that witnesses are motivated by their friendship with the opposition (in this case, the demons!—we shall return to this point below).

[76] Origen's own strategy, of quoting the words of the text and then proposing how the text would have been written if his opponents' interpretation were true ("Why, then, does the passage not say, 'The woman saw a petty demon *that was pretending to be* Samuel'"? [4.7]) employs this stock rhetorical technique, recommended by Cicero, *Inv.* 2.41.120.

[77] *Rhet. ad Her.* 2.6.9 recommends that in cross-examination one should demonstrate that the witness on the stand could not have known what happened.

through the woman's description of what she "saw" and Saul's inferences that identified the apparition as Samuel—not on the basis of his own eyewitness but of his interpretation of her (questionable) words. Having made this separation of words and event, and of the three characters (πρόσωπα), Eustathius systematically treats, and discredits, each of these "witnesses" in turn, before the eyes of the jury of his own readers.[78]

Saul

Proceeding like a prosecutor facing an opposing witness, Eustathius first points out that the king, in going to the ἐγγαστρίμυθος in the first place, was not only breaking his own judicial order banishing these practices from his kingdom but indeed violating the very law of God (Num 23:23). Hence, Eustathius asks, using the language of a courtroom contest of conflicting testimony: Who is more to be believed (ἀξιόπιστος/φερέγγυος): God, who thrust words into the mouth even of Balaam and who entrusted Moses with the task of penning the words of prohibition ("For there is no augury in Jacob, nor any divination in Israel"),[79] or Saul, a "witness (μάρτυς) who had tried to use such impious means" (2.9)?[80] Moreover, Eustathius insists, Saul is actually not even a witness, for the text itself indicates that he did not see anything[81] but relied on the woman's words. Since hearsay evidence is inadmissible, Saul can be dispensed with as a purported witness.[82]

---

[78] For a comparable treatment of a textual character as a witness, see, e.g., Aphthonius's sample ἀνασκευή, in which he contests the mythic claim that Daphne was the child of Ladon and Earth by questioning, τίνα τοῦ γένους ἔχουσα πίστιν ("what proof does she have of her ancestry?"; *Prog.* 5 [Rabe, *Aphthonius, Progymnasmata*, 11, lines 16–17]).

[79] See Young, *Biblical Exegesis*, 21–28; Neuschäfer, *Origenes als Philologe*, 1:276–85, on Origen's application to scripture of the schoolroom method of Ὅμηρον ἐξ Ὁμήρου σαφηνίζειν ("clarifying Homer from Homer"; e.g., *Princ.* 1.2).

[80] It is customary, of course, to discredit witnesses on the grounds of their bad moral conduct (see, e.g., Quintilian, *Inst.* 5.7.26).

[81] "Saul, since he was out of his mind, 'knew' from what he had heard (ἐξ ὧν ἀκήκοεν) that this was Samuel himself" (3.9); "would not Saul have seen him (οὐκ ἄρα ἑόρακεν αὐτὸν ὁ Σαούλ) rather than, as though struck with blindness, have wished to learn what sort of man he was from someone else?" (6.5).

[82] "In the case of hearsay evidence, it will be urged that those who produce such evidence are not really witnesses, but are merely reporting the words

The Woman

The discrediting of the testimony of ἡ ἐγγαστρίμυθος (the "belly-myther") spans the whole of Eustathius's lengthy treatise. As we have seen, she is evaluated first according to a nontextually supported assumption that the mantic arts are the work of ὁ δαίμων ("the demon" or "the devil") or some δαιμόνιον ("petty demon"). Indeed, both Origen and Eusebius state this repeatedly as though self-evident, although neither term appears in the LXX of 1 Kgdms 28—one clear indication of the "literal" limits of both interpretations.[83] Initially Eustathius flirts with a rhetorical question of which of the two witnesses his reader should grant credence: Saul or the boasting demon.[84] But then he sets up his real comparison, between the words of Jesus (a readily available witness who requires no special summons) to the effect that the devil is a liar (John 8:44), and the words of a demon, and brings Origen back to life to pronounce a judgment that redounds upon himself.[85] Hence the demonstration of the unreliability of the testimony of both Saul and the woman is made in terms of guilt by association: Saul is δαιμονιζόμενος ("demon-possessed"), and the woman is δαιμονῶσα ("acting under demonic influence"; 7.2). Hence the conclusion that "the knowledge of the demon-possessed man is

of unsworn persons" (*ut de auditionibus, non enim ipsos esse testes sed iniuratorum adferre voces*; Quintilian, *Inst.* 5.7.5).

[83] The grand assumption of Eustathius's argument, which is presented as requiring no proof, is, "Now it is impossible to dispute the fact that a demon does not bring up anyone's soul" (οὐ γὰρ ἔστιν ἀμφισβητεῖν ὅτι δαίμων οὐκ ἀνάγει ψυχὴν οὐδενός; 4.8). See discussion of this point in the preface, xv–xvii.

[84] "If one must believe either Saul, who was possessed by a demon (Εἰ δὲ δεῖ πιστεύειν ἢ τῷ δαιμονιζομένῳ Σαούλ), ... or a demon who boasted and promised to summon even the souls of the righteous from hell, let us judge for ourselves (κρίνωμεν παρ᾽ ἑαυτοῖς)" (4.1).

[85] 4.3. The extent to which this entire argument—pitting the credibility of one witness against another—is well rooted in ancient forensic techniques can be readily seen by juxtaposing it with this excerpt from Hermogenes, *Stat.* 3.19 (Rabe, 45, *Hermogenes, Opera*, lines 9–20): "Then he will not merely question the witnesses (ἀπαιτήσει τοὺς μάρτυρας), but discredit (διαβαλεῖ) them to the effect that one should not believe (μὴ δεῖ πιστεύειν) 'a slave who is by nature an enemy to his masters' ... and one should also pit witnesses against witnesses (ἀντιτιθέναι τοῖς μάρτυσι τοὺς μάρτυρας), as to which are more worthy of belief (πότεροι μᾶλλον ἀξιοπιστότεροι), and cross-examine them (ἀντεξετάζειν), as Demosthenes did against Konon."

only worth as much as the proclamation of the woman who served the words up for him."[86]

But can these words, part of holy scripture, be completely invalidated? Eustathius will later argue that the sacred author of the entire Bible (one single writer, for him) consistently and throughout prohibits necromantic activity and pronounces those involved in it accursed.[87] Here he wishes to emphasize that one of the methods that holy author used to encode this consistent attitude is to customarily include words and narratives about evil people who give false testimonies, but always signal to the reader their untrustworthiness by the titles with which they are first introduced (such as the prophets of Baal, who are said to "prophesy" in their contest with Elijah on Carmel, or Pharaoh's magicians, who are described as acting "in like manner" to Aaron's and Moses's divinely produced plagues on Egypt).[88] Since the divine author gave this woman the moniker ἡ ἐγγαστρίμυθος (the "belly-myther"), readers are supposed to know from the get-go— both by this clue and their own readerly savoir faire—that her words are not to be trusted. [89] "Even her name brought this to the forefront" (4.7).

[86] 7.3: ἡ γάρ τοι τοῦ δαιμονιζομένου γνῶσις ἀξία τοῦ κηρύγματος ἐτύγχανεν ἐκείνης τῆς καὶ τοὺς λόγους αὐτῷ διακονούσης (see also, e.g., 4.1, 7).

[87] That set of proofs, in chs. 24–26, involves the invocation of such scriptural "witnesses" (μαρτυρίαι) as Deut 18:9–12; Lev 20:27; and Isa 8:19–21 (introduced as μάρτυς ἄλλος ἀξιοφανής ["another distinguished witness"] in 25.8), which categorically forbid mantic practices (the fact that these texts in the LXX include the term ἐγγαστρίμυθος makes this point especially impressive). Eustathius complains that Origen deliberately avoids calling these witnesses, even though he knows them, but instead brings in irrelevant ones (26.1). Further, like any courtroom lawyer, Eustathius asks the jury of his readers to choose between these two sets of witnesses, because one or the other must be committing perjury. Hence they must either invalidate the words of holy scripture, or τὰ τῆς ἐγγαστριμύθου ῥήματα διαβαλεῖν ὡς ἕωλα καὶ ψευδῆ ("discredit the words of the belly-myther as worthless and false"; 25.3). The answer to this question is predetermined by the assumption that scripture does not self-contradict. But, Eustathius goes on, even if it did in this one instance, the majority witnesses should win the day: ταῖς δὲ πολλαῖς ἡ μία μάχεται ψῆφος; εἰ δ' ἄρα καὶ μάχη τίς ἐστιν, ἐπικρατοῦσιν αἱ πολλαί ("Does a single judgment conflict with the many? Well, then, if there is any contradiction, the passages in the majority prevail"; 25.3).

[88] On the *topos* that one should interpret a text in relation to its author's consistent way of writing, see, e.g., Cicero, *Inv.* 2.40.117.

[89] He writes, somewhat snidely, that the "narrative voice" writes ὡς πρὸς εἰδότας περὶ δαιμονώσης ὁμιλῶν ("on the assumption that he was conversing

Because the scriptural author gave this crone a name that contains the word μῦθος ("myth"), Eustathius will later argue (27–30), all readers in their right minds should know that she is completely unreliable. Indeed, through further scrutiny of the woman's testimony, Eustathius seeks to demonstrate that even on their own terms the words the woman employs can be shown to be logically untenable. For example, if Origen would like to claim that the reason Saul had to ask her to describe what she saw was because Samuel did not arise as a body but as a soul (ψυχή), Eustathius can entrap him by asking about the clothing she said Samuel had worn. "For I do not suppose you would in pretence speciously aver that the double cloak had remained upon the grave so many years until that very day, so that the prophet's soul could wear it lest he might go walking around naked" (6.7). If so, Eustathius submits, then Origen would have to admit the woman's words are not even literally true, but that the insignias she speaks of were meant to invoke not the reality, but the idea, of "priesthood."

Hence the ἐγγαστρίμυθος is the definitively untrustworthy witness, "for she was saying things other than what is really the case" (6.9). This definition of her speech—ἕτερα γὰρ ἔλεγεν παρὰ τὰ ὄντα—is extended to make very clear that Eustathius by his purportedly literal reading of the text (αὐτὸ τὸ τῆς ἱστορίας γράμμα)[90] has tarred her (and Origen, whom he has castigated as being her promoter)[91] with the worst of exegetical crimes: appropriating τὰ τῶν αἰσθητῶν ὀνόματα ("the names of perceptible things") for the task of designating τὰ νοητὰ πράγματα ("spiritual realities"; 6.9). Eustathius's charge is unmistakable—the woman is an allegorist! And in a court of law, allegory (thus defined) equals perjury.

This earlier, hinted slur against allegorical exegesis will be developed further in the treatise, when Eustathius overtly excoriates Origen's more usual allegorical practice on other biblical passages.[92] There it is revealed that, like Origen's ironic *inclusio* on the ἀναγωγή ("elevated sense"), Eustathius's treatise also is united

with people who know about a woman acting under demonic influence"; 4.8).

[90] 2.1; "the very letter of the narrative."

[91] See esp. 3.4, where Eustathius charges Origen with wishing to fill the church with "instruments of idolatry and inventions of necromancy" (and n. 104 below).

[92] See esp. chs. 21–22.

in a singular, cleverly executed hermeneutical goal. Under the guise of contesting Origen's unacceptably literal interpretation of a single passage, Eustathius brilliantly executes a sharp denunciation of Origenic allegorical method as being in collusion with such a "belly-myther." Eustathius cites Origen's exegesis of the Eden narrative in Genesis, which he had ostensibly treated under the category of μῦθοι, arguing that it is not about αἰσθητὰ ξύλα ("perceptible trees").[93] Shocked at this, Eustathius exclaims the bitter irony,

> in allegorizing them he does not shudder to call "myths" what God is said to have created and what Moses, the most trustworthy (πιστότατος) servant of God, wrote. But on the contrary, the very things "the myth fabricated in the belly" (ὁ μῦθος ἐν γαστρὶ πλαττώμενος) obscurely suggests are those that Origen confirms (βεβαιοῖ) by dogmatic fiat, demonstrating them to be true. Commending the words of the belly-myther as spoken by the Holy Spirit, he considers them worthy of remaining as unshakeable testimony, since he has attributed them to scripture by virtue of their appearing there. But the very revelations of God handed down by Moses he perverts the sense of, calling them "myths," not judging it right to abide by a literal interpretation (τῇ τοῦ γράμματος ἐκδοχῇ). (21.3–4)

So, the paradoxical implication is that in holding to an interpretation of 1 Kgdms 28 "by the letter," Origen winds up even here (or perhaps especially here!) a spokesman for allegorical interpretation, the mode of interpretive myth-making that Eustathius categorically rejects, because Origen literalizes the words of a woman "belly-myther" as though they were divine, literal truth. He does what she does, she does what he does: pull words out of the air to say that what is not there actually is. She (and Origen) uses the names of perceptible things (τὰ τῶν αἰσθητῶν ὀνόματα) to point to spiritual matters (τὰ νοητὰ πράγματα).[94]

---

[93] In no extant text does Origen call the Gen 2–3 narrative a μῦθος, a term he, like Eustathius, most often uses with derision (e.g., *Comm. Jo.* 13.17; *Cels.* 1.4.11; 1.37.34). This reference may be lost, or perhaps Eustathius's accusation is based upon what he takes to be the implication of Origen's allegorical method rather than his actual recourse to the term (for further references and discussion, see Eustathius translation, n. 71).

[94] 6.9, translation of the key terms following *PGL*, s.v. νοητός, II.E.2.

Employing a standard ancient exegetical practice that was itself not far from allegorization,[95] Eustathius etymologizes the word ἐγγαστρίμυθος to make his point.

> But not even her compound name convinces Origen of what sort of bearing she had. For if *"engastri-mythos"* ("belly-myther") is interpreted by derivation to indicate that "a myth (*mythos*) is fabricated in the belly (*en gastri*)," and if the composition of a myth is given shape, sheltered persuasively within the belly, then the name does not broadcast the truth but the exact opposite—a lie. Indeed, those who are conversant with various forms of literary reference know much better to what genre myth belongs. Even if Origen had introduced Greek mantic activity inadvertently, because he was seriously ill with the fever of superstition, nevertheless, I do not think I should beg off from giving at this point a brief refutation (ἐλέγξαι) of his lack of intelligence, since it is necessary. For the rhetorical handbooks (αἱ ῥητορικαὶ τεχνο-γραφίαι) clearly show that "a myth is a fabrication composed with persuasive attraction with an eye to some matter of vital importance and utility."[96] Doubtless, they say, it has been called a "fabrication" (πλάσμα), as derived from the verb "to have been fabricated" (πεπλάσθαι); this is commonly agreed upon, because it would no longer be considered a myth if it had truly happened. And if it is an improvised composition or act of myth-making, it stands convicted of being far from the truth indeed, while it fashions in speech a likeness of concrete events, though it is bereft in fact. For it seems to use persuasive speech to show that what does not exist does exist, and it introduces in narrative form a fabricated copy. (26.10–27.3)

This charge against mythic speech leads Eustathius to summon a surprise expert witness: no less an authority than Plato, who banished the poets from his republic, describing the epic po-

---

[95] For the common technique of etymologizing, see esp. the treatise on Greek theology by Cornutus and the valuable discussion in Glenn W. Most, "Cornutus and Stoic Allegoresis: A Preliminary Report," *ANRW* 2.36.3:2014–65; Long, "Stoic Readings of Homer." On etymology as the *topos* ἀπὸ τοῦ ὀνόματος ("from the name") as applied to proper names, see Aristotle, *Rhet.* 2.23.29.

[96] Compare Theon *Prog.* 1 (Spengel, *Rhetores Graeci*, 2:59, lines 21–22): "A myth is a false account that portrays the truth" (μῦθός ἐστι λόγος ψευδὴς εἰκονίζων ἀλήθειαν).

ems of Homer and Hesiod as works that "declare false myths" (μύθους ἀποφαίνει ψευδεῖς), despite their psychagogical role in education (παιδεία) and their sheer beauty in style and in thought (καλλιλεξία, εὐγλωττία). Consequently, by an argument *a maiore ad minus* (from Homer to hag), the words of the demon-colluding old crone should be interpreted as μυθοποιίαι ψευδεῖς ("false myth-making"), as the very name ἐγγαστρίμυθος quite clearly indicates (29.1). Indeed, even Greek school children are taught the meaning of ὀνοματοποιία ("name-coining"); surely the savvy, experienced reader would be alerted at once to be suspicious of any words from her![97] Hence the woman is completely repudiated from being any credible witness to the events she supposedly attests, and, along with her, Origen is implicated for his allegorism that mirrors her own technique —collusion with the demonic that leads people to say they see things that are not there.

"Samuel"

One "witness" is left in 1 Kgdms 28: the voice of "Samuel." This is an equally complicated matter, for Eustathius must deal with the fact—crucial to Origen's interpretation—that the apparition proclaims some prophecies that actually do come true within the larger biblical narrative. This was the basis for Origen's argument that it must really have been Samuel who was raised, since no *daimonion* would know about the future God had in store for the kingdom of Israel. Eustathius discredits the testimony of this phantasmal "witness" in a very clever fashion.[98] First, he points out that not all of the things reportedly said by the apparition actually came true. Those that did, he argues, such as the fact that God had torn the kingdom from the hand of Saul and given it to David, were true, not because they were the words of the demon, but because the *daimonion* had plagiarized them from Samuel's words

---

[97] Compare Cicero, *Inv.* 2.47.139: the one who argues against someone else's literal rendering should say that the text has been written such that the educated judiciary can fully understand it (*quod intellegeret quales viri res iudicaturi essent*). That is why the author did not have to spell everything out in composing the text. Even a child can read the simple words (*quod quivis puer facere posset*), but the document in question was written for those capable of higher understanding.

[98] On the use of "supernatural evidence" in a court case, see Quintilian, *Inst.* 5.7.36.

earlier in 1 Kgdms 15 (back when the real prophet lived; 12.1–9). In this way the *daimonion* who engaged in προσωποποιεῖσθαι ("personifying" Samuel) could have said things that were true—they just were not his own (12.8). Having thus dispensed with the theological (and forensic) problem of a *daimonion* telling true prophecies about the divine dispensation, Eustathius looks at the other things the *daimonion* said that he did *not* get by plagiarizing Samuel (i.e., those that do not appear earlier in the narrative in 1 Kgdms 15 as the words of the real Samuel). Most of those matters, Eustathius notes, in fact did not come to pass as the *daimonion* said, such as that Saul would on die "the next day" and his son Jonathan would die with him.[99] The remaining item said by the *daimonion* that he could not have cribbed from Samuel did come true, Eustathius admits, namely, that Saul would be μετ' ἐμοῦ ("with him," i.e., in hell). But Eustathius has a most ingenious way of pinning his opponent by this apparent counter-evidence: the phantom's words in that case were an act of proleptic plagiarism of the words Jesus would direct to the good thief in Luke's Gospel (23:43; see 14.6). In that context, because of the identity of the πρόσωπον speaking, it meant being "with Jesus" in heaven. Furthermore, the plagiarizing *daimonion*, in adopting Jesus' exact words, actually betrays his own identity, because Saul is clearly destined for hell, where he will be "with the devil," not with Christ. Hence the *daimonion*'s testimony, submitted to detailed cross-examination, fails to pass scrutiny but is discredited as either botched and hence inaccurate prophecy or sheer plagiarism that betrays the true demonic identity of the word thief.

Dividing what Origen sought to coalesce—the words of the text, which he parcels out to three different *personae*—Eustathius nevertheless still applies the same forensic criterion to each in succession: Are they true or not true? From this same "lie-detector" hermeneutic of the courtroom, Eustathius has sought to demolish each in turn as a liar—Saul, the "belly-myther," "Samuel"—and along with them his exegetical opponent Origen, who was so badly mistaken in regarding each as part of one seamless voice of divine truth, the Holy Spirit the author of all Scripture. Eustathius's reading is "literal" in that it claims for itself a more "true" render-

---

[99] 12.10–13.10. Saul died two days after (1 Kgdms 28:20–25); Saul died with three sons (1 Kgdms 31:2).

ing of the text by looking at what is actually there, not what is not there, but it is nonetheless in some sense the supremely figurative reading, given that Eustathius's ultimate purpose in his interpretation of this narrative is not to uncover the "facts" about the Endor event but to reject Origenic allegorism through a creative conceit of convicting Origen of the crime of the "belly-myther" of Endor: conjuring words and ideas from thin air.

CONCLUSIONS

The purpose of the present essay has been to propose that the standard map dividing patristic interpretation into two exclusive camps—the literal and the allegorial—had its origins in the way early Christian interpreters rhetorically presented their own readings. I have argued that this way of approaching biblical interpretation—as an ἀγών leading to a judgment that a text is either true or false—emerged quite naturally from the rhetorical education shared by the literate elite in late antiquity, which was, after all, the essential tool kit drawn upon by early Christian interpreters. Those trained in that rhetorical culture recognized that textual evidence may, in one case or another, be hostile or friendly, depending upon whether one takes a literal or more figurative approach to the text in question. They also knew that there were standard ways an orator was expected to defend the literal sense against its detractors or to uphold a sense beyond that of the literal. This rhetorical framing of the interpretive act as a tug of war with the text from opposing sides situates textual hermeneutics within a misleading, since deliberately simplistic, dualism as one seeks the high ground for oneself and the lowest for one's opponent, even as in some sense both tilt toward the middle. [100]

Both Origen and Eustathius defend their interpretation of the tale of the ἐγγαστρίμυθος by attempting to show that the contrary reading is based upon a pernicious and disastrous hermeneutic that would lead to absurd consequences. Eustathius

---

[100] Dawson critiques Daniel Boyarin for continually working with a "binary opposition" between literal and allegorical, body and spirit, which he contends is "formulated from a poststructuralist and postmodernist point of view," but (Dawson counters) is actually "distinctively modernist" (*Christian Figural Reading*, 48). However, as we can see, it is also clearly ancient.

has particular potency on this point because he seeks to revile and refute both Origen's "hyperliteralism" (as he characterizes it) in reading this story and his more customary allegorical method. Origen incipiently claims that his opponents are in effect changing the words of the text ("facing off against scripture"), since they are seeing things that are not there (such as that the woman saw a *daimonion* pretending to be Samuel), and, even more broadly, that once one allows that anything in scripture lies, then the truth of the whole is open to question. The rhetoric of literal versus less strict interpretations of textual evidence always, therefore, involves broad statements about textual hermeneutics in general, because each interpretive act becomes precedent (or at least potential precedent) for all others, even as it is defended by appeals to existing precedent. However, it must be pointed out, for both interpreters the argument by appeal to the consequences of this reading is not necessarily an absolute or thoroughly systematic commitment to that one mode of interpretation, but it is also a rhetorical convention, prescribed by the handbooks, for dealing with a specific exegesis of a given text that one finds troubling by calling on the slippery slope of consequences. This is, therefore, a commonplace argument that can be used either for an interpretation that is to the letter or for one that calls for a moderation of the literal sense by appeal to another consideration, such as the intent of the author.[101] That conventions of reading ingrained in the educational system are the backbone of these approaches is revealed by "the urbanity *topos*"[102] used by both authors, in which they state that "people who have actually had a lot of experience reading texts know...." With such insults hurled across the aisle (or the years!) one reader castigates the other for fumbling naïvely with the written evidence and, in so doing, exposing himself as a literary bumpkin who by such gross ignorance has (seemingly) disqualified himself from the company and conversation of educated men.[103] This frequently used line of invective boldly insists

---

[101] See, e.g., Cicero, *Inv.* 2.45.130–134.

[102] I use this phrase to refer to barbs against others and implicit claims for oneself as being well-educated and well-read. See also Mitchell, "Rhetorical Handbooks in Service of Biblical Exegesis."

[103] See the rich collection of material on the social dimensions of proper formation in the literary culture in Kaster, *Guardians of Language*, esp. 15–31, on how "the oldest article of faith in the literary culture" is the view that "we

that, if the opponent were really well-trained in literary studies, he would agree with the speaker. Hence, so the commonplace goes, he must either be merely prevaricating in propounding an interpretation he knows to be patently false, or he is actually not qualified to register an opinion in the first place.

Origen and Eustathius, as we have seen, articulate the exegetical stakes as absolute: true or false, right or wrong, literal or allegorical, with (theoretically and rhetorically) no grey area. This is especially because their methods are overtly apologetic—aggressively so—embracing the language and procedures of the courtroom, proceeding by standard forms of proof and refutation (κατασκευή and ἀνασκευή), and (ubiquitously) invective. Their exegetical work does not simply move from theoretical commitment to exegesis, but the invocation of the right theory for the interpretation on offer is part of the very practice of exegesis and the rhetorical presentation of it; there may be proclivities toward more literal or more allegorical readings, but not absolute fidelity.

In this case, the Alexandrine and the Antiochene alike comfortably adopt a self-conscious and direct prosecutorial approach to the pericope about the woman-mantic at Endor that employs the stylistic and substantive strategies of this agonistic approach to texts as witnesses.[104] But under this rhetoric of a simple choice—yes or no, true or false, literal or allegorical—each author is actually engaged in an argument of much more complex, nuanced, and clever proportions. And for both of them the case at hand is in some ways the pretext for larger hermeneutical and theological issues that they wish to press much more broadly, if not absolutely. Origen's homily is united in its paronomastic concern for ἀναγωγή ("elevation"), by which wordplay he cleverly seeks to hijack the literal meaning of 1 Kgdms 28 in service of an ultimately spiritual and revelatory meaning conveyed—that is, to those who can attend to τὰ ἀγόμενα ("the elevated meanings brought forth"). It is

---

are then as superior to the uneducated as they are to cattle" (17, in reference to Diomedes, *Grammatici latini* 1.299.18ff.).

[104] Eustathius is afraid that Christians may be induced by Origen's exegesis of this story to engage in mantic practices (3.4; 26.9) and adopt an undue credulity about "myths" that are lies coming from the devil (26.1–30.6). Origen is worried that, if doubt is cast on the veracity of this text, then believers may be dissuaded from the faith (2.5). Interestingly, their pastoral goals are not that divergent.

also an overt attempt to preserve the authority of scripture against
those who "face off against" (ἀντιβλέπειν) one narrative and hence
call into question the truth of the whole, which was written by the
Holy Spirit (2.29; 3.1–3). In the same way, Aphthonius advises
one who wishes to uphold the factuality of the Apollo-Daphne
myth to say that those who doubt it are speaking against (ἀντερεῖν)
the poets and, in turn, repudiating the divine Muses (and Apollo)
who inspired them.[105]

Eustathius's treatise, rather than containing an almost par-
enthetical, knee-jerk swipe at Origen's allegorizing (even though
its ostensible target was a rare instance of Origenic "literal" interpretation), can be understood as a quite deliberate, focused,
and thoroughly clever attempt to tar Origen with guilt by association in the very crime of the ἐγγαστρίμυθος whose testimony
Eustathius believes Origen blasphemously upholds over that of
the Holy Spirit, author of scripture. Like the "belly-myther"
with whom Eustathius allies him, Origen is guilty—whether pro-
fessedly upholding the literal or in his more usual "allegorical"
interpretations—of "saying what is not," of ignoring the divine
givens in scripture that he replaces with his own silly and old-
womanish myths. He becomes, for Eustathius, one who traffics
in the same kinds of verbal malfeasance as the devil himself.[106]
Though cast in the form of a truly "literal" reading of the passage, Eustathius has ironically read 1 Kgdms 28 as an allegory
about Origen and his exegesis, just as schoolmasters had used the
Daphne-Apollo narrative to encapsulate the essential hermeneutical dynamics of all the myths the poets tell about the gods.[107]

[105] Aphthonius, *Prog.* 6 (Rabe, *Aphthonius, Progymnasmata,* 14, lines 9–
12), quoted in n. 45 above.

[106] "Repeating himself with persuasive artifice he acted as though he
were conversing prophetically" (πιθανῇ δὲ τεχνοποιίᾳ ταυτολογῶν ὑπεκρίνατο
δὴ προφητικῶς ὁμιλεῖν; 12.8). This charge against the devil is a resounding echo
of what Eustathius says of Origen, including the accusation of using rhetorical
craft, the act of ταυτολογεῖν ("repeating oneself") and ὑποκρίνεσθαι ("hypocrisy,"
"play-acting"; for which, see especially 17.2 and further discussion in n. 72
above). Surely Eustathius could (and really does!) predicate of Origen what he
says of the devil: οἶδεν ἄρα τὰ γεγραμμένα κακομαθῶς ("he has a knowledge of
what is written, even though he is poorly trained"; 23.8; cf. 26.1, cited in n. 72
above).

[107] That the entire treatise had Origenic allegory in mind is broadly
hinted at in the *prooimion* (1.1–7), which introduces the problem that people

If this connection is more than an interesting parallel (as the conjuction of Eustathius and the rhetorician Aphthonius in Antioch,
with its famous Daphne, might suggest), then perhaps we have a
clue to why the ἐγγαστρίμυθος of 1 Kgdms 28 received this kind
of attention among Christian exegetes.[108] Perhaps it was their
Daphne myth.

have been induced by Origen's fame to "focus their attention on 'names' and not
on facts, as they should" (τοῖς ὀνόμασιν μᾶλλον, ἀλλ' οὐ τοῖς πράγμασι προσέχοντες ὡς δέον; 1.3). On the contrast between ὀνόματα and πράγματα as lying at
the heart of debate on allegory, see Eustathius 22.2: ἅπαντα μὲν ὡς ἔπος εἰπεῖν,
ἐκ τῶν ὀνομάτων ἀλληγορῶν ἀναιρεῖ τὰς τῶν πραγμάτων ὑποθέσεις ("To put it
generally, by allegorizing everything on the basis of 'names' Origen destroys the
settings of the actions"). After the present essay had been initially published, I
read the insightful argument of Connor, Dumbstruck, and saw that he, too, recognized that Eustathius had "[his] own non-literal mode of reading" (84).

[108] It was a ἱστορία διαβόητος ("[in]famous narrative") already by the
time of Origen (1.2), for whom "disbelief" in it was thought to run the danger of
εἰς ἀπιστίαν προτρέπει ("persuading toward disbelief") more comprehensively
(2.5).

Compositional Analyses

Margaret M. Mitchell

ORIGEN, *HOMILY 5 ON 1 KINGDOMS*[1]

I. Liturgical Preamble 1.1–3

Four passages read; which to choose? The Bishop makes the choice: τὰ περὶ τῆς ἐγγαστριμύθου ἐξεταζέσθω.

II. προοίμιον to ἐξέτασις ("examination")

Justification for the "Literal" Reading of This Text at the Outset 2.1–3

A. Premise: some texts do not touch us, some are "necessary for our hope"[2] 2.1

B. Articulation of two options in all textual interpretation: ἱστορία ("narrative sense") and ἀναγωγή ("elevated sense") 2.1–3

   1. Temporal distinction: ἀναγωγή reading "not yet arrived at" [hence a promise that it will be?] 2.1

   2. Epistemological distinction: "those who know how to elevate meaning" and those who can hear what others "elevate" 2.1

   3. Pragmatic distinction: between texts/readings that are "useful" [χρήσιμον/ὄφελος] and those that are not 2.2

   4. παραδείγματα: texts whose "usefulness" to all is in doubt[3] 2.2–3

      a. Lot and his daughters 2.2

---

[1] References to the text of Origen, *Homily 5 on 1 Kingdoms*, follow the chapter and paragraph enumerations in this volume (following Simonetti, *La Maga di Endor*).

[2] Later in the argument it will become clear that this refers to the promise about the afterlife.

[3] The text is ambiguous about whether the fault lies with (1) the passage itself; (2) the "narrative" or "elevated" reading of the same; (3) the readers (some or all). The rhetorical questions can be taken either as exclamations of the impossibility of finding a useful reading or as allowing the possibility.

b. Judah and Tamar 2.3

C. Premise: narrative of Saul and ἐγγαστρίμυθος "touches all" 2.3

D. Conclusion: its truth is necessary, "in accordance with the word" [κατὰ τὸν λόγον] 2.3

III. Division: Two Opposing Ways to Read This Text 2.4–4.1

A. Introduction of two options 2.4–5

1. Statement of sympathy with a troubling consequence of a reading κατὰ τὸν λόγον: if literal, then does a demon have power to raise such a righteous man as Samuel? 2.4–5

2. Momentary aporia [τί εἴπω;] 2.5

3. Rhetorical question supporting "literal" reading: Ἐγγέγραπται ταῦτα; 2.5

4. Statement of τὸ κρινόμενον (the point to be adjudicated): Ἀληθῆ ἐστιν ἢ οὐ ἔστιν ἀληθῆ; 2.5

5. Interpretive consequences at stake divide the two sides 2.5

a. Loss of faith [τὸ μὲν μὴ εἶναι ἀληθῆ λέγειν εἰς ἀπιστίαν προτρέπει] 2.5

b. Matter for investigation and point of doubt [τὸ δὲ εἶναι ἀληθῆ ζήτησιν καὶ ἐπαπόρησιν ἡμῖν παρέχει] 2.5

B. Introduction of the opposing case [the ἐναντίος λόγος] 3.1–4.1

1. Characterization of proponents 3.1

a. Positive [τινες τῶν ἡμετέρων ἀδελφῶν] 3.1

b. Negative [ἀντιβλέψαντες τῇ γραφῇ] 3.1; cf. οἱ φάσκοντες τὴν ἱστορίαν ταύτην μὴ εἶναι ἀληθῆ (3.1); ὁ μὴ βουλόμενος ἀγῶνα παραδέξασθαι ... (4.1)

2. Bringing them in by προσωποποιία ("personification") 3.2–5

a. Direct quotation of their proposition: Οὐ πιστεύω τῇ ἐγγαστριμύθῳ ... ψεύδεται 3.1

b. Brief recapitulation of their argument: the petty demon speaks false prophecy, as elsewhere in the Bible 3.1

c. Direct quotation of opponents' position 3.1–5

1) Introduction ("This is what those who claim the narrative is not true say") 3.1

2) Long anaphoric speech [Σαμουὴλ ἐν ᾅδου;] 3.2–5

a) Samuel a holy and blameless prophet, as many passages show (1 Kgdms 1:11; 1:22–23; 2:18–19; 3:4–14; 2:31–36; 12:17–18; 12:1–6) 3.2–3

       b) List of consequences [τί ἀκολουθεῖ] of Samuel be-
          ing in hell (patriarchs, other prophets, etc. in hell)
          3.4⁻5

3. Recapitulation of the division 4.1
    a. Characterization of opponent as a coward [ὁ μὴ βουλόμε-
       νος ἀγῶνα παραδέξασθαι] seeking the easy way out[4] 4.1
    b. Characterization of self: Origen will take on the ἀγών
       entailed in holding that Σαμουήλ ἐστιν ὄντως ὁ ἀναχθείς
       (implicit in 4.1)
    c. Methods contrasted 4.1
       1) Origen: "a right-minded approach" [εὐγνώμονα ἐν τῷ
          ἀκούειν τῶν γραφῶν] 4.1 (cf. 4.10)
       2) Opponent: a λόγος that is πιθανῶς καταβομβήσας ἡμῶν
          (a reference to the parodied anaphoric crescendo) καὶ
          ἀληθῶς δυνάμενος ταράξαι καὶ κινῆσαι ἡμᾶς 4.1
    d. Decision point for hearers (*divisio* in shorthand), ei-
       ther/or 4.1
       1) The one who rejects the ἀγών has understood the text
          [νενόηται ἡ γραφὴ τῷ τοῦτο μὴ παραδεξαμένῳ] 4.1
       2) He contradicts the text [ἐναντία δὲ λέγει τοῖς γεγραμμέ-
          νοις], even if from reputable motives 4.1
       3) Unstated inference setting up the argument of refu-
          tation: if they are wrong, by the logic of a disjunctive
          syllogism, *our* interpretation is the right one

IV. ἔλεγχος/ἀνασκευή, refutation of those who deny "the truth" of τὰ
γεγραμμένα 4.2–6.2

A. Principle of λύσις ἐκ προσώπου ("solution based on the speak-
    er") established 4.2
    1. Rehearsal of text [τίνα γάρ ἐστιν τὰ γεγραμμένα], followed by
       quotation of 1 Kgdms 28:11 4.2
    2. Question posed: "Whose persona is it that speaks?" [Τίνος
       πρόσωπόν ἐστιν τὸ λέγον;] 4.2
    3. Two possible answers allowed 4.2
       a. The Holy Spirit [τὸ πρόσωπον τοῦ ἁγίου πνεύματος (ἐξ οὗ
          πεπίστευται ἀναγεγράφθαι ἡ γραφή)] 4.2

---

    [4] This is consistent with a common refrain of characterizing them as
"fearful" (6.2, 6; 7.4).

    b. The persona of someone else [πρόσωπον ἄλλου τινός] 4.2

4. Proposition: the narrative persona = the persona of the author [τὸ διηγηματικὸν πρόσωπον = πρόσωπον τοῦ συγγραφέως] 4.2

5. Proof: invocation of the "urbanity *topos*," that those who have read widely know this to be always the case [ὡς ἴσασιν καὶ οἱ περὶ παντοδαποὺς γενόμενοι λόγους] 4.2

6. Conclusion 4.2

    a. Proposition: συγγραφεύς = τὸ πνεῦμα τὸ ἅγιον 4.2

    [b. Inference: unstated conclusion from these premises: τὸ διηγηματικὸν πρόσωπον = τὸ πνεῦμα τὸ ἅγιον]

B. λύσις ἐκ προσώπου applied to this passage 4.3–6.2

  1. What the Holy Spirit said (rehearsal of "testimony" of 1 Kgdms 28:11–14) 4.3–5

    a. "The woman said, 'whom shall I bring up for you'" 4.3

    b. "Bring up Samuel for me" 4.3

    c. "The woman saw Samuel, and the woman cried out with a loud voice and said" 4.3, reiterated 4.4

    d. "'Why have you deceived me' . . . and the woman said to Saul, 'I saw gods coming up from the ground . . . an old man is coming up, and he is wrapped in a double cloak, an ephod'" 4.4–5

  2. Objection from ὁ ἐναντίος λόγος introduced and refuted 4.6–9

    a. Since 2 Cor 11:14–15 testifies that Satan uses disguises, why is that not what is going on here? 4.6

    b. Counter-argument: the text would have been worded differently [διὰ τί οὐκ εἴρηται] if that were the case 4.6–9

      1) Why didn't the author say, "she saw a demon pretending [προσποιεῖσθαι] to be Samuel"? 4.7

      2) Why does it allow that Saul "knew that it was Samuel," rather than "thought [ἐνόμισεν] it was Samuel"? 4.7

      3) Why does text say εἶπεν Σαμουήλ . . . (instead of "τὸ δαιμόνιον said," or some such)? 4.8–9

      4) Proposition stated succinctly: "scripture said nothing otherwise" [ἡ γραφὴ οὐκ ἄλλως εἶπεν] 4.9

3. Proof of truthfulness of Samuel's words, which forms a transition from refutation to confirmation 4.9–6.2

   a. Rhetorical question to pin the opponent:[5] did the words of Samuel about the Israelite kingdom come true, or not? ['Ἀληθεύει ἢ ψεύδεται ταῦτα λέγων;] 4.9

   b. Rehearsal of text (1 Kgdms 28:16–17) 4.9

   c. Statement of the point to be adjudicated in the ἀγών: would a demon be able to prophesy truthfully about the Israelite kingdom, as Samuel does here? 4.9

   d. Charge: the ἐναντίος λόγος has no good answer to this key question 4.10; cf. 6.2

   e. Transition in argument signaled 4.10–5.1

      1) The first part of the proof—exegesis of the text — has raised big questions and cast doubts on the other interpretation (refutation largely accomplished) 4.10

      2) The second part of the proof—establishing "what awaits us after our departure from this world" (= "what is necessary for our hope")—still remains to be clarified 4.10

      3) Methodological reminder: the ἱστορία and ἐξέτασις are necessary for the larger goal of discerning "what our condition will be after we die" (linking of ἱστορία and ἀναγωγή; cf. 2.1–3) 5.1

   f. Completion of proof that Samuel's words were true 5.1–6.2

      1) Text rehearsed 5.1, 2, 3

      2) Proposition (repeatedly interspersed in textual quotations): a demon cannot know about the Davidic kingdom [δαιμόνιον οὐ δύναται εἰδέναι τὴν βασιλείαν Δαβίδ] 5.1, 3, 4 (cf. 4.9)

      3) Conclusion to subargument about the truth of Samuel's prophecy: Ταῦτα μὲν οὖν δηλοῖ ὅτι οὐκ ἔστιν ψευδῆ τὰ ἀναγεγραμμένα ... 6.1

C. Conclusion to λύσις ἐκ προσώπου 6.1–2

   1. ταῦτα μὲν οὖν δηλοῖ ... καὶ ὅτι Σαμουήλ ἐστιν ὁ ἀναβεβηκώς 6.1

---

[5] The words of Samuel were put on the table first to establish the wording of the text as not satisfying the view that this was the demon pretending to be Samuel. Now that they are out there, Origen sees a way to turn the tables on his opponent. He may be doing this *in medias res*, as the pause in 4.10 suggests.

2. Two difficult questions remain to be addressed (transition to next section of proof) 6.1

   a. What does the ἐγγαστρίμυθος do here? 6.1

   b. What does the ἐγγαστρίμυθος have to do with a righteous man like Samuel? 6.1; cf. 2.4 (Does her action mean after death *we* shall be under her power?)

3. Transitional taunt: opponent seeks to "flee the ἀγών," but Origen (in what follows) will tackle τὰ ζητούμενα head-on 6.2 (cf. 4.1)

4. Recapitulation of two main propositions 6.2

   a. Speaker of words is clear (disjunctive syllogism) 6.2

      1) "These are the words of scripture" [Τὰ δὲ ῥήματα τῆς γραφῆς ἐστιν] 6.2

      2) "Not spoken from the persona of the demon itself, but from the persona of scripture" [οὐκ ἔστιν ἐκ προσώπου τοῦ δαιμονίου αὐτοῦ ἀλλ' ἐκ προσώπου αὐτῆς] 6.2

   b. Consequences of the text being true 6.2

      1) The woman really did see Samuel (Samuel really was raised) 6.2

      2) Samuel really did say the prophetic words he is reported to have said [τὰ λελαλημένα ἀπὸ τοῦ Σαμουήλ] 6.2

V. λύσις τῶν ζητουμένων, "solution to matters requiring investigation": proof that there is no πρόσκομμα ("stumbling block") in this passage 6.3–9.11

A. "Samuel in hell" is not absurd 6.3–10

   1. Opening question: Πῶς οὖν λυόμενα τὰ τῆς ἐγγαστριμύθου φανεῖται τὰ κατὰ τὸν τόπον; 6.3

   2. Cross-examination of opponent 6.3–10

      a. Putting the personified opponent on the stand for questioning [Πυνθάνομαι τοῦ προειρηκότος τὰ πρότερα· Σαμουὴλ ἐν ᾅδου καὶ τὰ ἑξῆς, καὶ ἀποκρινάσθω πρὸς τὸ ἐπηρωτημένον] 6.3

      b. Lesser to greater argument: If Jesus went to hell, why not Samuel? 6.3–6

         1) Direct question [Τίς μείζων . . .] to counter the "bombastic" argument of the opponent (if Samuel in hell, then also Abraham, the prophets) 6.3

2) Forced confession from opponent: if you acknowledge that Christ was proclaimed ahead of time by the prophets you will not dare to deny that Ἰησοῦς Χριστὸς μείζων ἐστίν 6.4

3) Direct question: Was Christ in hell or not? 6.4

4) Will opponent contradict other witnesses who say Christ went to hell (Ps 15:10; Acts 2:27–31)? 6.5

5) Charge: opponent is afraid to say "yes," Jesus Christ was in hell 6.6

6) Opponent's presumed concession (under pressure) that Christ *was* in hell leads to a second line of questioning 6.6

c. Why *did* Christ descend to hell? 6.6–7

   1) Alternatives posed as direct questions to the opponent 6.6

      a) To prophesy to other souls there? [ἐκεῖ προφητεῦσαι καταβαίνει;] 6.6

      b) To conquer death or be conquered by it? [νικήσων (μὴ) νικηθησόμενος ὑπὸ τοῦ θανάτου;] 6.6

   2) Answer: "not as the servant of those who were there, but as their master" [οὐχ ὡς δοῦλος τῶν ἐκεῖ ἀλλ᾽ ὡς δεσπότης], as Ps 21 reminds us 6.6–7

   3) Conclusion [οὐκοῦν]: "the Savior has descended in order to save" 6.7

d. Proposition: since it was known beforehand that Christ would go to hell, it is not "absurd" [ἄτοπος] to think Moses and the prophets went there before him as forerunners 6.7–10

   1) Question: Did the prophets foretell this in advance, or did they only know of his earthly sojourn? 6.7

   2) Answer: he was προκηρυχθείς ("proclaimed ahead of time")—both here *and* there 6.7–9

      a) Moses proclaimed his coming "here" (Jn 5:46–47) 6.8

      b) Why wouldn't Moses have descended "there" (hell), too, to prophesy his coming? 6.9

      c) If by Moses, why not also by other prophets, including Samuel? 6.9

3) Proof by analogy against claim that it would be absurd for Samuel (and others) to have been in hell 6.9–10

   a) Physicians go where the sick are (What is absurd about that? [τί δὲ ἄτοπόν ἐστιν;]) 6.9
   b) Christ is the ἀρχίατρος 6.9
   c) παράδειγμα: the woman with the flow of blood 6.10
      1. "Many doctors" but one chief healer," Christ 6.10
      2. He healed what the others could not 6.10
      3. He exhorted her not to be afraid 6.10

4) Exhortation: "do not be alarmed!" 6.10 (see also next proof on undoing their fear)[6]

5) Conclusion: "Jesus has been in hell, and the prophets before him, and they proclaimed ahead of time Christ's coming" ['Ιησοῦς εἰς ᾅδου γέγονεν, καὶ οἱ προφῆται πρὸ αὐτοῦ, καὶ προσκηρύσσουσι τοῦ Χριστοῦ τὴν ἐπιδημίαν] 6.10

B. κατασκευή (constructive proof) that Samuel's being in hell is not a cause of fear, but hope, for believers 7.1–9.11

1. Introduction of Origen's own position: "I wish to say something else from this very scripture" [ἄλλο τι θέλω εἰπεῖν ἀπ' αὐτῆς τῆς γραφῆς] 7.1

2. Further proof in the text that the holy souls of all the prophets before Christ were in hell 7.1–2

   a. Rehearsal of text (her words): "I saw gods coming up from the earth" [εἶδον θεοὺς ἀναβαίνοντες ἀπὸ τῆς γῆς], not mere mortals 7.1
   b. Her reaction: "terror" 7.1
   c. Conjecture [τάχα]: *at that time* Samuel did not come up alone, but in the company of holy ones 7.2
   d. Proof by analogy 7.2
      1) "Here" (on earth) one "will be made holy with a holy person" (as Ps 17:26–27 shows) 7.2

---

[6] The alarm is that called for by the slippery slope of consequences in the bombastic speech of the ἐναντίος λόγος recited in 3.4–5 (cf. 4.1: ἀληθῶς δυνάμενος ταράξαι καὶ κινῆσαι ἡμᾶς). The consequences of the literal reading, Origen wishes to show, are actually positive (assurance of eschatological reward), not negative (all the prophets in hell as a kind of absurd doomsday scenario).

2) "There" (in hell) it is the same: the holy associate with the holy 7.2

3) Permitted exception *at that time*[7]: the holy (like Christ) consorted with the sinners to save them (cf. 6.6, 9) 7.2

4) Conjecture reiterated as conclusion: the holy souls of other prophets came up with Samuel 7.2

e. Added inquiry about angels 7.3–4

1) Question (anticipated): Did the holy souls have angels with them? 7.3

2) Answer: yes, either angels speaking in holy prophets (Zech 1:9) or alongside them 7.3

3) Reason: angels must go even to hell in service to those who are meant to be saved (Heb 1:14) 7.3

4) Rebuke of opponent: "Why are you afraid to say that every place (including hell) has need of Jesus Christ?" 7.4

3. The holy prophets were in hell for a good reason: to prophesy Christ's coming 7.4–8.1

a. Proposition: one who needs Christ needs also the prophets who prepared his way *everywhere* 7.4

b. παράδειγμα: John the Baptist prophetically proclaimed Christ in hell[8] 7.4–8.1

1) Choice of John as example that will prove the rest: "no one greater of all human beings" (Luke 7:28) 7.4

2) Rebuke of opponent: "Do not be afraid to say he went down to hell in order to proclaim the Lord ahead of time" 7.4

3) Scriptural testimony to John's prophetic insight ("he saw his glory") (Luke 7:18–20//Matt 11:2–3; John 1:14–15) 7.4–6

4) Rebuttal: John never lost the power of the Holy Spirit 7.6–11

---

[7] The then and now contrast here [καὶ εἰ ἄρα ποτέ], and earlier in 7.7 [τότε προφητεύσων] allows Origen to say that once saints were in hell, but only before the advent of Christ, not afterwards.

[8] On this tradition, found already in Tertullian, see Nautin and Nautin, *Origène*, 80 n.1.

      a) Errant view stated: the Holy Spirit must have left John since he had to ask if Jesus was the Christ 7.6 (repeated in 7.8)

      b) Characterization: a misunderstanding of the meaning of his words 7.6

      c) Proofs that John *did* know Christ 7.7–11

  c. Conclusion 8.1

    1) Denial of having digressed [παρεξέβην] or lost the thread of the argument 8.1

    2) Conclusion and restatement of σκοπός ("goal") of argument: confirmation [κατασκευάσαι] that "if all Christ's prophets, as forerunners of Christ, have descended to hell before Christ, then *in the same way* Samuel too has descended there" 8.1

4. Holy prophets remained holy in ethical purpose even in hell 8.1–3

  a. Proposition (and transition to next section of proof): Samuel did not descend ἁπλῶς ("in an ordinary way"),[9] but as a holy man [ἅγιος] 8.1

  b. Justification by maxim: "wherever a holy person might be, he is holy" 8.1

  c. παράδειγμα (from greater to lesser): Christ 8.2

    1) Rhetorical question [μήτι]: was Christ no longer Christ when in hell? 8.2

    2) Proof that he remained Son of God in netherworld (Phil 2:10) 8.2

    3) Conclusion: "Christ was Christ even when he was below" 8.2

    4) Explanation: when "below" in person, Christ was "above" with respect to ethical purpose [προαίρεσις] 8.2

  d. Inductive conclusion: like Christ, the prophets and Samuel "were able to be in the place 'below' but not be 'below' with respect to ethical purpose [προαίρεσις]" 8.3

5. The Holy Spirit was still with Samuel when he was in hell 8.3–9.6

  a. Cross-examination of opponent who denies a holy prophet like Samuel could be in hell 8.3–4

[9] As a "mere human being," as in 7.1.

1) Direct question: "Did the holy prophets prophesy things above the heavens?" 8.3

2) Counter-statement: Origen will not give a δαιμόνιον the authority to prophesy about the Davidic kingdom 8.3

3) Characterization by prophetic tag of his own: opponents [οἱ ταῦτα λέγοντες] "will come to know the matters of truth that are in this passage" 8.4

4) Charge: opponents cannot disprove that even a holy person will go where the sick are when salvation/health [σωτηρία] is at stake 8.4

5) Proofs by analogy, lesser to greater 8.5

   a) Physicians going onto the battlefield to aid the wounded 8.5

   b) The Word's requirements to Savior and prophets to go both to earth and to hell 8.5

b. Rebuttal against the argument that Samuel "jettisoned his prophetic gift" at death

1) Introduction: an argument Origen wishes to add [προσθετέον] 9.1

2) Syllogistic argument of opponent rehearsed: "if Samuel was a prophet, if the Holy Spirit abandoned him when he departed from this life, and if the prophetic gift abandoned him ..." 9.1

3) First proof: the future (after death) is the time of "perfection" in prophecy 9.1–2

   a) If opponent is right, then "the apostle" lied in 1 Cor 13:9–10 (unthinkable) 9.1

   b) Conclusion [οὐκοῦν]: "What is perfect is after this life" [τὸ τέλειον μετὰ τὸν βίον ἐστίν] 9.1

   c) παράδειγμα: Isaiah who prophesied "with all boldness" (Acts 4:29) 9.2

   d) Premise: Samuel's prophecies about the Davidic kingdom "extend to the perfection of prophecy" [ἐπὶ τὸ τέλειον τῆς προφητείας] 9.2

   e) Conclusion [οὖν]: "Samuel did not jettison the prophetic gift" at death [Οὐκ ἀπέβαλεν οὖν τὴν χάριν τὴν προφητικὴν Σαμουήλ] but brought it to perfection 9.2

4) Second proof: how the prophetic gift is really lost

a) Proposition: the Spirit only abandons those who do what is unworthy of it 9.4

b) Proof of proposition: David (Ps 51:11) 9.4

c) Premise: Samuel had not sinned 9.4

d) Conclusion: Samuel did not lose the prophetic gift, and hence had the Spirit, since it is the Holy Spirit that prophesies 9.4

5) Third proof: Samuel used the gift of prophecy as one should a "spiritual gift" 9.2–6

   a) Premise: prophetic gift is like the gift of speaking in tongues (according to 1 Cor 14:14) 9.2

   b) Premise: like tongues, prophecy should build up the church (according to 1 Cor 14:4) 9.3–4

   c) Conclusion: Samuel's prophecies fulfilled the requirement to build up the church 9.4–6

      1. Question: Whom did he build up? 9.4

      2. Answer: not those in heaven or angels who did not need it (physician analogy, with Matt 9:12) 9.5

      3. Premise: no gift of grace is idle, so someone needed it 9.5

      4. Bold declaration: the souls of the dead needed Samuel's prophetic gift there to proclaim the coming of Christ 9.6

6. Samuel's being in hell points to our going to heaven (then and now argument) 9.7–11

  a. Proposition: it was impossible for anyone to go to heaven before the arrival of Jesus Christ 9.7

  b. Proof: Gen 3:24—the fiery sword was blocking the way 9.7

  c. Question: Who could pass through and by what power? 9.8

  d. παραδείγματα: crossings only God could make happen 9.8

    1) God and pillar of fire crossing the sea (Exod 13:22; 14:24) 9.8

    2) Joshua (the Jesus-type) crossing the Jordan (Josh 3:16) 9.8

  e. παραδείγματα ἐναντία—people "then" who could not cross through flaming sword 9.8–9

     1) Not Samuel 9.8

     2) Not Abraham (seen by the rich man in Lk 16:23) 9.8–9

  f. Conclusion [οὖν/ὥστε]: the patriarchs, the prophets, and all the people were there in hell [ἐκεῖ] 9.10–11

     1) Awaiting the advent of Christ, who alone could open the way (John 14:6; 10:9) to paradise 9.10

     2) Awaiting fulfillment of the prophecy of Isa 43:2 about passing through fire (= the fiery sword) safely 9.10

     3) "Acting on God's providential plan" [οἰκονομίαν ποιοῦντες] while waiting 9.11

     4) Blocked from the future paradise, which will be the abode of the blessed, the elect, and the saints of God 9.11

VI. ἐπίλογος, Conclusion 10.1–5

A. Conclusion/recapitulation: "there is no stumbling block in this passage" [οὐδὲν οὖν πρόσκομμα κατὰ τὸν τόπον ἐστίν] 10.1

B. Two methodological pillars of proper understanding 10.2

  1. The text itself, which is "marvelously written" [θαυμασίως γέγραπται] (a reference to the ἱστορία; cf. 2.1–3) 10.2

  2. Inspired reading in which understanding comes [νενόηται][10] to "those to whom God has revealed it" [οἷς ἂν ὁ θεὸς ἀποκαλύψῃ] (a reference to the ἀναγωγή; cf. 2.1) 10.2

C. The secret meaning of the text revealed, as promised[11]

  1. Enigmatic proposition: "we" who have come to the end of the ages (Heb 9:26) have "something more" [περισσόν τι] (then and now argument) 10.1

  2. Exposition of the "something more" [περρισόν τι, πλέον τι] 10.2–5

    a. Question: τί περισσόν; 10.2

    b. Answer 10.2

     1) If "we" have lived good lives, we shall pass unharmed through the flaming sword into paradise 10.2

---

[10] Compare the division in 4.1.

[11] These are the ἅγιοι λόγοι μεγάλοι καὶ ἀπόρρητοι οἱ περὶ τῆς ἐξόδου promised in 4.10.

EUSTATHIUS OF ANTIOCH,
ON THE BELLY-MYTHER, AGAINST ORIGEN

I. προοίμιον 1.1–7

A. Literary Preface 1.1–3

  1. Direct address of Eutropius 1.1

  2. Praise (*captatio benevolentiae*) 1.1

  3. Eutropius's request: for Eustathius to give his γνώμη ἕνεκα τῆς ἐγγαστριμύθου 1.1

  4. Occasion and reason:

    a. Eutropius's dissatisfaction with Origen's view [οὐ γὰρ ἀρέσκεσθαι φὴς οἷς ἐξέδωκεν Ὠριγένης εἰς τήνδε τὴν ὑπόθεσιν] 1.3

    b. Others, not a few, are also vexed in their souls at this 1.2

    c. Some have been led by what Origen wrote to attend to ὀνόματα rather than πράγματα (i.e., allegorical rather than literal reading; cf. 21.6–7; 22.2–4, etc.) 1.3

B. Method for treatise announced and defended 1.4–7

  1. "Yoking Origen's interpretation with my explanation of the text" [πᾶσαν ὁμοῦ συζεῦξαι τὴν ἐξήγησιν αὐτοῦ τῇδε τῇ τοῦ γράμματος ὑπαγορίᾳ] 1.4

  2. "Side-by-side comparisons" παράλληλος σύγκρισις (justified by a series of exempla from horseracing, dance, and athletics) 1.5

  3. Result: literature-lovers can choose the better opinion of the two [τὴν ἀμείνονα γνώμην ἐξ ἀμφοῖν αἱρεῖσθαι τοὺς φιλολόγους] 1.5 (cf. ἵνα ἐξ ἑνὸς ὁποτέρου διαγινώσκηται τὸ προὖχον in 1.7–8)

  4. Order[12]

---

[12] This programatic statement does not correspond to the larger structural divisions in the treatise but to the general strategy followed throughout each subsection, of citing Origen's interpretation first and then engaging in rebuttal. The argument, as analyzed below, first goes through the biblical text in its order (part II) and then follows the progression of Origen's own argument, especially from where Eustathius thinks it breaks down (part III). The final section also engages other evidence within Origen's exegetical writings (see esp. 21.1–22.7). Hence τὰ Ὠριγένεια here may have a deliberately broad referent, pointing both to Origen's exegesis of this passage and to his wider œuvre and legacy.

    a. "Set forth Origen's interpretations first" [τὰ 'Ωριγένεια
       προτακτέον] 1.7

    b. "In proper order" [ἰδίᾳ τάξει] seriously attending to the
       opposing interpretation [τὸν ἀντιπίπτοντα νοῦν ἐκείνοις
       σπουδαστέον] 1.7

II. Text on trial: clarifying the "plain meaning" [τρανῶσαι τὸ σαφές]
2.1–16.2

A. Biblical text, first part (1 Kgdms 28:1–14): demolition of cred-
    ibility of woman and Saul as witnesses 2.1–9.14

    1. Starting point [ἀρκτέον] and method: rehearsal of text in its
       own narrative progression[13] [αὐτὸ τῆς ἱστορίας γράμμα] 2.1–
       3.9

    2. Propositions/προθέσεις

       a. Text does not say Samuel was brought up (3.8)

       b. Text only says woman boasted and Saul believed (3.9)

    3. Procedure for ἐξέτασις of the witness of/witnesses in the text
       4.1–5

       a. Purpose: κρίνωμεν παρ' ἑαυτοῖς the credibility of Saul and
         the woman (4.1)

       b. Examining those witnesses in the presence of their
         "lawyer," Origen (5.6: τῆς ἀθεμίτου μαντείας ὑποθήμων)
         4.2–5

         1) Accusations against Origen/opposing counsel

           a) "Stumbling from the truth" 4.2, 4 (cf. 3.5; 17.3
             βλασφημία)

           b) Contradicting Jesus (John 8:44) 4.3

           c) Contradicting the text 4.5; cf. 5.5

         2) Summoning Origen to speak: τί τοίνυν φής, ὦ 'Ωρίγενες
           (ἀνάγκη γὰρ ἐρέσθαι σε): 4.3 (and many times there-
           after)

    4. Cross-examination of Origen, step 1 4.5–10

       a. Origen's legal brief: these statements are true because
         they are the words of the Holy Spirit 4.5

       b. Invalidation of brief by "urbanity *topos*"—the words of
         the woman are given in character (as all sophisticated

---

[13] Twice in this section Eustathius leaps ahead to his argument of refutation but calls himself back on task (2.7–9; 3.3–5).

readers should know) 4.6–10

5. Cross-examination of Origen, step 2 4.10–9.14

   a. Origen's brief: a trial lawyer trick [ὡς πρὸς ἐναντίους δικανικῇ δεινότητι διαλεγόμενος] to state how the text *should
have been written* if the other side is right 4.10–5.2

   b. Refutation of Origen's brief 5.2–9.14

      1) Focus on *this* example of Origen's faulty reasoning 5.2

      2) Calling Origen to witness before God 5.3

      3) Direct cross-examination: What did she bring up? A
body or a soul? 5.3–6

      4) Trapped in the series of rapid-fire questions, the wit-
ness [Origen] will have to say it was a soul and thus
contradict himself and the text 6.1–7.6

      5) Origen tarred as guilty by association in the crimes of
his "clients"

        a) "Says things other than the case," "pronounc-
ing the names of perceptible things and indicating
spiritual matters," just like the ἐγγαστρίμυθος 6.9

        b) Sees nothing but speaks empty words, κουφολογία,
like Saul 7.6

      6) Origen wrong to say that the text does not explicitly
tell the reader not to trust the woman 7.7–9.14

        a) The story-writer [ὁ ἱστοριογράφος] gives a clue by
her very name, ἡ ἐγγαστρίμυθος, as to what sort of
πρόσωπον ("character/persona") she was 7.7

        b) Those who are not mad themselves understand
this 7.7

        c) The author did the same with the "knowledge" he
attributes to Saul, who was clearly out of his mind
7.8

        d) This is the general practice of the sacred author of
scripture 8.1–9.14

          1. In this case [αὐτὰ τὰ πράγματα] 8.1

          2. Other παραδείγματα/μαρτύρια 8.1–9.14

            α'. False prophets of Baal 8.1–9.1

            β'. False magicians of Egypt 9.1–13

        e) Inductive inference: same thing here—the woman
and Saul are clearly shown by the author not to be
trustworthy witnesses 9.14

B. Biblical text, second part (1 Kgdms 28:13–20): demolition of
credibility of Saul and "Samuel" as witnesses 10.1–16.2

   1. 1 Kgdms 28:13: "gods coming up from the earth" and Saul
      bowing down 10.1–18

      a. Text rehearsed 10.1

      b. Counter-statement: this is no true testimony by a pro-
         phet, but the devil giving false boasts 10.1–2

      c. Proofs: ἅγιαι μαρτυρίαι (Isa 14; Ezek 28; Dan 2) contra-
         vene devil's boast of having the power to raise souls from
         the dead 10.2–6

      d. Undeniable premise: only God has this authority 10.6

      e. Conclusion: no one in the company of the right-minded
         would "render a verdict that contradicts the holy testi-
         monies" 10.6

   2. 1 Kgdms 28:14: Saul's query of what the woman had seen,
      and her answer about the man "wrapped in a double cloak"
      10.7–18

      a. Text rehearsed 10.7

      b. Saul only a heresay witness, demon-besieged, who was
         "taken captive by [her] naming of the signs," not the
         presence of the real Samuel 10.8

      c. Proofs

         1) First: if it were Samuel he would have forbidden Saul
            to worship him (Matt 4:10) 10.9

         2) Second: then and now argument makes Saul's bow-
            ing down implausible here (did not bow down when
            a private citizen [1 Kgdms 9:3–21], would he when a
            king?) 10.10–11

         3) Third: Why bow down to Samuel but not to "gods"
            she mentioned first? 10.11–13

      d. Conclusions

         1) Saul was demon-driven, mentally blind 10.13

         2) The apparition was not Samuel, but the devil in dis-
            guise seeking worship, as usual (Matt 4//Luke 4)
            10.13–18

   3. 1 Kgdms 28:15a: "Samuel" pretending to be vexed at being
      called up "unwillingly" 11.1–9

      a. Text rehearsed 11.1–2

b. Counter-statement: not true testimony, but the devil lying in pretence 11.1–2

c. Proofs 11.3–8

   1) Proposition: those with mind of Christ not subject to demons against their will 11.3

   2) παράδειγμα ἐναντίον: Paul at Philippi (Acts 16) drove out a "Pythian prophetess" [πυθόμαντις] 11.4–8

d. Conclusion: "Samuel" was the devil in disguise, pretending to have been brought up against his will 11.9

4. 1 Kgdms 28:15b-e: Saul's request to "Samuel" and his initial response 11.10–12.1

  a. Text rehearsed 11.10

  b. Counter-statement: if this were the real Samuel, he would have answered Saul with a firmer rebuke and called him to repentance 11.10–11

  c. Proofs 11.12–15

    1) Real Samuel would be against necromancy (with Lev 19:31; 20:16) 11.12–14

    2) Real Samuel knew law from youth 11.15

    3) Real Samuel would have forestalled this dangerous precedent among the people 11.15–16

    4) The "bill of indictment" "Samuel" gave did not include the most grave charges against Saul 11.17–12.1

  d. Conclusion: this was the devil, not Samuel 11.16–12.1

5. 1 Kgdms 28:16–19: "Samuel's" prophecy to Saul 12.1–15.7

  a. Proposition: these words were not products of foreknowledge [πρόγνωσις] but plagiarism cast as prophecy 12.1–2

  b. Counter to Origen's reversal: he understands these old recycled prophecies as "apt and new prophetic utterances" 12.3

  c. Proofs that the devil is guilty of plagiarism 12.4–15.7

    1) 1 Kgdms 28:17–19: "The Lord will tear the kingdom out of your hand and will give it to your neighbor David ..." 12.4–9

     a) Text rehearsed 12.4

     b) "Clear meaning" shown in fact that these words were taken from 1 Kgdms 15, "word for word" [ἐπὶ λέξεως] 12.5–7

    c) Conclusion [οὖν]; charge rephrased three ways: devil "fashioned Samuel's words as his own" [ὡς ἴδια σχηματίζειν], "engaged in deceitful personification" [προσωποποιεῖν ἀπάτῃ], "repeated the same things with persuasive artifice" [πιθανῇ τεχνοποιίᾳ ταυτολογεῖν] 12.8

    d) Analogy with contemporary traveling soothsayers 12.9

        1. They research a few past events to amaze potential clients 12.9

        2. Once in, they make up all their "prophecies" about the future 12.9

        3. Goal: to steal (in this case, Saul's mind) 12.9

2) 1 Kgdms 28:19: "tomorrow, you and your son Jonathan will be with me, and the Lord will give the camp of Israel into the hands of the foreigners" 12.10–15.7

    a) Text rehearsed 12.10

    b) Premise: demon said these things on his own (not found in 1 Kgdms 15) 12.10

    c) Cross-examination proves these words give no evidence of foreknowledge 13.1–8

        1. Saul did not die "tomorrow" 13.1–3

        2. Saul was slain with three sons, not just Jonathan 13.4–5

        3. Faulty wording of threatened punishment, as devil tries to free-lance about the present: "handing over the camp" for Samuel's "the people will be divided" 13.6–7

        4. Conclusion: since not one thing the devil made up came true, he has no prophetic power 13.8

    d) Rebuttal of anticipated objection: the threat he made of war and death did come true 13.9–14.5

        1. Proposition: when the devil prophesies evil things that come to pass he is not "prophesying," since he is the cause, not the foreteller, of those events 13.9

        2. παραδείγματα 13.10–4.5

          α'. devil as war-monger against Job 13.10

β'. General rule: devil takes various shapes and guises 13.10

γ'. Crucial instance: 3 Kgdms 22:15–22 proves the lying spirit in the "mouth of the prophets" is an instrument of the devil and causes war and the death of a king in battle 14.1–5

e) Charge: demon's additions to Samuel's prophecies show impious blasphemy [ἐβλασφήμησεν ἀσεβῶς] 14.6–15.7

1. Proposition: "convicted of highest level of slander" [ἡ πρώτη διελέγχεται δυσφημία] 14.6

2. Proofs

α'. First: imitated words of Jesus to good thief (Lk 23:43) 14.6

β'. Second: wished to promote impiety by showing that evil and good have same postmortem reward 14.7

γ'. παραδείγματα ἐναντία that there is a great chasm between good and bad in afterlife 14.7–11

   i. No unity of opposites (2 Cor 6:14–15) 14.7

   ii. Lazarus and the rich man (Lk 16:19–31) 14.7–11

δ'. Inference: wicked Saul would not wind up in same place as Samuel, the saint 14.12–13

ε'. Amplification: further proofs of Saul's wickedness as greater than that of the rich man 15.1–2 (cf. 14.13)

ϛ'. Conclusion: "Samuel" = the devil 15.3–7

   i.   Saul would not be with Samuel 15.3

   ii. Prophecy to that effect a lie 15.3

   iii. Lord's prophets do not lie, but devil unmasked as liar 15.3

   iv. Saul's destiny in netherworld "with him," the devil, in his own habitat 15.4

   v.   Yoking fate of virtuous Jonathan and his wicked father a final proof of the "stitch-

ing together of lies" here 15.5–7

> 3) 1 Kgdms 28:20, "Saul hastened and fell fixed on the ground, filled with fear because of the words of Samuel" 16.1–2
>
>> a) Text Rehearsed 16.1
>> b) Narrator confirms the earlier words as being from the real Samuel 16.2
>>
>>> 1. Calls them "the words of Samuel" (i.e., from 1 Kgdms 15) 16.2
>>> 2. Phantom had plagiarized them 16.2
>>> 3. Saul's reaction of falling to the ground was appropriate nonetheless, because based on remembrance of their earlier delivery by the real Samuel 16.2

III. Origen's argument on trial 16.3–29.4

A. Origen's *Homily*, first part (*Hom. 5 on 1 Kgdms* 2.1–6.10)

> 1. Characterization 16.3–13
>
>> a. "Fashioning teachings on his own" [ἑαυτῷ δόγματα πλάττων] 16.3
>> b. Origen knew of the other view (ours!) but foolishly rejected it 16.3
>> c. Charge: did not studiously employ "due reverence" [ἡ ὀφειλομένη εὐλάβεια] in order to "ascertain accurately what is right" [ἀκριβῶσαι τὸ δέον] 16:3
>> d. Openly battles against the truth itself [αὐτῇ τῇ ἀληθείᾳ μάχεται προφανῶς] 16.3
>
> 2. Rehearsal of text of Origen's interpretation 16.3–9
> 3. Counter-statement: only God can raise souls from hell 16.10
> 4. Recapitulation of earlier argument about the text: the words there are not presented by the author as true 16.10–13
> 5. Conclusion: no one could prove the case Origen tries to (attributing the words to scripture), and scriptural examples are so plentiful we must stop here so as not to be knocked off point 16.13

B. Origen's *Homily*, second part (*Hom. 5 on 1 Kgdms* 6.3–9.11)

1. Context—the transition from one part of Origen's *Homily* to another[14]

   a. Origen paused because uncertain about his refutation (*Hom. 5 on 1 Kgdms* 4.10), repeated the old claims [ταυτολογεῖν] (*Hom. 5 on 1 Kgdms* 5.1–6.2), and then moved on to another idea [ἄλλη ἔννοια], from one form of deceit to another (*Hom. 5 on 1 Kgdms* 6.3–4) 17.1–2

   b. The "new idea"—the argument about Christ in hell (Origen, *Hom. 5 on 1 Kgdms* 6.3–4); we largely agree with this, but it is not the main point for dispute (cf. *Hom. 5 on 1 Kgdms* 6.2, 3) 17.2

   c. Counter-proposition: Origen has fled the real point; what should be disputed is not *if Samuel was raised* but *if a demon has the power to raise up a soul from hell* 17.2

   d. Charge: Origen is convicted of blasphemy [βλασφημία] and deceiving his hearers by artifice [ἀπαταλῇ ... τέχνη] 17.3 (cf. 21.1: Origen wishes to promote "ill-fated divination" [δυσδαίμων μαντεία]; he is in collusion with the impiety he defends [24.10; 25.1; 26.9])

2. Origen guilty of blasphemy[15] in his argument about Christ's descent into hell 17.3–20.6

   a. General characterization: "fleeing to the personage of Christ" [τὸ τοῦ Χριστοῦ πρόσωπον] (esp. *Hom. 5 on 1 Kgdms* 6.3–10) 17.3

   b. Charge: dared to compare Christ's descent to hell with that of holy men (*Hom. 5 on 1 Kgdms* 6.3–8.3) 17.3

   c. Accused readers of being afraid to say every place (even hell) has need of Christ (*Hom. 5 on 1 Kgdms* 7.4) 17.4

   d. Weaved in blasphemy [δυσφημία] by comparing Christ to an ordinary human being with respect to ethical purpose [προαίρεσις] (*Hom. 5 on 1 Kgdms* 8.2) 17.5–6

   e. Calumniated chorus of prophets, too, by leveling them with all people, good and bad (*Hom. 5 on 1 Kgdms* 8.3–9.6) 17.7

[14] The organization of Origen's homily is somewhat rough in 4.10–6.3, which is what Eustathius is seizing upon here.

[15] The structure reinforces the lexical parallels between Origen and the devil, both of whom are charged by Eustathius with blasphemy (see pp. cxxii–cxxiii for the list of parallels).

    f. Even more, he treated the Word of God as though it were like everyone else, which is utterly impious (*Hom. 5 on 1 Kgdms* 8.2) 17.8 19.4

        1) Origen misunderstood John 1:1—the superior quality [τὸ περισσόν] of the Word is his divinity, not his ethical purpose [προαίρεσις] 17.8–10

        2) Proof that the soul of Christ was in the netherworld and paradise at same time 18.2–19.3

            a) Salvation through the one to all, good and bad 18.2

            b) Testimony of John 3:13 that he will ascend and descend 18.3–4

            c) Because Christ's soul was united with God the Word, it was ubiquitous (John 1:1–18) 18.5–7

            d) Proof for those who reject the gospel can be found in Wis 18:14–16 that the Word from creation is everywhere by nature [τοιαύτη φύσις] 19.1–3

        3) Conclusion: Origen misunderstood and misrepresented both the source and extent of Christ's presence in his "offhand" [προχείρως] comments 19.4 (cf. 1.2)

    g. Origen's blasphemy against prophets and against angels fits with his treatment of Christ 20.1–6

        1) Origen was unafraid to say that ἡ ἐγγαστρίμυθος raised them, too (*Hom. 5 on 1 Kgdms* 7.1–3) 20.1–3

        2) Characterization: Origen in this proof speaks in "drunken folly" [παροινία] and "no less insanely [φρενοβλαβῶς] than the woman" 20.2, 4

        3) Proposition: Origen "poured contempt" [ἐκφαυλίζειν] on the prophets and "slandered" [διαβάλλειν] the order of angels 20.4

        4) Proof: angels are always in heaven with God, never down in hell 20.5–6

3. Origen guilty of blasphemy against God's words through allegorical exegesis = trafficking in "myths"[16] 21.1–29.4

    a. General proposition: after allegorizing [ἀλληγορῆσαι] all the rest of the Scriptures, he takes this text "according to

---

[16] Eustathius has left his strongest argument for last. That it is not a digression is clear from the presence of the charge against Origen's allegorization in the *prooimion* in 1.3 (teaching people to attend to ὀνόματα rather than to πράγματα, as they should).

the letter" ("literally" [ἐπὶ τοῦ γράμματος]) 21.1; repeated at 22.7

b. Characterization: "hypocritical" [θεσπίζων ὑποκρίσει]; "not right minded" [μηδὲ ... εὐγνωμόνως] even when he tries to interpret according to the letter (flashback to first part of proof) 21.1 (also cf. 22.7)

c. Proof by παραδείγματα that Origen commits blasphemy in allegorizing 21.2–22.7

  1) Origen's interpretation of trees in Gen 2:8 21.2–4

    a) τροπολογεῖν, "allegorizing" 21.2
    b) calls trees μῦθοι not αἰσθητά 21.2
    c) Proof that this is blasphemy 21.3–4

      1. God created them 21.3
      2. God entrusted Moses to write about them 21.3
      3. Utter irony! Accepts words of ἐγγαστρί-μυθος as true but thinks God's revealed word a μῦθος! 21.4 (cf. 22.7)
      4. allegorizing = "perverting the sense" [ἐνδιαλάττει τὴν ἔννοιαν] 21.4

  2) Other παραδείγματα of the same allegorizing error in Origen's exegetical writings 21.5–22.1

    a) Abraham's wells 21.5 [ἀλληγορεῖ ... μεταθεὶς εἰς ἕτερον νοῦν]
    b) Isaac, and Rebecca's jewelry [τροπολογεῖν ... ἅπασαν δὲ τὴν ὑπόθεσιν ἐκβιασάμενος ἐκείνην ... ἐσυκοφάντησεν] 21.6
    c) Job—he fastened on the "names" of his daughters [ὀνόματα κατετρίβη γραωδῶς] 21.7
    d) Lazarus—he allegorically "elevated" [ἀνήγαγεν ἀλληγορῶν] by demoting him from righteous man to everyman sinner 21.8–9
    e) John 10:31—tries to allegorize [πειρᾶται τροπολογεῖν] the stoning "again" but τοῦ εὐαγγελικοῦ καταψεύδεται γράμματος, for some strange reason missing entirely the first mention at John 8:59 (and "he thinks he knows all the scriptures!") 21.10–12
    f) Asseveration and authentication: many more examples could be found by consulting his works to

prove we have "fabricated" [πλάττειν] none of this
evidence or said nothing false 22.1

3) Problems of focusing on "names" [ὀνόματα] rather
than "facts" or "events" [πράγματα] (cf. 1.3) 22.2–4

  a) Destroys the plot-lines of events [ἐκ τῶν ὀνομάτων
ἀλληγορῶν ἀναιρεῖ τὰς τῶν πραγμάτων ὑποθέσεις] 22.2

  b) Creates moral confusion 22.2–4

    1. Proposition: different people (just and unjust)
can have the same name 22.2

    2. Ancient παραδείγματα (Judas, Zechariah, Ana-
nias) 22.3

    3. Contemporary παραδείγματα (immoral Jews
and "Greeks" who sport biblical names) 22.4

  c) Those who use τροπολογία have no method [ὁποίᾳ
μεθόδῳ;] for distinguishing unlike persons and
lifestyles from those who bear the same name 22.4

4) *Paraleipsis*[17]—Origen's faulty teaching on the resurrection as further proof of his blasphemy 22.5–6

  a) Not possible to catalogue here 22.5

  b) Evidence of his κακοδοξία 22.5

  c) Methodius has proven in writing that Origen's
teaching on the resurrection as form not body inadvisably aided heretics 22.6

5) Conclusion/recapitulation of charges and consequences 22.6–7

  a) "overturned everything by his allegories" 22.6

  b) "sown everywhere the seeds of evil teaching" [κα-
κοδοξία] 22.6

  c) ταυτολογεῖν with "boundless nonsense" 22.6

  d) Grand irony: Origen allegorizes everywhere *except* the passage about the ἐγγαστρίμυθος 22.7

  e) But (restatement of proposition of first section of
proof) even there he misses τὸ σαφές, "the plain
sense" 22.7

  f) Implication—Origen convicted of bad reading by
either method

---

[17] παράλειψις is the rhetorical figure of "pretended omission" (Herbert
Weir Smyth, *Greek Grammar* [rev. by Gordon M. Messing; Cambridge, Mass.:
Harvard University Press, 1956], §3036).

d. Origen's taking refuge[18] in supposedly pious reasoning results in worse blasphemy 23.1–26.9

  1) Characterization of this rhetorical move 23.1

    a) Adding new arguments to the earlier ones 23.1;[19] cf. 24.1

    b) "Fashioning excuses to expiate himself" [ἀφοσιώσει πλαττόμενος ἀποφυγάς] 23.1; cf. 26.8 and 24.1: "taking refuge in a cunning artifice" [εἰς τοῦτο κατέφυγε τετεχνασμένως]

  2) Rehearsal of Origen's argument: [the text must be true because] no demon could have prophetic knowledge of the fate of the Davidic kingdom 23.2

  3) Charge/slander: Origen hardly deserves a reputation for sound judgment 23.3; cf. 24.2

  4) Refutation: a demon *could* know about the Davidic kingdom 23.4–7

    a) God had testified to it in scripture 23.4, 7

    b) The anointing of David was corporeal and hence perceptible 23.4–5

    c) David had been publicly lauded for all to hear 23.4

    d) Greater to lesser argument: demons knew of the kingdom Christ ushered in (Matt 8:29; 4:6), so how much more so David's 23.6–7

  5) Counter-charge in form of rhetorical question— Which blasphemy is worse: to allow demons power to prophesy or power to raise the dead? 23.5

  6) σύγκρισις—Who really knows the Scriptures? 23.8–26.2

    a) The devil (as proven by his plagiarism, not prophecy), but he is "poorly trained" [κακομαθῶς] 23.8

    b) Origen supposed to, but in reality does not, for the scriptures prove that the devil cannot raise the

---

[18] Eustathius's repeated barb in this section about Origen's "fleeing" to desperate arguments (23.1; 24.1; 26.2, 5) is a direct response to Origen's original taunt against *his* opponents for purportedly trying to flee from the challenge of defending the text against the charge of falsehood [ἐκεῖνο ἔφυγεν ὁ τὸν πρῶτον λόγον εἰπών] (6.4–5).

[19] This is a reflection of the two-part argument of refutation within Origen's own homily, as can be seen in the compositional analysis of that work (above, pp. cxxv–cxxxviii).

dead and belly-mythers are liars 24.1–26.2

1. Rehearsal of Origen's argument that he cannot grant a demon power to prophesy 24.1

2. Restatement of counter-charge: illogical to grant a demon power to raise the dead but to deny it power to prophesy 24.2; cf. 23.5

3. Proposition and proof: even if the demon *could* prophesy, that would not justify the conclusion that it could raise the dead 24.2–5

   α'. Repetition of earlier premise: the demon did not actually prophesy 24.2; cf. 11.16–15.7

   β'. παράδειγμα ἐναντίον: Caiaphas (John 11:50–51) 24.3–5

4. Star witness must be heard: Moses proves by many passages that false prophets and diviners are abominable, impious, and untrue, and he justly calls for their punishment 24.6–25.2

5. Division: either Moses' testimony or that of the belly-myther is false. Which? 25.3

6. Even more abundant scriptural testimony [αἱ θεῖαι γραφαί] seals the conviction that the belly-myther's words are "worthless and false" [ἕωλα καὶ ψευδῆ] 25.3–12

   α'. Scripture does not contradict itself 25.3

   β'. Even if it did, the majority testimony should prevail 25.3

   γ'. But that rule not even needed in this case, for scripture renders "a single unanimous verdict" [ὁμοφώνῳ συνῳδίᾳ καταψηφίζονται] 25.3

   i.   Descriptions of both Manasseh and Josiah in 4 Kgdms by same author concur in rebuking necromancy 25.4–6

   ii. 1 Kgdms 28 does not contradict because her words not words of Holy Spirit but narrated of her (recapitulation of proof in II) 25.7

   iii. μάρτυς ἄλλος ἀξιοφανής, Isaiah also forbids necromancy 25.8–11

δ'. Conclusion: the law, "the highest guardian,"
offers definitive counter-evidence 25.12

7. Origen does not cite these passages 26.1
α'. Pretends not to know these μαρτυρίαι 26.1
β'. Piles up irrelevant passages instead 26.1
γ'. Reason: "poor training" [ἀμαθία] (like demon in 23.8, and as this proof has shown) or
"boldly trafficking with evil intent" [κακοθε-
λία] 26.1 (transition to next proof)

7) Origen put on the stand a last time to convict himself
of blasphemy[20] 26.2–9
a) Characterization of the "witness"
1. Offering hesitant and uncertain testimony
[ἀπορία] (*Hom. 5 on 1 Kgdms* 6.1) 26.2
2. Shifting the blame to another (scripture as author) (*Hom. 5 on 1 Kgdms* 6.2) 26.2
3. Evading the prosecutor's question: Who
brought Samuel up?[21] 26.2
b) Self-contradictory testimony[22] 26.3–7

[20] The charge of blasphemy was also made against the devil previously
(e.g., 14.6: ἐβλασφήμησεν ἀσεβῶς). See full references on the parallelism between the devil and Origen in Eustathius's argument on p. cxxii.

[21] Here Eustathius is disputing Origen's choice about which of τὰ κατὰ
τὸν τόπον ζητούμενα should be taken up (6.3, which Eustathius regards as *not*
answering the questions posed in 6.1).

[22] As with Origen's appearance in section II, Eustathius constructs this
on the basis of a combination of written testimony (from the earlier homily) and
oral testimony in his own personified words. It is also possible here that, in addition, Eustathius is referring to a second homily (now lost) that Origen published
on this text and showing it to be inconsistent with the earlier one (see Nautin and
Nautin, *Origène,* 210–12, for an attempted reconstruction of this "homily 6,"
and Declerk's identification of two fragments "aliunde non cognitum"). But the
strategy is similar enough to the earlier cross-examination of Origen and pronouncement of his having contradicted himself (6.1; 22.5; 26.5) that perhaps the
words are to be taken as further instances of Eustathius's personification. The
introduction with οἶμαι is supportive of this suggestion, and the verbs of speech
introducing "quotes" could be part of the impersonation. Harder to square with
this view are the past-tense verbs ἠρνήσατο (26.5), ἐσπούδασε (26.5), ἑάλω and
ὡμολόγησεν (26.6), but they may be used in a kind of judicial sense of what Origen has just done by these new testimonies produced through Eustathius. Either
way the argument is the same: comparing Origen with himself on one or more
occasions and finding him self-contradictory.

1. Refuted, Origen tries a second argumentative tack 26.3

2. Still avers Samuel was raised but now equivocates over whether we can be sure it was the belly-myther who did it 26.4–5

3. "Refuted to his face" [ἀντιπροσώπως ἐλεγχόμενος], Origen tries to deny it 26.5

4. Nakedly self-contradictory testimony, in an attempt to run away from the writ of accusation [ἡ ἐγκληματικὴ δίκη] 26.6

5. Eustathius orders the witness to say who did it, who raised "Samuel" [εἰπάτω] 26.6

c) The facts of the case: only Saul and the woman were there, and Saul went there to ask her to do it, so he could not have done it on his own 26.7

d) Division: either she performed the act, or it never happened 26.7

e) Judgment on cross-examination: perjury charge against Origen definitively proven, since "he introduces a lie as though it were the truth" 26.8 (same as the woman herself, 26.10)

f) Inference: Origen lies against the holy scriptures because he is the agent of impious divination [ἀσεβὴς μαντεία] 26.9

e. Rebuttal and reproof of Origen's unaccountable ignorance about how to understand "myth" 26.10–29.4

1) Proposition: the simple etymology of ἐγγαστρίμυθος tells that she engages in fiction, not truth, but Origen missed this 26.10

2) Riposte (via "urbanity topos"): "those who are conversant with various forms of literary reference know much better to what genre myth belongs" 26.10

3) Justification of "brief refutation" [ἐλέγξαι δι' ὀλίγων] of Origen's ἀξυνεσία here as necessary 27.1

4) Proof: genre "myth" fashions falsehood, not truth, as we all learned in school 27.2–28.5

a) Universally acknowledged evidence: the rhetorical handbooks [αἱ ῥητορικαὶ τεχνογραφίαι], which have clearly defined myth as "fabrication" [πλάσ-

μα] 27.2

b) Indisputable learnings in handbook definitions of myth:[23] myth "far from the truth," "bereft of concrete actions," and "impossible to confirm as fact" 27.3

c) Figurative embellishment by Eustathius, with commonplace of myth compared to painting 27.4–7

   1. Both use verisimilitude 27.4

   2. Both create dramatization, and in myth this involves giving characters speaking parts 27.4–5

   3. "Plausible speech" [εἰκοτολογία] using "personification" [προσωποποιία] is part of the art, like colors in painting 27.6

   4. But however beautiful, however varied, they are not true, but "inventions of poetic fancy" [ποιητικῆς οἰησικοπίας εὕρεσις] 27.7

d) Expert witness: the standard text on the question of "myth": Plato, *Resp.* 28.1–5

   1. Context of Plato's testimony: when asked to define "literary works inspired by the muses" 28.1 (cf. 28.5 dialogue between Socrates and Adeimantus)

   2. Rehearsal of literary testimony (*Resp.* 2.376E–377D) 28.1–29.1

      α'. Two forms of literature, the true and the false 28.1

      β'. Myth generally speaking false, but true in part 28.1

      γ'. Proof of need for censorship of false myths told to impressionable children 28.2–4

      δ'. False myths identified: Hesiod and Homer 28.5

      ε'. Poems of Homer and Hesiod have wide persuasive influence because of their place in the school curriculum [παιδεία] 29.1

---

[23] These are also commonplaces in the *progymnasmata*, as may be seen especially clearly in Aphthonius (of Antioch), *Prog.* 5–6, on ἀνασκευή (refutation) and κατασκευή (confirmation) (see Rabe, *Aphthonius*).

3. *A minore ad maius* conclusion [τοίνυν] 29.1–4

α′. If poems of Homer and Hesiod, as beautiful and influential as they are, arc false, how much more so the words of the belly-myther? 29.1

β′. Her words were "false myth-making" [μυθοποιίας ψευδεῖς] through demonic collusion 29.1

γ′. Final appeal to etymology as overt clue to meaning

   i. Her name has this sense 29.1

   ii. Greek boys know a meaningfully coined expression when they see one (why not Origen?!) 29.2

   iii. They also know the definition of myths (quoted from textbook above) as πλάσματα 29.2

   iv. Many παραδείγματα of false speech (Aesop's fables, children's rhymes, old hags' babbling into their cups) are well known 29.3

   v. The wise know to be suspicious even of "inspired poems" because of their questionable ethical content[24] 29.4

IV. ἐπίλογος (concise), drawing together conclusions [οὖν] of both sections of proof (II and III)

A. Proven: the "belly-myther" lied and did not raise Samuel 30-1-5

  1. The name gives her away 30.1

  2. The demon, lurking inside her, was an author of "mythic fictions" [μυθώδη πλάσματα] 30.1

  3. This fits with what we know of the devil's customary behavior: taking multiple forms and fictions to deceive 30.1–5

B. Proven: the devil did not raise Samuel either 30.5–6

  1. He cannot raise souls of prophets, the righteous, or angels 30.5

---

[24] A clear reference to Stoic allegorization of the Homeric myths and the charge that those myths depict the gods engaging in scandalous behavior.

2. He was with the angels only to be mocked (Job 41:25)
3. He has been crushed and laid low 30.5–6
4. Only God and the divine Son can raise souls from hell 30.6

C. [Inference: this event never happened, and anyone who says it did (i.e., Origen) is a liar and blasphemer like the belly-myther and like the demon who was at work in her.]

The "Belly-Myther" of Endor
Texts and Translations

Τοῦ ἁγίου Ἰουστίνου φιλοσόφου καὶ μάρτυρος πρὸς Τρύφωνα Ἰουδαῖον διάλογος

105. 1. Τὰ δὲ ἀκόλουθα τοῦ ψαλμοῦ· *Σὺ δέ, κύριε, μὴ μακρύνῃς τὴν βοήθειάν σου ἀπ' ἐμοῦ· εἰς τὴν ἀντίληψίν μου πρόσχες· ῥῦσαι ἀπὸ ῥομφαίας τὴν ψυχήν μου καὶ ἐκ χειρὸς κυνὸς τὴν μονογενῆ μου· σῶσόν με ἐκ στόματος λέοντος καὶ ἀπὸ κεράτων μονοκερώτων τὴν ταπείνωσίν μου·* ὁμοίως πάλιν διδασκαλία καὶ προαγγελία τῶν ὄντων αὐτῷ καὶ συμβαίνειν μελλόντων. μονογενὴς γὰρ ὅτι ἦν τῷ πατρὶ τῶν ὅλων οὗτος, ἰδίως ἐξ αὐτοῦ λόγος καὶ δύναμις γεγεννημένος, καὶ ὕστερον ἄνθρωπος διὰ τῆς παρθένου γενόμενος, ὡς ἀπὸ τῶν ἀπομνημονευμάτων ἐμάθομεν, προεδήλωσα. 2. καὶ ὅτι σταυρωθεὶς ἀπέθανεν, ὁμοίως προεῖπε. τὸ γὰρ *ῥῦσαι ἀπὸ ῥομφαίας τὴν ψυχήν μου καὶ ἐκ χειρὸς κυνὸς τὴν μονογενῆ μου· σῶσόν με ἐκ στόματος λέοντος καὶ ἀπὸ κεράτων μονοκερώτων τὴν ταπείνωσίν μου·* ὁμοίως μηνύοντος δι' οὗ πάθους ἔμελλεν ἀποθνήσκειν, τουτέστι σταυροῦσθαι· τὸ γὰρ *κεράτων μονοκερώτων* ὅτι τὸ σχῆμα τοῦ σταυροῦ ἐστι μόνου, προεξηγησάμην ὑμῖν. 3. καὶ τὸ *ἀπὸ ῥομφαίας* καὶ *στόματος λέοντος* καὶ *ἐκ χειρὸς κυνὸς* αἰτεῖν αὐτὸν τὴν *ψυχὴν* σωθῆναι, ἵνα μηδεὶς κυριεύσῃ τῆς ψυχῆς αὐτοῦ αἴτησις ἦν, ἵνα, ἡνίκα ἡμεῖς πρὸς τῇ ἐξόδῳ τοῦ βίου γινόμεθα, τὰ αὐτὰ αἰτῶμεν τὸν θεόν, τὸν δυνάμενον ἀποστρέψαι πάντα ἀναιδῆ πονηρὸν ἄγγελον μὴ λαβέσθαι ἡμῶν τῆς ψυχῆς. 4. καὶ ὅτι μένουσιν αἱ ψυχαὶ ἀπέδειξα ὑμῖν ἐκ τοῦ καὶ τὴν Σαμουὴλ ψυχὴν κληθῆναι ὑπὸ τῆς ἐγγαστριμύθου, ὡς ἠξίωσεν ὁ Σαούλ. φαίνεται δὲ καὶ ὅτι πᾶσαι αἱ ψυχαὶ τῶν οὕτως δικαίων καὶ προφητῶν

1. Justin Martyr,
Dialogue with Trypho 105

105. 1. The psalm (Ps 21) continues, "but you, Lord, do not keep your help far from me. Pay attention to my plea. Save my soul from the sword and my only begotten from the hand of the dog. Save me from the mouth of the lion and my humiliation from the horns of the unicorns" (Ps 21:20–22). Once more this is similarly a teaching and a foretelling of what belongs to him and what is going to happen. For he is the Only Begotten because he was with the Father of the universe, begotten from him in a special way as his Word and power. Later he became a human being through the virgin, as we have learned from the memoirs.[1] I have already demonstrated this. 2. The psalmist likewise also foretold that he would die by crucifixion. For the words "Save my soul from the sword and my only begotten from the hand of the dog. Save me from the mouth of the lion and my humiliation from the horns of the unicorns" similarly reveal by what suffering he was going to die, that is, by being crucified. For I have already explained to you that "the horns of the unicorns" refers to the form of the cross only. 3. And his request that his soul be saved from the sword, from the mouth of the lion, and from the hand of the dog was a prayer that no one should have dominion over his soul. This was so that when we come to our departure from life, we may ask the same thing of God, who is able to turn aside every shameless and evil angel from taking our souls. 4. And I have proved to you[2] that souls survive on the basis of the fact that even Samuel's soul was summoned by the belly-myther, as Saul requested. It appears also that all the souls of those who in this way were righteous and prophets used

---

[1] τὰ ἀπομνημονεύματα, the term Justin uses for the Gospels (in this case Matt 1:18–25 and Luke 1:26–38).

[2] Archambault's note reads, "The demonstration to which Justin refers depends upon the story of Saul summoning the shade of Samuel with the help of the pythoness of Endor: either it has disappeared or Justin's memory has failed him... This demonstration has disappeared with the lacuna of chapter 74 (see the introduction, p. lxxiv)." (Georges Archambault, *Justin: Dialogue avec Tryphon* [Paris: Picard et fils, 1909], 148–49).

ὑπὸ ἐξουσίαν ἔπιπτον τῶν τοιούτων δυνάμεων, ὁποία δὴ καὶ ἐν τῇ ἐγγαστριμύθῳ ἐκείνῃ ἐξ αὐτῶν τῶν πραγμάτων ὁμολογεῖται. 5. ὅθεν καὶ
ὁ θεὸς διδάσκει ἡμᾶς καὶ διὰ τοῦ υἱοῦ αὐτοῦ τὸ πάντως ἀγωνίζεσθαι
δικαίους γίνεσθαι, καὶ πρὸς τῇ ἐξόδῳ αἰτεῖν μὴ ὑπὸ τοιαύτην τινὰ δύναμιν ὑποπεσεῖν τὰς ψυχὰς ἡμῶν. καὶ γὰρ ἀποδιδοὺς τὸ πνεῦμα ἐπὶ τῷ
σταυρῷ εἶπε· *πάτερ, εἰς χεῖράς σου παρατίθεμαι τὸ πνεῦμά μου*, ὡς καὶ
ἐκ τῶν ἀπομνημονευμάτων καὶ τοῦτο ἔμαθον. 6. καὶ γὰρ πρὸς τὸ ὑπερ-
βάλλειν τὴν Φαρισαίων πολιτείαν τοὺς μαθητὰς αὐτοῦ συνωθῶν, εἰ δὲ
μή γε, ἐπίστασθαι ὅτι οὐ σωθήσονται, ταῦτα εἰρηκέναι ἐν τοῖς ἀπομνη-
μονεύμασι γέγραπται· *ἐὰν μὴ περισσεύσῃ ὑμῶν ἡ δικαιοσύνη πλεῖον τῶν
γραμματέων καὶ Φαρισαίων, οὐ μὴ εἰσέλθητε εἰς τὴν βασιλείαν τῶν οὐρανῶν.*

to fall under the authority of powers such as is acknowledged by the very facts in the case of that belly-myther. 5. Therefore, God also teaches us through his Son to struggle in every way to become righteous and to ask when we depart from life that our souls not fall beneath the sway of such a power. For when he gave up his spirit on the cross, he said, "Father, into your hands I commend my spirit" (Luke 23:46), as I have learned this also from the memoirs. 6. Moreover, when he urges his disciples to go beyond the way of life of the Pharisees and to understand that otherwise they will not be saved, it is written in the memoirs that he said, "Unless your righteousness exceeds that of the scribes and Pharisees, you will never enter the kingdom of heaven" (Matt 5:20).

Tertullianus, *De anima*

54. 1. Quo igitur deducetur anima, iam hinc reddimus. Omnes ferme philosophi, qui immortalitatem animae, qualiterqualiter volunt, tamen vindicant, ut Pythagoras, ut Empedocles, ut Plato, quique aliquod illi tempus indulgent ab excessu usque in conflagrationem universitatis, ut Stoici, suas solas, id est sapientium, animas in supernis mansionibus collocant. 2. Plato quidem non temere philosophorum animabus hoc praestat, sed eorum qui philosophiam scilicet exornaverint amore puerorum. Adeo etiam inter philosophos magnum habet privilegium impuritas. Itaque apud illum in aetherem sublimantur animae sapientes, apud Arium in aerem, apud Stoicos sub lunam. 3. Quos quidem miror, quod imprudentes animas circa terram prosternant, cum illas a sapientibus multo superioribus erudiri affirment. Ubi erit scholae regio in tanta distantia deversoriorum? Qua ratione discipulae ad magistras conventabunt tanto discrimine absentes? Quis autem illis postumae eruditionis usus ac fructus iamiam conflagratione perituris? 4. Reliquas animas ad inferos deiciunt. Hos Plato velut gremium terrae describit in Phaedone, quo omnes labes mundialium sordium confluendo et ibi desidendo exhalent et quasi caeno immunditiarum suarum grossiorem haustum et privatum illic aerem stipent.

    55. 1. Nobis inferi non nuda cavositas nec subdivalis aliqua mundi sentina creduntur, sed in fossa terrae et in alto va-

2. Tertullian, *On the Soul* 54–58

54. 1. Let us then now turn to the question where the soul will be led. Almost all the philosophers who assert the immortality of the soul, no matter how they understand it—such as Pythagoras, Empedocles, and Plato—all of them concede to it a period of time between its departure and the conflagration of the universe. The Stoics, for example, locate only their own souls, that is, the souls of the wise, in the highest dwellings. 2. Plato, however, rashly vouchsafes this to the souls not of philosophers but of those, indeed, who have adorned philosophy with the love of boys. For to such a great degree does impurity have a great claim to special rights among the philosophers. And so according to him wise souls are raised to the ether, according to Arius[1] to the air, and according to the Stoics to the region beneath the moon. 3. But I marvel at them because they place ignorant souls prostrate on the earth, since they affirm that they are instructed by the wise who are in much higher places. Where will there be a place for a school when their dwellings are so remote from one another? In what way will pupils resort to teachers when they are separated from one another by so great a division? Moreover, what use and enjoyment will they have in education after death if at any moment they are doomed to perish in the conflagration? 4. The philosophers hurl the rest of the souls to hell.[2] Plato in the *Phaedo*[3] described this as the bosom of the earth, where all the defects of worldly filth by flowing together and sinking down give off fumes and as though by the scum of their impurities make the atmosphere denser and in that place deprived of air.

55. 1. We do not believe that hell is a bare cavity or some kind of sewer opened beneath the earth. Rather, we believe it to

---

[1] Arius Didymus of Alexandria, first-century B.C.E. Stoic. In this chapter and elsewhere Tertullian appears to depend upon the doxographical materials collected in Soranus's *On the Soul*. See Tertullian, *An.* 6.6, and Waszink's introduction and notes (Jan Hendrik Waszink, *Tertullian: De anima* [2nd ed.: Amsterdam: Meulenhoff, 1947]). Pseudo-Plutarch's *De placita philosophorum* includes these materials.

[2] We have translated *inferi* (the lower regions) by "hell."

[3] Cf. *Phaed.* 111c–112e.

stitas et in ipsis visceribus eius abstrusa profunditas, siquidem
Christo in corde terrae triduum mortis legimus expunctum, id
est in recessu intimo et interno et in ipsa terra operto et in-
tra ipsam clauso et inferioribus adhuc abyssis superstructo. 2.
Quodsi Christus deus, quia et homo, mortuus secundum scrip-
turas et sepultus secundum easdem, huic quoque legi satisfecit
forma humanae mortis apud inferos functus, nec ante ascendit
in sublimiora caelorum quam descendit in inferiora terrarum,
ut illic patriarchas et prophetas compotes sui faceret, habes et
regionem inferum subterraneam credere et illos cubito pellere
qui satis superbe non putent animas fidelium inferis dignas, ser-
vi super dominum et discipuli super magistrum, aspernati, si
forte, in Abrahae sinu expectandae resurrectionis solacium capere. 3. 'Sed in hoc', inquiunt, 'Christus inferos adiit, ne nos
adiremus. Ceterum quod discrimen ethnicorum et Christiano-
rum, si carcer mortuis idem?' Quo ergo animam exhalabis in
caelum Christo illic adhuc sedente ad dexteram patris, nondum dei iussu per tubam archangeli audito, nondum illis quos
domini adventus in saeculo invenerit, obviam ei ereptis in aerem, cum his qui mortui in Christo primi resurgent? Nulli
patet caelum terra adhuc salva, ne dixerim clausa. Cum tran-
sactione enim mundi reserabuntur regna caelorum. 4. Sed in
aethere dormitio nostra cum puerariis Platonis aut in aere cum
Ario aut circa lunam cum Endymionibus Stoicorum? Immo,
inquis, in paradiso, quo iam tunc et patriarchae et prophetae
appendices dominicae resurrectionis ab inferis migraverint. Et

be a desolate expanse and a boundless space hidden in the innermost parts dug out in the earth. This is because we read that
Christ spent the three days of his death in the heart of the earth
(Matt 12:40), that is, in the innermost and interior recess opened
up in the earth itself and enclosed within it, yet built over still
lower depths. 2. Christ, although he is God, because he was also
a human being, died according to the scriptures and was buried
according to them (1 Cor 15:3–4). He also conformed to the condition of his humanity by experiencing the condition of those below
in the form of a human death. Nor did he ascend to the higher
parts of the heavens before he descended to the lower parts of the
earth (cf. Eph 4:9–10) in order to make the patriarchs and prophets
who were there his fellow heirs. If you grant this, then you have a
basis for believing that there is a subterranean lower region and
for fending off and elbowing away those who are so proud that
they think the souls of the faithful are undeserving of hell. These
people are servants above their master and disciples above their
teacher (Matt 10:24). They scorn to receive the consolation of the
resurrection if by chance it has to be awaited in Abraham's bosom
(Luke 16:22). 3. "But," they say, "Christ descended to hell so that
we should not go there. Besides, what difference would there be
between pagans and Christians if they have the same prison when
they die?" But then, to what end will you breathe forth your soul
to heaven while Christ is still sitting there at the Father's right
hand, when God's command through the archangel's trumpet has
not yet been heard (1 Thess 4:16; 1 Cor 15:22), when those whom
the Lord's coming will find in the world have not yet been caught
up to meet him in the air together with those who will rise first because they died in Christ (1 Thess 4:17)? So long as the earth is
preserved heaven lies open to no one—not to say it remains closed.
For it is when the world passes away that the kingdoms of the
heavens will be opened. 4. But will our sleep be in the ether with
Plato's corrupters of boys, or in the air with Arius, or in the region
beneath the moon with the Endymions of the Stoics?[4] "Certainly
not," you say, "but in paradise, where even now the patriarchs and
prophets are clinging to the Lord's resurrection, having passed out
of hell." How is it, then, that when the region of paradise was

---

[4] Waszink suggests there is a reference to Varro's satires on the
Endymions. Endymion was loved by the Moon and sleeps eternally.

quomodo Iohanni in spiritu paradisi regio revelata, quae subicitur altari, nullas alias animas apud se praeter martyrum ostendit? Quomodo Perpetua, fortissima martyr, sub die passionis in revelatione paradisi solos illic martyras vidit, nisi quia nullis romphaea paradisi ianitrix cedit nisi qui in Christo decesserint, non in Adam? 5. Nova mors pro deo et extraordinaria pro Christo alio et privato excipitur hospitio. Agnosce itaque differentiam ethnici et fidelis in morte, si pro deo occumbas, ut paracletus monet, non in mollibus febribus et in lectulis, sed in martyriis, si crucem tuam tollas et sequaris dominum, ut ipse praecepit. Tota paradisi clavis tuus sanguis est. Habes etiam de paradiso a nobis libellum, quo constituimus omnem animam apud inferos sequestrari in diem domini.

56. 1. Occurrit disceptatio, an hoc ab excessu statim fiat, an quasdam animas aliqua ratio detineat hic interim, an etiam receptas liceat postea ab inferis ex arbitrio vel ex imperio intervenire. 2. Nec harum enim opinionum suasoriae desunt. Creditum est insepultos non ad inferos redigi quam iusta perceperint, secundum Homericum Patroclum funus in somniis de Achille flagitantem, quod non alias adire portas inferum posset arcentibus eum longe animabus sepultorum. Novimus autem praeter poeticae iura pietatis quoque Homericae industriam. Tanto magis enim curam sepulturae collocavit, quanto etiam moram eius iniuriosam animabus incusavit, simul et ne quis defunctum domi detinens ipse amplius cum illo maceretur enormitate solacii dolore nutriti. Ita querellas animae insepultae ad utrum-

revealed to John in the spirit, it showed no other souls placed under the altar save those of the martyrs (Rev 6:9)? How is it that Perpetua, the boldest of martyrs, on the day of her passion when paradise was revealed to her saw there only the martyrs, unless because the sword that guarded the door to paradise yielded entrance to none save those who had died in Christ and not in Adam?[5] 5. A new death on behalf of God and an extraordinary one on behalf of Christ are met with a different and special accommodation. And so know that there is a difference in death between the pagan and the faithful Christian. If you meet your death on behalf of God, as the Paraclete advises, it is not in mild fevers and in beds but in martyrdom—if you take up your cross and follow the Lord, as he himself has taught (Matt 10:38; 16:24; Mark 8:34; Luke 14:27). Your blood is the complete key to paradise. You also have our book about paradise, where we have demonstrated that every soul is kept safe in hell until the day of the Lord.

56. 1. A dispute arises whether this happens immediately after death, whether some reason may keep certain souls here for a while, and whether it may be permitted some time afterwards for them to come back from hell by their own choice or upon command. 2. Indeed, persuasive reasons for these opinions are not lacking. People have believed that those unburied are not brought down to hell before they have received the ceremonies due them. According to Homer, Patroclus repeatedly asked Achilles in his dreams to give him burial rites because he could otherwise not enter the gates of hell, since the souls of those who had been buried kept him far away.[6] Moreover, we know that the diligence of Homer's piety is more than observing the laws of poetry. For he attached so great a care to burial that he even blamed its delay as harmful to souls, at the same time insisting that no one should torment himself with excessive consolation nourished by grief through keeping the body of the deceased with him at home too long. Thus, he shaped the complaints of the unburied soul with two aims in mind: that a speedy burial and the honor due

[5] The reference appears to be to the *Martyrdom of Perpetua and Felicitas* 11, which is a vision granted Saturus. He and Perpetua are carried "toward the east by four angels." They arrive at a garden where they are welcomed by four other angels and by several of those recently martyred. Chapter 12 appears to draw upon the throne vision of Rev 4–5.

[6] *Il.* 23.62–107.

que confinxit, ut instantia funeris et honor corporum servetur et memoria affectuum temperetur. 3. Ceterum quam vanum, ut anima corporis iusta sustineat, quasi aliquid ex illis ad inferos avehat? Multo vanius, si iniuria deputabitur animae cessatio sepulturae, quam pro gratia deberet amplecti. Utique enim tardius ad inferos abstrahi malet, quae nec mori voluit. Amabit impium heredem, per quem adhuc pascitur luce. Aut si qua pro certo iniuria est tardius sub terram detrudi, titulus autem iniuriae cessatio est sepulturae, perquam iniquum eam iniuria affici, cui non imputabitur cessatio sepulturae ad proximos scilicet pertinens. 4. Aiunt et immatura morte praeventas eo usque vagari istic, donec reliquatio compleatur aetatum, quacum pervixissent, si non intempestive obissent. Porro aut constituta sunt tempora unicuique, et constituta praeripi posse non credam, aut si constituta sunt quidem, dei tamen voluntate vel aliqua potestate mutilantur, frustra mutilantur, si iam impleri sustinentur, aut si non sunt constituta, nulla erit reliquatio temporum non constitutorum. 5. Adhuc addam: ecce obiit verbi gratia infans sub uberum fontibus, puta nunc puer investis, puta vesticeps, qui tamen octoginta annos victurus fuisset. Hos praereptos ut anima eius hic post mortem transigat, quale est? Aetatem enim non potest capere sine corpore, quia per corpora operantur aetates. Nostri autem illud quoque recogitent, corpora eadem recepturas in resurrectione animas in quibus discesserunt. 6. Idem ergo sperabuntur et corporum modi et eaedem aetates, quae corporum modos faciunt. Quo ergo pacto potest infantis anima hic transigere praerepta tempora, ut octogenaria resurgat in corpore mensis unius? Aut si hic necesse erit ea tempora impleri quae fuerant destinata, num et ordinem vitae, quem sortita sunt tempora pariter cum illis hic destinatum, pariter hic anima decurret, ut et studeat ab infantia pueritiae

to corpses should be preserved and that the powerful emotions caused by remembering the dead should be moderated. 3. However that may be, how is it not senseless to think that the soul of the body accepts due ceremonies as though it carried off something from them to hell? How much more senseless is it to suppose that the delay of burial be regarded as an injury to the soul, when it ought to be welcomed as a favor? For certainly the soul, which did not want to die, would prefer to be dragged down to hell in a more tardy way. It will love the impious heir because of whom it is still nurtured by the light. Even if the soul does indeed suffer any injury by not being taken down beneath the earth more quickly, nevertheless the ostensible motive for the injury is the delay of burial. It is exceedingly unjust that the soul should be affected by the injury, since the delay of burial will not be its fault but, obviously, has to do with the relatives of the one who died. 4. They also say that souls overtaken by an untimely death wander about here until the time when the remainder of their allotted years is completed, the age to which they would have lived had they not died unseasonably. Furthermore, one possibility is that the length of life has been established for each individual, and I do not believe that once established it can be cut short, or if it is indeed established but is broken off by God's will or by some other power, then it is broken off to no purpose if it still remains to be filled up. Another possibility is that the length of life has not been established, so that there will be no remainder of years not so constituted. 5. Let me add a further point. Suppose, for example, an infant still at its mother's breast died, think now of a boy before puberty, think of an adolescent who would nevertheless have lived eighty years. How can we imagine of those who have been cut off that their soul completes its time here after death? For the soul cannot acquire an age without a body, since the ages of life are a factor of what is done through bodies. Let our own people also consider this, that in the resurrection souls will get back the same bodies in which they died. 6. Therefore, the same conditions of bodies and the same ages are to be expected, since the age of life effects the conditions of bodies. Thus, in what manner can an infant's soul that has been cut off complete its span of life here so that it may rise again at the age of eighty in a body one-month old? Or if it will prove necessary that the span of life that had been appointed should be fulfilled here, will the soul here run through

delegata et militet ab adulescentia iuventae excitata et censeat a iuventa senectae ponderata, et fenus exprimat et agrum urgeat, naviget litiget nubat laboret aegritudines obeat et quaecumque illam cum temporibus manebant tristia ac laeta? 7. Sed haec sine corpore quomodo transigentur? Vita sine vita? Sed vacua erunt tempora solo decursu adimplenda. Quid ergo prohibet apud inferos ea impleri, ubi perinde nullus est usus illorum? Ita dicimus omnem animam quaqua aetate decesserit, in ea stare ad eum diem usque, quo perfectum illud repromittitur ad angelicae plenitudinis mensuram temperatum. 8. Proinde extorres inferum habebuntur quas vi ereptas arbitrantur, praecipue per atrocitates suppliciorum, crucis dico et securis et gladii et ferae; nec isti porro exitus violenti quos iustitia decernit, violentiae vindex. Et ideo, inquies, scelestae quaeque animae inferis exulant. Alteram ergo constituas, compello, aut bonos aut malos inferos: si malos placet, etiam praecipitari illuc animae pessimae debent; si bonos, cur idem animas immaturas et innuptas et pro condicione aetatis puras et innocuas interim indignas inferis iudicas?

57. 1. Aut optimum est hic retineri secundum ahoros aut pessimum secundum biaeothanatos, ut ipsis iam vocabulis utar quibus auctrix opinionum istarum magia sonat, Ostanes et Typhon et Dardanus et Damigeron et Nectabis et Berenice. 2. Publica iam litteratura est quae animas etiam iusta aetate sopitas, etiam proba morte disiunctas, etiam prompta humatione dispunctas evocaturam se ab inferum incolatu pollicetur. Quid

the stages of life correspondingly, since those stages had been appointed here in correspondence with the allotted span of life? Will the soul go to school as it passes from infancy to boyhood? Will it be a soldier when it is roused from adolescence to youth? Will it become a magistrate when it grows grave from youth to old age? Will it make a profit in business, plow the field, sail, go to court, marry, toil, suffer illnesses and whatever sorrows and joys are in store for it in its span of life? 7. Yet how can these activities take place without a body? Is there life without life? Still the span of life will be devoid of event, to be filled up only by its passage. Therefore, what will prevent it from being fulfilled in hell, where in the same way there is no use for these activities? So we say that every soul, no matter at what age it departs, remains in that state until that day when it is promised the perfection that is dispensed according to the measure of angelic fullness. 8. Similarly, those souls thought to be snatched away by violence, especially by savage punishments—I mean the cross, the axe, the sword, wild beasts—are held to be exiled from hell. But we do not regard those deaths as violent that justice, the avenger of violence, decrees. "So then," you will say, "all wicked souls are kept away from hell." Therefore, I challenge you to decide whether hell is good or bad. If it pleases you to say it is bad, then the souls that are most wicked should be thrown down there. But if it is good, why at the same time do you judge unworthy of hell the souls of infants, the unmarried, and those who in the present time were pure and blameless in accordance with the circumstances of their age?

57. 1. To be kept back here is either the best fate if it is along with the *ahori* or the worst fate if it is along with the *biaeothanati*,[7] if I may now use the terms with which magic, the founder of these opinions, resounds—with Ostanes, Typhon, Dardanus, Damigeron, Nectabis, and Berenice.[8] 2. There is now a widely available book that promises it can summon from their residence in hell souls that fell asleep at the right age, souls separated from their bodies by a virtuous death, and souls certified by a speedy

---

[7] *Ahori* transliterates ἄωροι, the untimely dead; *biaeothanati*, βιαιοθάνα-τοι, the suicides or those meeting with a violent death. See Arthur Darby Nock, "Tertullian and the *Ahori*," in *Essays on Religion and the Ancient World* (ed. Zeph Stewart; Oxford: Clarendon, 1972), 2:712–19.

[8] Waszink's notes identify all these figures save for Typhon. For the most part they are the supposed authors of magical writings.

ergo dicemus magian? Quod omnes paene, fallaciam. Sed ratio fallaciae solos non fugit Christianos, qui spiritalia nequitiae,
non quidem socia conscientia, sed inimica scientia novimus,
nec invitatoria operatione, sed expugnatoria dominatione trac-
tamus multiformem luem mentis humanae, totius erroris arti-
ficem, salutis pariter animaeque vastatorem; sic etiam magiae,
secundae scilicet idololatriae, in qua se daemones perinde mortuos fingunt, quemadmodum in illa deos. Quidni? cum et dii
mortui. 3. Itaque invocantur quidem ahori et biaeothanati sub
illo fidei argumento, quod credibile videatur eas potissimum
animas ad vim et iniuriam facere quas per vim et iniuriam sae-
vus et immaturus finis extorsit, quasi ad vicem offensae. 4. Sed
daemones operantur sub ostentu earum, et hi vel maxime qui in
ipsis tunc fuerunt, cum adviverent, quique illas in huiusmodi
impegerant exitus. Nam et suggessimus nullum paene hominem carere daemonio, et pluribus notum est daemoniorum
quoque opera et immaturas et atroces effici mortes, quas incur-
sibus deputant. 5. Hanc quoque fallaciam spiritus nequam sub
personis defunctorum delitescentis, nisi fallor, etiam rebus pro-
bamus, cum in exorcismis interdum aliquem se ex parentibus
hominis sui affirmat, interdum gladiatorem vel bestiarium, si-
cut et alibi deum, nihil magis curans quam hoc ipsum excludere
quod praedicamus, ne facile credamus animas universas ad inferos redigi, ut et iudicii et resurrectionis fidem turbent. Et tamen
ille daemon, postquam circumstantes circumvenire temptavit,
instantia divinae gratiae victus id quod in vero est invitus con-
fitetur. 6. Sic et in illa alia specie magiae, quae iam quiescentes
animas evellere ab inferis creditur et conspectui exhibere, non
alia fallaciae vis est: operatior plane, quia et phantasma praesta-
tur, quia et corpus affingitur; nec magnum illi exteriores oculos

burial. And so, what shall we say about magic? What almost everyone says: it is a fraud. Admittedly, the principle of the fraud has not escaped the notice of Christians alone. We, however, know the spiritual forces of wickedness not because of a shared complicity but because of a hostile understanding. It is not by effecting their summons but by mastering their expulsion that we deal with that scourge of the human mind, the contriver of all error, and equally the destroyer of salvation and of the soul. This is indeed what magic is like; it is clearly a second form of idolatry by which demons take the shape of dead people in just the same way they take the shape of gods in idolatry. And why not, since even the gods are dead? 3. And so the *ahori* and the *biaeothanati* are summoned as an argument for believing that it is quite likely that those souls that a savage and untimely end forcibly removed by violence and injury as retribution for some offense should be most powerful in subjecting souls to violence and injury. 4. But it is demons who are at work beneath the appearance of these dead, especially those who possessed them while they were still alive and who had driven them to deaths of this kind. For we have suggested that almost no one is exempt from a demon,[9] and most people recognize that it is the works of demons that bring about untimely and terrible deaths, which they attribute to demonic attacks. 5. If I am not mistaken, we also put to the test this deceit of the depraved spirit that hides itself in the persons of the dead, and we do so even by the facts. This is because in exorcisms sometimes the demon claims that the person it possesses is one of the ancestors, sometimes a gladiator or someone who fights with wild beasts, as also at other times it claims to be a god. It has no greater concern than to shut out that very point we preach, so that we may not find it easy to believe that all souls are brought down to hell and so that they may confound our belief in the judgment and the resurrection. Nevertheless, that demon, after it has tried to trick those standing around, unwillingly confesses what it really is, conquered by the assault of divine grace. 6. This is how it is also in that other form of magic that is believed to uproot from hell souls now resting there and to display them to open sight. The deceit has no other persuasive force. It is obviously quite effective both because a phantom is produced and because a body is associated with it. Nor is it a great task for the

---

[9] Tertullian, *An.* 39.

circumscribere, cui interiorem mentis aciem excaecare perfa-
cile est. 7. Corpora denique videbantur Pharaoni et Aegyptiis
magicarum virgarum dracones; sed Mosei veritas mendacium
devorat. Multa utique et adversus apostolos Simon et Elymas
magi; sed plaga caecitatis de praestigiis non fuit. Quid novi
aemulatio veritatis a spiritu immundo? Ecce hodie eiusdem Si-
monis haeretici tanta praesumptio se artis extollit, ut etiam
prophetarum animas ab inferis movere se spondeant. 8. Et cre-
do, quia mendacio possunt; nec enim pythonico tunc spiritui
minus licuit animam Samuelis effingere, post deum mortuos
consulente Saule. Absit alioquin, ut animam cuiuslibet sancti, nedum prophetae, a daemonio credamus extractam, edocti
quod *ipse satanas transfiguretur in angelum lucis*, nedum in
hominem lucis, etiam deum se asseveraturus in fine signaque
portentosiora editurus *ad evertendos, si fieri possit, electos.*
Dubitavit, si forte, tunc prophetam se dei asseverare et utique Sauli, in quo iam ipse morabatur, 9. ne putes alium fuisse
qui phantasma administrabat, alium qui commendabat, sed
eundem spiritum et in pseudoprophetide et in apostata facile
mentiri quod fecerat credi, per quem Sauli thesaurus illic erat
ubi et cor ipsius, ubi scilicet deus non erat. Et ideo per quem
visurum se credidit vidit, quia per quem vidit et credidit. 10.
Si et de nocturnis imaginibus opponitur saepe non frustra mortuos visos (nam et Nasamonas propria oracula apud parentum
sepulcra mansitando captare, ut Heraclides scribit vel Nym-
phodorus vel Herodotus, et Celtas apud virorum fortium busta
eadem de causa abnoctare, ut Nicander affirmat), non magis

demon to defraud the outward eyes, when it is quite easy for him to blind the inner sight of the mind. 7. Indeed, the serpents from the staffs of the magicians appeared as bodies to Pharaoh and the Egyptians, but the truth of Moses devoured the lie (Exod 7:8–12). Certainly Simon and Elymas the magicians opposed the apostles in many ways, but being struck blind was not the result of fraud (Acts 8:9–24; 13:8–11). What is strange about an unclean spirit's attempt to imitate the truth? Even today the presumption of this same heretic Simon exalts itself to such a degree that it guarantees it can remove the souls of the prophets from hell. 8. And I believe they can do this by lying, for it was of old no less permitted to the Pythian spirit to counterfeit the soul of Samuel when Saul consulted the dead after losing God (1 Kgdms 28). Quite apart from this let it be far from us to believe that the soul of any saint whatsoever, much less that of a prophet, was drawn forth by a demon, since we have been taught that "Satan himself may be changed into the form of an angel of light" (2 Cor 11:14), and much more into a man of light, and since at the end of the world he will claim that he is God and will produce such signs and great portents as "to overturn, if possible, the elect" (Matt 24:24). He scarcely hesitated of old to claim he was God's prophet, especially to Saul, whom he then himself possessed. 9. You should not suppose that there was one person who contrived the appearance and another who consulted it. Rather, it was the same spirit, both in the false prophetess and in the apostate, who easily lied about what he had already made them believe and by which Saul's treasure was where his heart was (Matt 6:21)—obviously, not where God was. And so Saul saw the one whom he believed he would see because he also believed the one through whom he saw. 10. But suppose it is objected on the basis of nocturnal apparitions that the dead often appear alive and not without purpose. (For the Nasamonians try to find special oracles by remaining near the tombs of their ancestors, as Heraclides or Nymphadorus or Herodotus have written. And the Celts for the same reason spend the night near the graves of their brave men, as Nicander affirms.)[10] We experi-

___

[10] The reference is to Herodotus 4.172. This and two other citations from Herodotus in the *De anima* probably derive from the dream book of Hermippus of Berytus, which Tertullian mentions in *An.* 46.11. See T. D. Barnes, *Tertullian: A Historical and Literary Study* (Oxford: Clarendon, 1971), 197. The whole of chapter 13 ("A Pagan Education") is a helpful discussion of Tertullian's

mortuos vere patimur in somnis quam vivos, sed eadem ratione mortuos qua et vivos et omnia quae videntur. Non enim quia videntur vera sunt, sed quia adimplentur. Fides somniorum de effectu, non de conspectu renuntiatur. 11. Nulli autem animae omnino inferos patere satis dominus in argumento illo pauperis requiescentis et divitis ingemiscentis ex persona Abrahae sanxit, non posse inde relegari renuntiatorem dispositionis infernae, quod vel tunc licere potuisset, ut Moysi et prophetis crederetur. 12. Sed etsi quasdam revocavit in corpora dei virtus in documenta iuris sui, non idcirco communicabitur fidei et audaciae magorum et fallaciae somniorum et licentiae poetarum. Atquin in resurrectionis exemplis, cum dei virtus sive per prophetas sive per Christum sive per apostolos in corpora animas repraesentat, solida et contrectabili et satiata veritate praeiudicatum est hanc esse formam veritatis, ut omnem mortuorum exhibitionem incorporalem praestrigias iudices.

58. 1. Omnis ergo anima penes inferos? inquis. Velis ac nolis, et supplicia iam illic et refrigeria: habes pauperem et divitem. Et quia distuli nescio quid ad hanc partem, iam oportune in clausula reddam. 2. Cur enim non putes animam et puniri et foveri in inferis interim sub expectatione utriusque iudicii in quadam usurpatione et candida eius? Quia salvum debet esse, inquis, in iudicio divino negotium suum sine ulla praelibatione sententiae; tum quia et carnis opperienda est restitutio ut consortis operarum atque mercedum. 3. Quid ergo fiet in tempore isto? Dormiemus? At enim animae nec in viventibus dormiunt; corporum enim est somnus, quorum et ipsa mors cum speculo suo somno. Aut nihil vis agi illic, quo universa humanitas trahitur, quo spes omnis sequestratur? Delibari pu-

ence the dead in dreams, but no more truly than the living. Rather, the dead appear in the same way as the living and everything that appears. For things are true not because they are seen but because they actually take place. Trust in dreams is proclaimed on the basis of their coming true rather than of what is seen in them. 11. Moreover, in the story of the poor man at rest and the rich man in torment the Lord in the person of Abraham has sufficiently confirmed that the gates of hell are open to no soul under any circumstances. It is impossible for anyone to be moved from there to report the condition of hell, something that could perhaps at that time have been permitted so that there might be belief in Moses and the prophets (Luke 16:19–31). 12. But even if the power of God has recalled some souls to their bodies as a confirmation of his authority, this will not be a reason for associating the faith with the impudence of magicians, the deceit of dreams, and the licentiousness of the poets. Besides, in the examples of resurrection, when God's power whether through the prophets or Christ or the apostles brings souls back to their bodies, an open judgment has been given with firm, tangible, and complete truth that this is a recognizable appearance of truth, so that you may condemn every incorporeal display of the dead as a fraud.

58. 1. Therefore, you ask, is every soul under the power of hell? Whether you answer yes or no, in that place there is already punishment and rest—you have the example of the poor man and the rich man. And because I have deferred some considerations to this part of the argument, I shall now take the opportunity of mentioning them in my conclusion. 2. For why are you unwilling to suppose that souls undergo both punishment and refreshment in hell during the time they await in a kind of anticipation and candidacy the twofold judgment of condemnation and acquittal? "Because," you say, "its case ought to be kept secure in the divine judgment without any preliminary sentence and also because the restoration of its flesh should be expected as something that shares in its deeds and deserts." 3. What then will happen during that time? Shall we sleep? I think not, since even when they are united with the living, souls do not sleep, for sleep belongs to bodies, as does death itself along with sleep its mirror. Or is it that you want nothing to happen in that place where the whole of human-

probable sources for his classical allusions. See also Waszink's notes.

tas iudicium an incipi? Praecipitari an praeministrari? Iam vero quam iniquissimum otium apud inferos, si et nocentibus adhuc illic bene est et innocentibus nondum! Quid amplius vis esse post, mortem confusa spe et incerta expectatione ludentem an vitae recensum iam et ordinationem iudicii inhorrentem? 4. Semper autem expectat anima corpus, ut doleat aut gaudeat? Nonne et de suo sufficit sibi ad utrumque titulum passionis? Quotiens inlaeso corpore anima sola torquetur bile ira taedio plerumque nec sibi noto? Quotiens item corpore afflicto furtivum sibi anima gaudium exquirit et a corporis tunc importuna societate secedit? 5. Mentior, si non de ipsis cruciatibus corporis et gloriari et gaudere sola consuevit. Respice ad Mutii animam, cum dexteram suam ignibus solvit; respice ad Zenonis, cum illam Dionysii tormenta praetereunt. Morsus ferarum ornamenta sunt iuventutis, ut in Cyro ursi cicatrices. Adeo novit et apud inferos anima et gaudere et dolere sine carne, quia et in carne et inlaesa si velit dolet et laesa si velit gaudet. Hoc si ex arbitrio suo in vita, quanto magis ex iudicio dei post mortem? 6. Sed nec omnia opera [optima] cum carnis ministerio anima partitur; nam et solos cogitatus et nudas voluntates censura divina persequitur. *Qui viderit ad concupiscendum, iam adulteravit in corde.* Ergo vel propter haec congruentissimum est animam, licet non expectata carne, puniri, quod non sociata carne commisit. Sic et ob cogitatus pios et benivolos, in quibus carne non eguit, sine carne recreabitur.

ity is carried down, where every hope is deposited? Do you think that judgment is anticipated or actually begun? Is it hastened on its way, or is it already administered? Indeed, how extremely unjust would the rest of the time in hell be if it were already good for the guilty but not yet for the innocent! Furthermore, what do you want there to be afterwards: death trifling with us by a vague hope and an uncertain expectation or an assessment of life already made and the fearful implementation of judgment? 4. Does the soul, then, always await the body so that it may sorrow or rejoice? Would it not even of itself have a sufficient claim to both emotions? How often when the body is unharmed is the soul by itself tormented by anger, wrath, and loathing, quite often unconsciously? Again, how often when the body is afflicted does the soul seek a secret joy and at that time withdraw from its troublesome association with the body? 5. I should be giving a false account if the soul by itself did not customarily both boast and rejoice over the very tortures of the body. Consider the soul of Mucius when he freely put his right hand in the fire. Consider the soul of Zeno when Dionysius's torments passed by it unnoticed. The bites of wild beasts are adornments for young manhood, as the scars of the bear were for Cyrus.[11] Likewise, even in hell the soul knows how both to rejoice and to sorrow without the flesh, since even when it was in the flesh it both sorrowed if it wished when the flesh was unharmed and rejoiced if it wished when the flesh was harmed. If this is possible by choice for the soul in this life, how much more will it be possible for it by God's judgment after death? 6. And yet the soul does not share all its best works with the instrument of the flesh, for God's appraisal searches out intentions by themselves and bare wishes: "Whoever has looked at a woman to lust after her has already committed adultery in his heart" (Matt 5:28). Therefore, because of this it is entirely fitting that the soul should be punished for what it committed apart from its association with the flesh without waiting for the flesh. Thus also it will be relieved without the flesh because of the pious and benevolent intentions

---

[11] The first two of these examples also occur in Tertullian, *Apol.* 50. The story of Mucius Scaevola is found in Livy 2.12–13. Zeno of Elea was a disciple of Parmenides; the tyrant is variously named. According to Clement of Alexandria (*Strom.* 4.56), Zeno refused to reveal a secret and, when tortured, bit off his tongue and spat it at the tyrant. Cyrus's scars are mentioned by Xenophon (*Cyr.* 1.4.8).

7. Quid nunc, si et in carnalibus prior est quae concipit, quae disponit, quae mandat, quae impellit? Et si quando invita, prior tamen tractat quod per corpus actura est; nunquam denique conscientia posterior erit facto. Ita huic quoque ordini competit eam priorem pensare mercedes cui priori debeantur. 8. In summa, cum carcerem illum, quem evangelium demonstrat, inferos intellegimus et novissimum quadrantem modicum quoque delictum mora resurrectionis illic luendum interpretamur, nemo dubitabit animam aliquid pensare penes inferos salva resurrectionis plenitudine per carnem quoque. Hoc etiam paracletus frequentissime commendavit, si qui sermones eius ex agnitione promissorum charismatum admiserit. 9. Ad omnem, ut arbitror, humanam super anima opinionem ex doctrina fidei congressi iustae dumtaxat ac necessariae curiositati satisfecimus; enormi autem et otiosae tantum deerit discere quantum libuerit inquirere.

in which it had no need of the flesh. 7. What shall we say now if even in the acts of the flesh the soul comes first because it forms a thought, adopts a disposition, gives a command, and puts it into action? Even if there are times when it is unwilling, nevertheless it first considers what is about to be done through the body. Thus, consciousness will never be later than what is done. And so it is also in accord with this order that the soul should be first to receive the deserts owed to it because it is first. 8. In short, since we understand hell to be that prison the Gospel points out and since we interpret the last penny as the least offense that must be expiated there in the time before the resurrection (Matt 5:25–26), no one will doubt that the soul receives some recompense at the hands of hell while it is being kept safe for the fullness of the resurrection, which includes the flesh. The Paraclete has also quite frequently pointed this out, provided someone accepts his words on the basis of the gracious gifts that have been promised.[12] 9. Now that, so far as I can judge, we have encountered every human opinion about the soul from the perspective of our faith's teaching, we have satisfied what is no more than a right and necessary curiosity. But there are as many great and idle points to learn as there is a desire to learn them.

---

[12] Tertullian probably alludes to the new revelations of the Spirit, received by the Montanists.

Μαρτύριον τοῦ ἁγίου Πιονίου
τοῦ πρεσβυτέρου καὶ τῶν σὺν αὐτῷ

12. 1. Ὅμως δ᾽ οὖν καὶ ἐν τῇ φυλακῇ πολλοὶ τῶν ἐθνῶν ἤρχοντο πείθειν θέλοντες, καὶ ἀκούοντες αὐτῶν τὰς ἀποκρίσεις ἐθαύμαζον. 2. εἰσῄεσαν δὲ καὶ ὅσοι κατὰ ἀνάγκην ἦσαν σεσυρμένοι τῶν Χριστιανῶν ἀδελφῶν πολὺν κλαυθμὸν ποιοῦντες, ὡς μέγα πένθος καθ᾽ ἑκάστην ὥραν ἔχειν αὐτούς, μάλιστα ἐπὶ τοῖς εὐλαβέσι καὶ ἐν καλῇ πολιτείᾳ γενομένοις, ὡς καὶ κλαίοντα τὸν Πιόνιον λέγειν· 3. Καινῇ κολάσει κολάζομαι, κατὰ μέλος τέμνομαι ὁρῶν τοὺς μαργαρίτας τῆς ἐκκλησίας ὑπὸ τῶν χοίρων καταπατουμένους καὶ τοὺς ἀστέρας τοῦ οὐρανοῦ ὑπὸ τῆς οὐρᾶς τοῦ δράκοντος εἰς τὴν γῆν σεσυρμένους, τὴν ἄμπελον ἣν ἐφύτευσεν ἡ δεξιὰ τοῦ θεοῦ ὑπὸ τοῦ ὑὸς τοῦ μονιοῦ λυμαινομένην· καὶ ταύτην νῦν *τρυγῶσι πάντες οἱ παραπορευόμενοι τὴν ὁδόν.* 4. *τεκνία μου οὓς πάλιν ὠδίνω ἕως οὗ μορφωθῇ Χριστὸς ἐν ὑμῖν, οἱ τρυφεροί μου ἐπορεύθησαν ὁδοὺς τραχείας.* 5. νῦν ἡ Σωσάννα ἐνεδρεύθη ὑπὸ τῶν ἀνόμων πρεσβυτέρων, νῦν ἀνακαλύπτουσι τὴν τρυφερὰν καὶ καλήν, ὅπως ἐμπλησθῶσι τοῦ κάλλους αὐτῆς καὶ ψευδῆ καταμαρτυρήσωσιν αὐτῆς. 6. νῦν ὁ Ἀμὰν κωθωνίζεται, Ἐσθὴρ δὲ καὶ πᾶσα πόλις ταράσσεται. 7. νῦν οὐ λιμὸς ἄρτου οὐδὲ δίψα ὕδατος, ἀλλ᾽ ἢ τοῦ ἀκοῦσαι λόγον κυρίου. 8. ἢ πάντως ἐνύσταξαν πᾶσαι αἱ παρθένοι καὶ ἐκάθευδον; 9. ἐπληρώθη τὸ ῥῆμα τοῦ κυρίου Ἰησοῦ· *ἆρα ὁ υἱὸς τοῦ ἀνθρώπου ἐλθὼν εὑρήσει τὴν πίστιν ἐπὶ τῆς γῆς;* 10. ἀκούω δὲ ὅτι καὶ εἷς ἕκαστος τὸν πλησίον παραδίδωσιν, ἵνα πληρωθῇ τὸ *παραδώσει ἀδελφὸς ἀδελφὸν εἰς θάνατον.* 11. ἆρα *ἐξητήσατο ὁ σατανᾶς ἡμᾶς τοῦ σινιάσαι ὡς τὸν σῖτον·* πύρινον δὲ τὸ πτύον ἐν τῇ χειρὶ τοῦ θεοῦ Λόγου τοῦ διακαθᾶραι τὴν ἅλωνα. 12. τάχα ἐμωράνθη τὸ ἅλας καὶ ἐβλήθη ἔξω καὶ καταπατεῖται ὑπὸ τῶν ἀνθρώπων. 13. ἀλλὰ μή τις ὑπολάβῃ, τεκνία, ὅτι ἠδυνάτησεν ὁ κύριος ἀλλ᾽ ἡμεῖς. 14. Μὴ ἀδυνατεῖ γάρ, φησίν, *ἡ χείρ μου τοῦ ἐξελέσθαι; ἢ ἐβάρυνε τὸ οὖς μου <τοῦ> μὴ εἰσακοῦσαι; ἀλλὰ τὰ ἁμαρτήματα ὑμῶν διϊστῶσιν ἀνὰ μέσον ἐμοῦ τοῦ θεοῦ καὶ ὑμῶν.* 15. ἠδικήσαμεν γάρ, ἔνιοι δὲ καὶ καταφρονήσαντες· ἠνομήσαμεν ἀλλήλους δάκνοντες καὶ ἀλλήλους καται-

12. 1. Nevertheless, while they were in prison many pagans came because they wanted to persuade them, and when they heard their responses, they were amazed. 2. As well, as many of the Christian brothers as had been dragged away by force came in. They made a great lament, since they were possessed by deep grief hour by hour, especially those who were devout and had lived a good life. So Pionius wept as he said: 3. "I am tormented by a new torture, and I am being torn limb from limb, when I see the pearls of the church being trampled by swine (Matt 7:6), the stars of heaven being dragged down to earth by the dragon's tail (Rev 12:4), and the vine that the right hand of God planted being destroyed by the solitary wild boar 'and now all those who pass by on the road strip it bare' (Ps 79:13). 4. 'My little children for whom I am again in the pain of childbirth until Christ is formed in you' (Gal 4:19), 'my tender ones have traveled rough roads' (Bar 4:26). 5. Now Susanna was ambushed by the lawless old men (Sus); now they are uncovering the tender and beautiful girl, to take their fill of her beauty and to bear false witness against her. 6. Now again is Haman made drunk (Esth 3:15), and Esther and the whole city are in terror. 7. Now there is no hunger for bread or thirst for water, but rather for hearing the word of the Lord (Amos 8:11). 8. Have all the virgins completely dozed off and fallen asleep (Matt 25:5)? 9. The word of the Lord Jesus is fulfilled: 'When the Son of Man comes, will he find faith on earth?' (Luke 18:8). 10. I also hear that each one hands over his neighbor, that the word might be fulfilled: 'Brother will hand over brother to death' (Mark 13:12). 11. Indeed, 'Satan has asked for us that he might sift us like wheat' (Luke 22:31), and the fiery winnowing fork is in the hand of the Word of God in order to cleanse the threshing floor (Matt 3:12). 12. Perhaps the salt has lost its taste and was thrown out and trampled by people (Matt 5:13). 13. But let no one suppose, my little children, that the Lord has been powerless; it is we who have been. 14. 'Is my hand, he says, powerless to rescue, or my ear hard of hearing? But your sins have made a division between my God and you' (Isa 59:1–2). 15. For we have done wrong, and some of us have indeed been scornful; we have acted lawlessly by backbit-

τιώμενοι· ὑπὸ ἀλλήλων ἀνηλώθημεν. 16. ἔδει δὲ ἡμῶν τὴν δικαιοσύνην περισσεύειν μᾶλλον **πλέον τῶν γραμματέων καὶ Φαρισαίων**.

13. 1. Ἀκούω δὲ ὅτι καί τινας ὑμῶν Ἰουδαῖοι καλοῦσιν εἰς συναγωγάς. διὸ προσέχετε μή ποτε ὑμῶν καὶ μεῖζον καὶ ἑκούσιον ἁμάρτημα ἅψηται, μηδέ τις τὴν ἀναφαίρετον ἁμαρτίαν τὴν εἰς τὴν βλασφημίαν τοῦ ἁγίου πνεύματος ἁμαρτήσῃ. 2. μὴ γίνεσθε ἅμα αὐτοῖς ἄρχοντες Σοδόμων καὶ λαὸς Γομόρρας, ὧν αἱ χεῖρες αἵματος πλήρεις. ἡμεῖς δὲ οὔτε προφήτας ἀπεκτείναμεν οὐδὲ τὸν Χριστὸν παρεδώκαμεν καὶ ἐσταυρώσαμεν. 3. καὶ τί πολλὰ λέγω ὑμῖν; μνημονεύετε ὧν ἠκούσατε <καὶ νῦν περαίνετε ἃ ἐμάθετε>. ἐπεὶ κἀκεῖνο ἠκούσατε ὅτι φασὶν οἱ Ἰουδαῖοι· Ὁ Χριστὸς ἄνθρωπος ἦν καὶ ἀνεπαύσατο ὡς βιοθανής. 4. εἰπάτωσαν οὖν ἡμῖν ποίου βιοθανοῦς πᾶς ὁ κόσμος μαθητῶν ἐπληρώθη; 5. ποίου βιοθανοῦς ἀνθρώπου οἱ μαθηταὶ καὶ ἄλλοι μετ' αὐτοὺς τοσοῦτοι ὑπὲρ τοῦ ὀνόματος τοῦ διδασκάλου αὐτῶν ἀπέθανον; 6. ποίου βιοθανοῦς ἀνθρώπου τῷ ὀνόματι τοσούτοις ἔτεσι δαιμόνια ἐξεβλήθη καὶ ἐκβάλλεται καὶ ἐκβληθήσεται; καὶ ὅσα ἄλλα μεγαλεῖα ἐν τῇ ἐκκλησίᾳ τῇ καθολικῇ γίνεται. 7. ἀγνοοῦσι δὲ ὅτι βιοθανής ἐστιν ὁ ἰδίᾳ προαιρέσει ἐξάγων ἑαυτὸν τοῦ βίου. 8. λέγουσι δὲ καὶ νεκυομαντείαν πεποιηκέναι καὶ ἀνηγειοχέναι τὸν Χριστὸν μετὰ τοῦ σταυροῦ. 9. καὶ ποία γραφὴ τῶν παρ' αὐτοῖς καὶ παρ' ἡμῖν ταῦτα περὶ Χριστοῦ λέγει; τίς δὲ τῶν δικαίων ποτὲ εἶπεν; οὐχ οἱ λέγοντες ἄνομοί εἰσι; πῶς δὲ ἀνόμοις λέγουσι πιστεύσῃ τις καὶ οὐχὶ τοῖς δικαίοις μᾶλλον;

14. 1. Ἐγὼ μὲν οὖν τοῦτο τὸ ψεῦσμα, ὃ λέγουσιν ὡς νῦν γεγονός, ἐκ παιδὸς ἡλικίας ἤκουον λεγόντων Ἰουδαίων. 2. ἔστι δὲ γεγραμμένον ὅτι ὁ Σαοὺλ ἐπηρώτησεν τὴν ἐγγαστρίμυθον καὶ εἶπεν τῇ γυναικὶ τῇ οὕτω μαντευομένῃ· **ἀνάγαγέ μοι τὸν Σαμουὴλ** τὸν προφήτην. 3. καὶ εἶδεν ἡ γυνὴ **ἄνδρα ὄρθιον ἀναβαίνοντα** ἐν διπλοΐδι, **καὶ ἔγνω Σαοὺλ ὅτι**

ing one another and by bringing charges against one another; we have been destroyed by one another. 16. But it was necessary that our righteousness 'exceed that of the scribes and Pharisees' (Matt 5:20).

13. 1. "I hear also that the Jews are inviting some of you into their synagogues. Therefore, take care that a sin both greater and uncompelled may not somehow take hold of you and that no one commit the unforgivable sin of blasphemy against the Holy Spirit (cf. Mark 3:29). 2. Do not become along with them rulers of Sodom and people of Gomorrah whose hands are filled with blood (Isa 1:10–11, 15). We neither slayed prophets nor handed over the crucified Christ. 3. But why should I speak at length on this point to you? Remember what you have heard, and now bring to fulfillment what you have learned. For you have also heard that the Jews say: Christ was a man, and he died a suicide.[1] 4. But let them tell us, what suicide has filled the entire world with his disciples? What man who has committed suicide has had disciples—and so many others after them—who died for the name of their teacher? 6. By what suicide's name for so many years have demons been cast out, are cast out, and will be cast out? And how many other wonders have taken place in the catholic church! 7. These people fail to recognize that a suicide is someone who by his own choice takes himself out of this life. 8. Again, they say that Christ practiced necromancy and divination with the cross.[2] 9. Yet what scripture of theirs or ours says this about Christ? Did any of the righteous ever say this? Are not those who say this lawless people? How then can anyone believe the lawless when they speak, rather than the righteous?

14. 1. "For my part, this lie, which they tell as though it just now had occurred, I have heard the Jews telling from my youth. 2. It is written that Saul asked the belly-myther and that he said to the woman who was divining through this means,[3] 'Bring up for me Samuel the prophet' (1 Kgdms 28:11). 3. And the woman saw 'a man coming up standing' and in a double cloak, and 'Saul knew

---

[1] βιοθανής can also mean "one who dies a violent death" (and is translated as such by Musurillo, *Acts of the Christian Martyrs*), but 13.7 below seems clearly to indicate that suicide is intended throughout this argument.

[2] Alternatively one could construe the grammar to say: "They say that necromancy has done it and raised Christ together with the cross."

[3] I.e., through νεκυομαντεία, "necromancy."

οὗτος Σαμουήλ, καὶ ἐπηρώτησε περὶ ὧν ἐβούλετο. 4. τί οὖν; ἠδύνατο ἡ ἐγγαστρίμυθος ἀναγαγεῖν τὸν Σαμουὴλ ἢ οὔ; 5. εἰ μὲν οὖν λέγουσιν ὅτι Ναί, ὡμολογήκασι τὴν ἀδικίαν πλέον ἰσχύειν τῆς δικαιοσύνης, καὶ ἐπικατάρατοί εἰσιν. 6. ἐὰν δὲ εἴπωσιν ὅτι οὐκ ἀνήγαγεν, ἄρα οὖν οὐδὲ τὸν Χριστὸν τὸν κύριον. 7. ἡ δὲ ὑπόδειξις τοῦδε τοῦ λόγου ἐστὶ τοιαύτη. πῶς ἠδύνατο ἡ ἄδικος ἐγγαστρίμυθος, ἡ δαίμων, ἀναγαγεῖν τὴν τοῦ ἁγίου προφήτου ψυχὴν τὴν ἀναπαυομένην ἐν κόλποις Ἀβραάμ; τὸ γὰρ ἔλαττον ὑπὸ τοῦ κρείττονος κελεύεται. 8. οὔκουν ὡς ἐκεῖνοι ὑπολαμβάνουσιν ἀνηνέχθη ὁ Σαμουήλ; μὴ γένοιτο. ἀλλ' ἔστι τοιοῦτό τι· 9. παντὶ τῷ ἀποστάτῃ γενομένῳ θεοῦ οἱ τῆς ἀποστασίας παρέπονται ἄγγελοι, καὶ παντὶ φαρμακῷ καὶ μάγῳ καὶ γόητι καὶ μάντει διαβολικοὶ ὑπουργοῦσι λειτουργοί. 10. **καὶ οὐ θαυμαστόν·** φησὶ γὰρ ὁ ἀπόστολος· **Αὐτὸς ὁ σατανᾶς μετασχηματίζεται εἰς ἄγγελον φωτός· οὐ μέγα οὖν εἰ καὶ οἱ διάκονοι αὐτοῦ μετασχηματίζονται ὡς διάκονοι δικαιοσύνης.** ἐπείπως καὶ ὁ ἀντίχριστος ὡς ὁ Χριστὸς φανήσεται. 11. οὐχ ὅτι οὖν ἀνήγαγε τὸν Σαμουήλ, ἀλλὰ τῇ ἐγγαστριμύθῳ καὶ τῷ ἀποστάτῃ Σαοὺλ δαίμονες ταρταραῖοι ἐξομοιωθέντες τῷ Σαμουὴλ ἐνεφάνισαν ἑαυτούς. 12. διδάξει δὲ αὐτὴ ἡ γραφή· λέγει γὰρ δῆθεν ὁ ὀφθεὶς Σαμουὴλ τῷ Σαούλ· Καὶ σὺ **σήμερον μετ' ἐμοῦ ἔσῃ.** 13. πῶς δύναται ὁ εἰδωλολάτρης Σαοὺλ εὑρεθῆναι μετὰ Σαμουήλ; ἢ δῆλον ὅτι μετὰ τῶν ἀνόμων καὶ τῶν ἀπατησάντων αὐτὸν καὶ κυριευσάντων αὐτοῦ δαιμόνων. ἄρα οὖν οὐκ ἦν Σαμουήλ. 14. εἰ δὲ ἀδύνατόν ἐστι τὴν τοῦ ἁγίου προφήτου ἀναγαγεῖν ψυχήν, πῶς τὸν ἐν τοῖς οὐρανοῖς Ἰησοῦν Χριστόν, ὃν ἀναλαμβανόμενον εἶδον οἱ μαθηταὶ καὶ ὑπὲρ τοῦ μὴ ἀρνήσασθαι αὐτὸν ἀπέθανον, οἷόν τέ ἐστιν ἐκ γῆς ἀνερχόμενον ὀφθῆναι; 15. εἰ δὲ ταῦτα μὴ δύνασθε ἀντιτιθέναι αὐτοῖς, λέγετε πρὸς αὐτούς· Ὅπως ἂν ᾖ, ἡμεῖς ὑμῶν τῶν χωρὶς ἀνάγκης ἐκπορνευσάντων καὶ εἰδωλολατρησάντων κρείττονές ἐσμεν. 16. καὶ μὴ συγκατάθεσθε αὐτοῖς ἐν ἀπογνώσει γενόμενοι, ἀδελφοί, ἀλλὰ τῇ μετανοίᾳ προσμείνατε τῷ Χριστῷ· ἐλεήμων γάρ ἐστι δέξασθαι πάλιν ὑμᾶς ὡς τέκνα.

that this was Samuel' (1 Kgdms 28:14) and asked him the questions that he wanted. 4. What, then? Was the belly-myther able to bring up Samuel or not? 5. If they say yes, they have admitted that wickedness has more power than righteousness, and they are accursed. 6. If they say 'she did not bring him up,' then they should not assert it of Christ the Lord.[4] 7. But the proof of this argument is as follows. How was the wicked belly-myther, herself a demon, able to bring up the soul of the holy prophet that was resting in the bosom of Abraham (cf. Luke 16:22)? For the lesser is commanded by the greater. 8. Then was Samuel brought up as these suppose? Certainly not. What happened is something like this. 9. Everyone who becomes an apostate from God is attended by apostate angels, and diabolical ministers assist every sorcerer, magician, wizard, and soothsayer. 10. 'And no wonder!' for the apostle says, 'Even Satan disguises himself as an angel of light. So it is not strange if his ministers also disguise themselves as ministers of righteousness' (2 Cor 11:14–15). Indeed, even the Antichrist will appear as Christ (cf. 1 John 2:18). 11. So then she did not bring Samuel up; rather, underworld demons who had taken on the likeness of Samuel manifested themselves to the belly-myther and to the apostate Saul. 12. Scripture itself will teach this. For the supposed 'Samuel' who appeared to Saul says, you, too, 'will be with me today' (cf. 1 Kgdms 28:19; Luke 23:43). 13. How can Saul the idolater be found together with Samuel? Surely it is clear that he is with the lawless demons that have deceived him and have become his masters. Consequently, therefore, it was certainly not Samuel. 14. But if it is impossible to bring up the soul of the holy prophet, how is it possible that Jesus Christ should appear rising up from the earth? He is in heaven; he is the one the disciples saw taken up there (Acts 1:9). And they died because they would not deny him. 15. And if you are unable to maintain this against them, tell them: however it may be, we are better than you, who committed fornication and idolatry without being forced to. 16. Do not yield to them because you are in despair, my brothers, but abide in Christ by repentance, for he is merciful in receiving you back again as his children."

---

[4] The grammar of this sentence aligns Christ not with the woman (in practicing necromancy) but with Samuel (in being [not] brought up by necromancy).

Ὠριγένους εἰς τὴν τῶν Βασιλειῶν ά

1. 1. Τὰ ἀναγνωσθέντα πλείονά ἐστιν, καὶ ἐπεὶ χρὴ ἐπιτεμνόμε-
νον εἰπεῖν, δ' εἰσὶν περικοπαί. ἀνεγνώσθη τὰ ἑξῆς τῶν περὶ Νάβαλ τὸν
Καρμήλιον· εἶτα μετὰ τοῦτο ἡ ἱστορία ἡ περὶ τοῦ κεκρύφθαι τὸν Δαβὶδ
παρὰ τοῖς Ζιφαίοις καὶ διαβεβλῆσθαι αὐτὸν ὑπ' αὐτῶν, ἐληλυθέναι δὲ τὸν
Σαοὺλ βουλόμενον λαβεῖν τὸν Δαβὶδ καὶ ἐληλυθότα ἐπιτηρῆσαι καιρόν,
ἐπεληλυθέναι τε τῷ Σαοὺλ τὸν Δαβὶδ καὶ εἰληφέναι, κοιμωμένου αὐτοῦ
καὶ τῶν φρουρούντων αὐτόν, τὸ δόρυ καὶ τὸν φακὸν τοῦ ὕδατος καὶ μετὰ
τοῦτο ἔλεγχον προσενηνοχέναι τοῖς πεπιστευμένοις μὲν φυλάττειν αὐτόν,
ἀποκοιμηθεῖσιν δέ. **2.** εἶτα [τὰ] ἑξῆς ἡ ἱστορία ἦν ἡ τρίτη, ὅτι κατέφυγε
πρὸς Ἀγ(χοὺς υἱὸν Ἀμμὰ)χ βασιλέα Γὲθ ὁ Δαβίδ, καὶ ὅσην εὗρε χάριν
παρ' αὐτῷ μετὰ τὰ πολλὰ ἀνδραγαθήματα ὁ Δαβίδ, πρὸς ὃν *ἀρχισωμα-
τοφύλακα θήσομαί σε* φησίν. ἑξῆς τούτοις ἦν ἡ ἱστορία ἡ διαβόητος ἡ
περὶ τῆς ἐγγαστριμύθου καὶ περὶ τοῦ Σαμουήλ, ὅτι ἔδοξεν ἀνενηνοχέναι
ἡ ἐγγαστρίμυθος τὸν Σαμουὴλ καὶ ὁ Σαμουὴλ προφητεύει τῷ Σαούλ.
3. τεσσάρων οὐσῶν περικοπῶν, ὧν ἑκάστη πράγματα οὐκ ὀλίγα ἔχει,
ἀλλὰ καὶ τοῖς δυναμένοις ἐξετάζειν δυνάμενα ἀσχολῆσαι ὥρας οὐ μιᾶς
συνάξεως ἀλλὰ καὶ πλειόνων, ὅτιποτε βούλεται ὁ ἐπίσκοπος προτεινάτω
τῶν τεσσάρων, ἵνα περὶ τοῦτο ἀσχοληθῶμεν. τὰ περὶ τῆς ἐγγαστριμύθου,
φησίν, ἐξεταζέσθω.

2. 1. Ἔνιαι μὲν ἱστορίαι οὐχ ἅπτονται ἡμῶν, ἔνιαι δὲ ἀναγκαῖαι
πρὸς τὴν ἐλπίδα ἡμῶν· οὕτω δ' εἶπον "ἱστορίαι", ἐπεὶ οὐδέπω φθάνομεν ἐπὶ τὰ τῆς ἀναγωγῆς, παντὶ τῷ εἰδότι ἀνάγειν ἢ ἀκούειν ἀναγομένων

4. Origen, *Homily on 1 Kingdoms 28*

1. 1. Many things have been read, and since I must speak briefly, there are four passages. In order, the events concerning Nabal the Carmelite were read (1 Kgdms 25). Then after this the narrative of how David hid himself among the Ziphites and was denounced by them, how Saul in his wish to capture David came and once there watched for an opportune time, and how David went to Saul and while he and his guards were sleeping took the spear and the water jar and after that offered a rebuke to those entrusted with guarding Saul but asleep on watch (1 Kgdms 26). 2. Next was the third narrative[1] of how David took refuge with the king of Gath, Achish the son of Ammach, and how he found such favor with him that after many feats of valor the king said to him, "I shall make you the commander of my bodyguard" (1 Kgdms 27:1–28:2). Next after these was the famous narrative concerning the belly-myther and concerning Samuel, how the belly-myther apparently brought up Samuel and how Samuel prophesies to Saul.

3. There are four passages, each of which involves no few subjects that—even for those capable of close examination—could occupy the time not just of one service, but of many. For this reason let the bishop[2] propose which of the four he wishes, so that we may be occupied with it.

"Let the matters concerning the belly-myther," he says, "be examined."

2. 1. There are narratives that do not touch us, and there are narratives that are necessary for our hope. I put it this way, "narratives," since we have not yet arrived at the benefits of the "elevated sense" for each person who knows how to "elevate" or

---

[1] The Greek word *historia*, more like the French *histoire*, can mean story or historical event. Origen will play with the meaning of the term in the homily, using it to refer to the passage and also to a reading of it according to "the literal sense." We adopt at the outset what seems to be the most neutral rendering, "narrative."

[2] The bishop is Alexander of Jerusalem, who had invited Origen to preach. Normally the bishop himself would have preached. See the Nautins' discussion in *Origène*, 61–66, and Simonetti's note, *La Maga di Endor*, 78.

χρήσιμα. 2. (τῶν οὖν τῆς ἱστορίας τινὰ μὲν χρήσιμα) πᾶσιν, τινὰ δὲ οὐ πᾶσιν. οἷον, ὡς ἐπὶ παραδείγματος, ἡ ἱστορία ἡ περὶ τοῦ Λὼτ καὶ τῶν θυγατέρων αὐτοῦ εἰ μέν τι κατὰ τὴν ἀναγωγὴν ἔχει χρήσιμον, θεὸς οἶδεν καὶ ᾧ ἂν χαρίσηται τοὺς λόγους ἐκείνους ἐξετάζειν· εἰ δὲ κατὰ τὴν ἱστο- ρίαν, ζητήσαις ἄν· τί γὰρ ὄφελός μοι ἐκ τῆς ἱστορίας τῆς περὶ τοῦ Λὼτ καὶ τῶν θυγατέρων αὐτοῦ; 3. ὁμοίως τί ὄφελός μοι ἁπλῶς λεχθεῖσα ἡ ἱστορία τοῦ Ἰούδα καὶ τῆς Θάμαρ καὶ τῶν κατ' αὐτήν; ἐπεὶ μέντοιγε ἡ ἱστορία ἡ περὶ τὸν Σαοὺλ καὶ τὴν ἐγγαστρίμυθον πάντων ἅπτεται, ἀναγκαία ἀλήθεια κατὰ τὸν λόγον. 4. τίς γὰρ ἀπαλλαγεὶς τούτου τοῦ βίου θέλει εἶναι ὑπὸ ἐξουσίαν δαιμονίου, ἵνα ἐγγαστρίμυθος ἀναγάγῃ οὐ τὸν τυχόντα τῶν πεπιστευκότων, ἀλλὰ Σαμουὴλ τὸν προφήτην; περὶ οὗ φησιν ὁ θεὸς διὰ τοῦ Ἰερεμίου· *οὐδ' ἂν Μωσῆς καὶ Σαμουὴλ πρὸ προσώπου μου, οὐδὲ τούτων εἰσακούσομαι*, περὶ οὗ φησιν ἐν ὕμνοις ὁ προφήτης· *Μωσῆς καὶ Ἀαρὼν ἐν τοῖς ἱερεῦσιν αὐτοῦ, καὶ Σαμουὴλ ἐν τοῖς ἐπικαλουμένοις τὸ ὄνομα αὐτοῦ· ἐπεκαλοῦντο τὸν κύριον, καὶ αὐτὸς εἰσήκουεν αὐτῶν, ἐν στύλῳ νεφέλης ἐλάλει πρὸς αὐτούς*, καὶ ἀλλαχοῦ· ἐὰν

to hear what is "elevated" by others.³ 2. But as regards the benefits of the "narrative sense," some benefits are for all people and some not for all people. Let us take the narrative about Lot and his daughters, for example (Gen 19:30–38). If it has a certain benefit according to the elevated sense, only God knows and the person to whom he grants the ability to investigate those words; if it has a benefit according to the narrative sense, you could search for it.⁴ Ask yourself: What is the benefit for me from the narrative about Lot and his daughters? 3. Likewise, what is the benefit to me from the narrative of Judith and Tamar and what happened to her, when simply read (Gen 38:1–30)?⁵ But since the narrative about Samuel and the belly-myther touches all people, then its truth is necessary in accordance with the word.⁶

4. For who, once delivered from this life,⁷ wishes to be subject to the authority of a petty demon so that a belly-myther might bring up not just any chance believer but Samuel the prophet? God said of him through Jeremiah, "Even if Moses and Samuel were before me, I will not hear even them" (cf. Jer 15:1). The prophet says of him in the Psalms, "Moses and Aaron are among his priests, and Samuel among those who call upon his name. They called upon the Lord, and he heard them. He spoke to them in the pillar of cloud" (Ps 98:6–7). And elsewhere, "If Moses and

---

³ ἡ ἀναγωγή, "the elevated meaning," is used by Origen for the allegorical sense (Grant, *Letter and Spirit*, 124). He may deliberately use this term here also as a wordplay on the biblical terminology for the "elevation" (ἀναγαγεῖν) of Samuel.

⁴ Nautin and Nautin, *Origène*, 171, call our attention to *Princ.* 4.2.2, where Origen refers to several passages, including the story of Lot's daughters, and implies that they are offensive in their narrative meaning and "are mysteries not understood by us." But see also *Cels.* 4.45, where Origen, while recognizing that many are offended by the story, by no means excludes the possibility of interpreting it spiritually and even appears to allow for the possibility of a beneficial meaning at the narrative level.

⁵ Here ἱστορία is used with both senses: of the passage itself and of the "plain sense" as contrasted with the elevated or spiritual meaning, reflecting Origen's distinction between the "letter" and the "spirit." The letter is what he takes to be the obvious meaning of the text and probably should not be too closely identified with what we might suppose to be the "literal" or "historical" meaning.

⁶ I.e., "literally" (κατὰ τὸν λόγον).

⁷ The fate of believers after death is Origen's ultimate concern in this homily, signaled here at the outset (see also 9.7; 10.2).

στῇ Μωσῆς καὶ Σαμουὴλ καὶ προσεύξωνται καὶ τὰ ἑξῆς. 5. ἆρ' οὖν, εἰ ὁ τηλικοῦτος ὑπὸ τὴν γῆν (ἦν) καὶ ἀνήγαγεν αὐτὸν ἡ ἐγγαστρίμυθος, ἐξουσίαν ἔχει δαιμόνιον ψυχῆς προφητικῆς; τί εἴπω; ἐγγέγραπται ταῦτα· ἀληθῆ ἐστιν ἢ οὐκ ἔστιν ἀληθῆ; τὸ μὲν μὴ εἶναι ἀληθῆ λέγειν εἰς ἀπιστίαν προτρέπει (χωρήσει ἐπὶ κεφαλὰς τῶν λεγόντων), τὸ δὲ εἶναι ἀληθῆ ζήτησιν καὶ ἐπαπόρησιν ἡμῖν παρέχει.

3. 1. Καὶ μὴν γοῦν ἴσμεν τινὰς τῶν ἡμετέρων ἀδελφῶν ἀντιβλέψαντας τῇ γραφῇ καὶ λέγοντας· οὐ πιστεύω τῇ ἐγγαστριμύθῳ. λέγει ἡ ἐγγαστρίμυθος ἑορακέναι τὸν Σαμουήλ, ψεύδεται. Σαμουὴλ οὐκ ἀνήχθη, Σαμουὴλ οὐ λαλεῖ. ἀλλ' ὥσπερ εἰσί τινες ψευδοπροφῆται λέγοντες· τάδε λέγει κύριος· καὶ κύριος οὐκ ἐλάλησεν, οὕτως καὶ τὸ δαιμόνιον τοῦτο ψεύδεται, ἐπαγγελλόμενον ἀνάγειν τὸν ὑπὸ τοῦ Σαοὺλ προστασσόμενον. *τίνα γὰρ ἀναγάγω; φησίν· Σαμουὴλ ἀνάγαγέ μοι.* ταῦτα λέγεται ὑπὸ τῶν φασκόντων τὴν ἱστορίαν ταύτην μὴ εἶναι ἀληθῆ. 2. Σαμουὴλ ἐν ᾅδου; Σαμουὴλ ὑπὸ ἐγγαστριμύθου ἀνάγεται ὁ ἐξαίρετος τῶν προφητῶν, ὁ ἀπὸ τῆς γενέσεως ἀνακείμενος τῷ θεῷ, ὁ πρὸ γενέσεως ἐν τῷ ἱερῷ λεγόμενος ἔσεσθαι, ὁ ἅμα τῷ ἀπογαλακτισθῆναι ἐνδυσάμενος ἐφοὺδ καὶ περιβεβλημένος διπλοΐδα καὶ ἱερεὺς γενόμενος τοῦ κυρίου, ᾧ παιδίῳ ἔτι ὄντι ἐχρημάτισεν ὁ κύριος λαλῶν; 3. Σαμουὴλ ἐν ᾅδου; Σαμουὴλ ἐν τοῖς καταχθονίοις ὁ διαδεξάμενος Ἡλὶ διὰ τὰ τῶν τέκνων ἁμαρτήματα καὶ παρανομήματα καταδικασθέντα ὑπὸ τῆς προνοίας; Σαμουὴλ ἐν ᾅδου, οὗ ὁ θεὸς ἐπήκουσεν ἐν καιρῷ θερισμοῦ πυρῶν, καὶ ὑετὸν ἔδωκεν ἐλθεῖν ἀπ' οὐρανοῦ; Σαμουὴλ ἐν ᾅδου ὁ τοιαῦτα παρρησιασάμενος, εἰ ἐπιθύμημά τινος ἔλαβεν; οὐκ ἔλαβεν τὸν μόσχον, οὐκ ἔλαβεν τὸν βοῦν, ἔκρινεν καὶ κατεδίκασεν τὸν λαὸν μένων πένης· οὐδέποτε ἐπεθύμησεν λαβεῖν τι

Samuel stand and pray, etc." (cf. Jer 15:1).[8] 5. Therefore, if such a great man were beneath the earth and the belly-myther brought him up, does a petty demon have authority over a prophetic soul? What shall I say? Are these things written?[9] Are they true, or are they not true? To say they are not true is an inducement to unbelief, and it will come down on the heads of those who say it. But to say they are true furnishes us with a matter for investigation[10] and an occasion for doubt.[11]

3. 1. Indeed, we know that some of our brothers have faced off against scripture and say, "I do not believe the belly-myther. The belly-myther says she has seen Samuel. She is lying.[12] Samuel was not brought up; Samuel does not speak. Rather, just as there are some false prophets who say 'thus says the Lord'— and the Lord has not spoken—so also this petty demon lies when it promises to bring up the one Saul designated. For it says, 'Whom shall I bring up?' 'Bring up Samuel for me'" (1 Kgdms 28:11). This is what those who claim the narrative is not true say: 2. "Samuel in hell? Samuel brought up by a belly-myther? He who was special among the prophets, who from birth was dedicated to God (1 Kgdms 1:11), who before birth was declared to live his future life in the temple, who when weaned was clothed with the ephod, wrapped in a double cloak, and became a priest of the Lord (1 Kgdms 1:22–23; 2:18–19), to whom while he was still a small boy the Lord gave spoken oracles (1 Kgdms 3:4–14)? 3. Samuel in hell? Samuel in the underworld—he who succeeded Eli because of his children's sins and transgressions, which were condemned by providence (1 Kgdms 2:31–36)? Samuel in hell—whom God heard at the time of the wheat harvest and made rain come down from heaven (1 Kgdms 12:17–18)? Samuel in hell—who publicly demanded whether he had taken anyone's prize possession? He took no calf; he took no bull; he judged and condemned the people while he remained poor; he never desired to take anything from

---

[8] Neither of the two apparent citations of Jer 15:1 agree with our LXX. Nautin and Nautin, *Origène*, 176–77, suggest that Origen has remembered the text in two forms and so mistakenly supposes there are two texts.

[9] Following the Nautins' punctuation in *Origène*. Simonetti, *La Maga di Endor*, does not make the sentence a question.

[10] ζήτησις, also "judicial inquiry."

[11] See Eustathius, *On the Belly-Myther* 16.4–5.

[12] See ibid., 16.7.

ἀπὸ τηλικούτου λαοῦ καὶ τοσούτου. 4. Σαμουὴλ ἵνα τί ἐν ᾅδου; ὁρᾶτε τί ἀκολουθεῖ τῷ Σαμουὴλ ἐν ᾅδου; Σαμουὴλ ἐν ᾅδου; διὰ τί οὐχὶ καὶ Ἀβραὰμ καὶ Ἰσαὰκ καὶ Ἰακὼβ ἐν ᾅδου; Σαμουὴλ ἐν ᾅδου; διὰ τί οὐχὶ καὶ Μωσῆς ὁ συνεζευγμένος τῷ Σαμουὴλ κατὰ τὸ εἰρημένον· *οὐδὲ ἐὰν στῇ Μωσῆς καὶ Σαμουήλ, οὐδὲ ἐκείνων εἰσακούσομαι*; 5. Σαμουὴλ ἐν ᾅδου; ἵνα τί μὴ καὶ Ἰερεμίας ἐν ᾅδου, πρὸς ὃν εἴρηται· *πρὸ τοῦ με πλάσαι σε ἐν κοιλίᾳ ἐπίσταμαί σε, καὶ πρὸ τοῦ σε ἐξελθεῖν ἐκ μήτρας ἡγίακά σε*; ἐν ᾅδου καὶ Ἡσαΐας, ἐν ᾅδου καὶ Ἰερεμίας, ἐν ᾅδου πάντες οἱ προφῆται, ἐν ᾅδου.

4. 1. Ταῦτα μὲν ἐρεῖ ὁ μὴ βουλόμενος ἀγῶνα παραδέξασθαι, ὅτι Σαμουὴλ ἐστιν ὄντως ὁ ἀναχθείς· ἐπεὶ δὲ δεῖ εὐγνώμονα εἶναι ἐν τῷ ἀκούειν τῶν γραφῶν, πιθανῶς καταβομβήσαντος ἡμᾶς τοῦ λόγου καὶ ἀληθῶς δυναμένου ταράξαι καὶ κινῆσαι ἡμᾶς, ἴδωμεν πότερόν ποτε νενόηται ἡ γραφὴ τῷ τοῦτο μὴ παραδεξαμένῳ, ἢ ἀπὸ ἐνδόξων μὲν ἐπιχειρεῖ, ἐναντία δὲ λέγει τοῖς γεγραμμένοις. 2. τίνα γάρ ἐστιν τὰ γεγραμμένα; *καὶ εἶπεν ἡ γυνή· τίνα ἀναγάγω σοι;* τίνος πρόσωπόν ἐστιν τὸ λέγον· *εἶπεν ἡ γυνή;* ἆρα τὸ πρόσωπον τοῦ ἁγίου πνεύματος, ἐξ οὗ πεπίστευται ἀναγεγράφθαι ἡ γραφή, ἢ πρόσωπον ἄλλου τινός; τὸ γὰρ διηγηματικὸν πρόσωπον πανταχοῦ (ὡς ἴσασιν καὶ οἱ περὶ παντοδαποὺς γενόμενοι λόγους) ἐστὶ πρόσωπον τοῦ συγγραφέως· συγγραφεὺς δ' ἐπὶ τούτων τῶν λόγων πεπίστευται εἶναι οὐκ ἄνθρωπος, ἀλλὰ συγγραφεὺς τὸ πνεῦμα τὸ ἅγιον τὸ κινῆσαν τοὺς ἀνθρώπους. 3. οὐκοῦν τὸ πνεῦμα τὸ ἅγιον λέγει· *καὶ εἶπεν ἡ γυνή "τίνα ἀναγάγω σοι;" καὶ εἶπεν· "Σαμουὴλ ἀνάγαγέ μοι"*. τίς λέγει· *καὶ εἶδεν ἡ γυνὴ τὸν Σαμουήλ, καὶ ἐβόησεν ἡ γυνὴ φωνῇ μεγάλῃ λέγουσα*; 4. ἐροῦμεν πρὸς ἐκεῖνον τὸν τοσαῦτα ἡμῶν

a people so mighty and so great (I Kgdms 12:1–6). 4. Why was Samuel in hell? Look at[13] what follows from Samuel's being in hell. Samuel in hell? Why not also Abraham, Isaac, and Jacob in hell? Samuel in hell? Why not also Moses, the one joined with Samuel according to what has been said, 'not even if Moses and Samuel take their stand will I listen even to them' (cf. Jer 15:1)? 5. Samuel in hell? Why not also Jeremiah in hell, to whom it was said, 'Before I formed you in the belly I knew you, and before you came forth from the womb I have consecrated you' (Jer 1:5)? In hell also Isaiah, in hell also Jeremiah, in hell all the prophets, in hell!"

4. 1. That is what someone will say who is unwilling to accept the trial that attends the fact that Samuel is really the one who was brought up. But since it is necessary to be right-minded in hearing the scriptures, although the other interpretation has bombarded us in a persuasive fashion and is able truly to trouble and disturb us, let us see whether the scripture has somehow been understood by the person who does not accept this[14] or whether, despite doing so with the best of intentions, he says things that directly contradict what is written.

2. What in fact are the words that stand written? "And the woman said, 'Whom shall I bring up for you?'" (I Kgdms 28:11). Whose persona is it that says, "the woman said"? Is it, then, the persona of the Holy Spirit by whom scripture is believed to have been written, or is it the persona of someone else? For, as those who are familiar with all sorts of writings know, the narrative persona throughout is the persona of the author. And the author responsible for these words is believed to be not a human being, but the author is the Holy Spirit who has moved the human beings to write. 3. Therefore, it is the Holy Spirit who says, "And the woman said, 'Whom shall I bring up for you?' And he said, 'Bring up Samuel for me.'" Who is it that says, "and the woman saw Samuel, and the woman cried out with a loud voice and said"? 4. We will say to that person who has bombarded us with such lita-

[13] Simonetti in *La Maga di Endor* takes the sentence as a question and so treats ὁρᾶτε as indicative ("Do you see what follows from Samuel being in hell?"). We are following the Nautins, *Origène*, and Declerck, *Eustathii Antiocheni Opera*, but either is possible as a way to state the rhetorical argument by appeal to consequences.

[14] I.e., the proposition that Samuel is truly the one who was raised.

καταβομβήσαντα καὶ μυρία εἰρηκότα ὡς ἄρα Σαμουὴλ οὐκ ἦν ἐν ᾅδου·
εἶδεν ἡ γυνὴ τὸν Σαμουήλ, ἡ διηγηματικὴ φωνὴ τοῦτο ἔφησεν, καὶ ἐβόησεν ἡ γυνὴ φωνῇ μεγάλῃ καὶ εἶπεν πρὸς Σαούλ· ἵνα τί παρελογίσω με;
καὶ σὺ εἶ Σαούλ. 5. καὶ εἶπεν αὐτῇ ὁ βασιλεύς· τί γάρ ἐστιν; μὴ φοβοῦ· τί
ἑόρακας; καὶ εἶπεν ἡ γυνὴ πρὸς τὸν Σαούλ· θεοὺς εἶδον ἀναβαίνοντας ἐκ
τῆς γῆς. καὶ εἶπεν αὐτῇ· τί τὸ εἶδος αὐτοῖς; καὶ εἶπεν αὐτῷ· ἀνὴρ πρεσ-
βύτερος ἀναβαίνων, καὶ αὐτὸς περιβεβλημένος διπλοΐδα [ἐφούδ]. λέγει
αὐτὴν ἑορακέναι καὶ τὸ ἱμάτιον τὸ ἱερατικόν. 6. οἶδα δὲ ὅτι ἐναντίου
ἐκ τοῦ λόγου λέγει· οὐ θαῦμα· αὐτὸς γὰρ ὁ σατανᾶς μετασχηματίζεται εἰς
ἄγγελον φωτός. οὐ μέγα οὖν, εἰ καὶ οἱ διάκονοι αὐτοῦ μετασχηματίζονται
ὡς διάκονοι δικαιοσύνης. 7. ἀλλὰ τί ἐστιν ὅπερ εἶδεν ἡ γυνή; τὸν Σαμουήλ. καὶ διὰ τί οὐκ εἴρηται· εἶδεν ἡ γυνὴ δαιμόνιον, ὃ προσεποιεῖτο
εἶναι Σαμουήλ; ἀλλὰ γέγραπται ὅτι ἔγνω Σαοὺλ ὅτι Σαμουήλ ἐστιν. εἰ
μὴ ἦν Σαμουήλ, ἔδει γεγράφθαι· καὶ ἐνόμισεν Σαοὺλ εἶναι αὐτὸν Σαμουήλ. νῦν δὲ γέγραπται· ἔγνω Σαούλ, οὐδεὶς δὲ ἔγνω τὸ μὴ ὄν· ἔγνω
οὖν Σαοὺλ ὅτι Σαμουήλ ἐστιν καὶ ἔπεσεν ἐπὶ πρόσωπον ἐπὶ τὴν γῆν καὶ
προσεκύνησεν. 8. εἶτα πάλιν τὸ πρόσωπον τῆς γραφῆς· καὶ εἶπεν Σαμουὴλ πρὸς Σαούλ· ἵνα τί παρώργισάς με τοῦ ἀναγαγεῖν με; εἶπεν φησὶν
ἡ γραφὴ ᾗ δεῖ πιστεύειν· εἶπεν Σαμουήλ· ἵνα τί παρώργισάς με τοῦ ἀναγαγεῖν με; εἶτα πρὸς τοῦτο ἀποκρίνεται Σαούλ· (θλίβομαι) σφόδρα· οἱ
ἀλλόφυλοι πολεμοῦσιν ἐν ἐμοί, καὶ ὁ θεὸς ἀπέστη ἀπ᾽ ἐμοῦ καὶ οὐκ ἀπεκρίθη μοι ἔτι, καίγε ἐν χειρὶ τῶν προφητῶν καὶ ἐν τοῖς ἐνυπνίοις ἐκάλεσα
τοῦ δηλῶσαί μοι τί ποιήσω. 9. πάλιν ἡ γραφὴ οὐκ ἄλλως εἶπεν, ἀλλ᾽
ὅτι αὐτὸς Σαμουὴλ ἔφη· καὶ ἵνα τί ἐπηρώτησάς με; καὶ κύριος ἀπέστη

nies and has said[15] that Samuel then was not in hell: "the woman saw Samuel." The narrative voice said this.

"And the woman cried out with a loud voice and said to Saul, 'Why have you deceived me? You are Saul!' 5. And the king said to her, 'What is it? Have no fear. What have you seen?' And the woman said to Saul, 'I saw gods coming up from the earth.' And he said to her, 'What is their appearance?' And she said to him, 'An old man is coming up, and he is wrapped in a double cloak, an ephod'" (1 Kgdms 28:11–14). She says that she has even seen the priestly vestment. 6. Now I know that the one who argues for the opposing interpretation cites the text, "It is no wonder, since even Satan disguises himself as an angel of light. So it is not strange if his ministers also disguise themselves as ministers of righteousness" (2 Cor 11:14–15). 7. But what is it that "the woman saw"? "Samuel."[16] Why, then, does the passage not say, "The woman saw a petty demon *that was pretending to be* Samuel"? But it is written, "Saul knew that it was Samuel." If it were not Samuel, it should have been written, "And Saul was under the impression that it was Samuel." But what it now says is "Saul knew." And no one knows that which does not exist. Therefore "Saul knew that it was Samuel and bowed with his face to the ground and worshiped him" (1 Kgdms 28:14–15). 8. The narrative persona of scripture then resumes, "And Samuel said to Saul, 'Why have you disturbed me in order to bring me up?'" Scripture, which it is necessary to believe, says, "He said." "Samuel said, 'Why have you disturbed me in order to bring me up?'" Then Saul replied to this, "I am in great distress; the foreigners[17] are warring against me, and God has turned away from me and no longer answers me either by the hand of prophets or by dreams, when I have called on him to reveal to me what I should do" (1 Kgdms 28:15).[18] 9. Again scripture said nothing other than that it was Samuel himself who said, "Why, then, have you asked me? The Lord has turned away from you" (1 Kgdms 28:16). Is he telling the truth or lying when

[15] Following Declerck, *Eustathii Antiocheni Opera*. Simonetti in *La Maga di Endor* adds μυρία, "thousands of times."

[16] For the rest of section 7, see Eustathius, *On the Belly-Myther* 5.1.

[17] The Septuagint's word for the Philistines.

[18] Our text of the LXX, however, reads "by the hand of prophets and by dreams, and now I have called upon you to make known to me what I should do."

ἀπὸ σοῦ. ἀληθεύει ἢ ψεύδεται ταῦτα λέγων· *κύριος ἀπέστη ἀπὸ σοῦ καὶ ἐγενήθη κατὰ σοῦ καὶ ἐποίησεν ἄλλον αὐτῷ, ὃν τρόπον ἐλάλησεν ἐν χειρί μου, καὶ διαρρήξει τὴν βασιλείαν ἐκ χειρός σου,* καὶ δαιμόνιον προφητεύει περὶ βασιλείας Ἰσραηλιτικῆς; 10. τί φησιν ὁ ἐναντίος λόγος; ὁρᾶτε ὅσος ἀγών ἐστιν ἐν τῷ λόγῳ τοῦ θεοῦ, χρείαν ἔχων καὶ ἀκροατῶν δυναμένων ἁγίων ἀκούειν λόγων, μεγάλων καὶ ἀπορρήτων τῶν περὶ τῆς ἐξόδου, ἔτι ἐπαπορουμένων τε τῶν προτέρων οὐδὲ τῶν δευτέρων σαφῶν ὄντων· ἀλλ' ὁ λόγος ἔτι ἐξετάζεται.

5. 1. Λέγω δὲ ὅτι ἀναγκαία καὶ ἡ ἱστορία καὶ ἡ ἐξέτασις ἡ περὶ αὐτῆς, ἵνα ἴδωμεν τί ἡμᾶς ἔχει μετὰ τὴν ἔξοδον. *λελάληκεν ἐν χειρί μου, καὶ διαρρήξει κύριος τὴν βασιλείαν ἐκ χειρός σου καὶ δώσει αὐτὴν τῷ πλησίον σου τῷ Δαβίδ.* δαιμόνιον δὲ οὐ δύναται εἰδέναι τὴν βασιλείαν Δαβὶδ τὴν ὑπὸ τοῦ κυρίου χειροτονηθεῖσαν. 2. *καθότι οὐκ ἤκουσας τὴν φωνὴν τοῦ κυρίου, οὐκ ἐποίησας ὀργὴν θυμοῦ αὐτοῦ ἐν Ἀμαλήκ.* ταῦτα οὐκ ἔστι ῥήματα θεοῦ; οὐκ ἔστιν ἀληθῆ; ἀληθῶς γὰρ οὐκ ἐποίησεν τὸ θέλημα κυρίου Σαούλ, ἀλλὰ *περιεποιήσατο* τὸν βασιλέα Ἀμαλὴκ *ζῶντα,* ἐφ' ᾧ καὶ πρὸ τῆς κοιμήσεως αὐτοῦ καὶ ἐπὶ τῆς ἐξόδου ὠνείδισεν Σα-

he says, "The Lord has turned away from you, has become your
enemy, and has appointed another for himself, just as he spoke
by my hand. And he will tear the kingdom out of your hand" (1
Kgdms 28:16-17)? Does a petty demon prophesy about the Israelite kingdom?[19]

10. What does the contrary interpretation say? See what a
great trial there is in God's word, which requires hearers able to
listen to words that are holy, great, and ineffable, words concerning our departure from this world. Still, although the arguments
of the former position are in doubt, those for the second interpretation are not yet clear.[20] Indeed, the passage needs further
examination, **5. 1.** and I say that both the narrative sense and the
examination of the passage[21] are necessary so that we may discern
what our condition will be after we depart from this life.

"He has spoken by my hand, and the Lord will tear the kingdom out of your hand and will give it to your neighbor, David"
(1 Kgdms 28:17). A petty demon is not able to know about the
kingdom that has been appointed to David by the Lord (1 Kgdms
16:1–13).[22] **2.** "Because you did not obey the voice of the Lord,
and did not carry out his fierce wrath against Amalek" (1 Kgdms
28:18). Are these not the words of God? Are they not true? For
truly Saul did not carry out the Lord's will but "allowed" the king
of Amalek "to remain alive" (1 Kgdms 15:9).[23] Samuel reproached
Saul for this both before his death (1 Kgdms 15:16–23) and in his
deceased state (1 Kgdms 28:16–19).

---

[19] See Eustathius, *On the Belly-Myther* 23.1.

[20] The Greek is difficult. Following the sense of the Nautins' French
translation in *Origène*, Origen means that objections mount against the view he
opposes, while he needs to say more to support his view that it is necessary that
it was really Samuel who appeared. In the language of the school exercises (*progymnasmata*) Origen is moving from ἀνασκευή to κατασκευή (see 8.1).

[21] Here again we have the word ἱστορία used in both of its senses (cf.
2.1–3).

[22] See Eustathius, *On the Belly-Myther* 23.1.

[23] Simonetti in *La Maga di Endor* follows Klostermann in conforming
the reading of M (περιέπει) to the LXX reading (περιεποιήσατο), and we have accepted this emendation. The Nautins, however, retain the reading of M ("treats
with respect"), even though their translation preserves the sense of the LXX. See
Origène, 187: "but that he showed the king of Amalek marks of respect and allowed him to live."

μουήλ τῷ Σαούλ· *καὶ διὰ τοῦτο τὸ ῥῆμα τοῦτο ἐποίησέν σοι κύριος ἐν τῇ ἡμέρᾳ ταύτῃ· καὶ δώσει κύριος καίγε τὸν Ἰσραὴλ ἐν χειρὶ ἀλλοφύλων.* 3. περὶ ὅλου λαοῦ θεοῦ δύναται δαιμόνιον προφητεῦσαι ὅτι κύριος μέλλει παραδιδόναι τὸν Ἰσραήλ; *καίγε τὴν παρεμβολὴν Ἰσραὴλ παραδώσει κύριος αὐτὴν ἐν χειρὶ ἀλλοφύλων. τάχυνον δὲ Σαούλ· αὔριον καὶ σὺ καὶ οἱ υἱοί σου μετ' ἐμοῦ.* 4. καὶ τοῦτο δύναται εἰδέναι δαιμόνιον, βασιλέα χειροτονηθέντα μετὰ χρίσματος προφητικοῦ, ὅτι αὔριον ἔμελλεν ἐξελεύσεσθαι ὁ Σαούλ τὸν βίον καὶ οἱ υἱοὶ αὐτοῦ μετ' αὐτοῦ; *αὔριον σὺ καὶ οἱ υἱοί σου μετ' ἐμοῦ.*

6. 1. Ταῦτα μὲν οὖν (δηλοῖ) ὅτι οὐκ ἔστιν ψευδῆ τὰ ἀναγεγραμμένα καὶ ὅτι Σαμουήλ ἐστιν ὁ ἀναβεβηκώς· τί οὖν ποιεῖ ἐγγαστρίμυθος ἐνθάδε; τί ποιεῖ ἐγγαστρίμυθος περὶ τὴν ἀναγωγὴν τῆς ψυχῆς τοῦ δικαίου; 2. ἐκεῖνο ἔφυγεν ὁ τὸν πρῶτον λόγον εἰπών (ἵνα γὰρ μὴ ἀγῶνα ἔχειν δοκῇ κατὰ τοσαῦτα ἄλλα τὰ κατὰ τὸν τόπον ζητούμενα) καὶ λέγει· οὐκ ἔστι Σαμουήλ, ψεύδεται τὸ δαιμόνιον, ἐπεὶ οὐ δύναται ψεύδεσθαι ἡ γραφή. τὰ δὲ ῥήματα τῆς γραφῆς ἐστιν· οὐκ ἔστιν ἐκ προσώπου τοῦ δαιμονίου αὐτοῦ, ἀλλ' ἐκ προσώπου αὐτῆς· *καὶ εἶδεν ἡ γυνὴ τὸν Σαμουήλ, εἶπεν Σαμουὴλ* τὰ λελαλημένα ἀπὸ τοῦ Σαμουήλ. 3. πῶς οὖν λυόμενα τὰ τῆς ἐγγαστριμύθου φανεῖται τὰ κατὰ τὸν τόπον; πυνθάνομαι τοῦ προειρηκότος τὰ πρότερα (Σαμουὴλ ἐν ᾅδου; καὶ τὰ ἑξῆς) καὶ ἀποκρινάσθω πρὸς τὸ ἐπηρωτημένον· τίς μείζων, Σαμουὴλ ἢ Ἰησοῦς ὁ Χριστός; τίς μείζων, οἱ προφῆται ἢ Ἰησοῦς ὁ Χριστός; τίς μείζων, Ἀβραὰμ ἢ Ἰησοῦς ὁ Χριστός; 4. ἐνθάδε μὲν οὐ τολμήσει τις τῶν ἅπαξ φθασάντων τὸν κύριον εἰδέναι Ἰησοῦν Χριστὸν τὸν ὑπὸ τῶν προφητῶν προκηρυχθέντα εἶναι εἰπεῖν ὅτι μείζων οὐκ ἔστιν ὁ Χριστὸς τῶν προφητῶν. ὅταν οὖν ὁμολογήσῃς ὅτι Ἰησοῦς Χριστὸς μείζων ἐστίν, Χριστὸς ἐν ᾅδου, ἢ οὐ γέγονεν ἐκεῖ; 5. οὐκ ἔστιν ἀληθὲς τὸ εἰρημένον ἐν Ψαλμοῖς, ἑρμηνευθὲν ὑπὸ

"And because of this word the Lord has done this thing to you today, and the Lord will also give Israel into the hands of the foreigners" (1 Kgdms 28:18–19). 3. Does a petty demon have the ability to prophesy about the entire people of God that the Lord was going to hand over Israel? "Indeed, the Lord will also give the camp of Israel into the hands of the foreigners. Hurry, Saul. Tomorrow both you and your sons shall be with me" (1 Kgdms 28:19).[24] 4. Does a petty demon have the power to know this— that a king had been appointed with the prophet's oil and that tomorrow Saul and his sons with him will depart this life? "To-morrow you and your sons shall be with me."

6. 1. All this demonstrates that the things written are not false and that it is Samuel who has come up. What, then, is the belly-myther doing here? What is the belly-myther doing regarding the bringing up of the righteous man's soul?[25] 2. This is the question the person giving the first interpretation tried to avoid (so that he might appear not to have any trial concerning the many other matters of dispute that must be raised about this passage). So he says, "It is not Samuel. It is the petty demon who lies, since scripture is not able to lie." But these are scripture's words. They are not spoken from the persona of the petty demon itself but from the persona of scripture: "the woman saw Samuel"; "Samuel said" the words that have been spoken by Samuel.

3. How, then, will clear solutions of these matters pertaining to the belly-myther in this passage come to light? I shall interrogate the person who has made the previous statements, who said earlier, "Samuel in hell? and the rest,"[26] and let him answer my question. Who is greater, Samuel or Jesus the Christ? Who is greater, the prophets or Jesus the Christ? Who is greater, Abraham or Jesus the Christ? 4. Now no one who has once come to know that the Lord Jesus is the Christ proclaimed ahead of time by the prophets will dare to say that Christ is not greater than the prophets. Therefore, when you confess that Jesus Christ is greater, was Christ in hell, or has he not been there? 5. Is what was spoken in the Psalms and interpreted by the apostles in their

---

[24] A rather free rendering of the LXX, with the important change of μετὰ σοῦ πεσοῦται to μετ' ἐμοῦ, which follows the Hebrew and the Lucianic text of the LXX.

[25] See Eustathius, *On the Belly-Myther* 26.2.

[26] See 3.1–5.

τῶν ἀποστόλων ἐν ταῖς Πράξεσιν αὐτῶν περὶ τοῦ τὸν σωτῆρα ἐν ᾅδου καταβεβηκέναι; γέγραπται ὅτι ἐπ᾽ αὐτὸν φέρεται τὸ ἐν πεντεκαιδεκάτῳ Ψαλμῷ· *ὅτι οὐκ ἐγκαταλείψεις τὴν ψυχήν μου ἐν ᾅδου, οὐδὲ δώσεις τὸν ὅσιόν σου ἰδεῖν διαφθοράν.* 6. εἶτα Ἰησοῦς μὲν Χριστὸς ἐν ᾅδου, φοβῇ δὲ εἰπεῖν ὅτι ναὶ καὶ ἐκεῖ προφητεῦσαι καταβαίνει καὶ ἔρχεσθαι πρὸς τὰς ψυχὰς τὰς ἑτέρας; εἶτα μετὰ τοῦτο ἐὰν ἀποκρίνηται ὅτι Χριστὸς ἐν ᾅδου καταβέβηκεν, ἐρῶ· Χριστὸς εἰς ᾅδου καταβέβηκεν τί ποιήσων; νικήσων ἢ νικηθησόμενος ὑπὸ τοῦ θανάτου; καὶ κατελήλυθεν εἰς τὰ χωρία ἐκεῖνα οὐχ ὡς δοῦλος τῶν ἐκεῖ, ἀλλ᾽ ὡς δεσπότης παλαίσων, ὡς πρώην ἐλέγομεν ἐξηγούμενοι τὸν κα΄ Ψαλμόν· *περιεκύκλωσάν με μόσχοι πολλοί, ταῦροι πίονες περιέσχον με· ἤνοιξαν ἐπ᾽ ἐμὲ τὸ στόμα αὐτῶν, ὡς λέων ἁρπάζων καὶ ὠρυόμενος. διεσκορπίσθησαν τὰ ὀστᾶ μου.* 7. μεμνήμεθα, εἴγε μεμνήμεθα τῶν ἱερῶν γραμμάτων· μέμνημαι γὰρ αὐτῶν εἰρημένων εἰς τὸν κα΄ Ψαλμόν. οὐκοῦν ὁ σωτὴρ κατελήλυθεν σώσων· κατελήλυθεν ἐκεῖ προκηρυχθεὶς ὑπὸ τῶν προφητῶν ἢ οὔ; ἀλλ᾽ ἐνθάδε μὲν προεκηρύχθη ὑπὸ τῶν προφητῶν, ἀλλαχοῦ δὲ κατέρχεται οὐ διὰ προφητῶν; 8. καὶ Μωσῆς αὐτὸν κηρύσσει ἐπιδημήσοντα τῷ γένει τῶν ἀνθρώπων, ὥστε λέγεσθαι καλῶς ὑπὸ τοῦ κυρίου καὶ σωτῆρος ἡμῶν· *εἰ ἐπιστεύετε Μωσεῖ, ἐπιστεύετε ἂν ἐμοί· περὶ γὰρ ἐμοῦ ἐκεῖνος ἔγραψεν. εἰ δὲ τοῖς ἐκείνου γράμμασιν οὐ πιστεύετε, πῶς τοῖς ἐμοῖς ῥήμασι πιστεύσητε;* καὶ ἐπιδεδήμηκεν τούτῳ τῷ βίῳ Χριστὸς καὶ προκηρύσσεται Χριστὸς ἐπιδημῶν τούτῳ τῷ βίῳ. 9. εἰ δὲ Μωσῆς προφητεύει αὐτὸν ἐνθάδε, οὐ θέλεις αὐτὸν κἀκεῖ καταβεβηκέναι, ἵνα προφητεύσῃ Χριστὸν ἐλεύσεσθαι; τί δέ; Μωσῆς μέν, οἱ δὲ ἑξῆς προφῆται οὐχί; Σαμουὴλ δὲ οὐχί; τί ἄτοπόν ἐστι τοὺς ἰατροὺς καταβαίνειν πρὸς τοὺς κακῶς ἔχοντας; τί δὲ ἄτοπόν ἐστιν ἵνα καὶ ὁ ἀρχίατρος καταβῇ πρὸς τοὺς κακῶς ἔχοντας; 10. ἐκεῖνοι ἰατροὶ μὲν ἦσαν πολλοί, ὁ δὲ κύριός μου καὶ σωτὴρ ἀρχίατρός ἐστι· καὶ γὰρ τὴν ἔνδον ἐπιθυμίαν, ἣ οὐ δύναται ὑπὸ ἄλλων θεραπευθῆναι, αὐτὸς θεραπεύει· ἥτις *οὐκ ἴσχυσεν ὑπ᾽ οὐδενὸς θεραπευθῆναι* τῶν ἰατρῶν,

Acts as a reference to the fact that the Savior descended to hell not true? It is written that the verse in Ps 15 refers to him: "You will not abandon my soul in hell, nor will you allow your holy one to see corruption" (Ps 15:10; Acts 2:27, 31). 6. Then Jesus Christ was in hell, but are you afraid to say yes and admit that he descends there to prophesy and to go to the other souls?

Then, moreover, if he answers "Christ has descended to hell," I shall say, what has Christ descended to hell to do? Was it to conquer death or to be conquered by it? He has descended to those regions not as the servant of those who were there but as their master in order to struggle for them, as we have recently said in interpreting Ps 21: "Many young bulls have encircled me, fat bulls have surrounded me. They opened their mouths against me like a ravening and roaring lion. My bones have been scattered" (Ps 21:13–15). 7. We remember these words, at least if we remember the sacred writings. Indeed, I remember well what was said about Ps 21.

Therefore, the Savior has descended in order to save. Was his descent there proclaimed by the prophets ahead of time or not? Or is it the case that the prophets proclaimed ahead of time that he would come here but that his descent anywhere else was not announced by the prophets? 8. Moses proclaims that he would come to dwell with the human race, so that it was rightly said by our Lord and Savior, "If you had believed Moses, you would have believed me, for he wrote about me. But if you do not believe what he wrote, how will you believe what I say?" (John 5:46–47). Christ has come to dwell in this life, and Christ is proclaimed ahead of time as coming to dwell in this life. 9. If, then, Moses prophesies him here, why do you not want Moses to have descended there, too, in order to prophesy that Christ will come? What then? Moses did so, but not the prophets that followed him? Not Samuel? Why is it absurd that physicians should descend to those who are sick? Why is it absurd that the chief of physicians, too, should descend to the sick? 10. Those physicians were many (Mark 5:26), but my Lord and Savior is the chief physician. Indeed, it is he who heals the inward concupiscence that cannot be healed by others. The woman who "could be healed by no one"

Χριστὸς Ἰησοῦς αὐτὴν θεραπεύει. *μὴ φοβοῦ*, μὴ θαμβοῦ· Ἰησοῦς εἰς ᾅδου γέγονεν, καὶ οἱ προφῆται πρὸ αὐτοῦ, καὶ προκηρύσσουσι τοῦ Χριστοῦ τὴν ἐπιδημίαν. **7.** **1.** Εἶτα καὶ ἄλλο τι θέλω εἰπεῖν ἀπ᾽ αὐτῆς τῆς γραφῆς. Σαμουὴλ ἀναβαίνει, καὶ τί τῷ Σαοὺλ λέγει ἑορακέναι ἡ γυνή; οὐ λέγει ἑορακέναι ἄνθρωπον· ἔπτηξεν τοῦτον ὃν εἶδεν. τίνα ὁρᾷ; *θεοὺς ἐγώ φησιν εἶδον, θεοὺς ἀναβαίνοντας ἀπὸ τῆς γῆς*. **2.** καὶ τάχα Σαμουὴλ οὐ μόνος ἀναβέβηκεν καὶ τότε προφητεύσων τῷ Σαούλ· ἀλλ᾽ εἰκός, ὥσπερ ἐνταῦθα *μετὰ ὁσίου ὁσιωθήσῃ, καὶ μετὰ ἀνδρὸς ἀθῴου ἀθῷος ἔσῃ, καὶ μετὰ ἐκλεκτοῦ ἐκλεκτὸς ἔσῃ*, καὶ εἰσὶν ἐνταῦθα διατριβαὶ ἁγίων μετὰ ἁγίων, οὐχὶ δὲ ἁγίων μετὰ ἁμαρτωλῶν, καὶ εἰ ἄρα ποτέ, ἐστὶ τῶν ἁγίων ἡ διατριβὴ μετὰ τῶν ἁμαρτωλῶν ὑπὲρ τοῦ καὶ τοὺς ἁμαρτωλοὺς σῶσαι, οὕτω τάχα καὶ ἀναβαίνοντι τῷ Σαμουὴλ συναναβεβήκασιν ἤτοι ἅγιαι ψυχαὶ ἄλλων προφητῶν. **3.** τάχα ζητήσεις εἰ ἄγγελοι ἦσαν ἐπὶ τῶν πνευμάτων αὐτῶν (ὁ προφήτης λέγει· *ὁ ἄγγελος ὁ λαλῶν ἐν ἐμοί*) ἢ ἄγγελοι ἦσαν μετὰ τῶν πνευμάτων συναναβεβηκότες, καὶ πάντα πληροῦται τῶν δεομένων σωτηρίας καὶ *πάντες εἰσὶ λειτουργικὰ πνεύματα εἰς διακονίαν ἀποστελλόμενα*

(Luke 8:43)—Christ Jesus heals her. "Do not fear" (Mark 5:36).[27] Do not be alarmed. Jesus has been in hell, and the prophets before him, and they proclaimed ahead of time Christ's coming.

7. 1. Next I wish to say something else from this very scriptural passage. Samuel comes up, and what does the woman say to Saul she has seen?[28] She does not say that she has seen a human being. She was terrified by what she saw. What did she see? She says, "I saw gods coming up from the earth" (1 Kgdms 28:13). 2. Hence perhaps Samuel has not come up alone even then to prophesy to Saul, but in all probability, just as here in this world "you will be made holy with a holy person and will be blameless with a blameless man and will be elect with someone elect" (Ps 17:26–27), there, too, the holy associate with the holy, but the holy do not associate with sinners—even if at that time the holy were associating with sinners in order to save sinners. In the same way, perhaps, holy souls of other prophets have come up together with Samuel when he came up.[29] 3. Perhaps you will inquire whether there were angels assigned to their spirits. (The prophet refers to "the angel who speaks in me" [Zech 1:9].) Or perhaps they were angels who came up with the spirits. The whole universe[30] is filled with those who need salvation, and "all are spirits in the divine

[27] These words come from the healing of Jairus's daughter (Mark 5:21–24, 35–43) rather than from the healing of the woman (Mark 5:25–34). They serve as a direct response to the "fear" Origen predicates of his opponent (6.6; cf. 7.4).

[28] The last clause is corrupt. M and T (see the preface, page viii with n. 3) read Ἰδοὺ Σαοὺλ λέγει ἑωρακέναι ψυχήν ("behold, Saul says he has seen a soul"?). We are following Simonetti's adoption in *La Maga di Endor* of Klostermann's conjectural emendation. The Nautins' conjecture in *Origène* is: Ἰδοὺ οὐ Σαμουὴλ λέγει ἑωρακέναι ἡ γυνή, οὐ λέγει ἑωρακέναι ψυχήν ("behold, the woman does not say she has seen Samuel; she does not say she has seen a soul"; references to the Greek text in Simonetti and the Nautins may be found *ad loc.*).

[29] Following Simonetti in *La Maga di Endor*, who retains the reading of M. T, however, begins the clause with τάχα καὶ εἰ ("perhaps even if...."). The Nautins in *Origène* apparently try to take account of this and note the repetition in 7.3: τάχα ζητήσεις εἰ. Their conjectural emendation is: οὕτω τάχα καὶ <ζητήσεις> εἰ ἀναβαίνοντι τῷ Σαμουὴλ συναναβεβήκασιν ἤτοι ἅγιαι ψυχαὶ ἄλλων προφητῶν <ἢ> τάχα ζητήσεις εἰ ἄγγελοι ἦσαν ἐπὶ τῶν πνευμάτων αὐτῶν.

[30] See Nautin and Nautin, *Origène*, 194 n.2: "'whole' including hell." Perhaps the Nautins take πάντα to refer to τὰ χωρία ἐκεῖνα in 6.6. We take it to be the same as πᾶς τόπος in 7.4, which encompasses the repeated antithesis in this argument between "here" (earth) and "there" (hell).

διὰ τοὺς μέλλοντας κληρονομεῖν σωτηρίαν. 4. τί φοβῇ εἰπεῖν ὅτι πᾶς τόπος χρῄζει Ἰησοῦ Χριστοῦ; χρῄζει τῶν προφητῶν ὁ χρῄζων Χριστοῦ·
οὐδὲ γὰρ Χριστοῦ μὲν χρῄζει, τῶν δὲ εὐτρεπιζόντων Χριστοῦ παρου-
σίαν καὶ ἐπιδημίαν οὐ χρῄζει. καὶ Ἰωάννης, οὗ μείζων ἐν γεννητοῖς
γυναικῶν οὐδεὶς ἦν κατὰ τὴν τοῦ σωτῆρος ἡμῶν μαρτυρίαν λέγοντος·
μείζων ἐν γεννητοῖς γυναικῶν Ἰωάννου τοῦ βαπτιστοῦ οὐδείς ἐστιν, μὴ
φοβοῦ λέγειν ὅτι εἰς ᾅδου καταβέβηκε προκηρύσσων μου τὸν κύριον, ἵνα
προείπῃ αὐτὸν κατελευσόμενον. 5. διὰ τοῦτο, ὅτε ἦν ἐν τῇ φυλακῇ καὶ
ᾔδει τὴν ἔξοδον τὴν ἐπικειμένην αὐτῷ, *πέμψας δύο τῶν μαθητῶν* ἐπυνθάνετο, οὐχί· *σὺ εἶ ὁ ἐρχόμενος;* (ᾔδει γάρ), ἀλλά· *σὺ εἶ ὁ ἐρχόμενος, ἢ
ἄλλον προσδοκῶμεν;* εἶδεν αὐτοῦ τὴν δόξαν, ἐλάλησεν πολλὰ περὶ τῆς
θαυμασιότητος αὐτοῦ, ἐμαρτύρησεν αὐτῷ πρῶτος· *ὁ ὀπίσω μου ἐρχόμενος ἔμπροσθέν μου γέγονεν,* εἶδεν αὐτοῦ τὴν δόξαν, *δόξαν ὡς μονογενοῦς
παρὰ πατρὸς πλήρης χάριτος καὶ ἀληθείας.* 6. τηλικαῦτα ἰδὼν περὶ Χριστοῦ ὀκνεῖ πιστεῦσαι, ἀμφιβάλλει καὶ οὐ λέγει· εἴπατε αὐτῷ· *σὺ εἶ ὁ
Χριστός;* νῦν μὴ νοήσαντες γάρ τινες τὰ εἰρημένα λέγουσιν· Ἰωάννης
ὁ τηλικοῦτος οὐκ ᾔδει Χριστόν, ἀλλ' ἀπέστη ἀπ' αὐτοῦ τὸ πνεῦμα τὸ
ἅγιον. 7. καὶ ᾔδει τοῦτον, ᾧ ἐμαρτύρησεν πρὸ γενέσεως καὶ ἐφ' ᾧ ἐσκίρτησεν, ἡνίκα ἦλθεν καὶ ἡ Μαρία πρὸς αὐτόν, ὡς ἐμαρτύρησεν αὐτῷ ἡ
μήτηρ αὐτοῦ λέγουσα· *ἰδοὺ γάρ, ὡς ἐγένετο ἡ φωνὴ τοῦ ἀσπασμοῦ σου εἰς
τὰ ὦτά μου, ἐσκίρτησεν ἐν ἀγαλλιάσει τὸ βρέφος ἐν τῇ κοιλίᾳ μου.* 8. οὗτος οὖν ὁ σκιρτήσας πρὸ γενέσεως Ἰωάννης, ὁ εἰπών· *οὗτός ἐστι περὶ οὗ
ἐγὼ εἶπον· ὁ ὀπίσω μου ἐρχόμενος ἔμπροσθέν μου γέγονεν καί· ὁ πέμψας
με εἰπέ μοι· ἐφ' ὃν ἂν ἴδῃς τὸ πνεῦμα καταβαῖνον καὶ μένον, οὗτός ἐστιν ὁ
υἱὸς τοῦ θεοῦ,* οὗτος, φασίν, οὐκέτι ᾔδει Ἰησοῦν Χριστόν; ἐν κοιλίᾳ ᾔδει

service sent to serve for the sake of those who are going to inherit salvation" (Heb 1:14).

4. Why are you afraid to say that every place has need of Jesus Christ?[31] What has need of Christ has need of the prophets. No, it cannot have need of Christ yet no need of those who prepared the way for Christ's presence and coming. Even in the case of John—than whom there was no one greater among those born of women, as our Savior testifies when he says, "among those born of women no one is greater than John the Baptist" (Luke 7:28)— do not be afraid to say that he has gone down to hell to proclaim my Lord ahead of time so as to foretell that he will come down. 5. This is why, when he was in prison and knew that his departure from this life was imminent, he sent two of his disciples not to inquire, "Are you the one who is coming?" (for he knew that). Rather, he inquired, "Are you the one who is coming, or are we to expect another?" (Luke 7:18–20, Matt 11:2–3). He saw his glory; he spoke many things about his marvelous nature; he was the first to testify about him, "He who comes after me ranks ahead of me" (John 1:15). He saw his glory, "the glory as of the Father's Only Begotten, full of grace and truth" (John 1:14). 6. Though he had seen such great marvels concerning Christ, he hesitates to believe. He doubts, but he does not say, "Ask him, 'Are you the Christ?'"[32]

Now some, not understanding these statements, say, "John, as great as he was, did not know Christ, but the Holy Spirit had left him."[33] 7. John did know the one to whom he testified before his birth and in whose presence he "leaped," when even Mary came to him, as his mother testified, saying, "For as soon as the sound of your greeting reached my ears, the infant in my womb leaped for joy" (Luke 1:44). 8. Therefore, this one who leaped before his birth, John, the one who said, "This is he of whom I said, 'He who comes after me ranks ahead of me'" (John 1:15, 30), and "the one who sent me said to me, 'He on whom you see the Spirit descend and remain, he is the Son of God'" (John 1:33-34), this is the one they say no longer knew that Jesus was the Christ? Indeed, he knew him in the womb.

---

[31] See Eustathius, *On the Belly-Myther* 17.4.

[32] The question of the high priest to Jesus in Mark 14:61, the mark of an unbeliever (see Nautin and Nautin, *Origène*, 195 n. 5).

[33] A reference to Marcion and his followers (see Nautin and Nautin, *Origène*, 80 n. 1; Simonetti, *La Maga di Endor*, 87–88).

γὰρ αὐτόν. ἀλλὰ δι' ὑπερβολὴν δόξης ὅμοιόν τι τῷ Πέτρῳ πεποίηκεν. 9. τί ὅμοιον; οὗτος μέγα τι ᾔδει περὶ τοῦ Χριστοῦ. τίς εἰμι; τίνα με λέγουσιν οἱ ἄνθρωποι εἶναι; ὁ δέ· τόδε καὶ τόδε. σὺ δὲ τί; σὺ εἶ ὁ Χριστὸς ὁ υἱὸς τοῦ θεοῦ τοῦ ζῶντος· ἐν ᾧ καὶ μακαρίζεται, ὅτι σὰρξ καὶ αἷμα οὐκ ἀπεκάλυψεν αὐτῷ, ἀλλ' ὁ πατὴρ ὁ ἐν τοῖς οὐρανοῖς. 10. ἐπεὶ οὖν μεγάλα ἤκουσεν περὶ Χριστοῦ καὶ μεγάλα ὑπελάμβανεν καὶ οὐ παρεδέξατο τὴν βοὴ(ν τὴν) θείαν τὴν πρὸς αὐτόν· ἰδοὺ ἀναβαίνομεν εἰς Ἱερουσαλήμ, καὶ τελειωθήσεται καί· δεῖ τὸν υἱὸν τοῦ ἀνθρώπου πολλὰ παθεῖν καὶ ἀποδοκιμασθῆναι ἀπὸ τῶν ἀρχιερέων καὶ πρεσβυτέρων, καὶ ἀποκτανθῆναι, καὶ τῇ τρίτῃ ἡμέρᾳ ἀναστῆναι, φησίν· ἵλεώς σοι, κύριε. 11. μεγάλα ᾔδει περὶ Χριστοῦ, οὐκ ἠθέλησεν παραδέξασθαι τὸ ταπεινότερον περὶ αὐτοῦ. τοιοῦτόν τινά μοι νόει καὶ τὸν Ἰωάννην. ἐν φυλακῇ ἦν μεγάλα εἰδὼς περὶ Χριστοῦ, εἶδεν οὐρανοὺς ἀνεῳγότας, εἶδεν πνεῦμα ἅγιον ἐξ οὐρανοῦ κατερχόμενον ἐπὶ τὸν σωτῆρα καὶ μένον ἐπ' αὐτόν· ἰδὼν τὴν τηλικαύτην δόξαν ἀμφέβαλλεν καὶ τάχα ἠπίστει διὸ οὕτως ἔνδοξος καὶ μέχρις ᾅδου καὶ μέχρις τῆς ἀβύσσου κατελεύσεται· διὰ τοῦτο ἔλεγεν· σὺ εἶ ὁ ἐρχόμενος, ἢ ἄλλον προσδοκῶμεν;

8. 1. Οὐ παρεξέβην οὐδὲ ἐπελαθόμην τοῦ προκειμένου, ἀλλὰ τοῦτο θέλομεν κατασκευάσαι ὅτι, εἰ πάντες εἰς ᾅδου καταβεβήκασι πρὸ τοῦ Χριστοῦ πρόδρομοι Χριστοῦ οἱ προφῆται Χριστοῦ, οὕτως καὶ Σαμουὴλ ἐκεῖ καταβέβηκεν· οὐ γὰρ ἁπλῶς, ἀλλ' ὡς ἅγιος. ὅπου ἐὰν ᾖ ὁ ἅγιος, ἔστιν ἅγιος. 2. μήτι Χριστὸς οὐκέτι Χριστός ἐστιν, ἐπεὶ ἐν ᾅδου ποτὲ ἦν; οὐκέτι ἦν υἱὸς θεοῦ, ἐπεὶ ἐν τῷ καταχθονίῳ γεγένηται τόπῳ, ἵνα πᾶν γόνυ κάμψῃ ἐν τῷ ὀνόματι Ἰησοῦ Χριστοῦ ἐπουρανίων καὶ ἐπιγείων καὶ

Nevertheless, for the sake of Christ's surpassing glory John did something similar to what Peter did. 9. Similar in what way? Peter knew something great about Christ. Who am I? "Who do people say that I am?" (Matt 11:13; Mark 8:24). Peter said, "Different people say different things." But what do you say? "You are the Christ, the Son of the living God." Peter is blessed for this response, "because flesh and blood did not reveal it" to him, "but the Father in heaven" (Matt 16:13–17). 10. Since, therefore, he heard great things about Christ and supposed great things, but did not accept the divine proclamation addressed to him, "See we are going up to Jerusalem, and everything will be accomplished" (Luke 18:31), and "the Son of Man must undergo great suffering, and be rejected by the chief priests and elders, and be killed, and on the third day rise again" (Luke 9:22),[34] for this reason he says, "God forbid it, Lord!" (Matt 16:22). 11. Peter knew great things about Christ, but he was unwilling to accept the more humiliating prospect for him. Understand, now, that John was also such a person as this. He was in prison after he had come to know great things about Christ. He had seen the heavens opened; he had seen the Holy Spirit coming down from heaven upon the Savior and remaining on him (Matt 3:16; John 1:32–33). Since he had seen such great glory, he was in doubt and perhaps disbelieving how it could be[35] that such a glorious one would descend to hell (Ps 15:10) and to the abyss (Rom 10:7). That is why he said, "Are you the one who is to come, or are we to expect another?" (Matt 11:3).

8. 1. I have not digressed, nor have I lost sight of the argument before me. But we want to establish the fact that if all Christ's prophets, as forerunners of Christ, have descended to hell before Christ, then likewise Samuel, too, has descended there. For he did not do so in an ordinary way, but as a holy man.[36] Wherever a holy person might be, he is holy. 2. Is Christ no longer Christ at that time when he was in hell? Was he no longer the Son of God when he was in the place under the earth "so that every knee should bend at the name of Jesus Christ, in heaven and on earth

---

[34] Origen may be citing the text from memory. His version of it does not correspond exactly to any of the Synoptic versions.

[35] With Simonetti, *La Maga di Endor* (and T and M), reading διό here, rather than the emendation εἰ ὁ suggested by Klostermann and followed by Nautin and Nautin, *Origène*.

[36] Cf. the citation of Ps 17:26–27 in 7.2.

καταχθονίων; οὕτως Χριστὸς Χριστὸς ἦν καὶ κάτω ὤν· ἵνα οὕτως εἴπω, ἐν τῷ κάτω τόπῳ ὤν, τῇ προαιρέσει ἄνω ἦν. 3. οὕτως καὶ οἱ προφῆται καὶ Σαμουήλ, κἂν καταβῶσιν ὅπου αἱ ψυχαὶ αἱ κάτω, ἐν τῷ κάτω μὲν δύνανται εἶναι τόπῳ, οὐ κάτω δέ εἰσιν τῇ προαιρέσει. πυνθάνομαι δέ· ἐπροφήτευσαν τὰ ὑπερουράνια; ἐγὼ δὲ οὐ δύναμαι διδόναι δαιμονίῳ τηλικαύτην δύναμιν, ὅτι προφητεύει περὶ Σαοὺλ [Σαμουὴλ] καὶ τοῦ λαοῦ τοῦ θεοῦ, καὶ προφητεύει περὶ βασιλείας Δαβὶδ ὅτι μέλλει βασιλεύειν. 4. εἴσονται οἱ ταῦτα λέγοντες τὰ τῆς ἀληθείας τῆς κατὰ τὸν τόπον· οὐχ εὑρήσουσιν παραστῆσαι πῶς (οὐκ) ἂν καὶ ἅγιος γένοιτο ὑπὲρ σωτηρίας τῶν κακῶς ἐχόντων εἰς τὸν τόπον τῶν κακῶς ἐχόντων. 5. ἰατροὶ γινέσθωσαν εἰς τοὺς τόπους τῶν καμνόντων στρατιωτῶν, καὶ εἰσίτωσαν ὅπου αἱ δυσωδίαι τῶν τραυμάτων αὐτῶν· τοῦτο ὑποβάλλει ἡ ἰατρικὴ φιλανθρωπία. οὕτω τοῦτο ὑποβέβληκεν τῷ σωτῆρι ὁ λόγος καὶ τοῖς προφήταις, καὶ ἐνθάδε ἐλθεῖν καὶ εἰς ᾅδου καταβῆναι.

9. 1. Καὶ τοῦτο δὲ προσθετέον τῷ λόγῳ ὅτι (εἰ) Σαμουὴλ προφήτης ἦν, καὶ ἐξελθόντος ἀπέστη ἀπ' αὐτοῦ τὸ πνεῦμα τὸ ἅγιον, καὶ ἀπέστη ἀπ' αὐτοῦ ἡ προφητεία, οὐκ ἄρα ἀληθεύει ὁ λέγων ἀπόστολος· *ἄρτι προφητεύω ἐκ μέρους, καὶ ἐκ μέρους γινώσκω· ὅταν δὲ ἔλθῃ τὸ τέ-*

and under the earth" (Phil 2:10)? Thus, Christ was Christ even
when he was below; so I might put it this way: when he was in
the place below, he was above with respect to ethical purpose.[37] 3.
Likewise, both the prophets and Samuel, even if they went down
where the souls below are, are able to be in the place below but are
not below with respect to ethical purpose.[38]

And I ask you: Did they prophesy things above the heavens?
For my part I cannot give such great power to a petty demon that[39]
he [as Samuel][40] might prophesy concerning Saul and the people
of God and prophesy concerning David's kingdom, that he was
going to reign.[41] 4. Those who say these things will come to know
the matters of truth in this passage.[42] They will not find a way of
explaining away the fact that even a holy person[43] has the potential to go to the place of the sick in order to save the sick.[44] 5. Let
physicians go into the places where soldiers are suffering and let
them enter wherever the stench of their wounds fills the air. The
physician's benevolence requires this. In the same way the Word
has required this of the Savior and the prophets—both that they
should come to this world and that they should go down to hell.

9. 1. For this reason, we must add to our argument the fact
that if Samuel was a prophet, if the Holy Spirit abandoned him
when he departed from this life, and if the prophetic gift abandoned him, then the apostle is not telling the truth when he says,
"Now I prophesy in part and I know in part, but when the perfect

---

[37] See Eustathius, *On the Belly-Myther* 17.4. The term προαίρεσις refers
to ethical disposition and the capacity to choose virtue over vice. Origen fore-
stalls the objection that only evildoers are in hell.

[38] See Eustathius, *On the Belly-Myther* 17.6.

[39] Simonetti in *La Maga di Endor* retains the reading of M (ὅτι), while
Nautin and Nautin, *Origène*, follow Eustathius, *On the Belly-Myther* 24 and
read ἵνα, changing the verbs to the subjunctive.

[40] Simonetti in *La Maga di Endor* includes in brackets the reading of M
[Σαμουήλ], but this may be a correction or dittography reflecting confusion with
the name Σαούλ that directly precedes. Eustathius omits it (24.1).

[41] See Eustathius, *On the Belly-Myther*, 24.1.

[42] Compare 6.3.

[43] ἅγιος is the reading of M. The Nautins' (*Origène*) emendation is ἰα-
τρός, physician.

[44] "Fail to go" reflects Klostermann's insertion of οὐκ, which Simonetti
in *La Maga di Endor* puts in brackets but uses in his translation. The negative
presumably conforms what Origen says here to what he said in 6.9.

λειον, τότε τὸ ἐκ μέρους καταργηθήσεται. οὐκοῦν τὸ τέλειον μετὰ τὸν βίον ἐστίν. 2. καὶ εἴ τι ἐπροφήτευσεν Ἡσαΐας, ἐκ μέρους ἐπροφήτευσεν μετὰ πάσης παρρησίας· μεμαρτύρηται δὲ τὰ ἐνθάδε ὁ Δαβὶδ ἐπὶ τὸ τέλειον τῆς προφητείας. οὐκ ἀπέβαλεν οὖν τὴν χάριν τὴν προφητικὴν Σαμουήλ. ὅτι δὲ οὐκ ἀπέβαλεν, οὕτως αὐτῇ ἐχρῆτο, ὡς οἱ γλώσσαις λαλοῦντες, ὥστε ἂν εἰπεῖν· *τὸ πνεῦμά μου προσεύχεται, ὁ δὲ νοῦς μου ἄκαρπός ἐστιν;* 3. καίτοι ἐκκλησίαν οὐκ οἰκοδομεῖ ὁ γλώσσῃ λαλῶν· καὶ γὰρ λέγει ὁ Παῦλος ὅτι ἐκκλησίαν οἰκοδομεῖ ὁ προφητεύων, αὐταῖς λέξεσι λέγων· *ὁ δὲ προφητεύων ἐκκλησίαν οἰκοδομεῖ.* 4. εἰ δὲ *ὁ προφητεύων ἐκκλησίαν οἰκοδομεῖ,* εἶχεν (δὲ) χάριν προφητικὴν (οὐ γὰρ ἀπολωλέκει αὐτὴν μὴ ἁμαρτήσας· μόνος γὰρ ἀπόλλυσι χάριν προφητικήν, ὃς μετὰ τὸ προφητεῦσαι πεποίηκεν ἀνάξια τοῦ πνεύματος τοῦ ἁγίου, ὥστ' ἐγκαταλιπεῖν αὐτὸν καὶ φυγεῖν ἀπὸ τοῦ ἡγεμονικοῦ αὐτοῦ· ὅπερ ἐφοβεῖτο τότε μετὰ τὴν ἁμαρτίαν καὶ ὁ Δαβίδ, καὶ ἔλεγεν· *καὶ τὸ πνεῦμα τὸ ἅγιόν σου μὴ ἀντανέλῃς ἀπ' ἐμοῦ),* εἰ τοίνυν τὸ πνεῦμα τὸ ἅγιον προφητεύει, καὶ Σαμουὴλ προφήτης ἦν, *ὁ δὲ προφητεύων ἐκκλησίαν οἰκοδομεῖ,* τίνα οἰκοδομεῖ; 5. εἰς οὐρανὸν προφητεύει; τίνι; ἀγγέλοις, τοῖς μὴ χρείαν ἔχουσιν; *(οὐ χρείαν ἔχουσιν) οἱ ἰσχύοντες ἰατρῶν, ἀλλ' οἱ κακῶς ἔχοντες.* δέονταί τινες τῆς προφητείας αὐτοῦ· οὐ γὰρ ἀργεῖ χάρις προφητική, οὐδὲν χάρισμα ἀργεῖ τῶν ἐν τῷ ἁγίῳ. 6. τῆς οὖν χάριτος τῆς προφητικῆς αἱ ψυχαὶ τῶν κοιμωμένων (τολμήσω καὶ εἴπω) ἐδέοντο. ἀλλ' ἐνθάδε μὲν χρείαν εἶχεν τοῦ προφήτου Ἰσραήλ· καὶ ὁ κοιμώμενος δέ, ὁ ἀπηλλαγμένος τοῦ βίου, χρείαν εἶχεν τῶν προφητῶν, ἵνα πάλιν οἱ προφῆται αὐτῷ κηρύξωσιν τὴν Χριστοῦ ἐπιδημίαν.

comes, then what is in part will come to an end" (1 Cor 13:9–10). Therefore, what is perfect is after this life. 2. And if Isaiah prophesied something, he prophesied with all boldness (cf. Acts 4:29) but in part. But the testimony Samuel gives here to David extends to the perfection of prophecy. Therefore, Samuel did not jettison the prophetic gift.

And because he did not jettison it, he used it in the same way as those who speak in tongues, so that he might have said, "My spirit prays, but my mind is unproductive" (1 Cor 14:14).[45] 3. And yet the person who speaks in a tongue does not build up the church. Indeed, Paul says that the one who prophesies builds up the church, putting it in these very words: "The one who prophesies builds up the church" (1 Cor 14:4). 4. We may suppose that "the one who prophesies builds up the church" and that Samuel had the prophetic gift.[46] For he did not lose it, since he had not sinned. The only one who loses the prophetic gift is the person who after prophesying has done what is unworthy of the Holy Spirit, with the result that the Spirit forsakes him and flees from his governing mind. This is what even David feared at the time after his sin. He said, "And do not take your Holy Spirit from me" (Ps 51:11). If, therefore, the Holy Spirit prophesies and Samuel was a prophet and "the one who prophesies builds up the church" (1 Cor 14:4), then whom did Samuel build up? 5. Does he prophesy to heaven? To whom? To the angels, who have no need of it? "Those who are well have no need of a physician, but those who are sick" (Matt 9:12). Some stand in need of his prophecy, for the prophetic gift is not idle—no gift of grace is idle in those who are holy. 6. Therefore, it is the souls of the dead, I shall dare to say, who need the prophetic gift. Now here on earth Israel had need of the prophet, but also the person who has died and been delivered from this life had need of the prophets so that once again the prophets might proclaim to him the coming of Christ.

---

[45] Following the Nautins' punctuation (*Origène*). Simonetti in *La Maga di Endor* treats the sentence as a question.

[46] Simonetti in *La Maga di Endor* places these sentences (down through the quotation from Ps 51) inside parentheses; the Nautins (*Origène*) have dashes marking an *anakolouthon*. We have unpacked the extended syntax in this way to show the integral role in the wider argument of the theme of keeping and losing the prophetic spirit, begun in the case of John.

7. ἄλλως τε καὶ πρὸ τῆς τοῦ κυρίου μου Ἰησοῦ Χριστοῦ ἐπιδημίας ἀδύνατον ἦν τινα παρελθεῖν ὅπου τὸ ξύλον τῆς ζωῆς, ἀδύνατον ἦν παρελθεῖν τὰ τεταγμένα φυλάσσειν τὴν ὁδὸν τοῦ ξύλου τῆς ζωῆς· *ἔταξεν τὰ Χερουβὶμ καὶ τὴν φλογίνην ῥομφαίαν τὴν στρεφομένην φυλάσσειν τὴν ὁδὸν τοῦ ξύλου τῆς ζωῆς.* 8. τίς ἠδύνατο ὁδοποιῆσαι; τίς ἠδύνατο τὴν φλογίνην ῥομφαίαν ποιῆσαι διελθεῖν τινα; ὥσπερ θάλασσαν οὐκ ἦν (οὐδενὸς) ὁδοποιῆσαι ἢ τοῦ θεοῦ καὶ τοῦ στύλου τοῦ πυρίνου, τοῦ στύλου τοῦ φωτὸς τοῦ ἀπὸ τοῦ θεοῦ, ὥσπερ τὸν Ἰορδάνην οὐκ ἦν οὐδενὸς ὁδοποιῆσαι ἢ Ἰησοῦ (τοῦ ἀληθινοῦ Ἰησοῦ τύπος ἦν ἐκεῖνος ὁ Ἰησοῦς), οὕτω διὰ τῆς φλογίνης ῥομφαίας Σαμουὴλ οὐκ ἠδύνατο διελθεῖν, οὐκ Ἀβραάμ. 9. διὰ τοῦτο καὶ Ἀβραὰμ βλέπεται ὑπὸ τοῦ κολαζομένου, καὶ *ὑπάρχων ἐν βασάνοις ὁ πλούσιος ἐπάρας τοὺς ὀφθαλμοὺς ὁρᾷ Ἀβραάμ, εἰ καὶ ἀπὸ μακρόθεν ὁρᾷ, ἀλλ' ὁρᾷ, καὶ τὸν Λάζαρον ἐν τοῖς κόλποις αὐτοῦ.* 10. περιέμενον οὖν τὴν τοῦ κυρίου μου Ἰησοῦ Χριστοῦ ἐπιδημίαν καὶ πατριάρχαι καὶ προφῆται καὶ πάντες, ἵν' οὗτος τὴν ὁδὸν ἀνοίξῃ. *ἐγώ εἰμι ἡ ὁδός, ἐγώ εἰμι ἡ θύρα.* ὁδός ἐστιν ἐπὶ τὸ ξύλον τῆς ζωῆς, ἵνα γένηται *ἐὰν διέλθῃς διὰ πυρός, φλὸξ οὐ κατακαύσει σε.* 11. ποίου πυρός; *ἔταξεν τὰ Χερουβὶμ καὶ τὴν φλογίνην ῥομφαίαν τὴν στρεφομένην φυλάσσειν τὴν ὁδὸν τοῦ ξύλου τῆς ζωῆς·* ὥστε διὰ τοῦτο περιέμενον οἱ μακάριοι ἐκεῖ, οἰκονομίαν ποιοῦντες καὶ μὴ δυνάμενοι ὅπου τὸ ξύλον τῆς ζωῆς, ὅπου ὁ παράδεισος ὁ τοῦ θεοῦ, ὅπου θεὸς γεωργός, ὅπου οἱ μακάριοι καὶ ἐκλεκτοὶ καὶ ἅγιοι θεοῦ, γενέσθαι.

10. 1. Οὐδὲν οὖν πρόσκομμα κατὰ τὸν τόπον ἐστίν, ἀλλὰ πάντα θαυμασίως γέγραπται καὶ νενόηται οἷς ἂν ὁ θεὸς ἀποκαλύψῃ. περισσὸν δέ

7. Above all, before the coming of my Lord Jesus Christ it was impossible for anyone to pass through to where the tree of life was; it was impossible to pass through the things appointed to guard the way to the tree of life. "He appointed the cherubim and a sword flaming and turning to guard the way to the tree of life" (Gen 3:24). 8. Who was able to make a way? Who was able to make anyone pass through the flaming sword? Just as it was in no one's power to make a way through the sea save for God and the pillar of fire, the pillar of the light that comes from God (Exod 13:22; 14:24), just as it was in no one's power to make a way through the Jordan save for Joshua (that Jesus[47] was the type of the true Jesus [Josh 3:16]), thus Samuel was not able to pass through the flaming sword, nor was Abraham. 9. That is why even Abraham is seen by the man being punished and why "in his torment the rich man looks up and sees Abraham." Even if "he sees him far away," nevertheless he does see him "and Lazarus in his bosom" (Luke 16:22–23). 10. Therefore, the patriarchs, the prophets, and everyone used to wait for the coming of my Lord Jesus Christ so that he might open the way. "I am the way" (John 14:6); "I am the door" (John 10:9). He is the way to the tree of life, so that it might happen that "if you pass through fire, the flame will not consume you" (Isa 43:2). 11. What sort of fire? "He appointed the cherubim and a sword flaming and turning to guard the way to the tree of life" (Gen 3:24). Consequently, it is for this reason that the blessed used to wait there, acting on God's providential plan[48] and unable to go where the tree of life is, where the paradise of God is, where God the gardener is, where the blessed and elect and holy ones of God are.

10. 1. Therefore, there is no stumbling block in this passage. Rather, everything is marvelously written, and its meaning has been understood by those to whom God has revealed it (cf. 1

---

[47] Origen is playing on the well-known fact that in Greek the name of "Joshua ben Nun" and "Jesus" are the same, 'Ιησοῦς.

[48] οἰκονομίαν ποιοῦντες. We are following Simonetti's interpretation in *La Maga di Endor*. The Nautins translate the phrase "exceptionally" but say: "Origen means that the place of the blessed is normally in heaven and that their sojourn in hell was a provisional exception" (*Origène*, 206 n. 1). Presumably, once Christ has harrowed hell, the exception is no longer necessary.

τι ἔχομεν ἡμεῖς οἱ ἐπὶ συντελείᾳ τῶν αἰώνων ἐληλυθότες. 2. τί περισσόν; ἐὰν ἀπαλλαγῶμεν ἐντεῦθεν, γενόμενοι καλοὶ καὶ ἀγαθοί, μὴ ἐπαγόμενοι τὰ τῆς ἁμαρτίας φορτία, διελευσόμεθα καὶ αὐτοὶ τὴν φλογίνην ῥομφαίαν, καὶ οὐ κατελευσόμεθα εἰς τὴν χώραν ὅπου περιέμενον τὸν Χριστὸν οἱ πρὸ τῆς παρουσίας αὐτοῦ κοιμώμενοι· διελευσόμεθα δέ, μηδὲν βλαπτόμενοι ὑπὸ τῆς φλογίνης ῥομφαίας. 3. *ἑκάστου δὲ τὸ ἔργον ὁποῖόν ἐστι, τὸ πῦρ αὐτὸ δοκιμάσει. εἴ τινος τὸ ἔργον κατακαήσεται, ζημιωθήσεται, αὐτὸς δὲ σωθήσεται οὕτως ὡς διὰ πυρός.* διελευσόμεθα οὖν· 4. καὶ πλέον ἔχομέν τι, καὶ οὐχὶ δυνάμεθα καλῶς βιώσαντες κακῶς ἀπαλλάξαι. οὐκ ἔλεγον οἱ ἀρχαῖοι οὐδὲ οἱ πατριάρχαι οὐδὲ οἱ προφῆται, ὃ δυνάμεθα ἡμεῖς εἰπεῖν, ἐὰν καλῶς βιώσωμεν· *κάλλιον γὰρ ἀναλῦσαι καὶ σὺν Χριστῷ εἶναι.* διόπερ οὕτως ἔχοντές τι πλέον καὶ πολὺ κέρδος ἐν τῷ ἐπὶ συντελείᾳ τῶν αἰώνων ἐληλυθέναι, πρῶτοι τὸ δηνάριον λαμβάνομεν. 5. ἄκουε γὰρ τῆς παραβολῆς, ὅτι *ἀρξάμενος ἐδίδου τὸ δηνάριον ἀπὸ τῶν ἐσχάτων·* οἱ δὲ πρῶτοι ᾤοντο *ὅτι πλεῖόν τι λήψονται.* σὺ οὖν πρῶτος, ὁ ἔσχατος ἐλθών, λαμβάνεις τοὺς μισθοὺς ἀπὸ τοῦ οἰκοδεσπότου ἐν Χριστῷ Ἰησοῦ τῷ κυρίῳ ἡμῶν, ᾧ ἡ δόξα καὶ τὸ κράτος εἰς τοὺς αἰῶνας τῶν αἰώνων. Ἀμήν.

Cor 2:10; Matt 11:25–27).[49] We who have come to the completion of the ages (Heb 9:26) have something more. 2. What is this something more? If we leave this life having been virtuous and good, not weighed down by the burdens of sin, we ourselves, too, shall pass through the flaming sword and shall not go down to the place where those who died before Christ's appearance used to wait for him. And we shall pass through completely unharmed by the flaming sword. 3. "The work of each, of what sort it is, the fire will test. If anyone's work is burned up, he will suffer loss, but he himself will be saved in this way as through fire" (1 Cor 3:13, 15). Therefore, we shall pass through. 4. Indeed, we have something more, and if we have lived life well, we cannot leave it badly. Neither the ancients nor the patriarchs nor the prophets said what we can say if we have lived life well: "It is better to depart and to be with Christ" (cf. Phil 1:23). Therefore, since we have something more and great gain (cf. Phil 1:21) by having come to the end of the ages, we are the first to receive the denarius[50] (Matt 20:8). 5. Listen to the parable: he gave them the denarius, "beginning with the last," but the first were assuming that "they will receive" something "more" (Matt 20:8, 10).[51] Therefore, you who have come last are the first to receive your wages from the master of the vineyard in Christ Jesus our Lord, to whom be glory and power forever and ever. Amen.

[49] This is the hermeneutic of the "elevated sense," as promised in 2.1–2; cf. 4.1.

[50] A coin unit representing a laborer's daily wage.

[51] Simonetti's demarcation (*La Maga di Endor*) of the words that are exact quotations from Matt 20:8, 10 within Origen's paraphrase is less exact than the Nautins' (*Origène*), which we follow here.

Τοῦ ἁγίου Εὐσταθίου ἀρχιεπισκόπου Ἀντιοχείας κατὰ Ὠριγένους διαγνωστικὸς εἰς τὸ τῆς ἐγγαστριμύθου θεώρημα

1. 1. Ἀεὶ μὲν ἄγαμαι τὸν ἀξιοφανῆ τῆς ἐνθέου πολιτείας σου ζῆλον, ὦ διαπρεπέστατε τῆς ὀρθοδοξίας ἱεροκῆρυξ Εὐτρόπιε· τὸ δὲ τῆς εὐσεβείας σου γνώρισμα πολλαχῶς ἐκπληττόμενος, οὐχ ἥκιστα καὶ περὶ τόδε μάλιστα τεθαύμακα τὸ μέρος, ὅτι σαφῶς ἀκριβῶσαι βούλῃ πῶς ἂν ἔχοιμι γνώμης ἕνεκα τῆς ἐγγαστριμύθου τῆς ἐν τῇ πρώτῃ τῶν Βασιλειῶν ἱστορουμένης· 2. οὐ γὰρ ἀρέσκεσθαι φῂς οἷς ἐξέδωκεν Ὠριγένης εἰς τήνδε τὴν ὑπόθεσιν. οὐ μὴν ἀλλ’ ἔγωγε καὶ ἄλλους εὖ οἶδ’ ὅτι μεμφομένους οὐκ ὀλίγους ἐφ’ οἷς ὡρίσατο προχείρως, ἀλλὰ συχνοὶ μέν εἰσιν οἱ δακνόμενοι τὰς ψυχάς, ἀσχάλλοντες οὐ μετρίως· 3. ἔσθ’ ὅτε δέ τινες οἷς ἔγραψεν ἐκεῖνος ὑπάγονται, τῇ προλαβούσῃ δοξοκοπίᾳ ῥᾷον ἀνατιθέμενοι, καὶ τοῖς ὀνόμασι μᾶλλον, ἀλλ’ οὐ τοῖς πράγμασι προσέχοντες ὡς δέον. 4. ἵν’ οὖν μὴ δόξαιμι κατ’ ἐμαυτὸν ἀγῶνα δικανικὸν εἰσάγειν, οὐκ ἀνοίκειον ἡγοῦμαι πᾶσαν μὲν ὁμοῦ συζεῦξαι τὴν ἐξήγησιν αὐτοῦ τῇδε τοῦ γράμματος ὑπαγορίᾳ, δι’ ἑκατέρου δὲ τρανῶσαι τὸ σαφές, ὡς ἂν μήτε τινὲς οἴοιντο συκοφαντεῖν ἡμᾶς τοὺς ὁπωσδήποτε δοξάσαι προαχθέντας, μήτ’ αὖ πάλιν ἀμφηρίστους εἶναι τὰς δόξας ἑκατέρων· 5. οἷόν τε γὰρ ἐκ τῆς παραλλήλου συγκρίσεως ἀντεξετάζειν μὲν ὅπως ἔχῃ δόξης ἑκάτερα τὰ μέρη, τὴν ἀμείνονα δὲ γνώμην ἐξ ἀμφοῖν αἱρεῖσθαι τοὺς φιλολόγους. 6. οὔτε γοῦν ἵππος ἀγωνιστὴς εἶναι κρίνεται δόκιμος, ἑαυτῷ τρέχων εὐσκελῶς, οὐδ’ εἰ σφόδρα κοῦφος ὢν ὥσπερ ὑποπτέρους ἐπιδείκνυται κινήσεις, οὔτ’ αὖ τις ἀθλητῶν ὠκύτατα τρέχειν ἐν σταδίῳ δυνάμενος οὔτε ἄλλος οὐδείς,

5. Eustathius, Bishop of Antioch, *On the Belly-Myther, Against Origen*[*]

1. 1. I am in constant admiration, Eutropius, of your reputable zeal for a godly way of life, you most distinguished and holy preacher of orthodoxy. Though I have often been struck by the marks of your piety, it is not the least of my marvels that you wish to ascertain clearly what opinion I might have about the belly-myther whose story is told in the first book of Kingdoms. 2. For you say that you are not satisfied with what Origen has published on this subject. For my part I know that there are not a few others who find fault with what he has set down so off-handedly. But there are a great many people who are vexed in their souls and distressed beyond measure, 3. while some are led astray by what he wrote, readily retreating under the influence of his earlier bid for popularity and focusing their attention on "names" and not on facts, as they should. 4. Therefore, lest I should appear to be introducing a forensic suit on my own behalf, I consider it not unsuitable to yoke together his entire interpretation with my explanation of the text and through each to make evident the plain sense.[1] This may keep some from supposing that we are making false accusations against people anywhere who have been persuaded to hold Origen's opinions; nor will they suppose that the opinions of each side are equally contestable. 5. For it is possible to carry out the investigation by a side-by-side comparison of how both sides stand in their opinions and for scholars to choose the better opinion from the two. 6. Indeed, no competitive racehorse is judged approved, however well-gaited, when it runs by itself—not even if it is exceptionally nimble and displays its moves as though on wings. This is also true of any athlete who can run swiftest in the stadium and of anyone else—the supple wrestler

---

[*] The full title is "A Critical Investigation on the Subject of the Belly-Myther, Against Origen."

[1] Eustathius apparently means that he is attaching a copy of Origen's homily (or homilies) to his treatise.

οὔτε παλαίων ὑγρῶς, οὔτε τραχύτατα παγκρατιάζων ἢ πυγμαχῶν, ἢ τὸν **ἀέρα δέρων** ἑωροκοπίαις ὑποκένοις· 7. ἀλλὰ συσταδὸν ἁρμόττει τὰ μαχόμενα τοῖς ἐναντίοις ἀντιστατεῖν, ἵν' ἐξ ἑνὸς ὁποτέρου διαγινώσκηται τὸ προὖχον. ὥστε τὰ μὲν Ὠριγένεια προτακτέον ἐν πρώτοις, ἰδίᾳ δὲ τάξει καὶ τὸν ἀντιπίπτοντα νοῦν ἐκείνοις ἐξετάσαι σπουδαστέον.

2. 1. Φέρε γοῦν αὐτὸ τὸ τῆς ἱστορίας γράμμα θεωρήσωμεν ὡς οἷόν τε κατὰ τὸ ἐφικτόν· ἐνθένδε ποθὲν ἀρκτέον. ὁπηνίκα μὲν ὁ Σαοὺλ ἄριστα προΐστατο τῆς τοῦ λαοῦ πολυανδρίας, ἐξῆρε πάντας τοὺς ἐγγαστριμύθους, ἔφη, καὶ τοὺς οὕτω καλουμένους ὀνόματι γνώστας, ἅτε δὴ λυμεῶνας ἐμφωλεύοντας ἐχθίστους. 2. ἐπειδὴ δὲ τραπεὶς ἐπὶ τὰ χείριστα πρὸς τοῦ ἀλιτηρίου πικρῶς ἠλαύνετο δαίμονος, ᾤχετο πάλιν ἐπὶ τὰ φάσματα τῆς μαντείας αὐτῶν, οἰκοδομῶν μὲν ὅσα κατέλυσεν ὀλίγῳ πρόσθεν, ἑαυτὸν δὲ καὶ διὰ τούτου παραβάτην ἐλέγχων. 3. ὡς γὰρ οἱ πέριξ ἀλλογενεῖς ὁμοθύμῳ σπουδῇ πολέμου γένεσιν ἀνεκήρυττον, ἀθροισθέντες μὲν ὡς ἔνι μάλιστα παμπληθεὶ τὰς φάλαγγας ἀντιπαρέταττον, ὅπλα δὲ γυμνώσαντες εἰς μάχην ἐξῆεσαν εὐρώστως. ὁ μέντοιγε σχέτλιος ἔδεισε Σαούλ, αὐτὸ τὸ τῆς παρεμβολῆς ἐπιτείχισμα πεφραγμένον ἰδὼν αὐτοφεί, καὶ τὸ σύμπαν εἰπεῖν **ἐξέστη** καταπλαγείς, ὡς ἡ θεία διαγορεύει γραφή. 4. μετὰ δὲ τοῦτο, φησίν, **ἠρώτα διὰ τοῦ κυρίου,** γνῶναι δηλαδὴ τὰ πρακτέα γλιχόμενος· **ὁ δὲ κύριος οὐκ ἀπεκρίνατο** τὸ παράπαν αὐτῷ διὰ τὰς τῆς ἀδικίας ὑπερβολάς, **οὔτε ἐν ἐνυπνίοις οὔτε ἐν δήλοις οὔτε ἐν τοῖς προφήταις,** ἀλλὰ μὴν ἐκείνῳ γε τὸ θεῖον οὐκ ἐχρημάτιζεν οὐδαμῶς, ἀθέμιτα δράσαντι. 5. τί δὲ μετὰ ταῦτα πράττει, τῆς ἀνωτάτω γυμνωθεὶς ἐπικουρίας; ἀντὶ τοῦ μᾶλλον ἐξιλεώσασθαι συχνοτέρα δεήσει καὶ καρτερᾷ ψυχολατρείᾳ, τοὐναντίον ἀποπηδήσας αὔξει μὲν τὰ τῆς ἀποστασίας ἐπιτηδεύματα, τοῖς δὲ παισὶν αὐτοῦ προσέταττεν γυναῖκα ζητήσειν ἐγγαστρίμυθον, ἵνα ἀφίκοιτο πρὸς αὐτὴν πευσόμενος ὡς ἐν μαντείῳ.

and the pancratiast or all-sport contestant[2] who fights the rough-
est, or the one who "beats the air" (1 Cor 9:26) with vain motions.
7. On the contrary, the contests unite them in close quarters to
stand against their opponents so that the superior of the two may
be determined. Thus, Origen's interpretations must be set forth
first, and then, in proper order, we must pay serious attention to
examining the interpretation that opposes them.

2. 1. Come, then, let us look at the very letter of the narrative as it is within our grasp to do so. This is the point from which
one should begin. When Saul was presiding well over the popu-
lous nation, scripture says that he expelled all the belly-mythers
and those who were called diviners, since these corrupters, lurking about, were much hated (1 Kgdms 28:3). 2. When, however,
he took a turn for the worse and was harshly carried away by the
vengeful demon, he went rushing back to the illusions of their divinatory art, thereby building up what he had shortly before torn
down and convicting himself also in this way of being a trans-
gressor (cf. Gal 2:18). 3. For when the foreigners round about
proclaimed with united zeal the beginning of war, after assembling
in a single great multitude, they drew up their troops in opposition
and baring their weapons went forth to battle with great might. To
be sure, the wretched Saul became frightened when he saw with
his own eyes that the enemy embattlement of his camp had been
set in place and, to put it succinctly, was "consumed by panic" (1
Kgdms 28:5), as the divine scripture relates. 4. After this, since he
longed to know clearly what should be done, he "inquired of the
Lord." But "the Lord did not answer him" at all because of the
magnitude of his wickedness—"not by dreams, or by portents,[3] or
by prophets" (1 Kgdms 28:6). Indeed, the divinity gave him absolutely no oracular response, since he had committed lawless deeds.
5. Thus stripped of aid from on high, what did he do next? Instead
of making greater supplications by longer prayers and more fer-
vent soul-searching, on the contrary he turned away and added to
his deeds of apostasy. He ordered his servants to seek out a woman
who was a belly-myther so that he might go to her in order to in-

---

[2] Following Declerck, *Eustathii Antiocheni Opera*, who retains the reading of M: παγκρατιάζων ἢ παμμαχῶν, treating the two words as synonyms.
Simonetti in *La Maga di Endor* adopts Klostermann's emendation of the last
word: πυγμαχῶν.

[3] δήλοις. The Hebrew is "Urim."

6. τῶν δὲ δὴ χειρίστων ὑπηρετῶν αὐτίκα δὴ μάλα καταμηνυσάντων τὴν ἔμπληκτον, ὁ μὲν Σαοὺλ ἀμελλητὶ μετασχηματίσας ἑαυτὸν καὶ τὰ τῆς ἐσθῆτος ἀμείψας ἐνδύματα δρομαῖος ᾤχετο, τὴν στρατιὰν ἐκλιπών. ὡς δὲ ἀφίκετο πρὸς αὐτὴν ἅμα δυοῖν ἀνδράσι νύκτωρ, ἀξιώσεις αὐτῇ προσεφέρετο τηνικαῦτα, **μάντευσαι δή μοι λέγων ἐν τῷ ἐγγαστριμύθῳ καὶ ἀνάγαγέ μοι φησὶν ὃν ἂν εἴπω σοι.** 7. τοιγαροῦν, εἴπερ ὁ Σαοὺλ ἐδεῖτο διὰ τῆς ἐγγαστριμύθου μαντεύσασθαι, φαίη τις ἂν ἀληθεῖς εἶναι τὰς ἐκείνου φωνάς. ἀλλ᾽ ἔστι τις ἀγνοῶν ὡς ἐκεῖνος ὑπὸ τοῦ δαίμονος ἀγρίοις ἠλαύνετο θυμοῖς, εἰς ἀνηκέστους ἐκτραπεὶς μαντείας καὶ διαβολικὰς μύθων ἐνεργείας; 8. τί γάρ; οὐκ ἀξιόπιστος μᾶλλόν ἐστιν ὁ θεὸς ὁ τοὺς μὲν λόγους εἰς τὸ στόμα τοῦ Βαλαὰμ ἐμβαλών, ἐπιτρέψας δὲ Μωσεῖ γράψαι ῥητῶς ἐν τοῖς Ἀριθμοῖς· **οὐ γάρ ἐστιν οἰωνισμὸς ἐν Ἰακώβ, οὐδὲ μαντεία ἐν Ἰσραήλ**; 9. εἰ τοίνυν ἀπαγορευτέα τὰ τοιάδε καθέστηκεν, οἷα δὴ βδελύγματα μυσερὰ καὶ τῆς ἐχθίστης εἰδωλολατρείας αἴτια, πῶς ἂν εἴη φερέγγυος [ὁ] μάρτυς ὁ τούτοις ἀνοσιώτατα χρήσασθαι πειραθείς; ἀλλὰ ταῦτα μὲν ὀλίγον ὕστερον ἐπαναλαβόντες ἐντελέστερον ἐροῦμεν· ἐπανιτέον δὲ πάλιν εἰς τὴν τοῦ γράμματος ἱστορίαν.

3. 1. Ὡς οὖν ἡ γυνὴ τὸν ἔκφρονα Σαοὺλ ἐθεάσατο, πλαττομένη μὴ εἰδέναι τὸν δυνάστην ἀνθυπέφερεν ὡς αὐτὸς ἄμεινον ἂν εἴη γινώσκων ὅσα πεποιήκει τοῖς περὶ ταῦτα δεινοῖς ὁ Σαούλ, **ὡς ἐξωλόθρευσε τοὺς ἐγγαστριμύθους ἔφη καὶ τοὺς ἐκφωνοῦντας ἀπὸ τῆς γῆς** 2. ἕνεκα δὲ τούτου **παγιδεύσασθαι** πρὸς αὐτοῦ τὴν ψυχὴν ἔφασκεν εἰς θάνατον. ἐπειδὴ δὲ πιστωσάμενος ὅρκῳ διεβεβαιώσατο μηδὲν αὐτὴν ὑποστῆναι σκαιόν, αὖθις ἐπιρρωσθεῖσα τῇ κακίᾳ παρρησιέστερον ἀποκρίνεται δήπουθεν ἡ γυνή· **τίνα φησὶν ἀναγάγω σοι;** 3. ποταπὴ καὶ ὁποία καὶ τίς ἡ κακοδαίμων ἐτύγχανεν αὕτη γραῦς, ἵνα ὑπόσχηται τὸν Σαμουὴλ ἐκ νεκρῶν ἀνάξαι; καὶ μήν, εἴ γε δεῖ τὸ τῆς ἀξίας ὑπερθεμένους εἰπεῖν, οὐχ ὁπωσοῦν ἠδύνατο προφητικὴν ἀνάξαι ψυχήν, ἀλλ᾽ οὐδὲ τῶν ἐπιτυχόντων οὐδενὸς οὐδ᾽ ὅλως, ἀλλ᾽ οὐδὲ μύρμηκος ἢ ψύλλης. οὐ γὰρ οἱ δαίμονες ἐξουσίαν ἔχουσιν

quire of her by divination (1 Kgdms 28:7). 6. When the servants, utter knaves, informed him at once of the mad woman, Saul without delay disguised himself and changed his clothes, and went off at a run, leaving the army behind. When he reached her at night together with two men, he then kept pressing her with the request, saying, "Divine for me by the belly-myther. Bring up for me," he said, "the one whom I name to you" (1 Kgdms 28:8). 7. To be sure, since Saul placed the request to receive divination through the belly-myther, someone could say that his words were true. But is there anyone who does not know that when Saul turned to deadly divination and the diabolic operations of myths,[4] he was being driven to savage rages by the demon? 8. What then? Is not God more worthy of belief—God, who put words into the mouth of Balaam and entrusted Moses to write expressly in Numbers: "For there is no augury in Jacob, nor any divination in Israel" (Num 23:23)? 9. Therefore, if such things as loathsome abominations and causes of hateful idolatry are established as prohibited acts, how could the witness who had tried to use such impious means be credible? But we shall take up these matters again a little later and shall speak more fully of them. Now we must turn back to the narrative as it is written.

3. 1. When, therefore, the woman saw Saul, who was out of his mind, maintaining a fiction that she did not recognize her ruler, she answered that he would better know "how many things Saul had done" to those skilled in such matters. She told him "how he had annihilated the belly-mythers and those who give oracles from the earth." 2. Because of this she said that he was "laying a snare" for her life to bring about her death (1 Kgdms 28:9). When Saul pledged by an oath and affirmed that she would suffer no harm, it was the woman, presumably, who, encouraged toward the evil act, answered more openly and said, "Whom shall I bring up for you?" (1 Kgdms 28:11). 3. What kind of woman and what kind of evil demon was this old crone that she promised to bring up Samuel from the dead? Indeed, even if we must in speaking pass over the matter of her worth, not only was she not able to bring up a prophet's soul but not even that of any ordinary person—not even that of an ant or a flea! For demons do not have authority over

---

[4] The first of many references to the meaning of the belly-myther's name. "Myths" are formed in her "belly" by demonic agency.

πνευμάτων τε καὶ ψυχῶν, ἀλλ' ὁ πάντων ὁμοῦ δεσπόζων θεός· ὥστε τῇ
θείᾳ δοτέον φύσει μόνῃ ἐξ ᾅδου μεταπέ μπεσθαι καὶ πάλιν ἀνακαλεῖσθαι
ψυχάς. 4. ἀλλ' ὁ κομψὸς Ὠριγένης, εἰδωλολατρείας ὄργανα καὶ νεκυο-
μαντείας εὑρήματα τῷ τῆς ἐκκλησίας ἐθέλων ἐπεισκυκλῆσαι χορῷ, τοῦ
θείου καταψεύδεται γράμματος. αὐτῆς γάρ τοι τῆς γραφῆς ἀναφανδὸν
ἐκβοώσης ὡς εἶπεν ἡ γυνὴ *τίνα ἀναγάγω σοι;* τοὐναντίον ἀντιστρέψας
οὗτος, "τὸ πρόσωπον," ἔφη, ταῦτα εἰρηκέναι "τοῦ ἁγίου πνεύματος."
5. εἶτα τοσοῦτον ἐξετράπη παρασυρείς, ὥστε οὐκ ἐρυθριᾷ τῷ ἁγίῳ πε-
ριτιθέναι πνεύματι τὰ τῆς ἐπιλήπτου ῥήματα· τοιαῦτα δὲ γυμνοτέρᾳ τῇ
γλώττῃ βλασφημῶν, εἰς τὸ πνεῦμα τὸ ἅγιον ἀναφέρει τὸ πᾶν, ἀξιοπίστῳ
τοὺς αὐτηκόους ὀνόματι καταιδέσαι πειρώμενος. 6. ἤρετο μὲν οὖν, ὡς
ἔφην, ἡ γυνή, καὶ καθάπερ ἐξουσίαν ἔχουσα τοῦ μεταπέμπεσθαι τοὺς νεκροὺς ἐκφωνεῖ· *τίνα φησὶν ἀναγάγω σοι;* τοῦ δὲ μαντευομένου φήσαντος
ἀναχθῆναι *τὸν Σαμουήλ,* αὖθις ἐπιφέρει· *καὶ εἶδεν ἡ γυνὴ τὸν Σαμουὴλ*
ἔφη *καὶ ἐβόησεν φωνῇ μεγάλῃ καὶ εἶπεν τῷ δυνάστῃ διὰ τί παρελογίσω*
με; καὶ σὺ εἶ Σαούλ. 7. ὡς δὲ ὁ βασιλεὺς ἔφησεν αὐτῇ *μὴ φοβοῦ* καὶ τὸ
τί ἑόρακας; ἐπάγει προσθείς, αὖθις ἀνθυπενέγκασα πάλιν ἡ πυθόμαντις
ἔφη· *θεοὺς ἑόρακα ἀναβαίνοντας ἐκ τῆς γῆς.* ἐπειδὴ δὲ καὶ τὸ τελευταῖον
ὁ δυνάστης ἤρετο, *τί ἔγνως;* εἰπών, αὐτίκα πάλιν ἀνθυπήνεγκε πρὸς ἔπος
ἄνδρα ὄρθιον ἀναβαίνοντα ἐκ τῆς γῆς, καὶ οὗτος ἀναβεβλημένος διπλο-
ίδα. 8. τί οὖν ἐπὶ τούτοις ἡ θεία διαγορεύει γραφή; *καὶ ἔγνω Σαοὺλ ὅτι*
Σαμουήλ ἐστιν οὗτος, καὶ ἔκυψεν ἐπὶ πρόσωπον αὐτοῦ ἐπὶ τὴν γῆν καὶ
προσεκύνησεν αὐτῷ. φαίνεται τοίνυν ὡς οὐδαμοῦ τὸ παράπαν ἡ τοῦ θείου
γράμματος ἔφησεν ἐκδοχὴ τὸν Σαμουὴλ ἀνῆχθαι διὰ τῆς ἐγγαστριμύθου·
9. ἀλλ' αὐτὴ μὲν προηγουμένως διὰ τοῦ ἐκβακχεύοντος αὐτὴν δαίμονος

spirits and souls, but the one who is Lord of all at once—God. As a result, the capacity to summon and to call souls up again from hell must be granted to the divine nature alone. 4. But that ingenious Origen, wishing to pile up instruments of idolatry and inventions of necromancy one after another on the chorus of the church, lies against the divine text. Indeed, even though scripture itself cries out quite openly that it was the woman who said "Whom shall I bring up for you?" turning it around in the opposite fashion, he said that *the persona of the Holy Spirit* has spoken it.[5] 5. Swept away, then, he was so far diverted from the right path that without a blush he attributes to the Holy Spirit the words of a woman caught up in a fit. Uttering such blasphemies with a naked tongue, he refers the whole thing to the Holy Spirit, attempting to shame those who heard it themselves by appeal to a trustworthy name. 6. As I have said, the woman posed the question and, as though she had power to summon the dead, exclaimed, "Whom," it says, "shall I bring up for you?" But after Saul, who was seeking the divination, said "Samuel is to be brought up," the narrative continues in turn, "and the woman saw Samuel," it said, "and she cried out with a loud voice and said" to the ruler, "Why have you deceived me? Indeed, you are Saul!" 7. When the king said to her, "Have no fear" and "What have you seen?" the narrative continues, and then the Pythian prophetess[6] spoke once more in reply, "I have seen gods coming up from the earth." When the ruler asked for the last time, saying, "What have you come to know?" she immediately replied to his statement, "A man coming up from the earth standing, and he is wrapped in a double cloak." 8. What, then, does the divine scripture relate after this? "And Saul knew that this was Samuel, and he bowed with his face to the ground and worshiped him" (1 Kgdms 28:12–14). Therefore, it is clear that nowhere at all has the plain sense[7] of the divine text said that Samuel was brought up through the agency of the belly-myther. 9. Rather, she proleptically declares through the agency of the de-

---

[5] Origen, *Hom. 5 on 1 Kgdms* 4.2–3.

[6] See Plutarch, *Def. orac.* 414E, where we learn that belly-mythers are "now" called *Pythones*. See below 11.8 and Eustathius's use of Acts 16:16.

[7] ἐκδοχή, literally "succession," in reference to texts means "interpretation" or "understanding in a certain sense" (LSJ, 505; *PGL*, 427). See also 4.5; 16.11; 21.2, 4, 11.

ἀποφθέγγεται δεῖν ἀνάγειν αὐτόν· εἶτα καὶ θεοὺς ἀνιόντας ἐπικομποῦσα θεωρεῖν, ἀπάτῃ μὲν ἐδίδου τὰ σημεῖα τἀνδρὸς εἰς ἐνέδραν, ὁ δὲ παράφρων ἔγνω Σαοὺλ ἐξ ὧν ἀκήκοεν ὡς αὐτὸς οὗτός ἐστι Σαμουήλ.

4. 1. Εἰ δὲ δεῖ πιστεύειν ἢ τῷ δαιμονιζομένῳ Σαοὺλ ὡς ἀληθῆ γνώσεως ἠκριβωκότι κατάληψιν, ἢ δαίμονι καυχωμένῳ καὶ ψυχὰς ὑπ- ισχνουμένῳ δικαίων ἐξ ᾅδου μεταπέμπεσθαι, κρίνωμεν παρ' ἑαυτοῖς ὅσης ἂν εἴη γε δυσφημίας ἀνάπλεα ταῦτα καὶ τὰ τοιαῦτα νοεῖν, ὦ κράτιστε ἀν- δρῶν Εὐτρόπιε· 2. πολὺ γάρ, ὡς ἔοικεν, Ὠριγένης τῆς ἀληθείας ἐσφάλη, καίτοι τοῦ δεσπότου ἡμῶν Ἰησοῦ περὶ τοῦ διαβόλου διαρρήδην εἰρηκό- τος *ἐκεῖνος ἀνθρωποκτόνος ἦν ἀπ' ἀρχῆς, καὶ ἐν τῇ ἀληθείᾳ οὐχ ἕστηκεν, ὅτι ἀλήθεια οὐκ ἔστιν ἐν αὐτῷ. ὅταν λαλῇ τὸ ψεῦδος, ἐκ τῶν ἰδίων λα- λεῖ, ὅτι ψεύστης ἐστὶν καὶ ὁ πατὴρ αὐτοῦ.* 3. τί τοίνυν φής, ὦ Ὠρίγενες ἀνάγκη γὰρ ἐρέσθαι σε; πότερον ἀληθῆ ταῦτά ἐστιν ἅπερ ἔφρασεν ὁ σω- τήρ, ἢ τοὐναντίον ἀνθυποφέρων ἐρεῖς; εἰ μὲν οὖν ἀληθεῖς οἱ τοῦ κυρίου τυγχάνουσι λόγοι, εἰωθότως ἄρα ὁ δαίμων ἐψεύσατο θρασυνόμενος· εἰ δὲ ἀψευδῆ τὰ τοῦ δαίμονος ὁρίζῃ ῥήματα, ψεύστην ἀποφῆναι τὸν κύριον ἐγ- χειρεῖς. 4. ὁρᾷς εἰς ὅσην ἐκπέπτωκεν ἀτοπίαν ὁ παρὰ σοὶ δογματιζόμενος ὅρος; ἄκοντες μὲν γὰρ ἔσθ' ὅτε τἀληθῆ λέγειν οἱ δαίμονες ἀναγκάζονται στρεβλούμενοι τοῖς πόνοις, οὐ μὴν ἑκόντες ἀψευδῶς εἴποιεν ἂν ὁτιοῦν. εἰ δὲ δὴ καὶ δικαίους ἀνάγειν ἐξ ᾅδου τοῦτον ὁριεῖταί τις ἀμελλητί, πῶς οὐκ ἄν γε εἴη σαφὲς ὡς ἀπάτῃ τὸ ψεῦδος ἀντεισάγει, βουλόμενος ἐκτραχηλιάσαι τινά; 5. ναί, φησίν, ἀλλ' οὐχ ὁ δαίμων ταῦτα εἴρηκεν, ἀλλ' ἡ διηγηματικὴ τοῦ συγγραφέως φωνή· συγγραφεὺς δὲ τῶν λόγων

mon raging with frenzy in her[8] that it is necessary to bring him up.
Then, boasting that she saw gods, too, coming up, she was deceitfully giving telltale signs of the man to trick him. And Saul, since
he was out of his mind, "knew" from what he had heard that this
was Samuel himself (1 Kgdms 28:14).

4. 1. If one must believe either Saul, who was possessed by
a demon, supposing him to have had an accurate and true grasp
of knowledge, or a demon who boasted and promised to summon
even the souls of the righteous from hell, let us judge for ourselves,
most excellent Eutropius, what great magnitude[9] of blasphemy it
is to think these and similar things. 2. For Origen, as it seems, has
stumbled far from the truth, despite the fact that our Lord Jesus
Christ said quite explicitly of the devil, "He was a murderer from
the beginning and does not stand in the truth, because there is no
truth in him. When he speaks a lie, he speaks according to his own
nature, for he is a liar and the father of the lie" (John 8:44). 3. Now
what do you say, Origen?[10] (For it is necessary to question you.)
Which is it: Are these words that the Savior spoke true, or will
you contradict them in your reply? If, therefore, the Lord's words
happen to be true, then the demon, as is his custom, boldly lied.
But if you affirm that the demon's words were not false, you are
attempting to declare the Lord a liar. 4. Do you see to how great
an absurdity the proposition that you teach has led? There are, of
course, times when the demons quite unwillingly are compelled to
tell the truth by being painfully tortured, but willingly, however,
they would not say anything whatsoever without lying. If, then,
someone will without hesitation affirm that this demon brings up
even righteous people from hell, how would it fail to be clear that
he is deceitfully introducing a lie in his wish to overthrow someone? 5. "Yes," Origen says, "but the demon has not spoken these
words; rather, it was the narrative voice of the author. And the

---

[8] M reads ἐκβακχεύοντος αὐτή. We are following Declerck, *Eustathii
Antiocheni Opera*, who adopts in a modified way Klostermann's emendation:
ἐμβακχεύοντος <ἐν> αὐτῇ. Simonetti's emendation in *La Maga di Endor* is: ἐμβακχεύοντος αὐτήν.

[9] Following Declerck, *Eustathii Antiocheni Opera*, who emends ἀνάπλεα
to ἀνάπλεον to avoid understanding the text to mean "to think these and similar
things filled with blasphemy."

[10] Following the punctuation of Declerck, *Eustathii Antiocheni Opera*,
rather than Simonetti's in *La Maga di Endor*.

εἶναι πεπίστευται τὸ πνεῦμα τὸ ἅγιον, ἀλλ' οὐκ ἄνθρωπος. εἶτ' οὐ νοεῖ πῶς ἐναντία φαίνει τῇ τοῦ διηγήματος ἐκδοχῇ; 6. κάλλιον γοῦν ἴσασιν οἱ παντοίοις σχολαιότερον ὁμιλήσαντες λόγοις ὡς ἡ διηγηματικὴ τοῦ συγγραφέως ὁμιλία ταῦτα ἐξέδωκεν, ἅπερ ἐδόκει πράττειν ἢ λέγειν τῷ μαντευομένῳ Σαοὺλ ἡ ἐγγαστρίμυθος· ἀμέλει περὶ ἐκείνης ἐκδιηγούμενος ὁ συγγραφεὺς καὶ τοὺς λόγους αὐτῆς ἐπὶ λέξεως ἐκτιθέμενος ἔφη *καὶ εἶπεν ἡ γυνή· τίνα ἀναγάγω σοι;* 7. τίς δὲ οὕτως εὐήθης ἐστὶν ὡς ὑποκρίνεσθαι μὴ νοεῖν ὅτι αὗται μὲν τοῦ συγγραφέως οὔκ εἰσιν αἱ φωναί, τῆς δὲ δαιμονώσης εἰσὶ γυναικός, ἧς καὶ τοὔνομα προὔταξεν; οὐδαμοῦ μέντοι βεβαιοῖ τοὺς λόγους αὐτῆς ὡς ἀληθεῖς, οὐδέ τις ἂν εἴη γε τοῦτο δεικνύναι δυνάμενος οὐδαμῶς. 8. ἀλλὰ μήν, εἴ γε δεῖ φιλαλήθως εἰπεῖν, ἡ διηγηματικὴ <φωνὴ> τοῦτο ἔφησε μόνον ὡς *εἶδεν ἡ γυνὴ τὸν Σαμουήλ.* οὕτω δὲ ταῦτα ἔγραψεν ὡς πρὸς εἰδότας περὶ δαιμονώσης ὁμιλῶν. οὐ γὰρ ἔστιν ἀμφισβητεῖν ὅτι δαίμων οὐκ ἀνάγει ψυχὴν οὐδενός, ὃς ὑπὸ τῶν εὐσεβῶν ἐξορκιζόμενος ἀνθρώπων ἐλαύνεται, πυροῦται, μαστίζεται καὶ φεύγει, τὸ σκήνωμα προλιπών. 9. ἀλλ' εἶδεν ἡ παραπλὴξ ὡς ἔπρεπεν αὐτῇ τὸ σχῆμα τῆς πεφαντασιοκοπημένης ὄψεως. εἴωθε γοῦν ὁ θὴρ εἰς πολυπροσώπους ἑαυτὸν ἐξαλλάττειν ἰδέας, ἵνα δὲ κατὰ τὸν ἁγιοφανῆ Παῦλον ἀποφθεγξάμενος εἴποιμ' ἄν· *αὐτὸς γὰρ ὁ σατανᾶς μετασχηματίζεται εἰς ἄγγελον φωτός· οὐ μέγα οὖν, εἰ καὶ οἱ διάκονοι αὐτοῦ μετασχηματίζονται ὡς διάκονοι δικαιοσύνης.*

10. Ὁ δὲ δογματιστὴς Ὠριγένης ὡς πρὸς ἐναντίους δικανικῇ δεινότητι διαλεγόμενος ἔταξεν μὲν καὶ τόδε τὸ χωρίον, οἰόμενος ἐκ τούτου περιγράφειν τοὺς τὴν ἀλήθειαν ἀντεισάγοντας, ἀτεχνίᾳ δὲ μᾶλλον ἢ τέχνῃ δοκῶν ἀνασκευάζειν αὐτὸ προσετίθει· 5. 1. καὶ "διὰ τί," φησίν, "οὐκ εἴρηται· εἶδεν ἡ γυνὴ δαιμόνιον ὃ προσεποιεῖτο εἶναι Σαμουήλ; ἀλλὰ

author of the words is believed to be the Holy Spirit—not a human being."[11] Does he not, then, understand how contradictory to the sense of the narrative his view appears? 6. Indeed, those who have spent more time becoming conversant with a wide range of literature know better that the narrative discourse of the author has put down these things that the belly-myther appeared to do or say to Saul, who seeks a divinatory word. Of course, the author, because he was telling a story about her and setting out her words in a style appropriate to her, said, "And the woman said, 'Whom shall I bring up for you?'" 7. Who is so simple-minded as to pretend not to understand that these are not the statements of the author but of the woman who was acting under demonic influence? Even her name brought this to the forefront. Nowhere does the author confirm her words as true, nor would anyone be able to prove this in any way at all. 8. To be sure, if we must at least speak as lovers of truth, the narrative voice[12] did make this one statement, to the effect that the woman "saw Samuel" (1 Kgdms 28:12). But the author said this on the assumption that he was conversing with people who know about a woman acting under demonic influence. Now it is impossible to dispute the fact that a demon does not bring up anyone's soul. A demon, when exorcized by pious people, is driven out, burned, whipped, and flees, leaving his dwelling behind. 9. But the mad woman saw, as was suitable for her, the shape of the vision she had conjured up. The monster, indeed, is accustomed to change himself into the form of many different people, so that I may say, speaking plainly in agreement with the saintly Paul, "Even Satan changes his form into an angel of light. So it is not strange if his ministers also change their form into ministers of righteousness" (2 Cor 11:14–15).

10. But that dogmatician Origen, arguing against his opponents with the skill of a trial lawyer, cited this passage, too,[13] thinking by it to circumvent those who were opposing him with the truth. Then, supposing he would refute it by artlessness[14] rather than by art, he adds, **5. 1.** *Why, then,* he says, *does it not say, "The woman saw a petty demon who was pretending to be Samuel"?*

---

[11] Origen, *Hom. 5 on 1 Kgdms* 4.2–4.

[12] Following Declerck, *Eustathii Antiocheni Opera*, who accepts Klostermann's insertion of "voice" on the basis of Origen, *Hom. 5 on 1 Kgdms* 4.4.

[13] Origen, *Hom. 5 on 1 Kgdms* 4.7.

[14] ἀτεχνίᾳ, that is, "artlessly rather than by the *ars rhetorica*."

γεγράφθαι," πρὸς ἐπὶ τούτοις ἔφησεν, "*ἔγνω Σαοὺλ ὅτι Σαμουήλ ἐστιν·*"
εἶτα πάλιν ἐπιφέρει προϊών· "εἰ μὴ ἦν Σαμουήλ, ἔδει γεγράφθαι· καὶ
ἐνόμιζεν Σαοὺλ εἶναι αὐτὸν Σαμουήλ. 2. νῦν δὲ γέγραπται· *ἔγνω Σαούλ.*
οὐδεὶς δὲ ἔγνω τὸ μὴ ὄν· ἔγνω οὖν *Σαοὺλ ὅτι Σαμουήλ ἐστιν καὶ ἔπεσεν*
ἐπὶ πρόσωπον ἐπὶ τὴν γῆν καὶ προσεκύνησεν αὐτῷ." ἵνα δὲ μὴ παρεκβὰς
ἐφ' ἕτερα τῶν παραδειγμάτων—ἐξ αὐτῶν ὧν ἔγραψεν ἐνταῦθα ποιήσο-
μαι τὴν ἐρώτησιν, εἶθ' οὕτως ἐπὶ τὰ λοιπὰ βαδιοῦμαι παραδείγματα.
3. καί μοι λέγε πρὸς θεοῦ· τί φῄς, ὦ 'Ωρίγενες; πότερον ἡ γυνὴ τὸν
Σαμουὴλ ἀνήγαγεν αὐτῷ σώματι ἤ τί γε σχῆμα σκιαγραφίας εἴδει περιβεβλημένον; εἰ μὲν οὖν ἀσώματον ἀνήγαγεν αὐτόν, οὐκ ἄρα τὸν Σαμουὴλ
ἀνέστησεν, ἀλλὰ πνεύματος ἰδέαν· ὁ γὰρ ἐκ ψυχῆς καὶ σώματος ἡρ-
μοσμένος οὗτός ἐστι Σαμουήλ, ὁ ἄνθρωπος ὁ κρᾶσιν ἔχων ἐξ ἀμφοῖν
ἀνάλογον. 4. εἰ δὲ ὁλόσωμον αὐτὸν ἀνήγαγεν τὸν ἄνδρα, πῶς οὐχ ἑόρακεν
αὐτὸν ὁ Σαούλ; εἰ γὰρ ἦν αὐτοψεὶ θεασάμενος αὐτόν, οὐκ ἂν ὡς ἀβλε-
πτῶν ἐξήταζε τὴν γυναῖκα, φάσκων αὐτολεξεὶ τὸ *τί ἑόρακας;* οὐκοῦν
εἰ μὲν ἀόρατος ἦν, ἀναμφίλογον ἀσώματος ἦν· εἰ δὲ ἀσωμάτῳ σχήματι
διεφαίνετο, τί δήποτε τοὐναντίον ἔφραζεν ἡ πυθόμαντις, ἑορακέναι μὲν
ἄνδρα ὄρθιον ἐκ τῆς γῆς ἀναβαίνοντα, διπλοΐδα δὲ κατὰ τὸ πρόσθεν ἔθος
ἀναβεβλημένον; 5. ἆρ' οὖν αὐτὰ τὰ πράγματα μάχεταί σου τοῖς λόγοις,
'Ωρίγενες· ὁ μέν γε Σαοὺλ οὐδὲν ὅλως ἑορακὼς ὡς περὶ φαντάσματος
ἀοράτου διαλεγόμενος ἐπυνθάνετο τὸ *τί ἑόρακας;* εἰπών, ἡ δὲ τοὐναντίον ὡς αὐτὸν ἄνθρωπον ἰδοῦσα κέκραγεν *ἄνδρα ὄρθιον ἀναβαίνοντα ἐκ*
τῆς γῆς, ὑπὲρ δὲ τοῦ πεῖσαι ὡς αὐτὸς ἄνθρωπός ἐστι, δίδωσιν αὐτῷ καὶ
σημεῖον ἐπιφθεγξαμένη *καὶ οὗτος ἀναβεβλημένος διπλοΐδα.* 6. τί οὖν, ὦ
τῆς ἀθεμίτου μαντείας ὑποθήμων, εἴπερ ἐτύγχανεν ἀνήρ, οὐκ εἶδεν αὐτὸν
ὁ Σαούλ; ἐκτὸς εἰ μή τι καὶ τὸ αἰσθητὸν ὄμμα τυφλώττειν αὐτὸν εἴποις,
ὥσπερ οὖν ἀμέλει καὶ τὸ τῆς ἐννοίας αὐτὸ τὸ νοητόν.

Moreover, he said that in addition to this, *it is written, "Saul knew that it was Samuel."* Then a little later he again goes on to say, *If it were not Samuel, it ought to have been written, "And Saul was under the impression that it was Samuel."* 2. *But what it now says is, "Saul knew." And no one knows that which does not exist. "So Saul knew that it was Samuel and bowed with his face to the ground and worshiped him."*[15] In order not to digress onto other examples, I shall formulate my questioning from the things he has written here, and then I shall proceed to the other examples. 3. Now, tell me in the presence of God, what do you say, Origen? Is it the case that the woman brought up Samuel in his very body, or was it some figure wrapped in the appearance of an illusion? Now, if she brought him up without a body, then it was not Samuel that she raised up, but the form of a spirit. For Samuel is a being composed of soul and body, since a human being has a proportionate mixture of both. 4. But if she brought the man up with his entire body, how is it that Saul has not seen him? For if he had seen him with his own eyes, he would not have quizzed the woman as though he did not see, saying in these exact words: "What have you seen?" Therefore, if Samuel was invisible, he was without a doubt bodiless. And if he had been transparent, in a bodiless form, why in the world would the Pythian prophetess say the opposite, namely, that she had seen "a man coming up from the earth standing, wrapped," as was his former custom "in a double cloak" (1 Kgdms 28:14)? 5. Therefore, the facts themselves fight against your words, Origen. Saul, since he had seen nothing at all, inquired as though speaking about an invisible phantom and said, "What have you seen?" And she, as though she had seen the man himself, cried out the opposite, "a man coming up from the earth standing." And in order to persuade Saul that it was the very man, she gives him also a sign by adding to her response: "and he is wrapped in a double cloak." 6. Why, is it then, Origen—you counsel for lawless divination—if it really were a man, that Saul did not see him? Surely you would not claim, would you, that he was blind in physical sight, also, just as he undoubtedly was in spiritual insight?[16]

---

[15] Origen, *Hom. 5 on 1 Kgdms* 4.7.

[16] Following the punctuation of Declerck, *Eustathii Antiocheni Opera*. Simonetti in *La Maga di Endor* does not make the sentence a question. Note that νοητός can mean "spiritual interpretation," as opposed to αἰσθητός, "literal" (*PGL*, 917E).

6. 1. Ἀλλ' ἴσως ἐρεῖς ἁλισκόμενος εὐπετῶς· αὐτὸ τὸ τῆς ψυχῆς ὄργανον ἀνθρωπόμορφον ἐσχηματίζετο κατὰ τὴν ὥραν, ἵνα ἐπιφανὲν ἐξείποι προφητικῷ μηνύματι τὸ μέλλον, οἷα δὴ κατὰ τοὺς ὕπνους ἐνίοτε πνεύματα καὶ ψυχαὶ τοῖς ἀνθρώποις ἐφίστανται, παμμελεῖ τοὺς ἀνθρωπείους ἐπιδεικνύμεναι χαρακτῆρας, οὐ μὴν ἀλλά γε καὶ διάφορα καὶ ποικίλα φοροῦντες ἐσθήματα καὶ σημασίας οὐλῶν ἢ τύπων ἢ μωλώπων ἐπιφερόμενοι καὶ πληγῶν ἢ τρώσεων. 2. εἰ τοίνυν ὁρίζῃ ψυχὴν ἀνῆχθαι μόνον, ἀλλ' οὐκ ἄνθρωπον αὐτῷ σώματι οὐδὲ γὰρ εἰ βούλῃ δίδωσί σοι τὸ γράμμα, μαχόμενα μὲν ἑαυτῷ θεσπίζων οὐκ αἰσθάνῃ, ταὐτὸν δὲ τοῦτό τις ἀνθυποφέρων ἐρεῖ σοι· τί δήποτε οὐκ εἶπεν ἡ γυνή· προφητικὴν εἶδον ψυχήν, ἀλλὰ τοὐναντίον ***ἄνδρα ὄρθιον***; 3. ᾧ γὰρ ἔφησθα τρόπῳ· "καὶ διὰ τί," λέγων, "οὐκ εἴρηται· εἶδεν ἡ γυνὴ δαιμόνιον ὃ προσεποιεῖτο εἶναι Σαμουήλ;" τούτῳ τῷ λόγῳ φαίην ἂν ἀνθυπενέγκας ἔγωγε· τίνος ἕνεκα ψυχῆς ἀναχθείσης οὐκ εἴρηκεν ἑορακέναι ψυχήν, εἴπερ οὕτως εἶχεν, ἀλλ' ἐκ τῶν ἐναντίων ***ἄνδρα*** καὶ τοῦτον ***ὄρθιον,*** ὅπερ ἐστὶ γνώρισμα σωματικῆς εὐεξίας; 4. οὐ γὰρ ἀμφίκυρτον οὐδὲ κεκυφότα γέροντα θεωρεῖν ἔφασκεν ἡ μαινάς, ἀλλ' ὄρθιον, ἐντεταμένον, ἀπηυθυμένον εἰς πόλεμον, ἀεὶ νεάζοντα περὶ τὰς τῆς κακίας ἀναδόσεις· ἀπάτη δὲ τὸν ἔκφρονα δελεάζουσα, σημείῳ μὲν ἔπειθεν αὐτὸν ὡς ἄνθρωπός ἐστιν ὁ ἀνιὼν ἐκ τῆς γῆς, ***ἀναβεβλῆσθαι*** δὲ αὐτὸν ἔφαινε ***διπλοΐδα.*** 5. τί οὖν εἴποι τις ἄν, εἴπερ αὐτῷ σώματι προκύπτων ἐτύγχανεν ἀνήρ, οὐκ ἄρα ἑόρακεν αὐτὸν ὁ Σαούλ, ἀλλὰ παρ' ἑτέρου βούλεται μαθεῖν ὁποῖός ἐστιν, ὡς ἀορασίᾳ πληγείς; οὐκοῦν αὐτὰ τὰ πράγματα κέκραγεν ὡς ἄνθρωπος μὲν οὐκ ἦν, ἀλλὰ σκιά τις ὡς ἔοικεν ἀφανής· οὐ γὰρ ἂν ἀόρατος ἦν. 6. εἰ δὲ νομίζεις, Ὠρίγενες, ὅτι ψυχὴ τοῦ Σαμουὴλ ἐτύγχανεν αὐτόθι, διὰ τί διπλοΐδα περιβεβλημένον ἑωρᾶτο τὸ φάσμα; προδήλῳ γοῦν ἐκφαίνεται σημασίᾳ ὡς ἅπαντα τὰ τῆς ἐσθῆτος ἐνδύματα καὶ σκεπάσματα σώμασι πλέον, ἀλλ'

6. 1. But caught, now, so readily in this trap, perhaps you will say that the very instrument of the soul was in the habit of taking shape in human form according to age, so that by its appearance the soul might foretell the future by prophetic foreshadowing. For example, sometimes in dreams spirits and souls appear to mortals, displaying the characteristics suited to human beings with all their members. Not only that, but they wear all sorts of different clothes and bear the signs of scars, beatings,[17] or bruises, even of blows or wounds. 2. Therefore, if you assert that only the soul was brought up but not the person with the body itself—though even if you want it to, the letter of scripture does not grant you the point—do you not perceive that you are laying down decrees that fight against themselves? Someone will respond to you with your very own objection. Why in the world did the woman not say, "I saw a prophetic soul" instead of the opposite, "a man standing"? 3. For by the tactic you appealed to when you said *why did not scripture say, "The woman saw a petty demon who was pretending to be Samuel,"*[18] by that same argument I should say in reply, why, if the soul was brought up, did she not say she had seen a soul, if that is what it was? But on the contrary, she said "a man" and him "standing," which is a characteristic mark of bodily health. 4. The mad woman did not say she saw an old man, bent over or stooping, but a man standing, on alert, arrayed for battle, and ever young in his concern for requiting evil. Trapping demented Saul by deceit, she persuaded him with a sign, that what was coming up from the earth was a man, and she made it known that he was "wrapped in a double cloak." 5. "What, then," someone might say, "if the man happened to emerge with his very body, would not Saul have seen him rather than, as though struck with blindness, have wished to learn what sort of man he was from someone else?" Therefore, the facts themselves cry out that it was not a human being but, as it seems, some kind of unseen shadow. For a human being would not have been invisible. 6. But if you suppose, Origen, that Samuel's soul happened to be right there, why was the apparition seen wrapped in a double cloak? Surely it is clear by obvious indications that all garments and coverings used

---

[17] Following Simonetti in *La Maga di Endor*, who accepts Klostermann's emendation: τύπων. Declerck, *Eustathii Antiocheni Opera*, retains the reading of M: κτύπων, "crash, bang, din."

[18] Origen, *Hom. 5 on 1 Kgdms* 4.7.

οὐ ψυχαῖς ἁρμόττει· 7. οὐ γὰρ οἴομαί σε φῆσαι μεθ᾽ ὑποκρίσεως ἀστα-
ϊζόμενον ὅτι μεμένηκεν ἡ διπλοῖς ἐπὶ τοῦ τάφου τοσούτοις ἔτεσιν ἄχρι
τῆσδε τῆς ἡμέρας, ἵνα ἡ ψυχὴ τοῦ προφήτου φορῇ, μή πῃ ἄρα γυμνὴ
βαδίζουσα διάγοι. καίτοιγε φαίη τις ἂν ὡς οὐδεὶς ἔοικεν ἀγνοεῖν ὅτι τοῖς
ἁγίοις ἀδιάφθορα πάρεστιν οὐρανόθεν ἐνδύματα φεγγοβόλοις ἐκλάμποντα
μαρμαρυγαῖς, ἀλλ᾽ οὐκ ἐσθῆτος ὑφάσματα ποικίλης εὐδιάφθορα. 8. εἰ δὲ
τὴν τοῦ Σαμουὴλ ὁρίζῃ ψυχὴν μὲν εἶναι τὴν ὀφθεῖσαν, ἱμάτιον μέντοι
φῇς ἱερατικὸν ἑορᾶσθαι κατὰ ἔννοιαν, ἵν᾽ ὁ τῆς ἱερουργίας ἔκδηλος εἴη
τρόπος ἀμφότερα δὲ ταῦτα νοητῶν ἐστι πραγμάτων ἴδια, συνέστηκεν
ὡς οὐδὲν ὑγιὲς οὐδὲ ἀληθὲς ἀπήγγελλεν ἡ μαινάς· 9. ἕτερα γὰρ ἔλεγεν
παρὰ τὰ ὄντα, τὰ τῶν αἰσθητῶν ὀνόματα παραφέρουσα καὶ τὰ νοητὰ
διαδεικνύουσα πράγματα. *ἄνδρα* γοῦν *ὄρθιον* ὀνομάζουσα καὶ περιβολῆς
ὑφαντὸν ἔσθημα χειρότευκτον, ἀόρατον ἐκ τῶν ἐναντίων εἰσῆγε πνεῦμα
φαντασιῶδες.

7. 1. Εἰπὲ τοίνυν, ὦ βέλτιστε δογματιστά, πῶς ἔγνω Σαοὺλ ὡς
αὐτὸς οὗτος ἐτύγχανε Σαμουήλ, ὁπηνίκα μηδὲ σκιᾶς εἶδεν μόριον, οὐχ
ὅπως ἀνδρὸς ἰδέαν; ἀλλ᾽ οὐκ ἐρυθριᾷς εἰρηκώς· "ἔδει γεγράφθαι· καὶ
ἐνόμιζε Σαοὺλ εἶναι αὐτὸν Σαμουήλ. νῦν δὲ γέγραπται· *ἔγνω Σαούλ*." 2.
εἶτα ὅτι μὲν ὁ δαιμονιζόμενος ἔγνω παρὰ δαιμονώσης ἀκούσας, ἄνω καὶ
κάτω λέγεις· ὅτι δὲ οὐδὲ ὅλως ἐθεάσατο, σιγῇ τὸ γράμμα κρύπτεις. 3.
οὐδαμοῦ δὲ δὴ παραφέρεις ἐν μέσῳ τὸν ἔλεγχον, ἀφελεῖς μὲν οἰόμενος
ἐξαπατᾶν ἀνθρώπους, εὕρημα δὲ μαντείας ἐπιτειχίζων ἅπασιν ἀσεβοῦς· ἡ
γάρ τοι τοῦ δαιμονιζομένου γνῶσις ἀξία τοῦ κηρύγματος ἐτύγχανεν ἐκείνης τῆς καὶ τοὺς λόγους αὐτῷ διακονούσης. 4. ἀλλ᾽ ἐπιστήμῃ καὶ συνέσει
φαίης ἂν ὡς ἔγνω μὴ θεασάμενος, ἀλλ᾽ οὐκ ἐνόμισεν· ἕκαστος γοῦν ἀνθρώπων ἀκοῇ μᾶλλον ἢ ὄψει πρᾶγμα παραλαβὼν οἴεται καὶ νομίζει,
τὸ σαφὲς οὐκ εἰδώς, ἄλλως τε κἂν ὑπὸ δαιμονῶντος ἀκούοι προσώπου·

for clothing are fitted to the body rather than to souls. 7. For I do not suppose you would in pretence speciously aver that the double cloak had remained upon the grave so many years until that very day, so that the prophet's soul could wear it lest he might go walking around naked. To be sure, someone might say that no one is likely to be ignorant of the fact that imperishable clothing from heaven, shining with flashing rays of light, is ready for the saints—not a varied wardrobe of garments that easily perish. 8. If you affirm that it was Samuel's soul that was seen, you would say as a consequence that his priestly cloak was seen in a spiritual way so that the fashion of priestly service would be manifest. (For both of these things are proper to spiritual matters.) If so, then it is established that the mad woman proclaimed nothing sound nor true. 9. For she was saying things other than what is really the case, allegedly pronouncing the names of perceptible things and indicating spiritual matters. For by naming "a man standing" and a hand-woven outer garment, she was representing an invisible and imaginary spirit from terms that denote the opposite.

7. 1. Tell me, then, my fine dogmatician, how did Saul know that this indeed was Samuel when at that time he did not even see a small part of a shadow, much less the form of a man? But you do not blush for having said *It ought to have been written, "And Saul was under the impression that it was Samuel," but as it is, it is written, "Saul knew."*[19] 2. Moreover, you say before and after this that the demon-possessed man "knew" because he heard from a woman acting under demonic influence, but you hide by your silence what the text actually says—that he saw absolutely nothing at all. 3. Nowhere do you bring forward any refutation of this point, supposing you will deceive simple people and fortifying for everyone the invention of impious divination. Indeed, the knowledge of the demon-possessed man is only worth as much as the proclamation of the woman who served the words up for him. 4. But you might say that even though he had not seen, he knew by understanding and comprehension (cf. Job 12:16) and it was not the case that he was "under an impression." Yet at any rate each person who grasps a fact by hearing rather than by sight thinks and forms an impression but does not know what is clearly the case, especially if he hears it from a person who is acting under demonic influence.

[19] Origen, *Hom. 5 on 1 Kgdms* 4.7.

μόνα γὰρ τὰ τοῦ θεοῦ βεβαιοῦνται ῥήματα πρὸς ἀκριβῆ κατάληψιν καὶ πίστεως ὀχυρότητα. 5. καὶ μὴν εἰ περὶ τῶν ἀνθρώπων ἔφησεν ὁ μελογράφος· *ἐγὼ εἶπα ἐν τῇ ἐκστάσει μου· πᾶς ἄνθρωπος ψεύστης* πόσῳ δὴ μᾶλλον, εἰ περὶ γυναικὸς ἐκδιηγοῖτό τις ἔκφρονος; εἶτα λέγεις ὅτι "οὐδεὶς ἔγνω τὸ μὴ ὄν," οἷα μειρακίοις ἄντικρυς ὁμιλῶν. 6. εἰπὲ τοίνυν πῶς ἔγνω τὸ ὄν, εἴπερ αὐτὸς οὐκ ἐθεάσατο πυνθανόμενος οὐ τὸν ἄνδρα τὸν ὄρθιον, οὐ τὸ ἐφοὺδ ὃ περιεῖχεν, οὐ τὸ ἀρχιερατικὸν ἱμάτιον; ἀλλ' ὁ οὐδὲν οὐδαμόθεν ὁρῶν ὑποκένοις ἀνερριπίζετο λόγοις, ὥσπερ οὖν ἀμέλει καὶ σὺ κουφολογίᾳ τοὺς ἀστάτους ἀναπτεροῖς. 7. ἀλλ' ὁ μὲν ἱστοριογράφος ὄνομα προθεὶς ἐγγαστριμύθου πρῶτον ἐδήλωσεν τὸ πρόσωπον ὁποῖόν ἐστιν, ἐμμανές. εἶθ' οὕτως αὐτὸ τὴν ὀπτασίαν ἑορακέναι διέγραφεν, ὡς πρέπει τοῖς εὖ φρονοῦσιν περὶ τοῦ παραπεπληγμένου νοεῖν· οὐδεὶς γὰρ ἂν ὑπολάβοι φρενοβλαβῆ τινα τὰ δέοντα θεωρεῖν. 8. ὁμοίῳ δὲ τρόπῳ καὶ τὸν ἔκφρονα Σαοὺλ ἔφησεν ἐγνωκέναι μαντευόμενον, ὡς ἄξιον ἂν εἴη περὶ ἐκείνου γε νοῆσαι τοῦ τοσαύταις ἐτῶν περιόδοις ἐλαυνομένου πικρῶς ὑπὸ τοῦ δαίμονος.

8. 1. Ἀλλὰ μὴν ὅτι γε ταῦτα τοῦτον ἔχει τὸν τρόπον αὐτὰ τὰ πράγματα βοᾷς ἀφίησιν ἐναργεῖς. ἵνα δὲ καὶ ἀφ' ἑτέρου τὰ ὅμοια συστήσαιμι παραδείγματος, φέρε τὴν ἐπὶ Ἡλίου τοῦ προφήτου προσαγάγωμεν ἱστορίαν. 2. ὁπηνίκα τοίνυν Ἡλίας ἐνθέῳ διήλεγχε ζήλῳ τοὺς ψευδοπροφήτας ὀκτακοσίους ὄντας πρὸς τοῖς πεντήκοντα τὸν ἀριθμόν, ἠξίου μὲν ἐν θυσίᾳ τὴν ἑκατέρων ἀντεξετάζεσθαι τάξιν, μηδένα δὲ πῦρ ἐπάγειν, ἀλλ' εὐχαῖς ἐπάγεσθαι πυρὸς ἐπιφοράν, ἵνα ἐκ τοῦ κατακομπαζομένου μετεώρου οὐρανόθεν ἔκδηλος μὲν ἂν εἴη πᾶσιν ὁ ἐπακοῦσαι δυνάμενος ἔμφλογι πυρὸς ἀποστολῇ θεός, ἐκ δὲ τούτου διαγινώσκηται τίς ἡ τοῦ

For only the words of God are confirmed for accurate understanding and rock-solid credibility. 5. If indeed the psalmist said of men, "I said in my consternation, 'Every man is a liar'" (Ps 115:2), how much more would one make such a judgment about a demented woman?[20] Then you say that *no one knows that which does not exist*,[21] as though you were conversing outright with schoolboys. 6. Tell me, then, how did he know what existed if when he inquired he did not see the man standing or the ephod he wore or the high-priestly robe? Rather, this man who saw nothing from any direction scattered empty words to the winds, just as you also doubtless give wings to unstable people by your thoughtless talk. 7. But the story-writer by setting forth the name "belly-myther" first disclosed the persona of this character[22] for what she was— mad. Then he went on to describe the persona that had seen the vision in a way appropriate for people of sound mind to understand that it was about a deranged woman. For no one would suppose that a brain-damaged woman would see what one ought to see. 8. In a similar fashion with the madman, Saul, the writer said that he "knew" when seeking divination, since it would be sufficient for readers to understand that this was about a man who was driven harshly by a demon for so many courses of years (1 Kgdms 10:9–13; 16:14–23).

8. 1. Moreover, the facts themselves cry out clearly that this is the fashion in which these events took place. Let me draw similar conclusions on the basis of another example. Let us, then, introduce the story of Elijah the prophet (3 Kgdms 18:19–40). 2. Now when Elijah, with a divinely inspired zeal, was refuting the false prophets, 850 in number, he asked that the arrangements of each station for the sacrifice be placed side by side and that fire be put to neither, but instead that the kindling of fire should be made by prayers, so that on the basis of airborne fire brought down from heaven the God who is able to hear might be made manifest to all by sending flames of fire. In this way it might be

---

[20] The word in the psalm is ἄνθρωπος ("man" or "human being"), but the logic of Eustathius's "from the greater to the lesser" argument appears predicated on the assumption that a woman would be more likely to be a liar than a man, so we translate it as "man" here.

[21] Origen, *Hom. 5 on 1 Kgdms* 4.7.

[22] πρόσωπον, "character," "person," or "persona" (the key term in Origen, *Hom. 5 on 1 Kgdms* 4.2–3).

κρείττονος ἐξουσία, καὶ πᾶσι φανερὸν ἂν εἴη γε τὸ ἄμεινον. 3. ὡς οὖν ἐπέταττε πρώτοις ἐπιτελεῖν ἐκείνοις, οἱ μὲν ἐπιλεξάμενοι βοΐδιον ἐμέλιζον εἰωθότως, ἐπικαλούμενοι δὲ δὴ τὸ τετράμορφον ἐμμελέτημα τοῦ καλουμένου Βάαλ οὐδὲν ἧττον ἔπραττον, οὐδὲν οὐδαμῶς. οὐ μὴν ἀλλά γε *καὶ κατετέμνοντο κατὰ τὸ ἔθος αὐτῶν μαχαίραις* ἔφη *καὶ σειρομάσταις ἕως ἐκχύσεως αἵματος.* 4. εἶτα ἐπὶ τούτοις ἡ διηγηματικὴ τοῦ συγγραφέως ἐπιφέρει βοή· *καὶ προεφήτευον ἕως παρῆλθε τὸ δειλινόν.* ἐπεὶ τοίνυν οὐ διέστειλε τὸ γράμμα πότερον ἀληθῆ προὐφήτευον ἢ ψευδῆ, παρὰ τοῦτο φαίη τις ἂν ἐκείνους εἶναι προφήτας ἀληθεῖς; 5. ἔδει γὰρ εἰρηκέναι κατὰ τὴν Ὠριγένους ἀπόφασιν· ἐπροεφήτευον ὡς ᾤοντο τῷ δοκεῖν, μηδὲν ἀληθὲς λέγοντες ἐπεὶ μηδὲ θέμις <λέγειν> ἐμπολιτεύεσθαι ἐν αὐτοῖς πρόγνωσιν, ἀλλ᾽ οὐκ ἀνεπιπλόκῳ καὶ καθαρᾷ προφωνῆσαι λέξει *καὶ προεφήτευον ἕως παρῆλθε τὸ δειλινόν.* 6. ἆρ᾽ οὖν ἀκολούθως ἐκ τῆς αὐτῆς τοῦ γράμματος ἱστορίας ἔστιν ἰδεῖν ὅτι ταῦτα ἐκείνοις ἐπέοικεν· εἰ γὰρ ὁ αὐτός ἐστιν ἑκατέρου ὁ συγγραφεύς, ὅμοιον ἐξ ἀμφοῖν ἀνάγει τὸν νοῦν. 7. ἀλλ᾽ ὥσπερ ἐνταῦθα τὸ τῶν εἰδωλολατρῶν ὄνομα προτάξας ἐδήλωσεν κατὰ ἔννοιαν ὅτι χρὴ περὶ τῶν τοιούτων ὑπολαμβάνειν ὡς εἰσὶν ψευδοπροφῆται λειπόμενοι προγνώσεως, οὕτω κἀκεῖ πρόσωπα δαιμονιζόμενα προτάξας καὶ μαντείας ἀθεμίτου δράματα, κατὰ ἀποσιώπησιν ἐμήνυσεν τί δέοι περὶ τῶν ἐκφρόνων δοξάζειν τοὺς ἔμφρονας.

determined what power the stronger divinity had, and the superior would be obvious to all. 3. Then when he ordered them to complete their sacrifice first, they selected their calf and cut it in pieces according to their custom, and, calling upon the tetramorphic idol of the one called Baal, they accomplished nothing less than nothing at all. Not only that, but scripture says, "as was their custom, they cut themselves with swords and lances until the blood gushed out" (3 Kgdms 18:28). 4. The narrative cry of the author[23] then continues, "They prophesied until the afternoon had passed" (3 Kgdms 18:29). Therefore, since the text of scripture did not define precisely whether they prophesied things that were true or false, would anyone say because of this that they were true prophets? 5. For the text ought to have said, according to Origen's negative rule,[24] "In appearance they prophesied as they saw fit, though they said nothing true (since foreknowledge is not a lawfully naturalized practice among them)." Instead, the text proclaims in words that are uncomplicated and clear, "They prophesied until the afternoon had passed." 6. Therefore, does it not follow that we can see from the very letter of the narrative that this case is just like the former?[25] For if it is the same author writing both passages, he draws out a similar sense from both. 7. Just as here, by first setting forth the name of the idolaters, he disclosed the meaning that it is necessary to assume that such people are false prophets lacking in foreknowledge; in exactly the same way in 1 Kgdms 28, by first setting forth the personae possessed by demons and the acts of unlawful divination, he indicated precisely by deliberate omission[26] what people in their right minds ought to think about those who are out of their minds.

---

[23] ἡ διηγηματικὴ τοῦ συγγραφέως βοή. Declerck, *Eustathii Antiocheni Opera*, treats the expression as a citation of Origen's homily, but there is no exact equivalent. Origen (*Hom. 5 on 1 Kgdms* 4.2) refers to the διηγηματικὸν πρόσωπον and the πρόσωπον τοῦ συγγραφέως; he also speaks (4.4) of the διηγηματικὴ φωνή and (4.8; 6.2) of the πρόσωπον τῆς γραφῆς. It seems more likely that Eustathius is simply paraphrasing Origen by using a common expression that conflates his various locutions for this same idea.

[24] That is, Origen's insistence that, if his opponents' view were correct, scripture would have been differently worded to make this clear (see Origen, *Hom. 5 on 1 Kgdms* 4.7).

[25] Following Declerck, *Eustathii Antiocheni Opera*, who makes the sentence a question, unlike Simonetti in *La Maga di Endor*.

[26] Eustathius's explanation predicates of the author of scripture the rhetorical figure ἀποσιώπησις.

9. 1. Ἀλλὰ τὰ τοιαῦτα μὲν εἰ παραφέροιμι μαρτύρια, τάχα ἴσως ὁ χρόνος ἡμᾶς ἐπιλείψει λέγοντας· ἄλλην δὲ μίαν παραδείγματος εἰκόνα προσθεὶς ἀρκεσθήσομαι. τοιγαροῦν ἐν τῷ τῆς Ἐξόδου κατασεσήμανται προγράμματι πῶς ἐπέταττε τοῖς ἀμφὶ Μωσέα καὶ Ἀαρὼν αὐτὸς ὁ κύριος εἰς ἔδαφος ἐκρίψειν τὴν ῥάβδον ἀντικρὺ Φαραώ, ἵνα εἰς ὄψιν ἀμείψασα τὸ σχῆμα σημείῳ καταπλήξοι φοβερῷ τοὺς Αἰγυπτίους. 2. ὡς δὲ τοῦτο ἐγίνετο παραδόξως, ὁ δυνάστης ἀνοίᾳ φενακιζόμενος ἀβούλῳ συνεκαλέσατο μὲν ὁμόσε *τοὺς σοφιστὰς καὶ τοὺς φαρμακοὺς Αἰγύπτου. ἐποίησαν δὲ καὶ οἱ ἐπαοιδοὶ τῶν Αἰγυπτίων ἔφη ταῖς φαρμακείαις αὐτῶν ὡσαύτως, καὶ ἔρριψεν ἕκαστος τὴν ἑαυτοῦ ῥάβδον, καὶ ἐγένοντο δράκοντες· καὶ κατέπιεν ἡ ῥάβδος Ἀαρὼν τὰς ἐκείνων ῥάβδους.* 3. ἔτι γε μὴν ἀναφερόμενόν ἐστιν ὡς αἷμά τε καὶ βατράχους *ἐποίησαν οἱ ἐπαοιδοὶ τῶν Αἰγυπτίων ὡσαύτως.* ἐπεὶ οὖν ἡ διηγηματικὴ μηδὲ δεῦρο διαιρεῖ φωνὴ τὰς ἑκατέρων τάξεις, ὡσαύτως δὲ καὶ τοὺς ἐπαοιδοὺς ἐξεῖπεν πεποιηκέναι, παρὰ τοῦτο φαίη τις ἂν ὅτι τὰ δεδραμένα τοῖς φαρμακοῖς ὅμοια τοῖς διὰ Μωσέως γενομένοις ἐστίν. 4. οὐ μὲν οὖν, εἴποι τις ἄν, ἀλλ' οὐδὲ θεμιτὸν ἂν εἴη λέγειν ὡς ἐξομοιοῦται τὰ περίεργα καὶ γοώδη τοῖς οὐρανίοις ἀπομιμήμασιν. ὅσα μέν γε διὰ Μωσέως ἐπράττετο τὴν ἀλήθειαν ἐκ τῶν δρωμένων ἐξέφαινεν, ὅσα δ' αὖ διὰ τῶν ἐπαοιδῶν ἐκαττύετο, τῷ δοκεῖν ἐφάνταζε τὰς ὄψεις· αὐτοτελῆ γὰρ ἔλεγχον ἐκ τῆς ἀδρανείας ἐπεφέρετο τὸ ψεῦδος, ἐπεὶ πῶς ἡ μία κατέπιεν ῥάβδος ἄφνω τὰς πολλὰς ἐκείνας; 5. οὐδέ γε θέμις ἐστὶν ἐννοεῖν ὡς ἐκ τῶν ἀψύχων ἐκεῖνοι ῥάβδων ἐμψύχους ἠδύναντο δράκοντας ἀποτελεῖν ἀθρόως· ἀμείνους γὰρ ἂν ἦσαν ἴσως ἡμῶν οἱ τὰ νεκρὰ δυνάμενοι ψυχῶσαι ξύλα. τάχα δὲ οὐδὲ Μωσῆς παράδοξον ἔπραττεν ἂν οὐδέν, εἰ τὰ παραπλήσια τούτοις εἰργάζετο. 6. καίτοι πῶς οὐ δίκαιον ἀδρανῆ φαίνειν αὐτὰ δι' αὐτοῦ τοῦ γραφικοῦ μηνύματος; εἰ γὰρ ἀμυνόμενος τοὺς Αἰγυπτίους ὁ θεὸς ἅπαντα μὲν ἐπεκελεύετο τὰ ῥεῖθρα τῶν ὑδάτων εἰς αἷμα μεταβάλλεσθαι τιμωρίας χάριν, οἱ δὲ τοιαύταις αἰκιζόμενοι πληγαῖς εἰς αἵματος ἰδέαν ἀμείβουσι τοὺς ὀχετοὺς ὡσαύτως, αὔξειν ἐπιτεχνώμενοι τὸ πάθος, ἕνεκα τίνος ἀξιοῦσι καὶ δέονται πιεζόμενοι τῇ δίψῃ

9. 1. Indeed, if I were to continue to cite testimonies like these, time would probably quickly run out for me while I was speaking. I shall content myself with adding one other image as exemplary proof. In the written text of Exodus it has been noted down how the Lord himself commanded Moses and Aaron and their colleagues to throw the staff to the ground before Pharaoh so that when it changed its form into a serpent it might astonish the Egyptians with a fearful sign. 2. When this happened miraculously, the ruler, tricked by his ill-advised folly, summoned together "the wise men and sorcerers of Egypt." Scripture says, "And the magicians of the Egyptians did likewise by their charms. Each one threw down his own staff, and they became serpents. And Aaron's staff swallowed up their staffs" (Exod 7:11–12). 3. It is as well reported that "the magicians of the Egyptians likewise" produced blood and frogs (Exod 7:22; 8:7). Therefore, since not even here does the narrative voice distinguish the commands of the two sides and does declare that the magicians did "likewise," from the comparison would anyone say that the deeds of the sorcerers are similar to those accomplished through Moses?[27] 4. "Surely not!" one might say. But neither would it be legitimate to claim that the arts of magic and sorcery faithfully imitated heavenly exemplars. What was accomplished by Moses displayed the truth by what was done, but what was stitched together by the magicians conjured up images in appearance only. For the lie convicts itself by its sheer unreality, since how did one staff suddenly swallow up those many other staffs? 5. Nor is it right to suppose that they were able from lifeless staffs to produce living serpents all at once. For those able to give life to dead pieces of wood in that case would probably have been more powerful than we. But perhaps not even Moses would have done anything miraculous if he had accomplished feats like theirs. 6. Yet how is it not right to show that these deeds were not real when scripture itself indicates this? For if God, in taking vengeance on the Egyptians, commanded all the flowing waters to be turned to blood as punishment, and if those tormented by such plagues likewise turned streams into the form of blood, by this contrivance increasing the suffering, why

---

[27] Following the punctuation of Declerck, *Eustathii Antiocheni Opera*. Simonetti in *La Maga di Endor* does not make the sentence a question. We continue to follow the punctuation of Declerck, *Eustathii Antiocheni Opera*, in section 4.

καθαρισθῆναι τὰ κατὰ πᾶσαν Αἴγυπτον ὕδατα τῆς αἱμοφόρου μίξεως ; 7. ἢ αὖ πάλιν ἀπειροπληθεῖς ἄφνω θεασάμενοι βατράχους, τί δήποτε παραιτούμενοι τοὺς ὄχλους αὐτῶν αὖθις ἔπλαττον ἄλλους, εἰ μὴ τῶν μὲν ὡς ἐν σκιᾷ καὶ φαντασίας εἴδει φαινομένων οὐκ ἐπεφρόντιζον, ὑπὸ δὲ τῶν ἄλλων ἔργῳ δεικνυμένων ἐλυμήναντο δεινῶς ; 8. οὐδεὶς γὰρ ἂν ἕλοιτο τῷ πολεμίῳ πλήθει ἕτερον προστιθέναι πλῆθος ἀναρίθμητον ἀντὶ τοῦ νεολέκτους στρατολογεῖν εἰς συμμαχίαν δορυφόρους, οὐδὲ ἐπεγεῖραι πυρετῷ πυρετὸν ἀπαλλαγῆναι τοῦ πρώτου γλιχόμενος, οὐδὲ πληγῶν ἀφορήτων βίᾳ μαστιζόμενος ἄλλας ἑαυτῷ προσεπιφέρειν πληγάς, ἀνεθῆναι τούτων ἀφέσει καθαρᾷ καὶ πρεσβείᾳ καὶ δεήσει προσλιπαρῶν· 9. ἀλλ' οὐδὲ τῶν οἴκοι πιπραμένων, ἀντὶ τοῦ σβεστήρια καταψεκάζειν ὄργανα, τοὐναντίον ἔλαιον ἢ πίτταν ἐπιχέων εἰς ἄμετρον μὲν ὕψος ἐγείρει τὴν φλόγα, φλεγομένη δὲ μεῖζον τὸ πάθος αὔξει καὶ πῦρ ἄρδει κατὰ πυρὸς ἀπειροκάλως. 10. οὕτως ἄρα, δι' ὧν ἐφιλοτιμοῦντο πράττειν οἱ φαρμακοί, διὰ τούτων ἐναργεῖς ἐξέφερον ἐλέγχους ὡς οἰησικοπίᾳ φαντασιώδει ψυχαγωγεῖν ᾤοντο δεῖν ἑαυτούς. ἔστιν γοῦν αὐτόθεν οὐ χαλεπῶς ἰδεῖν ὅτι καὶ νυνὶ πολλῷ πλείονα καὶ μείζονα τούτων ἐν τοῖς θεάτροις οἱ ψηφοπαῖκται δρῶσιν εἰωθότως. 11. ἀλλ' ὅμως αὐτοσχεδίῳ δυνάμει τούτων ἄντικρυς ἁλισκομένων ἑώλων, οὐδὲν ἧττον ἡ διηγηματικὴ προγράφει φωνή **καὶ ἐποίησαν οἱ ἐπαοιδοὶ τῶν Αἰγυπτίων ταῖς φαρμακείαις αὐτῶν ὡσαύτως.** ἔδει τοίνυν, ὡς ὁ δογματιστὴς ἐνομοθέτησεν Ὠριγένης, εἰπεῖν· ἐποίησαν δὲ τὰ παραπλήσια τῷ δοκεῖν οἱ ἐπαοιδοὶ τῶν Αἰγυπτίων, ἀλλὰ μὴ λέγειν **ὡσαύτως,** ἵνα μή τις ὑπολάβοιεν ἂν ὡς ἐξ ὁμοίας ὁρμᾶται δυνάμεως. 12. εἰ γὰρ ὅμοια τοῖς ἀμφὶ Μωσέα πράττειν οἷοί τε ἦσαν, οὐκοῦν ὡσαύτως ἠδύναντο τοὺς ἐναντίους ἀμύνασθαι τοῖς ἴσοις, ὥστε τοὺς ἀγῶνας ἑκατέρωθεν ὑπάρχειν ἀντιπάλους. εἰ δ' οὐδένα δι' ὧν ἐσχημάτιζον ἔβλαπτον, ἀποκέχρηται μὲν ἄρα τῷ ῥήματι, πρόδηλα δὲ τὰ τῆς ἀψύχου φαντασίας ἐκτυπώματα. 13. οἷα δὴ κἀνταῦθα τὸ τῶν ἐπαοιδῶν ὄνομα προτάξας ὁ συγγραφεὺς καὶ τὰ τῆς φαρμακείας ἐπιτηδεύματα, διέδειξεν ὡς οὐ χρεὼν ἂν εἴη τὸ παράπαν ἀμφισβητεῖν ὅτι τοῖς μάγοις ἕκαστα περιεργίᾳ δια-

would they ask and pray, hard pressed by thirst, for the waters throughout all Egypt to be cleansed of the blood-bearing mixture? 7. Moreover, if they suddenly saw an unlimited number of frogs, why in the world when they were asking for relief from these multitudes would they fashion more, unless they had no concern about frogs that appeared only in a shadow and an imaginary form, while they were harmed terribly by the others that in actuality appeared? 8. For no one would choose to add to a hostile multitude another innumerable multitude instead of enlisting a guard of allied fresh recruits. Nor does anyone add one fever to another, hoping to be delivered from the first. And if one is whipped by the force of unbearable blows, he does not draw more blows upon himself even as he is importunately begging by pure appeal, intercession, and prayer to be freed from them. 9. Moreover, when someone's house is on fire, if he pours oil or tar on it instead of applying the means for quenching the fire, he heightens the flames beyond measure, and as it burns all the more fiercely, it increases the suffering, and because of his rash move fire pours down upon fire. 10. In the same way, therefore, through the very deeds they were ambitious to perform, the sorcerers produced clear proofs that they assumed they had to persuade people by an unreal fantasy. It is not difficult to see at once that even now the jugglers in the theaters customarily perform many more and greater feats than those sorcerers did. 11. But as the latter are openly caught out because of their rough-handed skill, so it is with the sorcerers of old. For the narrative voice no less clearly proclaimed earlier of them, "And the magicians of the Egyptians did likewise by their charms." Now, as Origen the dogmatician has decreed, it ought to have said, "The magicians of the Egyptians did things similar in appearance"—not said "likewise"—lest someone should suppose that their deeds were set in motion by a similar power. 12. But if they were the kind of men able to accomplish deeds like Moses and his colleagues, surely they would likewise have been able to take vengeance on their opponents with equivalent feats, so that the contests would be evenly matched. But if they harmed no one by the forms they roused, then the wording was sufficient and the figments of a lifeless imagination perfectly evident. 13. The author, by setting forth from the outset the name of "the magicians" and the devices "of sorcery" (Exod 7:10), has demonstrated that there would be no need at all to dispute the fact that each of these

πράττεται γοώδει. 14. τοιαῦτα καὶ τὰ τῆσδε τῆς ἱστορίας ἀπογράφεται δράματα· αὐτὸς γὰρ ἐγγαστρίμυθον ὀνομάσας, εἶτα καὶ μαντικῆς εὑρή- ματα διελέγχων ἀσεβῆ, δαιμονιζομένου τε τὸ πρόσωπον ἀποδείξας εἶναι τὸ μαντευόμενον, αὐτοτελῶς ἐξέφηνεν ὅτι φαντασιοκοπίαις ἕκαστα διε- πράττετο κιβδήλοις. Ἀλλὰ ταῦτα μὲν ἡμῖν οὕτω νοητέον.

10. 1. Ἴωμεν δὲ πάλιν ἐξελίττοντες ἐπὶ τὰ τῶν λόγων ἴχνη. τί οὖν; ὡς ἤρετο τὴν ἐγγαστρίμυθον ὁ Σαοὺλ τὸ *τί ἑόρακας;* εἰπών, ἐν πρώτοις ἡ παραπλὴξ ἀνθυπενέγκασα βοᾷ· *καὶ θεοὺς ἑόρακα ἀναβαίνον- τας ἐκ τῆς γῆς.* 2. ἐπειδὴ γὰρ ἐβούλετο παντοίως ἐκτραχηλιάσαι τὸν ἄνδρα συναρπάσας ὁ διάβολος, ἐπειρᾶτο δεικνύναι σαφῶς ὅτι τὸ δαι- μόνιον ἐπ' ἐξουσίας εἶχεν οὐχὶ μίαν μόνον ἀνάξαι δικαίου ψυχήν, ἀλλὰ καὶ πάσας ὁμοῦ τὰς τῶν ἁγίων ἀνδρῶν. ὁ δὲ ἐκ τῶν ἐναντίων τὴν τῶν δαιμόνων ἐν ταὐτῷ στρατιὰν ὁπλίσας καὶ σύνοδον ἐν μιᾷ ῥοπῆς ὥρα συ- στησάμενος ἐκόμπαζε, πεῖσαι καὶ διὰ τοῦδε τοὺς ἅπαντας ἐθέλων ὡς αὐτὸς εἴη θεὸς ὁ συναγωγεὺς τῶν ἄλλων. 3. ὅτι δ' οὖν οἰκείᾳ χρώ- μενος ἀπονοίᾳ θεοποιεῖν εἴωθεν ἑαυτόν, ὁ μὲν Ἡσαΐας ἀντιπροσώπως ἐλέγχων αὐτὸν ἱεροφωνίᾳ κηρύττει προφητικῇ· *σὺ δὲ εἶπας ἐν τῇ καρδίᾳ σου· εἰς οὐρανὸν ἀναβήσομαι, ἐπάνω τῶν ἀστέρων θήσω τὸν θρόνον μου, καθιῶ ἐν ὄρει ὑψηλῷ ἐπὶ τὰ ὄρη τὰ ὑψηλὰ τὰ πρὸς βορρᾶν, ἀναβήσομαι ἐπάνω τῶν νεφελῶν, ἔσομαι ὅμοιος τῷ ὑψίστῳ.* 4. μαρτυρεῖ δὲ τούτοις ὅμοια καὶ διὰ τοῦ προφήτου φθεγγόμενος Ἰεζεκιὴλ αὐτὸς ὁ κύριος ἄν- τικρυς· *ἀνθ' ὧν ὑψώθη ἡ καρδία σου, καὶ εἶπας· θεός εἰμι ἐγώ, κατοικῶ ἐν καρδίᾳ θαλάσσης, σὺ δὲ εἶ ἄνθρωπος καὶ οὐ θεός.* ἀντὶ τούτου μὲν ὅσας αὐτῷ τιμωρίας ἀπειλεῖ, ῥᾷόν ἐστιν ἐκ τῶν ὑποκειμένων ἰδεῖν· ὅτι δὲ τοιούτοις ἐπερείδεται φάσμασι κομπολογῶν ἑκάστοτε, θείᾳ δεδήλωται ψηφοφορίᾳ. 5. τοιγαροῦν, εἴπερ ὁ δαίμων οἷός τε ἦν ἀνάξαι τοὺς ὀνόματι θεοὺς ἀνακικλησκομένους, οὐκ ἀνάγκη νοεῖν ὅτι μείζων τῶν ἀναγομένων ὁ ἀνάγων ἐστίν; εἰ δὲ προύχει τῶν ὁσίων οὗτος, ἀκόλουθον ὑπολαμ- βάνειν ὅτι καὶ τούτου πάλιν αὐτὸς ὁ ἀρχιδαίμων. 6. εἰ δὲ ταῦτά τις

deeds was accomplished by magicians using the art of magic. 14. The dramatic actions of the narrative we are speaking about are set in writing in just this way also. For by naming her "belly-myther" and then by reproving the impious devices of divination and showing that the persona seeking divination is possessed by a demon, the narrator has made it absolutely clear that each of these acts was accomplished by spurious illusions. This is the manner in which these elements of the narrative are to be understood.

10. 1. But let us resume our step-by-step unfurling of the narrative. What then? When Saul asked the belly-myther, saying, "What have you seen?" at first the deranged woman cried out in answer, "I have seen gods coming up from the earth" (1 Kgdms 28:13). 2. For when the devil, after snatching the man up, wished to throw him over by various devices, he tried to give him clear proof that the petty demon had it in his power to bring up not only a single soul of a righteous man but all the souls of the holy men at once. But on the contrary it was the devil, the one who had armed the cohort of demons in that place and brought them all together at that critical moment, who was making this boast, because he wished also by this means to persuade everyone that he—the convener of the others—was a god. 3. Hence it is for the fact that by his own foolishness he was accustomed to make himself God that Isaiah reproves him to his face. He proclaims in his sacred prophetic voice, "You said in your heart, 'I will ascend to heaven; I will raise my throne above the stars; I will sit on the lofty mountain, above the lofty mountains that face north; I will ascend above the clouds; I will be like the Most High'" (Isa 14:13–14). 4. The Lord himself, speaking openly through the utterance of the prophet Ezekiel, gives testimony similar to this, "Because your heart has been lifted up and you have said, 'I am God; I will dwell in the heart of the sea,' yet you are a man and not God" (Ezek 28:2). It is easy to see from what he says next the sort of punishments God threatens him with in return, even as it has been revealed by divine decree that the devil relies upon such apparitions in every instance when he boasts. 5. Therefore, if the demon were of a type able to bring up those called "gods," would it not be necessary to think that the one who brings up is greater than those brought up? And if the demon is superior to the holy ones, it follows that we should suppose the leader of demons himself is in turn superior to him. 6. If someone were to grant these premises,

ἀποδώσειεν, ἀναντιρρήτῳ δυνάμει συνίστησιν ὡς αὐτός ἐστιν *θεὸς θεῶν*
ὁ τοῖς ὑπηρέταις τοῖς ἑαυτοῦ τοιαύτην ἀπονέμων ἐξουσίαν, ὥστε πνεύματα καὶ ψυχὰς ἐξ ᾅδου μεταπέμπεσθαι δικαίων. ἀλλὰ ταῦτα μὲν οὐδείς
πω τῶν εὖ φρονούντων ὁριεῖται τὸ σύνολον, ἵνα μὴ ταῖς ἁγίαις ἐναντία
ψηφιεῖται μαρτυρίαις. 7. ἐπειδὴ δὲ τὸ δεύτερον ὁ παραπλὴξ ἤρετο καὶ
συνάψας εἶπεν τῇ γυναικί *τί ἔγνως;* αὐτίκα πάλιν ἀνθυπενέγκασα πρὸς
τὴν ἐρώτησιν ἔφησεν· εἶδον *ἄνδρα ὄρθιον ἀναβαίνοντα ἐκ τῆς γῆς, καὶ
οὗτος ἀναβεβλημένος διπλοΐδα.* 8. μηδένα δὲ τὸ παράπαν ἰδών, ὡς αὐτήκοος ἐγένετο τῶν λόγων, *ἔγνω* μὲν κατὰ τὴν ἔννοιαν τὴν ἑαυτοῦ τοῦτον
εἶναι *Σαμουήλ,* ἅτε δὴ πολιορκούμενος ὑπὸ τοῦ δαίμονος ἔνδοθεν· ὡς δὲ
τῇ τῶν σημείων ὀνομασίᾳ συνηρπάσθη, τηνικαῦτα τὸ πρόσωπον ὑποκλί-
νας ἐπὶ τῇ γῇ *προσεκύνησεν αὐτῷ.* 9. πρῶτον μὲν οὖν ὀρθότατα φαίη τις
ἄν· εἰ Σαμουὴλ ἐτύγχανεν ἐκεῖνος, ἀλλὰ μὴ μεταμορφωθεὶς ὁ πολύτρο-
πος ὄφις, ἀνθυπενέγκας ἔφρασεν ἂν εὐσεβεῖ λογισμῷ· *κυρίῳ τῷ θεῷ σου
προσκυνήσεις καὶ αὐτῷ μόνῳ λατρεύσεις.* 10. δεύτερον δὲ πάλιν εἴποιμ᾽
ἄν· ὁπηνίκα Σαμουὴλ τοῦ παντὸς ἦρχε λαοῦ καὶ προφήτης ἐτύγχανεν
ἔκκριτος, ὁ Σαοὺλ ἰδιωτεύων ἔτι καὶ τὰς τοῦ πατρὸς ὄνους ἀναζητῶν
ἀπῄει μὲν ὡς αὐτὸν ἐρωτήσων οἷα προφήτην ἕνεκα τῶν ἀπολομένων
ὑποζυγίων, οὐδαμοῦ δὲ φαίνεται προσκυνήσας αὐτῷ, καίτοι χρῄζων αὐτοῦ καὶ προφανῶς ὑποκείμενος οἷα καθηγεμόνι λαοῦ. 11. πῶς οὖν ὁ τότε
μὴ προσκυνήσας ὡς ἰδιώτης ἄρχοντι, νῦν ἐκ τῶν ἐναντίων ὁ βασιλεὺς
ἰδιωτεύοντι προσκυνεῖ; τρίτον δ᾽ ἐπὶ τούτοις ἔχω λέγειν· τί δήποτε, θεοὺς
ἀναβαίνοντας ἀκούσας οὐδενὶ τούτων προσεκύνησεν, ὅτε δὲ τὸν ἄνδρα ὄρ-

he would establish with undeniable force that it is "the God of gods" (Dan 2:47) himself who assigns to his own servants such authority as to summon the spirits and souls of the righteous from hell. Yet no one who belongs to the company of the right-minded will assert this at all, lest he render a verdict that contradicts the holy testimonies.[28]

7. Now when the deranged man asked a second question, taking the conversation further, he said to the woman, "What have you come to know?" Immediately she again answered his question and said, "I saw a man coming up from the earth standing, and he is wrapped in a double cloak" (1 Kgdms 28:14). 8. And even though he saw no one at all, he was a hearsay witness[29] to her words. He "knew" in his own mind that it was "Samuel" inasmuch as he was thoroughly besieged by the demon within. And when he was taken in by the naming of the signs, then he bowed with his face to the ground and "worshiped him." 9. Therefore, first of all, one may say quite rightly that if it had been Samuel and not the multifarious serpent transformed, he would have replied with pious reasoning, "It is to the Lord your God that you shall bow down, and him alone you shall serve" (Matt 4:10). 10. In the second place, I should say that when Samuel ruled over the whole people and was a distinguished prophet, Saul, still a private citizen, when trying to find his father's donkeys, went off to inquire of him as a prophet because of the lost animals (1 Kgdms 9:3–21). But nowhere does he appear to have bowed down[30] to him even though he needed his help and was quite obviously subject to him as the governor of the people. 11. How is it, therefore, that the one who when he was a private citizen did not bow down to him as ruler, now on the contrary when king does bow down before him, a private citizen?

In addition to these points, I have a third. Why in the world, after hearing that there were gods coming up, did he bow down

---

[28] That is, according to the implication of the text it is really the devil of devils that brings up the "gods," and not the God of gods. Though it logically follows that God could give his servants power to bring up the righteous from hell, it would be wrong to draw this conclusion, since only God himself can bring them up.

[29] Literally, an "ear-witness."

[30] προσκυνήσας is better translated "bow down" than "worship" in this context.

θιον ἀκήκοεν ἀναβεβηκότα, τηνικαῦτα προσκυνήσας ὑπέκυψεν; 12. καὶ
μήν, ὡς Ὠριγένης ἀπεφήνατο τολμηρῶς, εἴπερ ἄγγελοί τινες ἦσαν ἐκ
τούτων ἢ χοροὶ προφητῶν, ἔδει τοῖς κρείττοσι καὶ πλείοσι πρῶτον ὑποπεσεῖν, οὐχὶ δὲ τὸν μὲν ἕνα θεραπεῦσαι, τοὺς δὲ πλείους ὑπεροψίας ἀνοίᾳ
προλιπεῖν. 13. ἢ γὰρ ἀγνοητέον ὡς αἱ φλογοείκελοι τῶν ἀγγέλων ἄξιαι
τῶν ἀνθρώπων ἀεὶ μακρῷ καλλίους εἰσίν; οὐκοῦν ἐκ πάντων ὁμοῦ τῶν
ἔργων εὐχερῶς ἔστιν ἰδεῖν ὅτι τὸν ἡγεμόνα μὲν νοῦν ἐτύφλωττεν ὁ Σαοὺλ
ὑπὸ τοῦ δαίμονος ἐλαυνόμενος, ὁ δὲ διάβολος εἰς διαφόρους ἐξήλλαττεν
ἑαυτὸν ἰδέας ὑπὸ τοῦ δυνάστου προσκυνηθῆναι πραγματευόμενος, ἵνα ἐκ
τούτου πλείστους ὅσους ἐξαπατήσοι λεληθότως ὑποκύπτειν αὐτῷ. 14.
καὶ τί γε δὴ ξένον ἐστὶν εἰπεῖν, ὅπου γε καὶ τὸ τοῦ Χριστοῦ πρόσωπον
εἰσιδὼν ἔργῳ μὲν ἔνδοθεν ἑώρα καὶ πράξει θεὸν καὶ φύσει θεοῦ γνήσιον
υἱόν, ἄνθρωπον δὲ καθαρόν, ἄχραντον, ἀκηλίδωτον ἐξωτάτω περικεί-
μενον ἐποπτεύων καὶ ναοῦ χρῆμα περικαλλές, ἀφιερωμένον, ἀσύλητον,
οὐδὲν ἧττον ἐκπειράσων αὐτὸν ἀμελλητὶ προσῄει θεομαχῶν εἰωθότως;
15. ὡς δὲ τὰ πρῶτα καὶ τὰ δεύτερα καθ' ἑαυτοῦ προκαλεσάμενος ἡτ-
τήθη ῥαγεὶς ἀθλίως, αὖθις εἰς ἄλλο μεταλλάξας ἦθος ὑποδεικνύναι μὲν
αὐτῷ πᾶσαν τὴν τοῦδε τοῦ κόσμου περιγραφὴν ἐπεχείρει καὶ τὰς βασιλείας αὐτῆς, ἀπονοίᾳ δὲ καὶ ψευδηγορίᾳ θρασυνόμενος ἐκόμπαζε *ταῦτα
πάντα σοι δώσω, ἐὰν πεσὼν προσκυνήσῃς μοι.* 16. τοιαύτας μὲν οὖν ὁ
ἀσεβὴς ἔρρηξε δεῦρο φωνάς, οἰόμενος εἰς ὀργὴν ἐκκαλέσασθαι τὰ τῆς
ἀνεξικακίας ἤθη, καὶ διὰ τοῦ τοιοῦδε δοκῶν ἐπιλαμβάνεσθαι. μακροθυ-
μίᾳ δὲ κατεσίγασε τὸν ἀλάστορα θεοπρεπῶς ὁ κύριος· ἴδιον γὰρ ἂν εἴη
θεῷ πάντα ἀνεξικάκως φέρειν. 17. εἰ τοίνυν αὐτῷ τῷ κυρίῳ τοιαῦτα
προσοῖσαι ῥήματα παρ' οὐδὲν ἡγήσατο, πῶς οὐκ ἔστι σαφὲς ὅτι προσ-
κυνεῖσθαι βουλόμενος ἴσα θεῷ ταῦτα διεπράττετο; 18. τοῦτο μέν, οἶμαι, τοῖς εὖ φρονοῦσι κατάφωρον ὑπάρχει πᾶσιν, ὅτι διὰ γυναικὸς ἐμ-

to none of them, but when he has heard a man was coming up standing, then he bowed down and worshiped?[31] 12. And yet, as Origen boldly decrees, if some of them were angels or choruses of prophets, he ought first to have fallen down before them as better and more numerous and not have done service to the single individual, while leaving out the greater number by foolish disdain. 13. For is it possible to be ignorant of the fact that the flamelike dignity of angels is always far better than that of humans? Therefore, on the basis of all these facts taken together, it is quite easy to see that Saul, because he was driven by the demon, was blind in his governing mind. And the devil changed himself into various forms, exerting himself in the effort to be worshiped by the ruler so that in this way he might trick as many people as possible into bowing down to him unawares. 14. Indeed, what is strange about saying this? When the devil beheld the persona of Christ, he saw within it God in deed and action and God's genuine Son in nature. On the other hand, he looked upon him clothed on the outside as a pure man, undefiled, spotless, a marvel of a temple, all beautiful, consecrated, inviolate. Nevertheless, he approached him without hesitation to tempt him, since it is his custom to join battle with God. 15. When he challenged Christ the first and the second time on his own, he was miserably broken and defeated. When once more the wretch turned to another way of tempting him, he undertook to show Christ the entire circumference of this world and its kingdoms, and in his folly and lying speech he confidently boasted, "I will give you all these things, if you will fall down and worship me" (Matt 4:9). 16. Such, then, were the sorts of statements the impious one let loose on that occasion. He thought he would provoke to anger Christ's customary forbearance and supposed that in this way he would get hold of him. But the Lord in a manner suitable to God silenced the avenging demon by his patient endurance, for it is proper to God to bear everything with forbearance. 17. Therefore, if the devil thought nothing of addressing such words to the Lord himself, how is it not clear that he was doing so because he wished to be worshiped equally with God? 18. This, I suppose, is evident to all people who are in their right mind: that through the agency of the mad woman the devil

---

[31] προσκυνήσας ὑπέκυψεν, a reference to 1 Kgdms 28:14, translated elsewhere as "bowed (with his face to the ground) and worshiped."

μανοῦς ἠπάτησεν τὸν ἔκφρονα δυνάστην ὑποκύψειν αὐτῷ παρὰ τὸ δέον. **11.** 1. Ἔτι δὲ διαληπτέον αὐτὰ τὰ τούτοις ὑποκείμενα καθεξῆς. ὡς οὖν ὁ Σαοὺλ ὑπεκλίθη τῷ φάσματι προσκυνήσας, αὖθις ὑποκρίνεται πεπονθέναι βίαν ὁ δολομήτης, εἰς τὸ σχῆμα τοῦ Σαμουὴλ ἀμείψας ἑαυτόν· 2. εἶτα μετὰ εἰρωνείας ἀποκρίνεται σκυθρωπότερον, *ἵνα τί παρηνώχλησάς μοι φάσκων ἀναβῆναι;* ταῦτα δὲ πλαττόμενος ἀπαρεμφάτως ἐβούλετο σημαίνειν ὅτι καὶ ἄκοντα τὸν προφήτην ὁ δαίμων ἠδύνατο μεταπέμπεσθαι, καὶ κατ' αὐτοῦ τοιαύτην ἔχειν ἐξουσίαν. 3. εἶτα τοσοῦτον ἀμβλυωποῦσί τινες, ὡς οὐ δύνασθαι νοεῖν ὅτι τοὺς δαίμονας ἐν τῷ θείῳ φυγαδεύουσιν ὀνόματι πάντες οἱ τὰ τοῦ Χριστοῦ φρονοῦντες εἰλικρινῶς, οὐχὶ δὲ τοὐναντίον ὡς ὑποκείμενοι τούτοις ἄκοντες ἀναβαίνουσιν ἐξ ᾅδου, μεταπεμπόμενοι πρὸς αὐτῶν; 4. εἰ δέ τις οἴεται τὸ τῆς ἐγγαστριμύθου δαιμόνιον οὐδεπώποτε φυγαδεύεσθαι, προὖχον ἁπάντων ὁμοῦ τῶν ἄλλων, ἀναδραμέτω μὲν εἰς τὰς τῶν ἀποστόλων Πράξεις, ἐπ' αὐτῶν δὲ τῶν χωρίων ἐμβατεύσας ἰδέτω πῶς ὁ περίοδος ἱεροκῆρυξ ἀφίκετο Παῦλος εἰς Φιλίππους· 5. ὡς δὲ τὴν καλουμένην ἐφώτισε Λυδίαν εὐσεβείας ἐπιγνώσει, τηνικαῦτα μὲν ᾤχετο τὰς εὐχὰς ἀνοίσων, *ἐγένετο δὲ παιδίσκην ἀπαντῆσαί τινα* φησὶν *ἔχουσαν πνεῦμα πύθωνος, ἥπερ ἐργασίαν πολλὴν παρεῖχεν τοῖς κυρίοις αὐτῆς μαντευομένη. τοιγαροῦν αὕτη κατακολουθήσασα τῷ Παύλῳ* καὶ τοῖς ἀμφ' αὐτὸν *ἐβόα γεγωνότως· οὗτοι οἱ ἄνθρωποι δοῦλοι τοῦ θεοῦ τοῦ ὑψίστου εἰσίν, οἵτινες καταγγέλλουσιν ὑμῖν ὁδὸν σωτηρίας· καὶ τοῦτο ἐπὶ πολλὰς ἔπραττεν ἡμέρας.* 6. ἀλλ' ὁ μὲν δαίμων ἀοράτῳ μάστιγι στρεβλούμενος ἄκων ἠναγκάζετο τοιαύτας ἀφιέναι φωνάς, ὁ δὲ Παῦλος οὐκ ἀξιόπιστον εἶναι τὴν ἐκείνου μαρτυρίαν ἐννοήσας ὀρθότατα, *διαπονηθεὶς ἔφη τῷ πνεύματι, παραγγέλλω σοι λέγων ἐν ὀνόματι Ἰησοῦ Χριστοῦ ἐξελθεῖν ἀπ' αὐτῆς.* εἶτα τὸ πρᾶγμα διηγούμενος ὁ συγγραφεὺς ἐπιφέρει, *καὶ ἐξῆλθεν λέγων αὐτῇ τῇ ὥρᾳ.* 7. θεασάμενοι οὖν *οἱ κύριοι τῆς θεραπαινίδος ὡς ἐκποδὼν ᾤχετο τῆς ἐργασίας αὐτῶν ἡ ἐλπίς, ἐπιλαβόμενοι τὸν Παῦλον καὶ τὸν Σίλαν εἵλκυσαν εἰς τὴν ἀγορὰν ἐπὶ τοὺς ἄρχοντας* ὕβρεσι δὲ καὶ πληγαῖς αἴτιοι γεγόνασι, συκοφαντίᾳ στάσεις ἐπεγείραντες. 8. εἰ τοίνυν ὁ Παῦλος ἐπιτιμήσας τῷ πνεύματι

tricked the demented ruler into bowing down to him in violation of what is right.

11. 1. The verses that follow still remain to be discussed in order. When, then, Saul bowed down and worshiped the phantom, the crafty one, having changed himself into the form of Samuel, pretended that he was suffering under compulsion. 2. Then, dissembling, he answered rather sulkily, saying, "Why have you disturbed me by bringing me up?" (1 Kgdms 28:15). By fabricating these words he wanted indirectly to show that the demon was able to summon up the prophet even against his will and had this kind of authority against him. 3. Then are some people so blind that they cannot understand that all those who sincerely have the mind of Christ set demons to flight by means of the divine name, rather than the opposite, as though, being subject to the demons, unwillingly they come up from hell at their summons? 4. If anyone supposes that the petty demon belonging to the belly-myther was never put to flight because it excelled all the others taken together, let him turn quickly to the Acts of the Apostles. And when he has set foot on that very terrain, let him see how that sacred preacher Paul in his circumnavigation arrived at Philippi. 5. When he had enlightened the woman called Lydia with the knowledge of true religion, he then went to offer up prayers. The text says, "it happened that we met a certain slave-girl who had a spirit of a Python," who "brought her owners a great deal of money by performing divination." Therefore, "when she had followed Paul" and his companions, she cried out resoundingly, "These men are slaves of the Most High God, who proclaim to you the way of salvation." And she kept doing "this for many days" (Acts 16:16–19). 6. But the demon, tormented by an invisible whip, was being compelled against its will to utter such statements as these, and Paul rightly understood that its testimony was not worthy of trust. "Very much annoyed," he said "to the spirit, 'I order you in the name of Jesus Christ to come out from her'" (Acts 16:18). Then the author continues his narrative of the event. "And it came out that very hour." 7. But when the "owners" of the servant girl saw that their hope of making money was gone, "they seized Paul and Silas and dragged them into the marketplace before the authorities" (Acts 16:18–19). They were subjected to insults and blows on the false charge that they were stirring up sedition. 8. Now if Paul drove the Pythian prophetess

τὸν πυθόμαντιν ἀθρόως ἐξήλασεν ἐν αὐτῇ τῇ ῥοπῇ, τὸ δὲ πνεῦμα τῇ τοῦ ῥήματος ἀπέδρασεν ἐξουσίᾳ μὴ δυνάμενον ὑποστῆναι τὸν τῆς γλώσσης ἦχον, εἰπάτω παριὼν εἰς τοὔμφανὲς ὁ τῷ τοιῷδε συνιστάμενος ὅρῳ, ποταπῇ δυνάμεως ἀρετῇ τὸν ὁμόδοξον τῷ Παύλῳ Σαμουὴλ ἄκοντα μετακαλούμενος ὁ δαίμων ἀνήγαγεν ἐξ ᾅδου. 9. ἀλλ᾽ οὐκ ἂν ἔχοι δεικνύναι τούτων οὐδὲν ἀληθές· ὥστε καὶ διὰ τῶνδε μάλα ῥᾳδίως ἔστιν ἰδεῖν ὅτι μεταμορφωσάμενος ἠγόρευε τῷ Σαοὺλ ὁ δολομήτης, *ἵνα τί παρηνώχλησάς μοι;* φήσας. ὑπηνίττετο γὰρ ὅτι παρὰ βούλησιν ἄκων ἀνέβαινεν, οὐ θέλων, ἀλλὰ ἀνάγκῃ καὶ βίᾳ, καθάπερ ὑπ᾽ αὐτοῦ μεταπεμφθῆναι τοῦ κρείττονος ἐπιταχθείς. 10. ὁ δὲ δυνάστης ἀνθυπενέγκας ἔφη· *θλίβομαι σφόδρα, καὶ οἱ ἀλλόφυλοι πολεμοῦσιν ἐν ἐμοί, καὶ ὁ θεὸς ἀφέστηκε φησὶν ἀπ᾽ ἐμοῦ καὶ οὐκ ἀκήκοέν μου ἔτι, οὔτ᾽ ἐν χειρὶ τῶν προφητῶν οὔτε ἐν ἐνυπνίοις· καὶ νῦν κέκληκά σε γνωρίσαι μοι τί ποιήσω.* πάλιν οὖν ἀποκριτέον· εἰ Σαμουὴλ ὁ περίβλεπτος ἐτύγχανε προφήτης, οὐκ ἂν ἐσωφρόνισε τὸν ἄνδρα νουθετῶν; 11. οὐκ ἂν εἶπεν αὐτῷ τὸ πρῶτον· εἰπέ μοι, σχέτλιε πάντων ἀνθρώπων, εἰ περιέστηκαν οἱ ἀλλογενεῖς εἰς πόλεμον ἀντιπαραταττόμενοι συσταδόν, εἴπερ ὁ θεὸς ἀφέστηκεν ἀπὸ σοῦ καὶ τὸ παράπαν οὐκ ἐπακήκοέν σου, οὔτε δὲ προφῆται πρεσβεύοντες ὑπὲρ σοῦ κατήδεισαν, οὔτε ὄναρ οὔτε ὕπαρ ἀπεκαλύφθη σοι τὸ δέον, οὐ ταύτῃ μᾶλλον ὤφελες ἐξιλεούμενος ὑποκλιθῆναι θεῷ καὶ πενήτων ἐλεημοσύναις ἀπολούσασθαι τὰ τῶν ἐγκλημάτων αἴτια, μήτι γε δὴ καταφεύγειν ἐπὶ μάντιν ἐγγαστρίμυθον καὶ μανιώδει μαντικῇ τὰ τῆς εὐσεβείας ἀντικαταλλάττεσθαι σύμβολα καὶ καθ᾽ ἑαυτοῦ τὸ πάθος αὐξῆσαι διττῶς; 12. ἢ γὰρ οὐ διανοητέον ὅτι τὰ τοιάδε μιάσματα ῥητῶς ἀπηγόρευσεν ὁ θεός, ἐν τῷ Λευϊτικῷ διὰ Μωσέως εἰπών· *οὐκ ἐπακολουθήσετε τοῖς ἐγγαστριμύθοις, καὶ τοῖς ἐπαοιδοῖς οὐ προσκολληθήσεσθε μιανθῆναι ἐν αὐτοῖς· ἐγώ εἰμι κύριος ὁ θεὸς ὑμῶν;* ἀλλ᾽ οὐκ ἀσεβῆ τάδε τὰ βδελύγματα νομίζεις, ἐναντία τῷ θεῷ δραματουργεῖν ἐγχειρῶν; 13. ἄκουε καὶ μεθ᾽ ἕτερα τοῦ θεοῦ χρησμῳδοῦντος ἐπὶ τῷ τοιῷδε τολμήματι· *καὶ ψυχὴ* φησὶν *ἥτις ἂν ἐπακολουθήσῃ τοῖς ἐγγαστριμύθοις ἢ ἐπαοιδοῖς ὥστε ἐκπορνεῦσαι ὀπίσω αὐτῶν·* ὁποῖα καὶ τίνα πείσεται προσθείς, ἐπέφρασε προϊών· *ἐπιστήσω*

out in an instant by rebuking the spirit, and if the spirit ran off at
the authority of his word because it could not withstand the sound
of his tongue, let whoever recommends the judgment I am reject-
ing come out in the open and explain by what great act of power
the demon with a summons brought up Samuel from hell against
his will—Samuel, who is as reputable as Paul. 9. But he could
not show anything of this to be true. As a result, it is in this way
quite easy to see that the crafty one had changed his form when he
addressed Saul and said, "Why have you disturbed me?" For he
was trying to imply that he had come up contrary to his purpose
against his will, not willingly but by necessity and compulsion as
though he were being summoned up at the command of someone
mightier than he. 10. The ruler replied, "I am in great distress, for
the foreigners are warring against me, and God has turned away
from me," the text says, "and no longer answers me, either by the
hand of prophets or by dreams; so now I have summoned you to
tell me what I should do" (1 Kgdms 28:15). Once again, then, this
calls for an answer: if it were Samuel the famous prophet, would
he not have called the man to his senses by admonishing him? 11.
Would he not first have said to him, "Tell me, most wretched of all
men, if the foreigners have taken their stand drawn up all united in
hostile ranks for war, if 'God has deserted you' and 'does not answer' you at all, if the prophets acting as your ambassadors have
observed nothing, no dream, no vision, has revealed to you what
you ought to do, ought you not rather here bow down to God
in propitiation, wash off from yourself the causes of the accusations against you by giving alms to the poor and not fleeing to a
belly-mything mantic and exchanging the tokens of right religion
for manic divination and doubly increase your own suffering? 12.
Indeed, should you not be mindful that God expressly prohibited such polluting acts when he said through Moses in Leviticus,
'You shall not resort to belly-mythers, and you shall not cleave to
magicians to be defiled by them. I am the Lord your God' (Lev
19:31)? But do you not suppose these abominations to be impious, since you are attempting to devise actions that are directly
contrary to God? 13. Hear also God's subsequent oracle against
this shameless act. He says, 'And the soul that resorts to belly-
mythers or magicians to commit fornication with them'—he goes
on to declare in addition what and what kind of suffering it will
experience, saying, 'I will set my face against that soul, and I will

τὸ πρόσωπόν μου, φάμενος, *ἐπὶ τὴν ψυχὴν ἐκείνην καὶ ἀπολῶ αὐτὴν ἐκ τοῦ λαοῦ αὐτῆς.* 14. εἰ οὖν ἀρχῆθεν νομοθετήσας ὁ θεὸς αὐστηροῖς ἀπέστειλε προγράμμασι τοὺς ταῖς τοιαύταις ἐγκαλινδουμένους ἐπαοιδαῖς ἢ μαντείαις, ἀπειλεῖ δὲ σκυθρωπὰ καὶ φρικώδη κολαστήρια κατὰ τῶν ἁλισκομένων ἐπὶ τῇ δίκῃ φοβερῶς, οὐ τὸν ἀνακείμενον ἐξ ἁπαλῶν ὀνύχων αὐτῷ τῷ θεῷ καὶ νομοφύλακα βέβαιον ἔδει περὶ τούτων ἐγκαλέσαι πρῶτον; 15. ἀλλ᾽ ὁ νομομαθὴς ἐκ μειρακίου καὶ τὰς νομικὰς ἀκριβῶσαι γραμμὰς ἀκρότατα δυνηθεὶς οὐκ ἂν ἐπεζήτησε τὸ πταῖσμα, μή πῃ ἄρα διὰ τούτου τινὲς εἰς μανικὰς ἐξελκυσθῶσι μαντείας, ἀπάτῃ συληθέντες ἀθλίως; 16. ἀλλὰ τούτων μὲν οὐδὲν οὔτε εἶπεν οὔτε ἐζήτησεν οὐ γὰρ ἦν ὁ Σαμουήλ, ἀλλ᾽ ὁ τὰ τοιάδε δράματα τυρεύων ἀνέκαθεν, ἐπὶ δὲ τούτοις ἀποκρίνεται, τὸ πρόσωπον τοῦ προφήτου ὑποδύς, *ἵνα τί λέγων ἐπερωτᾷς με, καὶ κύριος ἀφέστηκεν ἀπὸ σοῦ καὶ γέγονεν μετὰ τοῦ πλησίον σου; καὶ πεποίηκέν σοι κύριος καθὰ ἐλάλησεν ἐν χειρί μου.* 17. ταῦτα μὲν οὖν ὡς ἐχθρὸς ἅμα καὶ ἐκδικίαν ὑποτυπούμενος εἰσάγειν ἀναγινώσκει τὰ τῆς κατηγορίας ὑπομνήματα.

12. 1. Θεωρητέον δὲ πῶς αὐτὰ τὰ συνεκτικὰ παρεὶς ἐγκλήματα πλάττεται μὲν ὑποκρίσει δεικτικώτερα φθέγγεσθαι, μηδὲν δὲ προγνώσεως ἄξιον εἰπὼν ἐκεῖνα δευτεροῖ τετεχνασμένως, ὅσα περιὼν ὁ Σαμουὴλ ἔτι προὔλεγε συνενεχθῆναι τῷ Σαούλ, ἅπερ ὡς ἤδη γεγονότα προανεφώνει προφητεύων. 2. ἀλλὰ μὴν ὅ γε φήσας αὐτῷ *τί ἐπερωτᾷς με;* διαρρήδην ὁμολογεῖ ταῦτα καὶ πρότερον εἰρηκέναι· ταυτολογεῖ δὲ δὴ τὰ πρῶτα διὰ τῶν ἔπειτα βεβαιῶν ἐπὶ προσχήματι γοωδῶς. 3. Ὠριγένης δὲ τοὐναντίον αὐτὰ τὰ πάλαι τῷ προφήτῃ προαναφωνηθέντα ῥήματα παραλαβὼν ἐπὶ λέξεως ὡς ἄρτια καὶ καινὰ προφητείας ἀποφθέγματα διορίζεται, διά τοι τοῦτο βούλεται τὸν Σαμουὴλ ἀνῆχθαι, καίτοι τῆς γραφῆς ἄντικρυς ἐλεγχούσης αὐτόν, ὥς γε συνομολογεῖ καὶ αὐτὸς ἐν μέρει

destroy it from its people'"[32] (Lev 20:6). 14. Therefore, if God, when he gave the law, from the beginning banished with harsh edicts those who harness themselves to such magicians or diviners and threatens those who are caught and fearfully convicted with gloomy and terrifying punishments, ought not the man who was dedicated to God himself from his childhood and was a steadfast guardian of the law have first of all laid charges against these crimes? 15. Surely the one instructed in the law from his youth, the one who was able to interpret with the greatest accuracy the books of the law, would he not have searched out the error, lest somehow by it people should be dragged into manic mantic divination, miserably carried off by deceit? 16. But he neither said nor asked any of these things—for he was not Samuel but the one who cunningly devised such actions from the beginning—but in the face of these things he replies, putting on the persona of the prophet and saying, "Why, then, do you ask me, since the Lord has turned from you and has joined your neighbor? The Lord has done to you just as he spoke by my hand" (cf. 1 Kgdms 28:16–17). 17. Thus, he introduces these words as though he were an enemy, and at the same time, drafting the punishment to introduce, he reads the bill of indictment.

12. 1. It must be observed how, passing over what are the essential charges, the devil fabricates subordinate arguments to utter in pretence. But saying nothing worthy of foreknowledge, he craftily repeats what Samuel when alive had already foretold would happen to Saul, pronouncing this in the course of prophesying events ahead of time as though they had already taken place. 2. Moreover, the one who said to him, "Why do you ask me?" confesses explicitly his words to be what Samuel had previously said (cf. 1 Kgdms 15:23, 28). Thus, he says the same things, confirming the initial statements by subsequent events as a cloak for his sorcery. 3. But Origen, on the contrary, because he takes the words pronounced long ago by the prophet according to the letter, defines these words as apt and new prophetic utterances. Accordingly, for this reason he wants Samuel to have been brought up, even though scripture openly refutes him, as he himself joins

[32] It is not entirely clear where Samuel's imagined speech ends. But the reference in 11.14–15 would appear to be to Samuel (cf. 1 Kgdms 2–3), implying that Eustathius is now explaining why, if Samuel had really appeared to Saul, he would have said what is found in 11.11–13.

τοπικῶς. 4. ἀλλὰ τί μετὰ ταῦτα προσετίθει πάλιν, ὁπηνίκα τῷ δυνάστῃ διελέγετο, τὸ φάσμα; *διαρρήξει κύριος τὴν βασιλείαν ἐκ χειρός σου
καὶ δώσει αὐτὴν τῷ πλησίον σου τῷ Δαβίδ. διότι οὐκ ἤκουσας τῆς φωνῆς κυρίου καὶ οὐκ ἔπλησας θυμὸν ὀργῆς αὐτοῦ ἐν Ἀμαλήκ, διὰ τὸ ῥῆμα
τοῦτο ἐποίησεν κύριος τοῦτό σοι τῇ ἡμέρᾳ ταύτῃ καὶ δώσει κύριος τὸν
Ἰσραὴλ μετὰ σοῦ εἰς χεῖρας ἀλλοφύλων.* 5. εἰ δέ τις ἀκριβῶσαι βούλοιτο
τὸ σαφές, ἐπανίτω μὲν ἐπὶ τὴν τοῦ γράμματος ἱστορίαν ὀλίγῳ πρόσθεν
ἀναδραμών, αὐτὸ δὲ τὸ χωρίον ἀναπτύξας, ἔνθα τὸν Ἀμαλὴκ ἡττήσας
ἐσφετερίσατο τὰ κράτιστα τῶν σκύλων καὶ τὰς ἐκ τούτων ᾤετο δεῖν ἀνα-
φέρειν ὁλοκαυτώσεις ὡς ἀπαρχάς. 6. ἀκριβολογίᾳ δὲ τρανοτέρᾳ ζητῶν
ἐπιστημόνως εὑρήσειεν ἂν ὡς ἅπαντα τὰ ῥήματα ταῦτα κατ' ἐκεῖνο καιροῦ προεῖπεν ἐπὶ λέξεως ὁ Σαμουήλ· ἔφη γὰρ ὅτι καὶ *διέρρηξεν κύριος
ἐκ χειρὸς αὐτοῦ τὴν βασιλείαν,* ὁπότε καὶ τὸ τοῦ διπλοϊδίου πτερύγιον
ἐπιλαβόμενος ὁ δυνάστης ἐδίχασε. 7. προύλεγε δ' αὐτῷ πρὸς ἐπὶ τούτοις μὲν ὡς ἤμελλεν ἡ βασιλεία δοθήσεσθαι *τῷ πλησίον* αὐτοῦ *τῷ μᾶλλον
ὑπὲρ αὐτὸν ἀγαθῷ.* προύφήτευε δὲ καὶ τίνα τρόπον ἔδει τὸν Ἰσραὴλ ἕνεκα
τούτου διασχισθήσεσθαι καὶ μηκέτι ἐπιστρέψαι. ταῦτα δὲ φήσας ὁμοῦ
τοῖς ἔργοις ἐβεβαίου τὰ λεκτέα· μετ' οὐ πολὺ γὰρ ἐκ θείας ἀποσταλεὶς
ἐπικρίσεως ἔχρισε βασιλέα τὸν Δαβίδ. 8. ἆρ' οὖν οὐδὲν ἀπήγγελλεν ξένον
ὁ διὰ τῆς ἐγγαστριμύθου λεγόμενος ἀνῆχθαι, τὰ δὲ ὑπὸ τοῦ Σαμουὴλ εἰρημένα πρότερον ὡς ἴδια μὲν ἐσχημάτιζε προσωποποιῶν ἀπάτῃ, πιθανῇ
δὲ τεχνοποιίᾳ ταυτολογῶν ὑπεκρίνατο δὴ προφητικῶς ὁμιλεῖν. 9. ἀλλ'
ὥσπερ ἀγύρται <καὶ> μάντεις ἐπὶ πλουσίων ἰέναι θύρας ἐπειγόμενοι τὰ
μὲν ἤδη παροδεύσαντα τοῦ βίου πράγματα πολυπευστοῦντες ἀνιχνεύουσι
λεληθότως, αὐτὰ δὲ τὰ πρὸ πολλοῦ γεγονότα λέγειν αὐτοσχεδίως ὑπο-
νοούμενοι παραχρῆμα μὲν ἐκπλήττουσι τοὺς αὐτηκόους, εἰς εὐήθη δὲ
πίστιν αὐτοὺς ὑπαγόμενοι περὶ τῶν μελλόντων ἅπερ ἐθέλουσι πλάττου-
σιν οὕτως ἄρα καὶ τὸ τῆς ἐγγαστριμύθου φάσμα μεταμορφούμενον αὐτὰ

in admitting in several places.³³ 4. Furthermore, what does the phantom declare after this when addressing the ruler? "The Lord will tear the kingdom out of your hand and will give it to your neighbor, David, because you did not obey the voice of the Lord and did not carry out his fierce wrath against Amalek. Because of this word the Lord has done this thing to you today. And the Lord will give Israel along with you into the hands of the foreigners" (1 Kgdms 28:17–19). 5. If someone wants to have an accurate understanding of the clear meaning, let him go to the narrative of scripture, turning back a little before this passage and opening at the place where after defeating Amalek Saul appropriated for himself the best of the spoils and was thinking that he should offer whole burnt offerings from it as firstfruits. 6. If he inquires in a skilled manner with keener precision, he would find that Samuel previously said all these things, word for word. For he said also that "the Lord had torn the kingdom from" Saul's "hand," when the ruler, catching hold of the hem of Samuel's double cloak, tore it. 7. And in addition to these things Samuel foretold to him that the kingdom was going to be given to his "neighbor, the one better than" he. And he prophesied as well in what way Israel would be torn in two on account of this and no longer return (1 Kgdms 15:27–29). After saying these things he confirmed the words with deeds, for not long afterwards he was sent by divine determination and anointed David king (1 Kgdms 16). 8. Therefore, we must conclude that the one said to have been brought up by the belly-myther related nothing strange. Rather, engaging in deceitful impersonation, he disguised the words Samuel had said earlier as his own, and by repeating them with persuasive artifice he acted as though he were conversing prophetically. 9. This is just like, when begging priests and soothsayers rush with eagerness to the doors of rich people,³⁴ they secretly track down by much inquiry the events that have already taken place in their lives. Guessing what to say in an offhand way about what happened long ago, they immediately astonish their audience, and carrying them away into simple-minded credulity, they fabricate whatever they wish about the future. In just the same way, also the phantom of the belly-

---

³³ Presumably, because Origen does not always accept the letter of scripture as useful.

³⁴ There is here an allusion to and partial citation of Plato, *Resp.* 364b: "begging priests and soothsayers go to rich men's doors."

μὲν ἐξηγόρευε τὰ προφητικὰ τοῦ Σαμουὴλ ἀποφθέγματα, τῷ δὲ δοκεῖν ᾤετο προφητεύειν οὐδὲν ἐπιστάμενον, ἀλλὰ τὰ μὲν ἀλλότρια προὔταττεν ὡς ἴδια καὶ κατέπληττε τὸν ἀλάστορα, διὰ δὲ τούτων εὐχερῶς ὑπεσύλα καὶ τὸν νοῦν ἔκλεπτεν ἐκείνου.

10. τί οὖν ἄλλο μετὰ ταῦτα προσετίθει; **καὶ σὺ φησὶν αὔριον καὶ ὁ υἱός σου Ἰωνάθαν μετ᾽ ἐμοῦ, καὶ τὴν παρεμβολὴν Ἰσραὴλ δώσει κύριος εἰς τὰς χεῖρας ἀλλοφύλων.** ἀλλὰ ταῦτα μὲν ἐῴκει λέγειν ὁ δαίμων ὡς ἴδια. **13**. 1. Ζητητέον δὲ πότερον ἀληθῆ προὔλεγεν, ὡς ᾤετο, καὶ πότερον ἀπὸ στόχου καὶ συγκυρίας ἀπήγγελλεν, καὶ πρὸς ἐπὶ τούτοις εἰ προεγνωκέναι τούτων ἠδύνατό τινα. πρῶτον μὲν οὖν οὐ φαίνεται τῇ ἑξῆς ἡμέρᾳ διαφθαρεὶς ὁ Σαούλ, ὡς ἔφασκε τὸ φάσμα φθεγγόμενον. 2. εἰ γὰρ ἀκούσας τῶν λόγων ἐκ τῆς ἄγαν ἀθυμίας **οὐκ ἔφαγεν ἄρτον ὅλην τὴν ἡμέραν καὶ ὅλην τὴν νύκτα** φησὶν **ἐκείνην**, ὡς ἡ θεία διαγορεύει γραφή, μετὰ δὲ τοῦτο παραινοῦσα πάλιν ἡ γυνὴ προὔτρεπεν ἐδωδῆς ἅψασθαι, προκειμένης ὁδοῦ, πρόδηλον ὅτι τῇ δευτέρᾳ δήπουθεν ἡμέρᾳ μετὰ τὴν πάννυχτον καὶ πανήμερον ἐκείνην ἀσιτίαν ἔπεισε μὲν αὐτόν, εἰς τοὔδαφος ἐρριμμένον ἐκλύτως, ἀναστῆναι καὶ καθεσθῆναι κοσμιώτερον ἐπὶ τοῦ δίφρου, τὸ δὲ μοσχάριον ὅπερ εἶχε γαλαθηνὸν ἀμελλητὶ λαβοῦσα σφάττει, ὀψοποιοῦσα δὲ καὶ πέττουσα τοὺς ἀζύμους, ηὐτρέπιζεν ἐδωδάς. 3. ἐπειδὴ δὲ προσέφερεν αὐτῷ καὶ τοῖς ἀμφ᾽ αὐτὸν ἀριστοποιήσασα σπουδαίως, ὁ μὲν αὐτόθι σιτίων ἐλάβετο προτραπείς· ἀνάγκη δὲ νοεῖν ὡς εἰς ἄλλας ἀφίκετο νυκτερίους ὥρας, εἴπερ ᾤχετο νυκτὸς ἐκεῖθεν ἐξορμήσας. ὥστε τοῦτο μὲν αὐτοτελῶς ἐλέγχεται ψευσάμενος ὁ δαίμων· οὐ γάρ, ὡς εἶπεν (**αὔριον ἔσῃ σὺ μετ᾽ ἐμοῦ**), γέγονεν οὕτως, ὁπηνίκα τὴν ἑξῆς αὐτόσε διέτριψεν ἡμέραν ἄσιτος, εἶτα τῇ δευτέρᾳ τῆς ἐδωδῆς ἁψάμενος ἐβάδισεν εἰς τὸ στρατόπεδον. 4. οὐχὶ δὲ τοῦτο μόνον ἁλίσκεται παρὰ τὸ γεγονὸς εἰρηκώς, ἀλλὰ καὶ τὸν Ἰωνάθαν ἔφη μονώτατον ὁμοῦ τῷ πατρὶ κατα-

myther in disguise declared the actual prophetic sayings of Samuel and supposed he would appear to be prophesying even though he understood nothing. Thus, he put forward the words of another as his own and struck Saul, the wretch, with astonishment; by them with great ease he secretly took away and stole his mind.

10. What else, then, does he add after this? "And tomorrow," he says, "you and your son Jonathan will be with me. And the Lord will give the camp of Israel into the hands of the foreigners" (1 Kgdms 28:19). But the demon seems to have said these things as his own. 13. 1. Now we must investigate whether he foretold the truth, as Origen supposed, whether he related this by conjecture and coincidence, and in addition whether he was able to have foreknowledge of any of these things. First, then, Saul does not appear to have died the next day, as the phantom said when prophesying. 2. For when Saul had heard these words, because of his great despondency "he did not eat bread all day and for the whole of that night," as the divine scripture relates. After this the woman, giving advice once more, sought to persuade him to taste some food, since he had a journey ahead of him. If we take account of this, it is presumably quite clear that it was on the second day after that fast of a whole day and night that she convinced him, when he had fallen unnerved to the ground, to get up and sit on a chair in a more orderly fashion. She quickly took and slaughtered the fatted young calf she had, prepared and baked unleavened cakes, and got the food ready. 3. When she had made the meal in haste and offered it to Saul and those with him, Saul, yielding to persuasion, partook of the provisions right away. We must understand that if he departed in a hurry from there "during the night," then the time had arrived at a second set of night hours (1 Kgdms 28:20–25).[35] As a result, the demon is convicted of his own accord by this lie, for it did not happen in the way he said—"Tomorrow you will be with me"—since he had spent the full next day right there, fasting. Then it was on the second day, after tasting the food, that he went back to the army. 4. Not only is the devil caught having said this contrary to what happened, but he also said that only Jonathan together with his father would end up with him. But on the con-

---

[35] Although it is not entirely clear, it would seem that Saul's fast includes the night he consulted the belly-myther and the day following. In any case, the night in verse 25 is clearly a second night. "Tomorrow" has already gone by.

λῆξαι πρὸς αὐτόν· ἐκ δὲ τῶν ἐναντίων ἡ διηγηματικὴ τοῦ γράμματος ἀγορεύει φωνῇ τὸν Σαοὺλ ἅμα τρισὶν ἀπεσφάχθαι παισίν, ἀλλ᾽ οὐχ ἑνὶ μόνῳ, ὡς ἔφησεν ἐκεῖνος. 5. οὐκοῦν ἀπορίᾳ προγνώσεως οὐδὲν ἀληθὲς ἐξεῖπεν ὁ δαίμων· οὐ γὰρ ἂν ἐναντία τῶν γεγονότων ἀπήγγελλεν, ἀλλὰ τὰ τῷ Σαμουὴλ εἰρημένα πρότερον, ὡς ἔφην, ὑπεκκλέψας, ὀλίγα ἄττα προσετίθει τούτοις, ἐκ τῶν εἰκότων ὁμοιότροπα συμπλέξας. 6. οὕτως ἄρα καὶ θάνατον ἠπείλει τῷ δυνάστῃ, ταῖς ἐκείνου φωναῖς ἀποχρώμενος. ἀλλ᾽ ἔτι γε καὶ τὴν τοῦ Ἰσραὴλ ἐκδοῦναι παρεμβολὴν ὑπισχνεῖτο, τῷ τὸν προφήτην ἐμβριθῶς εἰρηκέναι διασχισθήσεσθαι τὸν λαόν. 7. ὁρῶν οὖν ἐπιτετειχισμένα πολέμου μηχανήματα καὶ τὸν τοῦ λαοῦ προεστῶτα περιδεῆ, προσέτι δὲ καὶ καταλειφθέντα πρὸς αὐτοῦ τοῦ θεοῦ δι᾽ ὧν ὁ δυνάστης ὡμολόγει στοχαζόμενος ὅτι δεῦρο περαιοῦται τὸ τοῦ προφήτου κήρυγμα, πρὸς τὰς ἐνεστώσας ὑπεκρίνατο κινήσεις ἀναφωνεῖν. 8. ὅσα μέντοι προσέθηκεν ἴδια καθ᾽ ἑαυτά, φανερῶς ἑάλω ψευσάμενος· οὔτε γὰρ τὴν τοῦ θανάτου δεδύνηται προειπεῖν ἡμέραν, οὔτε τὰς τῶν υἱέων τοῦ Σαοὺλ ἀναιρέσεις, ὧν ἐπὶ ὀνόματος ἐμνημόνευσεν ἡ γραφή. ἐκ δὲ τούτων οὐ χαλεπῶς ἂν εἴη νοεῖν ὡς οὐδὲν ἴδιον οὐδὲ ἀληθὲς ἀπήγγελλεν τὸ πνεῦμα, ὅσα δὲ τοῦ Σαμουὴλ ὑπεξέκλεπτε ῥήματα, ταῦτα σφετεριζόμενον ᾤετο προφητεύειν. 9. ἀλλὰ μάλιστα μὲν οὐκ ἔστιν εἰπεῖν ὅτι τοῦτο προύφήτευεν ἀψευδῶς· εἰ δ᾽ ἄρα καὶ πολέμου γένεσιν ἀνεκήρυττεν καὶ τὰ τῆς αἱματεκχυσίας ἀνήκεστα ῥεύματα, τίς ὁ τῶν ἁπάντων αἴτιός ἐστι πολέμων; 10. οὐχ ὁ διάβολος; οὐκ αὐτὸς ἐξῃτήσατο τὸν Ἰώβ; οὐκ ἐπήγειρεν αὐτῷ πόλεμον ἐξαίφνης ἀκήρυκτον; οὐ μεταμορφούμενος ἄλλοθι ἄλλως αὐτάγγελος ἅμα καὶ μάρτυς ἐγίγνετο καὶ πολέμαρχος, εἰς τὰ τῶν ἀνθρώπων ἐνδόσθια παρεισδύς;

14. 1. Ἀλλὰ ἀσαφὲς εἶναι τὸ τοιοῦτο σχῆμα νενόμισται τοῖς πολλοῖς· ἰτέον οὖν ἀκολούθως εἰς τὰ τῆς τρίτης τῶν Βασιλειῶν ἴχνη. φαίνεται τοίνυν ὅπως ὁ προφήτης ἐπερωτᾶται Μιχαίας ὑπὸ τοῦ Ἀχαάβ· ἀλλ᾽ ἐπειδήπερ ἠναγκάζετο τἀληθῆ λέγειν ἀπαρακαλύπτως, ἑορακέναι μὲν ἔφασκε **τὸν κύριον ἐπὶ θρόνου καθήμενον**, εἶτα καὶ **στρατιὰς** ἑστάναι

trary, the narrative voice of the text recounts that Saul was slain together with three sons and not only one, as he said (1 Kgdms 31:2). 5. Therefore, the demon declared nothing true, since he was at a loss for foreknowledge—for he would not have proclaimed what was contrary to what happened—rather, as I have said, having stolen the things Samuel had said earlier, he added to them a few particulars, interweaving them with verisimilitudes based on what was likely to happen. 6. In this way, then, he threatened the ruler with death, misappropriating Samuel's words. Moreover, the demon promised the handing over of the Israelite camp, while the actual prophet (Samuel) had said forcefully that the people will be divided.[36] 7. Therefore, when he saw the instruments of war drawn up and the leader of the people terrified and still more even forsaken by God himself, conjecturing from what the ruler confessed that Samuel's proclamation was coming to pass here, he pretended to address the present occurrences. 8. Nevertheless, he is caught openly lying by statements he added that were all his own, since he was neither able to predict the day of death nor the slaying of Saul's sons whose names scripture has laid up in memory. For these reasons it would not be difficult to understand that the spirit declared not even a single thing of his own that was true but that he secretly stole the words of Samuel and by appropriating them as though his own, supposed he was prophesying. 9. But most important, one cannot say that he prophesied in this respect without lying. Even if he did proclaim the beginning of war and the unbearable streams of bloodshed, who is the cause of all wars? 10. Is it not the devil? Did he not ask for Job? Did he not suddenly raise up an undeclared war against him? Does he not transform himself into different shapes at different times and become at one and the same time a self-appointed messenger, a witness, and a warlord slipping into the inner parts of people?

14. 1. But such a use of disguise has been thought by many to be unclear. We must consequently turn to subsequent events in 3 Kingdoms. There it is shown how the prophet Micaiah was questioned by Ahab, but when he was compelled to speak the truth in an unveiled manner, he said that he "saw the Lord sitting on his

---

[36] The LXX of 1 Kgdms 15:29 has "Israel will be divided in two" instead of "the people will be cut in two." Is Eustathius suggesting that the devil has misunderstood the prophecy, referring it to Israel's defeat at Mount Gilboa instead of to the division of the kingdoms after Solomon?

περὶ αὐτὸν οὐρανίους ἔκ τε δεξιῶν ἅμα καὶ εὐωνύμων· 2. ὁμοῦ δὲ τῇ τῆς ὄψεως ἱστορίᾳ καὶ φωνῆς ἔφησεν ἀκηκοέναι τοιᾶσδέ τινος· *τίς ἀπατήσει τὸν Ἀχαὰβ καὶ ἀναβήσεται εἰς Ῥεμμὸδ Γαλαὰδ καὶ πεσεῖται ἐκεῖ;* τηνικαῦτα δέ φησιν (ἵνα τὰ ἐν μέσῳ παραλείψας ἐρῶ τὸ ζητούμενον) *ἐξῆλθε πνεῦμα καὶ ἔστη ἐνώπιον κυρίου καὶ εἶπεν· ἐγὼ ἀπατήσω αὐτόν.* 3. ὡς δὲ ὁ κύριος ἀνθυπενέγκας ἔφρασεν *ἐν τίνι;* ἀνθυποφέρει πάλιν· *ἐξελεύσομαι καὶ ἔσομαι πνεῦμα ψευδὲς ἐν στόματι πάντων τῶν προφητῶν αὐτοῦ.* πρὸς ταῦτα μὲν οὖν εἴρηκεν ὁ κρείττων· *ἀπατήσεις, καί γε δυνήσῃ· καὶ νῦν ἰδοὺ* φησὶν *ἔξελθε καὶ ποίησον οὕτως.* ὁ δὲ προφήτης αὐτὰ ταῦτα τῷ βασιλεῖ διηγούμενος εὐθέως ἐπιφέρει· *δέδωκεν ὁ θεὸς πνεῦμα ψευδὲς ἐν στόματι πάντων τῶν προφητῶν σου τούτων, καὶ ἐλάλησεν κύριος ἐπὶ σὲ κακά.* 4. τοιγαροῦν εἴπερ ἀνάγκη νοεῖν οὐκ ἀγαθόν, ἀλλὰ πονηρὸν εἶναι τοῦτο τὸ πνεῦμα τὸ τῆς ψευδηγορίας αἴτιον, ἀκόλουθον ὑπολαμβάνειν αὐτὸ τοῦτο διαβολικὸν ὄργανον ὑπάρχειν. εἰ δὲ κυρίως ἀποδείκνυται τοῦτο εἶναι, προακήκοεν ἄρα πῶς ἤμελλεν ὁ μιαρὸς Ἀχαὰβ εἰς πόλεμον ἀπιὼν ἀποθνήσκειν· 5. αὐτὸ γὰρ ἠξίωσε τὸ ψεῦδος ἀντὶ τῆς ἀληθείας ἐμβάλλειν, ἵνα πολέμου γένεσιν αὐτουργήσῃ καὶ διαφθείρῃ τὸν ἄδικον αἰσχίως. ὥστε καὶ διὰ τούτων ἀποδείκνυται τῶν ἔργων ὅτι τὰ κακὰ τοῖς ἀδίκοις ἐπιφερόμενα προμεμάθηκεν ὁ διάβολος, ἐπειδὴ τῶν ἐχθίστων ὁ δραματουργὸς αὐτός ἐστιν ἁπάντων.

6. Ἐπὶ μέντοι τοῦ Σαοὺλ ὅσα προσθεὶς ἀφ᾽ ἑαυτοῦ συνέζευξεν τοῖς τοῦ Σαμουὴλ ἀποφθέγμασιν, οὐ μόνον ἐψεύσατο πιθανῶς, ἀλλὰ καὶ ἐβλασφήμησεν ἀσεβῶς. ἐνθένδε ποθὲν ἡ πρώτη διελέγχεται δυσφημία· πρῶτον μέν, ὅτι κατὰ μίμησιν, ὡς ὁ κύριος ἔφη τῷ λῃστῇ τὸ κράτος ὁμολογήσαντι τῆς βασιλείας αὐτοῦ, *σήμερον ἔσῃ μετ᾽ ἐμοῦ* λέγων *ἐν τῷ παραδείσῳ,* ταὐτὸν δὴ τοῦτο καὶ τῷ Σαοὺλ ἐκπληρώσαντι τὰς μανικὰς αὐτοῦ μαντείας ἔφησεν ὁ δολομήτης· *αὔριον ἔσῃ σὺ μετ᾽ ἐμοῦ καὶ Ἰωνάθαν ὁ υἱός σου.* 7. δεύτερον δὲ βούλεται δεικνύναι διὰ τούτων ὅτι μηδὲν ὁ δίκαιος ἀδίκου διαφέρει, τὰς τῶν εὐσεβῶν ἐκκόψαι προθυμίας ἐπιτεχνώμενος. οὐδεὶς δὲ ἔοικεν ἀγνοεῖν ὅτι μηδεμία συνυπάρχει κοινωνία *πιστῷ μετὰ ἀπίστου,* ἢ αὖ πάλιν ὅπως ὁ πλούτῳ κατατρυφήσας ἀπλήστῳ πόρρω

throne," then also "the host" of heaven standing "beside him to the right and the left." 2. Together with the narrative of his vision he said he also heard someone's voice like this, "Who will deceive Ahab, so that he will go up to Ramoth-gilead and fall there?" Then he said (I am leaving out the intervening part so I can speak to the issue under discussion), "A spirit came forward and stood before the Lord, and said, 'I will deceive him.'" 3. And when the Lord said in reply, "How?" he replied in turn, "I will go out and be a lying spirit in the mouth of all his prophets." The Great One then said these words, "You shall deceive him, and you shall succeed; now go out and do it." When the prophet had narrated these very things to the king, he immediately continued, "God has put a lying spirit in the mouth of all these your prophets, and the Lord has spoken evil against you" (3 Kgdms 22:15–23). 4. Consequently, if we must understand that the spirit responsible for the lie was not good but evil, it follows that we must suppose it to be the very instrument of the devil. And if it is authoritatively demonstrated that this is the case, then it had heard ahead of time how Ahab, a man defiled, was going to go off to battle to meet his death. 5. For the spirit saw fit to introduce this very lie instead of the truth so that it might on its own bring about the beginning of war and destroy the wicked one shamefully. Therefore, it is proven by these acts, too, that the devil has prior notice of the evils inflicted upon wicked people, since he is himself the contriver of everything that is most hateful.

6. Certainly, in the case of Saul, in the things the devil added on his own and joined to Samuel's actual utterances he not only lied persuasively but also impiously blasphemed. He is convicted of the highest level of slander by the following considerations. First, that he imitated what the Lord said to the thief who confessed the power of his kingdom, "Today you will be with me," he said, "in Paradise" (Luke 23:43). This is the exact same thing the crafty one said to Saul, who had brought to completion his manic mantic pursuits, "Tomorrow you and Jonathan your son" will be "with me." 7. Second, he wanted to show by these words that the righteous person fares no differently from the wicked, scheming to cut off all ethical motivation that the pious have. No one is likely not to know that there is no fellowship "between a faithful and an unfaithful person" (2 Cor 6:14–15) or, moreover, of how the person who has luxuriated in insatiable wealth has been set

τῆς τοῦ Λαζάρου διαίτης ἀπεκρίθη, καίτοι μηδὲν ὅμοιον ἐκείνῳ δράσας. 8. ἀλλ' οὗτος μὲν οὐδὲν πώποτε μετέδωκεν τῷ πενομένῳ, τὸ παράπαν οὐδέν, οὔτε περιττευμάτων οὔτε ψιχῶν εἰς τοὔδαφος ἐκριπτομένων, ἀλλ' οὐδ' ἐλυμήνατο τὸν ἄνδρα πληγαῖς, οὐ μάστιξιν αἰκισάμενος ἐδίωξε περαιτέρω που γῆς. 9. ἀλλ' ὅμως, ἐπειδὴ μετήλλαξαν ἄμφω μετάραντες ἐντεῦθεν, ὁ μὲν εἰς κόλπους ἔληξε τοῦ προπάτορος Ἀβραάμ, ὁ δὲ ταῖς ἀκοιμήτοις ἐδόθη φλοξὶν τοῦ πυρός. ὡς οὖν ἐν τῷ ᾅδῃ βασανιζόμενος ἐφλέγετο, πόρρωθεν μὲν ὁρᾷ τὸν προπάτορα, θεωρεῖ δὲ καὶ τὸν *Λάζαρον ἐν τοῖς κόλποις αὐτοῦ·* 10. τῇ δὲ δὴ φλογὶ πυρούμενος, ἐκθύμως ἠξίου τὸν Ἀβραάμ, ὅπως ἐκπέμψῃ τὸν πένητα πρὸς αὐτόν· ἐδεῖτο γάρ, ἵν' ἀφικόμενος ὁ Λάζαρος τὸ μὲν ἄκρον ὕδατι βάψῃ τοῦ δακτύλου, καταψύξῃ δὲ τὴν γλῶτταν αὐτοῦ, νοτίδος ἐπαφυσάμενος ἰκμάδα· πυροφόροις οὖν ἀλγυνόμενος ὀδύναις ἐπρέσβευε τοιαῦτα μεθ' ἱκετείας ὁ τάλας. 11. ἐπειδὴ δὲ πρὸς ἔπος ἀποκρινάμενος ὁ προπάτωρ ἕκαστον ἐν ἑκάστῳ μέρει τὰς ἀξίας ἔφαινεν ἀμοιβὰς ἐπάθλου χάριν εἰληφέναι, τηνικαῦτα προσθεὶς ἐπεφθέγξατο· *καὶ ἐπὶ πᾶσι τούτοις μεταξὺ ἡμῶν καὶ ὑμῶν χάσμα φησὶν ἐστήρικται μέγα, ὅπως οἱ θέλοντες διαβῆναι ἔνθεν πρὸς ὑμᾶς μὴ δύνωνται, μηδὲ οἱ ἐκεῖθεν πρὸς ἡμᾶς διαπερῶσιν.* 12. εἰ τοίνυν ἐστὶ χάσματος ἰδέα διείργουσα μεταξὺ δικαίων ἠδ' ἀδίκων, ὥστε μὴ δύνασθαι τοὺς ἔνθεν ἐκεῖσε διαπορθμεῦσαι μήτε δεῦρο τοὺς ἐκεῖθεν ἀφικέσθαι, συνέστηκεν ὡς ὁ Σαοὺλ ἄδικος ὢν οὐκ ἔστι μετὰ προφήτου Σαμουήλ· 13. εἰ γὰρ ὁ πλούσιος οὐ δύναται μετὰ τοῦ πένητος εἶναι, καὶ ταῦτα μηδὲν ἀδικήσας μηδὲ διώξας αὐτόν, ἀλλὰ μὴ μεταδοὺς αὐτῷ προχείρως ἐξ ὧν εἶχεν, πόσῳ δὴ μᾶλλον ὁ σχέτλιος ἀνὴρ ἀνάξιός ἐστι τῆς τῶν ἁγίων ἀπολαῦσαι κοινωνίας;

15. 1. Ἀλλ' οὐ διανοητέον ὅπως αἰσχροῦ μὲν ἕνεκα κέρδους ἀθετεῖ τὸ θεῖον ἐπίταγμα, δαίμονι δὲ πληγεὶς ἀνιάτως ἐλαύνεται βασκανίᾳ, τὸν ἁγιοπρεπῆ διώκει Δαβὶδ οὐδενὶ κόσμῳ πρέποντι, καίτοι ψαλμῳδίᾳ προφητικῇ τὴν ἀγριότητα τοῦ ἐμβακχεύοντος ἐν αὐτῷ δαίμονος ἡμεροῦντα, 2. τοὺς ἱερεῖς ἀποσφάττει τοῦ κυρίου τριακοσίους ὄντας πρὸς τοῖς πεντήκοντα τὸν ἀριθμόν, ἀφίσταται τοῦ θεοῦ μαντευόμενος ἀσεβῶς; εἰ δὲ

far apart from Lazarus's way of life (Luke 16:19–31), even though he had done nothing similar to Saul. 8. But the rich man never shared anything with the poor man—nothing at all, neither from his abundance nor from the crumbs that fell to the ground. And yet he did not mistreat the man with blows, nor by torturing him with whips did he chase him off somewhere beyond the earth. 9. But, nevertheless, when they were both taken from here, they were translated; one rested in the bosom of forefather Abraham, while the other was handed over to unceasing flames of fire. Then when the rich man was being tormented in the hell-fire, from afar he sees the forefather and beholds also "Lazarus in his bosom." 10. And while he was being burned in the flames, he fervently asked Abraham to send the poor man to him, for he was begging for Lazarus to come and "dip the tip of" his "finger in water and cool" his "tongue," drawing for himself a drop of liquid. So the miserable man, suffering grievously in fiery agony, made these pleas with supplication. 11. When the forefather in response to his statement pointed out that each man had received his fitting reward in each place as recompense, he then went on to say, "Besides all this, between us and you," it says, "a great chasm has been fixed, so that those who want to pass from here to you cannot do so, nor can those from there cross over to us" (cf. Luke 16:26). 12. Therefore, if a sort of chasm is lying between the righteous and the wicked, so that those on this side are not able to pass through to there and those on that side cannot get here, it is established that Saul, being wicked, is not with the prophet Samuel. 13. For if the rich man cannot be with the poor man—even though he had not injured or pursued him but merely failed to share readily with him from what he had—how much more is the wretched man Saul unworthy to enjoy the fellowship of the saints.

15. 1. Must we not, however, consider how Saul disregarded the divine command for the sake of shameful gain (1 Kgdms 15:9), how when he was incurably struck by the demon, he was led by malign influence to pursue the suitably holy David in a thoroughly unsuitable fashion, even though it was David who tamed the savagery of the demon raging within him by his prophetic psalmody (1 Kgdms 19:9), 2. how he slaughtered the priests of the Lord— 350 priests in number (1 Kgdms 22:18),[37] how he committed

---

[37] The LXX has 305.

ταῦτα καὶ τὰ τούτοις ἀδελφὰ διεπράξατο, πῶς οἷόν τε νομίζειν ὅτι μετὰ τοῦ θαυμασιουργοῦ κατέληξε Σαμουήλ, ὃς ἐν ὥρᾳ θέρους ὑετὸν ἠξίωσε γενέσθαι, καὶ παρ' αὐτὸ κατεσκεδάσθη πλῆθος ἀμέτρητον ὑδάτων; 3. εἰ δὲ οὐκ ἔστιν εἰπεῖν ὅτι Σαοὺλ ἐστιν μετὰ τοῦ Σαμουήλ, ἐψεύσατο μὲν ὁ λέγων αὐτῷ· *αὔριον ἔσῃ σὺ μετ' ἐμοῦ*. τοιγαροῦν εἰ ψεύστης ὁ ταῦτα εἰρηκὼς ὑπάρχει, πρόδηλον ὡς οὐκ ἔστιν ὁ Σαμουὴλ οὗτος· οὐ γὰρ ἂν οὕτως ἀφρόνως ὁ τοῦ κυρίου ψεύσαιτο προφήτης, ὥστε τὰ τοιαῦτα δίχα διαπτυσσόμενα ῥήματα γυμνὸν ὑποδεικνύει τὸν πολυπρόσωπον ἐνδοτάτω θῆρα κρυπτόμενον. 4. αὐτὸς γοῦν ἐστιν ὁ κατασπάσας εἰς τοῦ ταρτάρου χάσμα καὶ τὸν ἐμμανῆ Σαούλ· ὅθεν οἰκείως αὐτῷ προσεφθέγγετο κρατήσας· *αὔριον ἔσῃ μετ' ἐμοῦ*. 5. διττῷ δὲ συστῆσαι τρόπῳ πειρώμενος ὡς οὐδέποτε δίκαιος ἀδίκου διαφέρει, καὶ τὸν Ἰωνάθαν ἅμα τῷ πατρὶ τὸν αὐτὸν ἐκείνῳ κλῆρον ἀπενέγκασθαι συνωμολόγει, καίτοι μὴ συνενεχθέντα τῇ τούτου ὠμότητι. 6. τίς δὲ τῶν ὄντων ὑποκρίνεται μὴ νοεῖν ὅτι κράτιστα βιώσας ὁ τοῦ προφήτου Δαβὶδ ἐραστής, ἀλλὰ μὴ διῶξαι δίκαιον ἀδίκως ἐγχειρήσας, οὐ τὴν αὐτὴν ἀποφέρεται τῷ διώξαντι μισθοφορίαν; 7. οὐ γὰρ ἀποθανεῖται, τὸ ξύμπαν εἰπεῖν, υἱὸς ὑπὲρ ἀδίκου πατρός. ἀλλὰ μὴν ἐλέγχεταί γε καὶ διὰ τοῦδε τοῦ μηνύματος ὁ ψευδορράφος.

16. 1. Ἀπαραλείπτῳ δὲ τάξεως ἀκολουθίᾳ προσθεὶς ἔφησεν ὁ συγγραφεὺς ὅτι *καὶ ἔσπευσε Σαοὺλ καὶ ἔπεσεν ἑστηκὼς ἐπὶ τὴν γῆν καὶ ἐφοβήθη σφόδρα λέγων ἀπὸ τῶν λόγων Σαμουήλ*. 2. ἐκείνους γὰρ οἶδε τοῦ Σαμουὴλ εἶναι τοὺς λόγους, οὓς προεφήτευσε μὲν αὐτῷ σώματι καὶ γλώττῃ παρών, τὸ δὲ φάσμα τούτους ἀνελέξατο τοὺς λόγους καὶ προὔφερεν ὡς ἰδίους· ὧν ὁ δυνάστης ὑπομνησθείς, καὶ τὰ τοῦ πολέμου σύμβολα θεωρῶν ἄντικρυς ἱδρυμένα, περιδεὴς ἐγεγόνει, τὸ πέρας αὐτῶν ἐννοῶν. 3. ἀλλ' Ὠριγένης ἑαυτῷ δόγματα πλάττων, εἰδὼς ὅτι πλεῖστοι μὲν ὅσοι

apostasy from God by impiously seeking divination? If he carried out these deeds and those like them, how is it possible to suppose that he ended up with Samuel, the wonder-worker who asked for rain at harvest time and because of it a boundless supply of water was poured down at just that moment (1 Kgdms 12:18)? 3. So if it is not possible to say that Saul is with Samuel, then the one who said to him, "Tomorrow you will be with me" lied. And consequently, if the one who has said these things was a liar, it is perfectly clear that this was not Samuel. For the Lord's prophet could not have lied in so foolish a fashion.[38] Consequently, such words, rolled out for the second time, provide a glimpse of the many-faced beast hidden inside. 4. He it is, then, who dragged also the madman Saul down into the chasm of the netherworld, where, holding sway on his own terrain, he directed the statement to Saul: "Tomorrow" you will be "with me." 5. Trying to establish by a double stratagem that there is no difference between a righteous and a wicked person, he promised that Jonathan, too, together with his father would receive the same lot as he, even though he had not been allied with his savagery. 6. Who among the living pretends not to understand that the one who loved the prophet David, having lived an excellent life, never attempting an unrighteous persecution of a righteous man, does not receive the same reward as the one who did persecute him? 7. For, generally speaking, a son will not die on behalf of a wicked father (see Ezek 18:19–20; Deut 24:16). Thus, the one who stitches lies together stands convicted also by this reference.

16. 1. Without interrupting his orderly sequence, the author goes on to say, "And Saul hastened and fell fixed on the ground, and was filled with great fear because of the words of Samuel" (1 Kgdms 28:20). 2. For Saul knew those to be the words of Samuel, which he had prophesied to him when present in body and in voice,[39] but the phantom had picked up these words and was presenting them as his own. When the ruler remembered them and saw the signs of war set up openly, he became terrified, knowing what their end would be. 3. Now Origen, fashioning teachings on his own, knows that there are a great many people who reach

---

[38] ἀφρόνως, an emendation Simonetti in *La Maga di Endor* accepts. Declerck, *Eustathii Antiocheni Opera*, retains the reading of M (ἀχρόμως), understanding it to be ἀχρώμως, "shamelessly."

[39] Literally, "tongue" (γλῶττα).

τυγχάνουσιν οἱ ταῦτα ψηφιζόμενοι, πρὸς δὲ τοὺς ἀντιλέγοντας αὐτῷ διαλεγόμενος, οὐκ ἐσπούδασε μετὰ τῆς ὀφειλομένης εὐλαβείας ἀκριβῶσαι
τὸ δέον· ἀλλά γε τὸ τῆς ἐγγαστριμύθου δρᾶμα "πάντων ἅπτεσθαι" προλέγων καὶ "τὴν ἀλήθειαν" εἰς τὴν ἐξέτασιν "ἀναγκαίαν" ἐπικαλούμενος,
αὐτῇ τῇ ἀληθείᾳ μάχεται προφανῶς. 4. εἶτα τοῦ Σαμουὴλ ἐγκώμια δι-
εξιών, ὅσα περὶ αὐτοῦ διαλαλοῦσιν αἱ θεῖαι γραφαί, τηνικαῦτα πάλιν
ὑπὸ τὴν τοῦ δαίμονος ἐξουσίαν ἀποφαίνων αὐτὸν αὐτοῖς ῥήμασι καὶ αὐταῖς ἐπέφραζε συλλαβαῖς· "ἆρ᾽ οὖν <εἰ> ὁ τηλικοῦτος ὑπὸ τὴν γῆν ἦν
καὶ ἀνήγαγεν αὐτὸν ἡ ἐγγαστρίμυθος, ἐξουσίαν ἔχει δαιμόνιον ψυχῆς
προφητικῆς;" 5. ἀλλὰ ταῦτα μὲν ὡς ἐπαπορῶν ἢ τάχα ἴσως ἐρόμενος
ὑπονοεῖται λέγειν ἐνίοτε παρά τισιν· ἵνα δὲ διὰ τῶν ἔπειτα συστήσειεν
ἐπιλόγων ὅτι ταῦτα οὕτως ἔχει, λευκοτέρᾳ προσετίθει φράσει "τί εἴπω;"
κεκραγὼς "ἐγγέγραπται ταῦτα·" φησὶν "ἀληθῆ ἐστιν ἢ οὐκ ἔστιν ἀληθῆ;
6. τὸ μὲν μὴ εἶναι ἀληθῆ λέγειν εἰς ἀπιστίαν προτρέπει χωρήσει ἐπὶ
κεφαλάς," φάμενος, "τῶν λεγόντων, τὸ δὲ εἶναι ἀληθῆ ζήτησιν καὶ ἐπαπόρησιν ἡμῖν παρέχει." 7. μετὰ δὲ τοῦτο πάλιν βεβαιῶν ἀνεπισκέπτως
ἅπερ εἰσαγγέλλει, καὶ τὰς τῶν ἀντιδοξούντων αὐτῷ γνώμας ἐκτιθέμενος
ἐπιφέρει· "καὶ μὴν ἴσμεν τινὰς τῶν ἡμετέρων ἀδελφῶν ἀντιβλέψαντας τῇ
γραφῇ καὶ λέγοντας· οὐ πιστεύω τῇ ἐγγαστριμύθῳ, λέγει ἡ ἐγγαστρίμυθος ἑορακέναι τὸν Σαμουήλ, ψεύδεται." καὶ πολλά γε πρὸς ἐπὶ τούτοις
ἕτερα. 8. διὰ δὲ τούτων ἀπαρακαλύπτως ἐπιτιμᾷ τοῖς ἀποφαίνουσι ψευδῆ
τὰ τῆς ἐγγαστριμύθου μαντεύματα, καὶ καταρώμενος ἐπὶ κεφαλὰς ἀναφέρει τῶν ἀπιστούντων αὐτῇ. ῥᾷστα μέντοι πεῖσαι τοὺς εὐχερεῖς ἐθέλων
αὐτὴ περιάπτει τῇ γραφῇ τὸ διήγημα, "γέγραπται ταῦτα," λέγων, "ἢ οὐ
γέγραπται;" 9. συλλογιστικῇ δὲ δεινότητι χρώμενος ἐπάγει δευτερῶν,
"ἀληθῆ ταῦτά ἐστιν ἢ οὐκ ἔστιν ἀληθῆ;" καίτοι τὸ μὲν οὐκ ἀνῆχθαι τὴν
τοῦ προφήτου ψυχὴν "ἐπαπόρησιν ἡμῖν," ἔφη, "παρέχει καὶ ζήτησιν."

the same verdict on this as we do. But in debating with his opponents he did not exert the reverence one ought in ascertaining
accurately what is right. Rather, by saying first that the dramatic
episode of the belly-myther *touches all people*, even though he pronounces the *truth necessary* for an examination,[40] he quite openly
battles against the truth itself. 4. Then, recounting the praises of
Samuel just as the divine scriptures declare them of him and reasoning once again that he was under the authority of the demon,
he goes on to state in these very words and syllables, *Therefore, if*[41]
such a great man were beneath the earth and the belly-myther brought
him up, does a petty demon have authority over a prophetic soul?[42] 5.
But whether feigning doubt or just asking questions, he is presumably speaking at a certain time to some audience. And so that he
may establish by the inferences that follow that these matters are
in fact the case, he expresses himself more lucidly by adding, *What*
shall I say?—crying out he says—*Are these things written? Are they*
true, or are they not true? 6. *To say they are not true is an inducement*
to unbelief, and it will come down on the heads of those who say it. But
to say they are true furnishes us with a matter for investigation and
an occasion for doubt.[43] 7. After this, again confirming without examination what he is declaring, he continues by setting forth the
opinions of those who take the view opposite to his. *Indeed, we*
know that some of our brothers have faced off against scripture and
say, "I do not believe the belly-myther. The belly-myther says she has
seen Samuel. She is lying."[44] And he adds many other statements
besides these. 8. Through them in an unveiled manner he rebukes
those who declare the mantic pronouncements of the belly-myther
to be lies, and he raises up curses on the heads of those who do not
believe her. Moreover, in his wish easily to persuade the heedless,
he attributes the tale to scripture itself. *Are these things written?*
he says, *or not written?* 9. Employing syllogistic cleverness he sec-
onds the point: *Are they true, or are they not true?* Furthermore,
while he admits that the prophet's soul having been brought up
furnishes us with an occasion for doubt and a matter for investiga-

[40] Origen, *Hom. 5 on 1 Kgdms* 2.3.
[41] "If" (εἰ), missing from M, is supplied from the text of Origen's homily.
[42] Origen, *Hom. 5 on 1 Kgdms* 2.5.
[43] Ibid.
[44] Ibid., 3.1.

αὐτὸ δὲ τὸ τὰ τοιαῦτα διδόναι τῷ δαίμονι πόσης ἀσεβείας ἐστὶ μεστόν,
οὐκέτι λέγει ζητῶν οὐδὲ προσέχει τὸν νοῦν ἀκράτῳ πληγεὶς ἀσυνεσίᾳ.
10. θεῷ γὰρ ὑπάρχει μόνῳ τοιαύτη ἐξουσίᾳ ἐπιτάσσειν, ὥστε ψυχὰς ἐξ
ᾅδου μεταπέμπεσθαι καὶ καλεῖν. ἀνθυπενεκτέον οὖν ἐνταῦθα πάλιν· ἐν
μὲν ταῖς ἱεραῖς ἀνείληπται ταῦτα γραφαῖς, οὐ μὴν ἐξ ἰδίου προσώπου τὸ
τοιοῦτο διαπεπρᾶχθαι γράμμα προὔλεγεν ὁ συγγραφεύς· οὐ γὰρ ἂν ἐκ-
κλησίαζεν ἡ βίβλος, ἐναντία ταῖς προφητικαῖς ἀντιβοῶσα φωναῖς, ὥς γε
καὶ πρόσθεν ἐδείξαμεν καὶ μικρὸν ὕστερον ἐροῦμεν. 11. ἀλλὰ δὴ τὰ τῆς
ἐγγαστριμύθου διεχάραττε ῥήματα καὶ τὴν ἐμμανῆ τοῦ δυνάστου *γνῶσιν*
ἔργοις ἀγνωσίας ἀποδεδειγμένην ἀνάπλεον· εἰ γὰρ οὕτως ἁρμόσει ταῖς
ἁγίαις ἐπισκῆψαι γραφαῖς, οὐκοῦν, ἐπειδὴ φασιν ὅτι καὶ θεὸν ἄντικρυς
ὁ διάβολος ἑαυτὸν ἀναγορεύει, παρὰ τοῦτο δεήσει πιστεύειν αὐτῷ, τῇ
διηγηματικῇ τοῦ γράμματος ἐκδοχῇ τὸ πᾶν ἀνατιθέντας, ὡς Ὠριγένης
εἰσηγεῖται; 12. καὶ τοῦτο γὰρ εἰς αὐτὰς ἀναγέγραπται τὰς γραφάς. ἢ αὖ
πάλιν, ἐπειδὰν ὑπερηφανίᾳ χρώμενος ἀμέτρῳ πᾶσαν ὁμοῦ τὴν τοῦδε τοῦ
κόσμου περιγραφὴν ἤτοι καὶ τὰς βασιλείας αὐτῆς ἰδίας εἶναι λέγοι, παρὰ
τοῦτο φαίη τις ἂν ὡς ἄρα προσήκει νοεῖν ὅτι δημιουργὸς αὐτός ἐστιν
ἁπάντων; 13. οὐ μὲν οὖν, εἴποι τις ἄν· ἡ γάρ τοι διηγηματικὴ διεχά-
ραξε φωνὴ τὰς ἐκείνου μεγαληγορίας, οὐ μὴν ἀληθεῖς ἀποφαίνει αὐτάς,
οὐδ᾽ ἔστι τοῦτο δεῖξαι δυνάμενος οὐδεὶς οὐδαμῶς. ἀλλὰ μυρία μὲν ἔστι

tion,[45] the very granting of such power to the demon is full of such great impiety that he no longer speaks as one investigating the matter, nor one focusing his mind on it, but as one struck with unmitigated ignorance. 10. For it belongs to God alone to give orders with such authority that he can summon and call souls from hell. Therefore, we must cross-examine Origen's interpretation, in turn, once more. These things have been taken up into sacred scripture, but the author by no means foretells in his own persona that what is written[46] took place. For the book would in that case not have been read in the church, if it cried out things that stand in direct opposition to the prophetic voices, as we have already demonstrated and shall say a little later. 11. But indeed, the author has set in character the words of the "belly-myther" and the insane "knowledge" (1 Kgdms 28:14) of the ruler, which by his actions is proven to be full of ignorance. For if it will be fitting to examine the holy scriptures this way, then is it the case that, when they say that the devil openly proclaims himself even to be God, we will because of this be obliged to believe him because we attribute everything to the narrative sense of the text, as Origen proposes? 12. For this, too, is written in the scriptures themselves (Ezek 28:2). Or again, when the devil in his immeasurable arrogance says that the whole circumference of this world together with its kingdoms belongs to him (Matt 4:8–9; Luke 4:5–6), would anyone, at least if he had any sense, say because of this that the devil is the creator of all things? 13. Surely no one would say this. For in truth the "narrative voice"[47] has characterized his boastings and declares them not true. Nor is there ever anyone who is able to prove this in any way whatsoever. Indeed, it is possible to look at countless such examples as these, but we cannot bring them all forward, lest we

---

[45] In Origen, *Hom. 5 on 1 Kgdms* 2.5 the questions and doubts have to do with the opinion that Samuel *was* brought up. If Eustathius has not misunderstood Origen, "not" must be removed from the text (so our translation). Klostermann, followed by Declerck, *Eustathii Antiocheni Opera*, posits a lacuna before the citation from Origen's homily. He fills it by appealing to Origen's text: "Furthermore, while he admits that to say the prophet's soul was not brought up *leads to unbelief*, yet to say that it was brought up *furnishes us with questions and doubts....*"

[46] The reading of M: γράμμα. Brockmeier emends to πρᾶγμα or δρᾶμα.

[47] This is the same expression found in Origen *Hom. 5 on 1 Kgdms* 4.4: διηγηματικὴ φωνή, used here as equivalent to narrative sense (ἡ διηγηματικὴ ἐκδοχῇ).

τοιαῦτα πρὸς ἐπὶ τούτοις ἰδεῖν, οὐχ οἷόν τε δὲ πάντα παράγειν, ἵνα μὴ μακρηγορίᾳ δόξωμεν ἐκκρούεσθαι τοῦ ζητήματος.

17. 1. Ὡς οὖν ἐδόκει τοῖς ὀρθότατα φρονοῦσιν οὐ μετρίως ἐπιτιμᾶν, αὖθις ὑπεκκλέψας ἐπ' ἄλλην ἀπεπήδησεν ἔννοιαν, ἐδεινοποίει δὲ δημαγωγῶν ὅτι φάσκουσι πρὸς τοῖς ἄλλοις ὡς εἴη φρικῶδες ὑπολαβεῖν ἐν ᾅδου γεγονέναι τὸν εὐκλεῆ Σαμουήλ, ὃς ἐκκρίτῳ προφητείας ἀξίᾳ τετίμηται. 2. τοῦτο μὲν οὖν ἄνω καὶ κάτω ταυτολογεῖ γραωδῶς, ἐξ ἄλλων εἰς ἄλλα μεταχειρίζεσθαι τοὺς αὐτηκόους ἀπάτῃ τεχνώμενος. ἡμεῖς δὲ περὶ τούτων οὐ διαφερόμεθα, περὶ ὧν ἅπασιν συνομολογητέα καθέστηκεν, ἀλλ' ὧν ἕνεκα κυρίως ἀμφισβητεῖν ἐγνώκαμεν· οὐ γὰρ εἰ Σαμουὴλ γέγονεν ζητητέον, ἀλλ' εἰ τοιαύτην ἔχει δαίμων ἐξουσίαν, ὥστε δικαίων ἀνακαλεῖσθαι ψυχὰς ἐξ ᾅδου καὶ πάλιν ἀποπέμπειν. 3. ἐπεὶ τοίνυν ἐπ' αὐτοφώρῳ ληφθεὶς ἑάλω βλασφημίας ἐπαντλῶν αἰκίᾳ τὰς τῶν ἀκροατῶν ἀκοάς, ἀπατηλῇ μὲν ὑπεκκλίνει τέχνῃ, καταφεύγει δὲ δῆθεν ἐπὶ τὸ τοῦ Χριστοῦ πρόσωπον, ἵν' ἀντεξετάσας αὐτὸ τοῖς ἁγίοις ἀνδράσιν ἀποδείξειεν ὅτι καὶ αὐτὸς εἰς ᾅδου κατῆλθεν ὁ Χριστὸς ὁμοῦ τοῖς ἄλλοις ἅπασιν. 4. ἀλλὰ γὰρ ὡς ἀπεδείκνυε τοῦτο καὶ δὴ καὶ κατ' ἄνδρα παραινῶν ἐπεφθέγγετο, "τί φοβῇ," λέγων, "εἰπεῖν ὅτι πᾶς χρῄζει τόπος αὐτοῦ τε τοῦ Χριστοῦ καὶ τῶν προφητῶν;" ὀλίγα ἄττα διὰ μέσου τάττων ἄλλην ἐπιπλέκει δυσφημίαν, ἐκφαίνων ὅτι "καὶ κάτω" τυγχάνων ὁ

seem by a long digression to be driven away from our investigation.

17. 1. Since he did not think he had sufficiently rebuked those who had the most orthodox opinions,[48] Origen stole away and turned to another idea. He used terrifying rhetoric in haranguing that they declare to others how frightening it would be to accept that the famous Samuel, who had been honored with the distinguished office of prophecy, should be in hell.[49] 2. He says this same thing over and over like an old crone, contriving to lead his audience by deceit from one camp to the other. Now we do not disagree about some things—that is, what is established as the common confession—but we recognize the things about which it is proper to engage in dispute. What needs to be investigated is not whether it was Samuel[50] but whether a demon had such authority as to call up the souls of the righteous from hell and send them back again. 3. Therefore, caught in the act, Origen has been convicted of blasphemy by cascading assaults on the ears of his audience.[51] He stoops to a deceptive artifice and, indeed, takes refuge in the personage of Christ so that, by comparing him side by side with the holy men, he may show that even Christ himself went down to hell together with all the rest.[52] 4. Moreover, when he had demonstrated this, he directed his advice to each reader in turn and said, *Why are you afraid to say that every place has need of Christ* himself and of *the prophets?*[53] Introducing a few other points in the meantime, he weaves into his argument another blasphemy, declaring that even when *Christ* was *below, so as to put it this way,* he says, *when he was in the place below, he was above with*

---

[48] See Origen, *Hom. 5 on 1 Kgdms* 4.10.

[49] Ibid., 3.2.

[50] See ibid., 6.1–2, where Origen seems to waver about which of the many "matters of dispute" (τὰ ζητούμενα) about the passage require attention and resolution.

[51] This is a reference to the anaphoric "bombast" Origen delivers in his personification of the "opposing interpretation" in *Hom. 5 on 1 Kgdms* 3.2–5.

[52] Origen, *Hom. 5 on 1 Kgdms* 6.2–3. Eustathius is accusing Origen of failing to make it clear whether or not the belly-myther brought up Samuel by turning the question to a point that all would admit, namely, that Christ descended into hell.

[53] Ibid., 7.4.

Χριστὸς "ἵν' οὕτως εἴπω," φησίν, "ἐν τῷ κάτω τόπῳ ὤν, τῇ προαιρέσει ἄνω ἦν." 5. ὡς περὶ ἀνθρώπου δὲ μόνου προσομιλῶν ἀλλ' οὐκέτι καὶ τῆς θείας αὐτοῦ στοχαζόμενος φύσεως, ἐν τοῖς κατωτάτω μὲν αὐτὸν ἔφασκεν ἀφῖχθαι, προαιρέσει δὲ δήπουθεν ἄνω βεβηκέναι, καθάπερ οὖν ἀμέλει καὶ τοὺς ἄλλους ἀνθρώπους. 6. "οὕτω," γὰρ ἔφη, "καὶ οἱ προφῆται καὶ Σαμουήλ, κἂν καταβῶσιν ὅπου αἱ ψυχαὶ φησὶν αἱ κάτω, ἐν τῷ κάτω μὲν δύνανται εἶναι τόπῳ, οὐ κάτω δέ εἰσι τῇ προαιρέσει." κουφολογίᾳ δὲ δὴ περιηχήσας ἀπειροπληθεῖ τὸν κόσμον, οὐδὲ τοῦτο ξυνίησιν ὅτι πᾶς ὁστισοῦν ἀνθρώπων, εἰ καὶ σφόδρα σχέτλιός ἐστιν, ἐν ᾅδου κατελθὼν ἄων τῇ προαιρέσει καθέστηκεν. 7. οὐδεὶς γοῦν ἂν εἴη γε δικαίων οὐδ' ἀδίκων, ὃς οὐ γλίχεται τῶν ἀνωτάτω μὲν ἑκάστοτε διατριβῶν ἔχεσθαι, τῶν δὲ καταχθονίων ἀπηλλάχθαι τόπων. εἰ τοίνυν ἅπαντες ὁμοῦ οἱ καταχθέντες εἰς ᾅδου τῶν ἄνω φορῶν ἐρῶσι προαιρέσει, κἂν οὐ πάνυ δικαίου τινὲς ἐπεμελήσαντο βίου, ποταπὸν ἀξίωμα τοῦ προφητικοῦ διεσάφει χοροῦ; 8. τί δὲ τὸ περιττὸν ἀπήγγελλε τοῦ κυρίου, πᾶσιν ὅμοιον ἀποφαίνων αὐτόν; ἀλλ' οὕτως ἀμαθῶς ἐξήχησε τὴν φωνήν, οὐκ ἐννοήσας ὅτι θεὸς ὢν ὁ λόγος, οὐ προαιρέσει μᾶλλον, ἀλλ' ἀρετῇ τῆς θεότητος ἁπανταχοῦ πάρεστιν ἀθρόως. 9. εἰ δὲ καὶ τὰ μάλιστα τὸν ἔκκριτον ἑαυτοῦ ναὸν ἐπέτρεψε λυθῆναι, τριήμερον μὲν αὐτίκα πάλιν ἀνήγειρε καινοπρεπῶς, ἡ δὲ ψυχὴ τοῦδε τοῦ ἀνθρωπείου σκηνώματος εἰς τὰ κατώτατα κατελθοῦσα μέρη τῆς γῆς, ἀνεπέτασε τὰς ἐκεῖσε πύλας ἀθρόᾳ ῥοπῇ καὶ τὰς αὐτόθι καθειργμένας ἀνῆκε ψυχάς· 10. οὕτω δὲ θεσπεσίᾳ κεκραταίωται δυνά-

respect to ethical purpose.[54] 5. As though speaking of a mere man with no longer any regard even for his divine nature, he said that he came to the lowest regions but that he had doubtless gone above *with respect to ethical purpose.* Of course, this is just like the rest of humanity. 6. For Origen said, *Likewise, both the prophets and Samuel, even if they went down where the souls below are, are able to be in the place below but are not below with respect to ethical purpose.*[55] He makes the world echo round with his boundless supply of idle talk and does not even understand that any person whatsoever, even if he is an utter wretch, when he descends to hell, is established above by ethical purpose. 7. Certainly there could not be anyone among either the righteous or the unrighteous who does not yearn constantly to have his dwelling in the highest place and to be delivered from the regions of the netherworld. Therefore, if all those who were brought down to hell together desire the fruitful lands[56] above by ethical purpose—even those who have taken no trouble at all to lead a righteous life—then what sort of honorable rank for the chorus of prophets is Origen explicating? 8. What does he relate as the superior quality[57] the Lord had, when he declares him to be like everyone else? Thus, he has made his voice echo in such an uneducated fashion because he did not understand that "the Word," being "God" (John 1:1), is present at one time everywhere not so much by ethical purpose as by the excellence of his divinity. 9. And if he permitted even his own most distinguished temple to be destroyed, then on the third day he immediately raised it again in a novel way, and the soul of this human tabernacle, having descended to the lowest "parts of the earth" (cf. Eph 4:9), threw wide the gates there in a single moment and brought up the souls that had been imprisoned there. 10. Thus, his soul was strengthened by divine power because of the constant

---

[54] Ibid., 8.2. προαίρεσις is "free will" or "choice" exercised in an ethically positive manner.

[55] Ibid., 8.3.

[56] The text is τῶν ἄνω φορῶν. Declerck in *Eustathii Antiocheni Opera* suggests a parallel with Plato, *Leg.* 747a, where the discussion concerns the ascent and descent of musical notes and motions. But φορός can mean "fruitful," and we might supply τόπων from the preceding sentence. Klostermann emends to ἄνω χορῶν.

[57] τὸ περιττόν, "something more" (likely a play on Origen's emphasis on the term at the end of his own homily (see *Hom. 5 on 1 Kgdms* 10.1, 4, and 5).

μει διὰ τὴν τοῦ θεοῦ καὶ λόγου συνουσίαν, ὥστε καὶ παντέφορον ἔχειν ἐξουσίαν.

18. 1. Ἀλλὰ μὴν ἔγωγε πείθομαι καὶ τούτου τεκμήριον εἶναι σαφές, ὁπηνίκα μὲν εἰς τοὺς καταχθονίους ἀφικνεῖτο τόπους, ἐν ταὐτῷ δὲ καὶ τὴν τοῦ λῃστοῦ ψυχὴν αὐθήμερον εἰσῆγεν εἰς τὸν παράδεισον. 2. εἰ γὰρ δι᾽ ἑνὸς ἀνθρώπου τοῖς ἅπασιν ὑπῆρξεν ἀνθρώποις ἡ σωτηρία, πρόδηλον ὡς ἡ ψυχὴ τὰς ὁμογενεῖς ἀναλυτροῦται ψυχάς, ἅμα μὲν εἰς τὰ καταχθόνια κατιοῦσα μέρη τοῦ χάους, ἅμα δὲ καὶ τῇ ἀρχαιοτάτῃ τοῦ παραδείσου πάλιν ἀποκαθιστῶσα νομῇ τὸν ὑπεισδύντα τῷ κράτει τῆς ἀηττήτου βασιλείας. 3. ἀκόλουθα δὲ καὶ πρὸ τούτων ὁ τοῦ θεοῦ παῖς ἐμαρτύρετο, προλέγων ὅτι *καὶ οὐδεὶς ἀναβέβηκεν εἰς τὸν οὐρανὸν εἰ μὴ ὁ ἐκ τοῦ οὐρανοῦ καταβάς, ὁ υἱὸς τοῦ ἀνθρώπου ὁ ὢν ἐν τῷ οὐρανῷ.* 4. τοιγαροῦν εἴπερ ἔφασκε τὸν ἐκ τοῦ ἀνθρωπείου γένους ὁρμώμενον εἰς οὐρανὸν μὲν ἀναβεβηκέναι μονώτατον ἐκ πάντων, ἐκ δὲ τῶν ἐκεῖσε πάλιν καταβεβηκέναι ἐνθάδε, καὶ δεῦρο βεβηκότα φοιτᾶν ἐν οὐρανῷ, συνέστηκεν ὅτι ψυχῆς ἀρετῇ ταῦτα ἔπραττεν ὁ ἄνθρωπος ἐκκρίτως. 5. ἡ γὰρ ἁγία τοῦ Χριστοῦ ψυχή, τῷ θεῷ συνδιαιτωμένη καὶ λόγῳ, πάντα μὲν ἐκπεριπολεῖ συλλήβδην, εἰς αὐτὸν δὲ βέβηκεν τὸν ἀνώτατον οὐρανόν, εἰς ὃν οὐδεὶς ἄλλος ἀνῆλθε τῶν ἀνθρώπων. ἀλλὰ ταῦτα εἰς αὐτὴν ἀνήρτηται τὴν ἀνθρωπείαν ἰδέαν, ἣν ὁ θεὸς ἐφόρεσε καὶ λόγος. 6. ὅτι δὲ πανταχοῦ πάρεστιν ἀθρόως ὁ τοῦ θεοῦ παῖς, οὐχ ἥκιστα καὶ περὶ τούτου μάρτυς ἕστηκεν Ἰωάννης, αὐτήκοος μὲν ὑπάρχων αὐτοῦ τοῦ Χριστοῦ, βοᾷ δὲ γεγονότως αὐτολεξεί *θεὸν οὐδεὶς ἑόρακεν πώποτε· ὁ μονογενὴς υἱὸς ὁ ὢν εἰς τὸν κόλπον τοῦ πατρός, ἐκεῖνος ἐξηγήσατο.* 7. καὶ μὴν εἰ δεῦρο παρὼν ἐπεφοίτα σωματικῶς ὁ Χριστός, ὁπηνίκα τούτους ἀπήγγελλεν Ἰωάννῃ τοὺς λόγους, ὁ δὲ τὰς τούτου ῥήσεις ὑποδεξάμενος ἐκήρυττε μὲν αὐτὸν ἐν τοῖς κόλποις εἶναι τοῦ πατρός, ἐστιώμενον ἐπὶ γῆς αὐτῷ σώματι, πῶς οὐκ ἐννοητέον ὅτι καὶ τῶν οὐρανῶν ἐπιβεβήκει τῷ τότε, καὶ ὡς κόλπων εἴσω διαιτώμενος καὶ τῇ γῇ θεοπρεπῶς ἐπεδήμει καὶ πᾶσιν ὁμοῦ παρῆν οἷα θεός;

association of God the Word so that he, too, had authority that extended everywhere.

18. 1. Moreover, for my part I am persuaded that there is a clear proof of this. When the soul of Christ came to the regions of the netherworld, at the same time it also led the soul of the thief on that very day to paradise (Luke 23:43). 2. For if through one man salvation began for all people, it is perfectly clear that his soul ransomed souls of the same kind, at once both by going down to the chaotic subterranean regions and by restoring to the most ancient plot of paradise the thief, who entered it secretly by the might of Christ's unconquerable kingdom. 3. Even before this the Son of God gave corroborating testimony when he proclaimed, "No one has ascended into heaven except the one who descended from heaven, the Son of Man who is in heaven" (John 3:13; cf. Eph 4:10). 4. Therefore, since he said that the one who sprang from the human race alone of all ascended into heaven and from there descended here again and a second time went to roam about in heaven, it is established that the Man was accomplishing these deeds in a distinctive way by the excellence of his soul.[58] 5. For Christ's holy soul, since it lives united with God the Word, travels all regions at once, and it has gone into the very highest heaven, into which no other human being has gone up. Yet all this has been bestowed upon the human form that God the Word bore. 6. And of the fact that the Son of God is present everywhere at a single time, John above all stands as a witness: he heard Christ himself with his own ears, and he cries out with a loud voice in these very words, "No one has ever seen God. It is the only begotten Son who is in the bosom of the Father who has made him known" (John 1:18). 7. Moreover, if Christ when present here was going about in bodily fashion at the moment he proclaimed these words to John, and if John, who received Christ's words, preached that he was in the bosom of the Father when he was a guest on earth in an actual body, how could it fail to be understood that even then he was both mounted above the heavens, residing in the bosom of the Father, and was also sojourning on earth in a way suitable for God, and was present to all at the same time as God?

---

[58] Eustathius appears to imagine that the human Christ at his ascension took the penitent thief's soul to paradise, then descended in order to harrow hell, and finally returned to heaven. He bases this interpretation on equating the subject of John 3:13 ("the Son of Man") with the assumed Man, who "ascended," then "descended," and finally is "in heaven."

19. 1. Εἰ δέ τις Ἰουδαϊκὴν ἀρρωστῶν ἀβλεψίαν τὰς εὐαγγελικὰς οὐ προσίεται φωνάς, ἐπακτέον αὐτῷ τὰ τοῦ Σολομῶντος ἀποφθέγματα καὶ ῥητέον ὧδέ πως· *ἡσύχου γὰρ σιγῆς περιεχούσης τὰ πάντα καὶ νυκτὸς ἐν ἰδίῳ τάχει μεσαζούσης, ὁ παντοδύναμός σου λόγος ἀπ᾽ οὐρανοῦ ἐκ θρόνων βασιλείων, ξίφος ὀξὺ τὴν ἀνυπόκριτον ἐπιταγήν σου φέρων, στὰς ἐπλήρωσε θανάτου τὰ πάντα· καὶ οὐρανοῦ μὲν ἥπτετο, βεβήκει δὲ ἐπὶ γῆς.* 2. εἰ τοίνυν ὁ μονογενὴς υἱὸς αὐτοῦ τοῦ θεοῦ λόγος ἀναγορεύεται καὶ θεὸς ὁμοδόξῳ συνῳδίᾳ, δι᾽ οὗ γεγόνασιν ἄγγελοι καὶ οὐρανοὶ καὶ γῆ καὶ θάλατται καὶ βυθοὶ καὶ φωστῆρες οὐρανοδρόμοι καὶ συλλήβδην εἰπεῖν ἅπασα τῶν γενητῶν ἡ σύστασις, οὕτως δὲ δικαίᾳ κρίσει σωφρονίζων ἅπαντας θρόνου μὲν οὐρανόθεν ἔχεται τῆς ἀϊδίου βασιλείας, ὀξείᾳ δὲ τιμωρεῖται δίκῃ τοὺς ἀδίκους (ἀλλὰ μὴν ἔργῳ καὶ πράξει παντοδύναμος ὤν, ἅτε δὴ θεὸς καὶ θεὸς λόγος, *οὐρανοῦ μὲν ἥπτετο, βεβήκει δὲ ἐπὶ γῆς* ἐν ταὐτῷ), θεότητος ἀρετῇ δηλονότι πάντα πληροῖ πανταχῶς. 3. οὐκοῦν εἰ τοιαύτης ἐπείληπται φύσεως, ἀσεβοῦσι μὲν οἱ νομίζοντες ἀβουλίᾳ τόπῳ καὶ ῥητῷ τινι χωρίου μορίῳ περιγράφεσθαι τὸ θεῖον, ἀμαθίᾳ δὲ μᾶλλον ἢ φρονήσει κοσμίᾳ φθέγγεται προχείρως Ὠριγένης ὅτι κατελθὼν εἰς τὰ κατώτατα μέρη τῆς γῆς ὁ Χριστὸς ἄνω "τῇ προαιρέσει" διέτριβεν· 4. οὐ γὰρ ἐνόησεν ὅτι θεὸς ὢν οὐ τοσούτῳ προθυμίᾳ γνώμης ἄνω τῷ δοκεῖν [ἐπιθυμίᾳ] παρῆν, ὅσῳ θειότητος ἐνεργείᾳ τοῖς ἅπασιν ὡς ἕνι μάλιστα πάντα πληροῖ πανταχῶς.

20. 1. Ἀλλὰ τοιαῦτα μὲν ἁρμόττει περὶ τοῦ Χριστοῦ δοξάζειν ἐκεῖνον, ὃς ὑπὸ δαίμονος ὁρίζεται ψυχὰς ἀνάγεσθαι προφητικάς· ἡ δὲ πυθόμαντις ὡς ἐθεάσατο τοὺς ὁμογαστρίους αὐτῇ δαίμονας, οἷα δή τι-

19. 1. But if someone, afflicted with the blindness of the Jews, does not accept the words of the Gospel, we must bring Solomon's words against him. They read something like this, "For while gentle silence enveloped all things, and night in its swift course was now half-gone, your all-powerful Word leaped from heaven, from the royal throne, carrying the sharp sword of your authentic command. He stood and filled all things with death, and he touched heaven, but he stood on earth" (Wis 18:14–16).[59] 2. Therefore, if the only begotten Son of God himself is proclaimed God the Word in perfectly consenting concord, he through whom angels, heavens and earth, seas, depths, the stars that course through the heavens, and, in sum, the entire fabric of creation came into being, then by just judgment recalling all people to their senses, from heaven he takes hold of the throne of the eternal kingdom, while with a sharp decree he punishes the unjust. Moreover, being all-powerful in work and deed inasmuch as he is God and God the Word, "he touched heaven, but he stood on earth" at the same time; it is clear that he fills all things (cf. Eph 4:10) in all ways by the excellence of his divinity. 3. Therefore, if he possesses such a nature, those who thoughtlessly suppose that what is divine is circumscribed by a place and by any particularly defined territory are downright impious. Hence, it is by lack of learning rather than by orderly thinking that Origen offhandedly says[60] that Christ after he went down to the lowest parts of the earth (cf. Eph 4:9) remained above *with respect to ethical purpose.*[61] 4. For Origen did not understand that Christ, being God, was present above not so much by the zeal of his ethical intent in the face of apparent desire as by the working of divinity, generally and particularly, by which he certainly fills all things in all ways.

20. 1. Yet it is fitting that Origen hold such opinions about Christ, since he is the one who pronounces that prophetic souls are brought up by a demon. Now when the Pythian prophetess saw demons who were biological kin to her, in order to elevate the

---

[59] Eustathius omits part of verse 15: "a stern warrior." The omission seems deliberate, since the passage is applied to the incarnation, which brings salvation rather than doom. It appears that Eustathius understands verse 16a ("He stood and filled all things with death"; Καὶ στὰς ἐπλήρωσεν τὰ πάντα θανάτου) to mean "he stood and filled all the places of death."

[60] προχείρως (cf. 1.2).

[61] Origen, *Hom. 5 on 1 Kgdms* 8.2.

νας ὁμοκοιλίους ἀδελφοὺς ἐπαίρουσα τὰ ὁμομήτρια γένη, βοᾷ· *θεοὺς ἑό-*
ρακα ἀναβαίνοντας ἐκ τῆς γῆς. 2. ἀλλ' ὁ μεγαληγόρος οὐκ ἔδεισεν Ὠριγένης εἰπεῖν ὅτι τὸ δαιμόνιον οὐχὶ τὴν τοῦ προφήτου μόνον ἀνήγαγεν
ψυχήν, ἀλλὰ μήτι γε καὶ ἄλλαι "συναναβεβήκασιν," ἔφη, "ψυχαὶ προφητῶν ἅγιαι"· μὴ κορεσθεὶς δὲ τῇ τοσαύτῃ παροινίᾳ καὶ τοὺς ἀγγέλους
ὡρίσατο συναναβεβηκέναι τοῖς πνεύμασιν αὐτῶν· εἴρηκε γὰρ ὅτι τῆς
τῶν δεομένων ἕνεκα σωτηρίας ἀνῆσαν ἐνθάδε. 3. μεγίστας οὖν, ὡς ἔοικεν, Ὠριγένης ἐλπίδας ὑποτίθεται τοῖς ἀγγέλοις καὶ προφήταις ἤτοι καὶ
παντὶ τῷ τῶν ἁγίων ὁμόσε χορῷ, πρῶτον μὲν εἰσάγων ὡς ὑπὸ δαίμονος
ἐξουσίαν εἰσίν, ἔπειτα δὲ μηνύων ὅτι διὰ μαινάδος ἀνήχθησαν ἐνταῦθα
γυναικός, ἰατρεῦσαι τοὺς πάσχοντας οἷα δεσμῶται προαχθέντες. 4. οὔτι
γέ μοι δοκεῖ μεῖον ἐκείνης ἀποφθέγγεσθαι φρενοβλαβῶς· ἔργῳ γὰρ οὕτως οἰκτρῶς ἐξεφαύλισε τοὺς ἁγίους ἄνδρας, οὐδὲ τὸ τῶν οὐρανοπετῶν
ἀγγέλων ᾐσχύνθη τάγμα διαβαλεῖν· 5. ἢ δεικνύτω τρανῶς ὁ τῷ τοιούτῳ
συνιστάμενος ὅρῳ πόθεν λαβὼν ἐκ τῆς γῆς ἔφησεν ἀνιέναι τοὺς ἐν τοῖς
οὐρανοῖς ἑστιωμένους ἀγγέλους· οὐ γὰρ οὗτοι κατεληλύθασιν εἰς ᾅδου
λυτηρίους ἐπαγόμενοι τοῖς αἰχμαλώτοις ἀφέσεις, ἀλλ' ὁ Χριστός, ἐπειδὴ
καὶ νικηφόρον οὗτος ἵδρυσε κατὰ τοῦ πολεμίου τρόπαιον, καὶ τὰς τῶν
αἰχμαλώτων ἀποσπάσας λείας αὐτῷ σώματι μεταρσίως ἀνῆλθεν εἰς οὐ-
ρανούς. 6. ἄγγελοι δὲ τῷ θεῷ παρεστᾶσιν ἑκάστοτε, τὰς ὀφειλομένας
ἐκτελεῖν ἐπειγόμενοι λατρείας, ἀλλ' οὐχὶ τὸν ᾅδην οἰκοῦσιν.

21. 1. Ἀλλ', ὡς ἔοικεν, Ὠριγένης ὑποκρίνεται μὴ νοεῖν, ἵνα δυσδαίμονα παρασκευάσῃ μαντείαν· εἶτα πάσας ἀλληγορῆσαι τὰς γραφὰς

status of these types of kindred demons, who were like brothers from the same womb,[62] she cried out, "I have seen gods coming up from the earth." 2. But that braggart Origen was not afraid to say that the petty demon did not bring up the soul of the prophet Samuel alone but much more, as he says, other *holy souls of ... prophets have come up together with* him.[63] Not satisfied with such drunken folly he also pronounced that the angels came up together with their spirits, for he said that they came up here for the sake of the salvation of those in need (cf. Heb 1:14).[64] 3. Therefore, so it seems, Origen places highest hopes in the angels and the prophets, indeed in the entire chorus of holy ones together. First he introduces the view that they are subject to a demon's authority. Then he indicates that they were brought up here by the mad woman, brought forward in the manner of captives to heal those who were suffering. 4. He seems to me to speak at least no less insanely than the woman. Let it stand proven,[65] then, that he has in this way miserably poured contempt on those holy men and has not been ashamed to slander the order of the angels who wing their way around heaven. 5. Or let him show clearly, since he is fixed in this opinion, what is the source of his statement that the angels who dwell in the heavens come up from the earth. For the angels are not the ones who have gone down to hell to bring redemptive pardon to the captives (cf. 1 Pet 3:19). Rather, it is Christ who, when he set up his trophy of victory against the enemy, dragged off the captives as his plunder and went up bodily on high to the heavens.[66] 6. The angels at all times stand near God, incited to fulfill their due services. But they do not dwell in hell.

21. 1. Yet, as it seems, Origen pretends not to understand, so that he may promote ill-fated[67] divination. Accordingly, though

---

[62] "Biological kin" (ὁμογάστριοι), "kindred demons" = "demons from the same mother" (ὁμομήτρια), and "from the same womb" (ὁμοκοίλιοι) play upon the belly-myther's name.

[63] Origen, *Hom. 5 on 1 Kgdms* 7.2. We are following the punctuation of Declerck, *Eustathii Antiocheni Opera*, instead of that of Simonetti in *La Maga di Endor*, who makes the sentence a question.

[64] A paraphrase of Origen, *Hom. 5 on 1 Kgdms* 7.3.

[65] Following Declerck, *Eustathii Antiocheni Opera*, who retains the reading of M (ἔστω). Simonetti in *La Maga di Endor* emends the text to ἔργῳ.

[66] Cf. Ps 67:19; Eph 4:8–9; Col 2:15.

[67] The word is δυσδαίμονα. Note the wordplay on "demon."

ἐγχειρήσας οὐκ ἐρυθριᾷ τοῦτο μόνον ἐπὶ τοῦ γράμματος ἐκδέχεσθαι θεσπίζων ὑποκρίσει, καίτοι μηδ' αὐτῷ σώματι προσέχων εὐγνωμόνως. 2. ἀλλὰ δὴ περὶ τοῦ παραδείσου διαλεγόμενος, ὃν ἐφύτευσεν ὁ θεὸς ἐν Ἐδέμ, εἶτα καὶ τίνα τρόπον ἐξανέτειλε τὰ καρποφόρα ξύλα διηγεῖσθαι βουλόμενος ἐπέφερε πρὸς τοῖς ἄλλοις· ὅταν ἀναγινώσκοντες ἀναβαίνωμεν ἀπὸ τῶν μύθων ἔφη καὶ τῆς κατὰ τὸ γράμμα ἐκδοχῆς <καὶ> ζητῶμεν τίνα τὰ ξύλα φησὶν ἐστὶν ἐκεῖνα, ἃ ὁ θεὸς γεωργεῖ, λέγομεν ὅτι οὐκ ἔνι αἰσθητὰ ξύλα ἐν τῷ τόπῳ. 3. ταῦτα δὲ δὴ τροπολογῶν οὐ φρίττει μύθους ὀνομάζειν, ὅσα δεδημιουργηκέναι μὲν ἱστορεῖται θεός, ὁ δὲ πιστότατος τοῦ θεοῦ θεράπων ἔγραψε Μωσῆς· ἀλλ' ἐκ τῶν ἐναντίων, ἅπερ ὁ μῦθος ἐν γαστρὶ πλαττόμενος ἀφανῶς ὑπηχεῖ, ταῦτα δογματικῷ βεβαιοῖ προγράμματι, δεικνύων ἀληθῆ. 4. τὰ μέν γε τῆς ἐγγαστριμύθου ῥήματα διὰ τοῦ ἁγίου πνεύματος εἰρῆσθαι συνιστῶν ἀσάλευτα μένειν ἀξιοῖ, τῇ γραφῇ τῷ δοκεῖν ἀναθείς· αὐτὰ δὲ τὰ τοῦ θεοῦ διὰ Μωσέως ἐκδοθέντα μηνύματα μύθους ὀνομάσας ἐνδιαλλάττει τὴν ἔννοιαν, οὐ δικαιῶν ἐμμένειν τῇ τοῦ γράμματος ἐκδοχῇ. 5. ἀλλ' οὐχὶ τὰ ὑπὸ τοῦ

he took it in hand to allegorize all the scriptures, he does not blush
to understand this passage alone according to the letter, declaring
his interpretation hypocritically, even though he does not pay attention to the body of scripture right-mindedly.[68] 2. Yet when he
discusses the paradise God planted in Eden and then wants to describe in what manner he brought forth the fruit-bearing trees,
among other things he adds the statement, "When in our reading we ascend from myths," he said, "and from the literal sense,
and we search out what those trees are that it says that God cul-
tivates," he says, "we say that there are not perceptible trees in
the place."[69] 3. In allegorizing[70] them he does not shudder to call
"myths"[71] what God is said to have created and what Moses, the
most trustworthy servant of God, wrote. But on the contrary, the
very things "the myth fabricated in the belly" obscurely suggests
are those that Origen confirms by dogmatic fiat, demonstrating
them to be true. 4. Commending the words of the belly-myther as
spoken by the Holy Spirit, he considers them worthy of remaining
as unshakeable testimony, since he has attributed them to scripture by virtue of their appearing there. But he perverts the sense of
the very revelations of God handed down by Moses, calling them
"myths," not judging it right to abide by a literal interpretation.
5. Does he not allegorize the wells dug by Abraham and by those

[68] For Origen's view of the triple sense of scripture as body, soul, and
spirit, see *Princ.* 4.2.4–6. For "right-mindedly," see Origen, *Hom. 5 on 1 Kgdms*
4.1.

[69] The citation may be from Origen's lost commentary on Genesis (but
see n. 71). The last phrase in the citation ("*in the place*") could mean instead "in
the [scriptural] passage." The term τόπος can have both meanings (*PGL*, 1806).

[70] Several expressions refer to the spiritual interpretation. Here we find
τροπολογῶν. In 21.1 Eustathius uses the verb ἀλληγορῆσαι. Hence, he appears
to regard "allegory" and "tropology" as synonymous. See also 21.10, where he
uses θεωρεῖν; θεωρία can also refer to the spiritual meaning.

[71] In his extant writings Origen does not use the term μῦθος in reference
to scripture in this way (see p. cxv, n. 93), but excoriates it in much the same
terms as Eustathius (see, e.g., *Hom. Gen.* 28.14–17; *Princ.* 4.2.1; discussion of
Origen's eschewal of the term in Robert M. Grant, *The Earliest Lives of Jesus*
[New York: Harper & Brothers, 1961], 65–66). Either the preceding sentence is
an accurate quotation from a lost commentary of Origen's on Genesis that counters his usual practice, or Eustathius has here drawn an inference from Origen's
allegorical interpretation—that it treats the text as a myth—and has fashioned
speech in character at this point, as elsewhere in his treatise, where he puts Origen on the stand.

Ἀβραὰμ ὀρωρυγμένα φρέατα καὶ τῶν ἀμφ' αὐτὸν ἀλληγορεῖ, καὶ τοσοῦτον ἀποτείνας λόγων ἐσμὸν ἅπασαν ὁμοῦ τὴν πραγματείαν αὐτῶν
ἀναιρεῖ, μεταθεὶς εἰς ἕτερον νοῦν, καίτοι τῶν φρεάτων ἐπὶ χώρας ἔτι
καὶ νῦν ὄψει φαινομένων; 6. οὐχὶ τὰ τοῦ Ἰσαὰκ καὶ τὰ τῆς Ῥεβέκκας
ἐτροπολόγησε πράγματα, τὰ μὲν ἐνώτια καὶ ψέλλια "λόγους" εἶναι "χρυ-
σοῦς" εἰρηκώς, ἅπασαν δὲ τὴν ὑπόθεσιν ἐκβιασάμενος ἐκείνην ἐπὶ τοῦ
νοητοῦ παραλαβὼν ἐσυκοφάντησεν; 7. περὶ δέ γε τοῦ πολύτλα προσο-
μιλήσας Ἰώβ, ἀντὶ τοῦ θαυμάσαι τὴν ὑπομονήν, ἐπαινέσαι τοὺς πόνους,
εὐφημῆσαι τὴν ἀριστείαν, ἀποδέξασθαι τὴν πίστιν, ἐκφράσαι τὰ τῆς καρ-
τεροψυχίας ὑποδείγματα, προτρέψασθαι διὰ τούτου τοὺς νεολέκτους εἰς
ἀρετήν, εὐψυχίᾳ καὶ ῥώμῃ φρονήσεως ὁπλίσαι τοὺς ἀγωνιστὰς ἀνδρείως
ὑπὲρ τῆς εὐσεβείας ἀθλεῖν, ἀφέμενος ἐκείνου, μετεώρως εἰς τὰ τῶν θυγατέρων ὁρμήσας ὀνόματα κατετρίβη γραωδῶς. ἀλλ' οἷα μὲν ἐφλυάρησεν
εἰς τὸ τῆς Ἡμέρας ὄνομα καὶ Κασσίας ἤτοι καὶ τὸ τῆς Ἀμαλθείας κέ-
ρας, οὐδὲ λέγειν οἷόν τε· χλεύης γάρ ἐστι παντοίας ἀνάπλεα. 8. περὶ δὲ
τοῦ Λαζάρου γράφων, ἀντὶ τοῦ δοξάσαι τὴν τοῦ Χριστοῦ μεγαλουργίαν
καὶ διὰ τούτων ἀποδεῖξαι σαφῶς ὅτι θεός ἐστιν ὁ τὸν ὀδωδότα νεκρὸν
ἐκ τῶν μνημάτων ἐξουσίᾳ μεταπεμψάμενος καὶ τῇ τοῦ ῥήματος ἀφέσει
τὰ διωδηκότα σώματα ψυχώσας, οὐδὲν μὲν ἕνεκα τούτου λέγει, Λάζαρον δὲ τὸν τοῦ κυρίου φίλον, ὃν οὐκ ἀπεικότως ἠγάπα δι' ἀρετήν, εἰς τὸν

around him?⁷² Does he not by prolonging his speech into such a
great swarm of words at the same time destroy their entire fac-
tual basis by turning to another sense, even though the wells can
still to this day be seen on the land?⁷³ 6. Did he not give an allegory of events involving Isaac and Rebekah by saying that the
earrings and bracelets are "golden words,"⁷⁴ and in doing violence
to the entire setting⁷⁵ of the narrative by taking it in a spiritual
sense, has he not slandered it? 7. And when he preached on long-
suffering Job, instead of marveling at his endurance, praising his
labors, extolling his excellence, commending his faith, describing
examples of his strength of spirit, instead of exhorting new recruits to virtue through this man, instead of arming contestants
with courage and strength of mind to fight bravely for piety—he
dismissed all those tasks and, lost in the clouds, wasted his time
running off to the names of Job's daughters like some old crone.⁷⁶
The kind of nonsense he spoke about the names "Day," "Cassia,"
and "Horn of Amaltheia" is not even possible to tell, for it is filled
with all sorts of ridiculous statements. 8. When he writes about
Lazarus,⁷⁷ instead of glorifying the mighty deed of Christ and
through that showing clearly that God is the one who summoned
the stinking corpse from the tomb by his authority and who by dis-
charging a word brought to life bodies in a state of decay, he says
nothing about this. Rather, by allegorical elevation⁷⁸ he interprets

⁷² Cf. Origen, *Hom. Gen.* 7.5; 10.2; 11.3; 12.5 and 13 (see Louis Doutreleau, ed., *Origène, Homélies sur la Genèse* [SC 7 bis; Paris: Cerf, 1976], ad loc.).
⁷³ That is, Judea, the holy land.
⁷⁴ Gen 24:22. Origen, *Hom. Gen.* 10.4 (Doutreleau, *Origène*, 270): "Vult
enim aurea in auribus verba suscipere et aureas actus in manibus habere" ("For
she [Rebekah] wishes to receive golden words in her ears and to hold golden
deeds in her hands").
⁷⁵ The term literally means what "underlies" a narrative (ὑπόθεσις).
Other possible translations include "subject matter" or "plot-line" (for the latter, see Robert M. Grant, *Irenaeus of Lyons* [London: Routledge, 1997], 47–49).
⁷⁶ Job 42:14 LXX. Origen's commentary on Job is lost.
⁷⁷ Origen's *Comm. Jo.*, book 28, preserves what remains of his comments
on John 11. Origen does not deny that Christ actually raised Lazarus, but he
does allegorize the raising of Lazarus as a rising up from sin. Cf. 28.6–7. See
Trigg, "Eustathius of Antioch's Attack on Origen," 232–33.
⁷⁸ ἀνήγαγεν ἀλληγορῶν. Eustathius is making a play here on the literal
"elevation" of Lazarus and the Origenist allegory (termed "elevation," ἀναγωγή;
see Origen, *Hom. 5 on 1 Kgdms* 2.1).

ἀσθενοῦντα καὶ τεθνεῶτα ταῖς ἁμαρτίαις ἀνήγαγεν ἀλληγορῶν. 9. οὐδεὶς δὲ κατὰ τοῦ δικαίου ταῦτα εἶπεν οὔτ᾽ ἔγραψεν· οὐ γὰρ ἂν οὕτως ἐκκρίτως ἔστεργεν ὁ κύριος αὐτόν, εἰ μὴ θεσπεσίας ἐξῆπτο πολιτείας. 10. οὐκ ἔλαττον δὲ καὶ τὸ τῆς λιθοβολίας δρᾶμα θεωρῶν ἐπειδὴ καὶ τοῦτο πειρᾶται τροπολογῆσαι τοῦ εὐαγγελικοῦ καταψεύδεται γράμματος, "οὐ πάνυ τι," λέγων, "εὕραμεν, ζητήσαντες ἐν τοῖς πρὸ τούτου, ὅτι ἐβάστασαν οἱ Ἰουδαῖοι λίθους ἵνα λιθάσωσιν αὐτόν·" εἶτα μετ᾽ ὀλίγα φησίν· "εἰ γὰρ **πάλιν ἐβάστασαν,** πρότερον ἐβάστασαν." 11. ἄνω δὲ καὶ κάτω βούλεται κατασκευάσαι μὴ προηγεῖσθαι καὶ ἄλλην ὁμοίως ἐκδοχήν, ἵνα συστήσειεν ὅτι λόγους, ἀλλ᾽ οὐχὶ λίθους ἐβάστασαν ἀμελλητὶ κατ᾽ αὐτοῦ, καίτοι τοῦ εὐαγγελιστοῦ πρόσθεν εἰρηκότος **ἦραν οὖν λίθους ἵνα βάλωσιν ἐπ᾽ αὐτόν.** 12. ὡς δὲ ταῦτα προὔγραψεν, ἐν τῷ μεταξὺ πέντε που καὶ τριάκοντα πρὸς τοῖς ἑκατὸν στίχους ὑπερβάς, ἐπιφέρει προσθείς· **ἐβάστασαν οὖν πάλιν οἱ Ἰουδαῖοι λίθους, ἵνα λιθάσωσιν αὐτόν.** ἀλλὰ ταῦτα μὲν ἐν διττοῖς ἀναγέγραπται χωρίοις, ἐν διαφόροις δὲ φαίνεται πεπραγμένα καιροῖς ἀπὸ τοῦ μὴ τὰς αὐτὰς ἔχειν τῶν ῥημάτων ἐπιπλοκὰς ἢ συζυγίας· ἀλλ᾽ Ὡριγένης ὁ πάσας οἰόμενος εἰδέναι τὰς γραφὰς οὐκ ἀνέγνω τοῦτο, καὶ ταῦτα γράφων εἰς ὅλον ὁμοῦ τὸ εὐαγγέλιον ἐπὶ λέξεως.

22. 1. Εἰ δέ τις ὑπολαμβάνει ταῦτα πλάττειν ἡμᾶς, αὐταῖς ταῖς εὐαγγελικαῖς ἐντυχὼν ἀποφάσεσι καὶ τοῖς ἐκπονηθεῖσιν αὐτῷ περὶ τοῦτο σπουδάσμασιν, εὑρήσει μηδὲν ἡμᾶς εἰρηκέναι ψευδές. 2. ἀλλὰ τί δεῖ περαιτέρω λέγειν; ἅπαντα μὲν ὡς ἔπος εἰπεῖν, ἐκ τῶν ὀνομάτων ἀλληγορῶν

Lazarus, the friend of the Lord, whom he loved with good reason for his virtue, as referring to the man who is sick and dead in his sins. 9. But no one has said or written these things against that righteous man. For the Lord would not have loved him in such an indiscriminating way had he not cleaved to a divinely decreed way of life. 10. No less is it also the case that Origen lies about the Gospel text by looking for a hidden meaning in the story about the stoning, since he tries to allegorize even it. He says, "We do not actually find when we examine what comes before this that the Jews had taken up stones so that they might stone him." Then a little later he says, "For if *they took them up again* (John 10:31), they had taken them up before."[79] 11. Again and again Origen wants to demonstrate that no other sense can equally be brought forward, so that he might establish that it was words and not stones they took up against him immediately. All this despite the fact that the Evangelist had said earlier, "Then they picked up stones to throw at him" (John 8:59). 12. Since the Evangelist wrote this first, then after an interval of 135 lines,[80] he continued by adding, "The Jews took up stones again to stone him" (John 10:31). But these things have been recorded in two places, and the actions seem to have taken place at different times, since they do not have the same combination and conjunction of the words. Yet Origen, who thinks he knows all the scriptures, did not know this, writing these things also against the Gospel as a unified whole in its plain sense.

22. 1. Now if someone supposes that we are fabricating these things, if he consults the Gospel statements themselves and the commentaries carefully worked out by him[81] about this, he will find that we have said nothing false. 2. But why must we say

---

[79] Eustathius's second citation begins a fragment that has been preserved from one of the lost books of Origen's commentary (A. E. Brooke, *The Commentary of Origen on S. John's Gospel* [Cambridge: Cambridge University Press, 1896], 2:283–84, frg. 74). In this fragment Origen ignores John 8:59 and asks why "again" has been added in 10:31. His answer is that the reviling of Jesus in 10:19–20 refers to a previous spiritual "stoning." Eustathius presumably regards John 8:59 as the first stoning, even though the vocabulary in 8:59 differs from that in 10:31 (ἦρον | βάλωσιν as opposed to ἐβάστασαν | λιθάσωσιν).

[80] Presumably the reference is to the lines in the manuscript Eustathius is using.

[81] Eustathius assumes readers may consult Origen's commentaries for themselves.

ἀναιρεῖ τὰς τῶν πραγμάτων ὑποθέσεις, οὐδὲ τοῦτο ἐννοῶν, ὅτι πολλαὶ
μέν εἰσιν ὁμωνυμίαι δικαίων ἠδ᾽ ἀδίκων, οὐχ οἷόν τε δὲ τὰς ἀνομοίους
τοῦ βίου πολιτείας ἐκ τοῦ ἑνὸς ὡσαύτως ὀνόματος κρίνεσθαι. 3. ἔστιν
γοῦν Ἰούδας ὁ προδότης καὶ θάτερος Ἰούδας ἀπόστολος, ἢ αὖ πάλιν
Ζαχαρίας ἀδικώτατος βασιλεὺς καὶ Ζαχαρίας ἕτερος ὁ προφήτης, οὐ
μὴν ἀλλὰ καὶ ὁ βληθεὶς ἐν τῇ καμίνῳ τοῦ πυρὸς Ἀνανίας, ἔτι δὲ παρὰ
τοῦτον ἄλλος Ἀνανίας ὁ διώκων μὲν ἐκκλησίαν ἀντὶ τοῦ διώκεσθαι,
προστάττων δὲ τύπτεσθαι τὸν ἀπόστολον, ᾧ καὶ καταντικρὺ πρὸς ἔπος
ὁ Παῦλος ἀντεφθέγξατο· *τύπτειν σε μέλλει ὁ θεός, τοῖχε κεκονιαμένε.*
καὶ σὺ κάθῃ κρῖναί με κατὰ τὸν νόμον, καὶ παρανομῶν κελεύεις με τύπτε-
σθαι; 4. τοιγαροῦν, εἴπερ ὀνόματι τὰ πράγματα κρίνεται, λεγέτωσαν οἱ
ταῖς τοιαύταις ἐπερειδόμενοι τροπολογίαις ὁποίᾳ μεθόδῳ τὰς ἀνομοίους
ἐπιστήμας ἢ πολιτειῶν ἀναγωγὰς ἐκ τῆς ὁμωνυμίας ἀξιοῦσιν ἑρμηνεύειν.
ἀμέλει πολλοὶ μὲν ἔτι καὶ τήμερον Ἰουδαῖοι προπατόρων ἢ προφητῶν
ὀνόματα περιβαλλόμενοι δρῶσιν ἀθέμιτα, πολλοὶ δὲ καὶ παρ᾽ Ἕλλησιν
Πέτροι καὶ Παῦλοι καλούμενοι πράττουσιν ἀνήκεστα.

5. τὰ μὲν τοίνυν ὑπόκενα τῶν λόγων Ὠριγένους οὐχ ἥκιστα καὶ
διὰ τῆς τοιαύτης ἁλίσκεται κουφολογίας. ὅσα δὲ τῆς ἀναστάσεως ἕνεκα
κακοδόξως εἰσηγεῖται, δηλῶσαι μὲν ἐπὶ τοῦ παρόντος οὐχ οἷόν τε. Με-
θόδιος γὰρ ὁ τῆς ἁγίας ἄξιος μνήμης ἔγραψεν ἀποχρώντως εἰς τόδε
τὸ θεώρημα, καὶ διέδειξέ γε <ἀνα>φανδὸν ὅτι τοῖς αἱρεσιώταις ἔδωκε
πάροδον ἀβούλως, ἐπὶ εἴδους, ἀλλ᾽ οὐκ ἐπὶ σώματος αὐτοῦ τὴν ἀνά-
στασιν ὁρισάμενος. 6. ἀλλ᾽ ὅτι μὲν ἅπαντα τροπολογίαις ἀνέτρεψε καὶ
τὰ τῆς κακοδοξίας ἔσπειρεν ἑκασταχοῦ σπέρματα ῥᾷόν ἐστιν ἰδεῖν, ἄνω
δὲ καὶ κάτω ταυτολογῶν ἐπλήρωσε τὴν οἰκουμένην ἀμέτρῳ φλυαρίᾳ. 7.
τοιαύτῃ δὲ δὴ μεθόδῳ συνήθως ἀλληγορῶν ἅπαντα πανταχῶς, οὐχ οἷός

anything beyond this? To put it generally, by allegorizing everything on the basis of "names," Origen destroys the settings of the
actions. Nor does he understand that many of the same names ap-
ply to just or unjust people, so it is impossible for different ways
of life to be judged the same on the basis of a single name. 3.
Thus, there is Judas the betrayer and the other Judas, the apostle, or again Zechariah the most wicked king (4 Kgdms 15) and
another Zechariah the prophet. Not only that, but there is even
one Ananias who was thrown into the furnace of fire (Dan 3:19–20)
and still another Ananias besides him who persecuted the church
instead of being persecuted and who ordered the apostle to be
struck. Paul directly returned his statement: "God will strike you,
you whitewashed wall! Are you sitting there to judge me according to the law, and yet in violation of the law you order me to be
struck?" (Acts 23:3). 4. Therefore, if things are judged by a name,
let those who lean upon such allegories explain by what method
they think it right to interpret from the same name professions or
references to ways of life that are lawless or upright.[82] Doubtless
there are still to this day many Jews who are endowed with the
names of the forefathers or the prophets and yet commit unlawful deeds. Just so, there are many even among the Greeks called
Peter and Paul who commit pernicious deeds.

5. Accordingly, the emptiness of Origen's words is caught
out not least of all by such light banter. But it is not possible at
the present moment to expose the many unorthodox[83] opinions
he introduces concerning the resurrection. For Methodius, who
is worthy of holy memory, has sufficiently written about Origen's
very doctrine and has clearly demonstrated before the eyes of all
that Origen inadvisably gave an opening to the heretics when he
defined the resurrection as one of form but not of the body itself. 6.
But it is easy to see that he has overturned everything by his allegories and has sown everywhere the seeds of unorthodox teaching;
saying the same thing over and over again, he has filled the whole
world with boundless nonsense. 7. Though he customarily allego-
rized absolutely everything by this method, it was only the words

---

[82] Following the variant reading of M (ἀνομους, with no accent) rather
than ἀνομοίους, the reading accepted by Simonetti in *La Maga di Endor* and by
Declerck in *Eustathii Antiocheni Opera*.

[83] Literally "badly thought" (κακοδόξως; cf. κακοδοξία in 22.6), "hereti-
cal" (*PGL*, 695). Cf. ὀρθοδοξία, which Eustathius ascribes to Eutropius in 1.1.

τε ἐγένετο τὰ τῆς ἐγγαστριμύθου τροπολογῆσαι ῥήματα μόνον, οὐδ' αὖ τὸ σαφὲς ἐξ αὐτῆς ἱστορῆσαι τῆς ἀκολουθίας. 23. 1. Ἀλλὰ τί πρὸς ἐπὶ τούτοις εἰσήγαγεν, ἀφοσιώσει πλαττόμενος ἀποφυγάς ; ἐπειδήπερ ἐδόκει τὸ φάσμα τῷ Σαοὺλ εἰρηκέναι· **διαρρήξει κύριος τὴν βασιλείαν ἐκ χειρός σου,** πρὸς ταῦτα πιθανολογῶν ἀνθυπέφερεν ὡς οὐ χρεὼν εἴη νοεῖν ὅτι "δαιμόνιον προφητεύει περὶ βασιλείας Ἰσραηλιτικῆς." 2. ἤδη δὲ καὶ πρόσθεν ἔφαμεν ὅτι ταῦτα τὰ ῥήματα τῷ Σαμουὴλ εἰρημένα πρόσθεν ἔκλεψεν ὁ δαίμων, ἵνα δὴ τὸν ἔκφρονα Σαοὺλ ἐξαπατήσας ἴδια δόξῃ λέγειν. ἀλλ' οὗτος οὐ προσποιεῖται τὰ τοιάδε τοῦ διαβόλου δράματα γιγνώσκειν. ὡς οὖν ἐδόκει προλέγειν ὅτι διαρραγήσοιτο τοῦ παραπλῆγος ἡ βασιλεία, τηνικαῦτα προσετίθει· **καὶ δώσει αὐτὴν τῷ πλησίον σου τῷ Δαβίδ.** ὁ μέντοιγε πολυΐστωρ Ὠριγένης ἐνταῦθα κινηθεὶς ἔφη· "δαιμόνιον δέ," λέγων, "οὐ δύναται εἰδέναι τὴν βασιλείαν Δαβὶδ τὴν ὑπὸ κυρίου χειροτονηθεῖσαν." 3. ἀλλ' ἔμοιγε θαυμάζειν ἔπεισιν ὅπως οὗτος ἀποφέρεται δόξαν ἐπ' εὐβουλίᾳ παρὰ τοῖς πολλοῖς, ὡς ἔμφρων ἅμα καὶ γνώμης ἄριστος. εἰ μὲν οὖν ἄδηλος ἦν ἡ βασιλεία, ἐξῆν ἂν ἴσως ἄγνοιαν ὑποκρίνεσθαί τινα σκηπτόμενον· 4. εἰ δὲ μεμαρτύρητο μὲν ὑπὸ τοῦ θεοῦ, κέχριστο δ' ἐπὶ τούτοις ὑπὸ τοῦ Σαμουήλ, ἔν τε τοῖς πολέμοις ἀριστεύων ἀεὶ γαμβρὸς ἀναδέδεικτο τοῦ βασιλέως, ὥστε τούτῳ μὲν τὰς χορευούσας ἀναθεῖναι τὰς **μυριάδας,** τῷ δὲ Σαοὺλ ἀποδοῦναι τὰς **χιλιάδας,** εἰ δὲ ταῦτα καὶ τὰ τοιαῦτα καθεστήκει σαφῆ, τί ξένον ἢ τί παράδοξον ἦν, εἰ τὴν οὖσαν καὶ κεχειροτονημένην ὑπὸ τοῦ κυρίου διὰ τοῦ προφήτου βασιλείαν ἐπεγίνωσκεν ὁ δαίμων ; 5. ἢ γὰρ οὐ διανοητέον εἴ γε δεῖ λέγειν ἐξ ὑπερβολῆς ὅτι τὰ σωματικὰ μόνον οἶδεν ὡς ἡ τοῦ ἐλαίου χρίσις αἰσθητὴν ἔχει τὴν τῆς ἀφῆς ἐπιφοράν; ἀλλὰ ταῦτα μὲν οὐδεὶς ἀμφιλέξει πρόδηλα καθεστάναι πᾶσιν· ἵνα δὲ τὸ ὑπερβάλλον ἐρῶ προσθεὶς εἰ καὶ μὴ <τὰ> τοιαῦτα καθεστήκει σαφῆ· πότερον ἂν

of the belly-myther that he was unable to allegorize. Yet even here he did not explicate what is the plain sense on the basis of its logical sequence.

23. 1. But what has he added to the previous arguments, fabricating excuses to expiate himself? Since the phantom seemed to say to Saul, "The Lord will tear the kingdom out of your hand," he responded to this by crafting the specious argument that it would not be right to understand that *a petty demon was prophesying about the kingdom of Israel.*[84] 2. We have already said before that the demon stole these words that had been spoken by Samuel earlier so that, deceiving the demented Saul, he might appear to be speaking his own words. But Origen pretends he does not know such actions of the devil. When the demon seemed to foretell that the kingdom would be torn away from the deranged king, he then added, "and he will give it to your neighbor David." However, the learned Origen, moved by this, said expressly, *A petty demon is not able to know about the kingdom that has been appointed to David by the Lord.*[85] 3. For my part this leads me to marvel that Origen has pulled off still a reputation for sound judgment in the eyes of many people, as though he were sensible and had the best judgment. If then the rulership were undisclosed, it would perhaps have been possible for someone to feign a supposed ignorance. 4. But if testimony had been given by God, and in addition David had been anointed by Samuel, and because he was always the bravest in battles David had been publicly proclaimed as King Saul's son-in-law, and as a result the women in chorus attributed to David "ten thousands" but gave Saul "thousands" (1 Kgdms 18:7)—if these and facts like them were clearly established, why would it be strange or marvelous if the demon had found out about David's kingdom and its having been appointed by the Lord through the prophet? 5. For if it is necessary to say by way of exaggeration that the demon knows only corporeal things, should it not be kept in mind that anointing with oil is a tactile application that is perceptible? But surely no one will dispute that these things have been established in the sight of all. But, so that I might say what is of overriding importance, I should add that, even if these things

---

[84] Origen, *Hom. 5 on 1 Kgdms* 4.9. Origen's point, of course, is that it is actually Samuel who says this.

[85] Ibid., 5.1.

εἴη μεῖζον πρὸς σύγκρισιν τὸ γνῶναι τὴν τοῦ Δαβὶδ βασιλείαν, ἢ ψυχὰς ἐξ ᾅδου προφητικὰς ἀνάξαι; 6. καίτοι τοῦτο καὶ ἐπὶ τοῦ κρείττονος
ἀποδέδεικται προσώπου· καὶ γὰρ καὶ ἐπὶ τοῦ Χριστοῦ στρεβλούμενοι
καὶ ἄκοντες ἐκβοῶσιν οἱ δαίμονες, αὐτολεξεὶ *τί ἡμῖν καὶ σοί* κεκραγό-
τες *υἱὲ τοῦ θεοῦ; ἦλθες πρὸ καιροῦ ἀπολέσαι ἡμᾶς;* τὸ δὲ ψυχὰς ἐξ ᾅδου
μεταπέμπεσθαι καὶ χοροὺς ἀγγέλων οὐρανοπετεῖς ἐν ταὐτῷ μετακαλεῖ-
σθαι μόνος ἐξουσίαν ἔχει διαπράττεσθαι θεὸς καὶ ὁ θειότατος αὐτοῦ παῖς,
ἄλλος δὲ τὸ παράπαν οὐδείς. 7. εἰ οὖν τὴν ἀόρατον τοῦ θεοῦ βασιλείαν
ἔγνωσαν ἁγίῳ πνεύματι χρισθεῖσαν, οὐ πολλῷ πλέον ἐπιγνῶναι τὴν τοῦ
Δαβὶδ ἐδύναντο διὰ χρίσματος ἀναδειχθεῖσαν αἰσθητοῦ καὶ καταχύσεως
ὁρατῆς; ἀλλ' οὐκ ᾔδει τὰ πεπραγμένα καὶ γραφαῖς ἀνακείμενα περὶ τοῦ
Δαβὶδ ὁ ἀλιτήριος, ὅς γε καὶ τῷ κυρίῳ περιβαλλομένῳ τὸ σῶμα προσελ-
θὼν ἔφη τολμηρῶς· *εἰ υἱὸς εἶ τοῦ θεοῦ, βάλε σεαυτὸν κάτω· γέγραπται γὰρ
ὅτι τοῖς ἀγγέλοις αὐτοῦ,* φησίν, *ἐντελεῖται περὶ σοῦ καὶ ἐπὶ χειρῶν ἀροῦ-
σίν σε, μήποτε προσκόψῃς πρὸς λίθον τὸν πόδα σου;* 8. οὐκοῦν εἴπερ
ἐκ τῶν ἁγίων ὑποτυποῦται γραφῶν ὁμιλεῖν, οἶδεν ἄρα τὰ γεγραμμένα
κακομαθῶς· εἰ δὲ τούτων ἐν γνώσει καθέστηκεν, οὐκ ἄρα τὴν τοῦ Δαβὶδ ἠγνόει βασιλείαν, ἢ τοῖς ἱεροῖς ἐγκεχάρακται γράμμασιν· ὥστε τὰ
γεγραμμένα λέγων ὁ δαίμων οὐδὲν ἐπροφήτευσεν οὐδαμῶς.

24. 1. Ἀλλ' ὁ πολύφημος Ὠριγένης, οὐδ' ὁτιοῦν εὑρίσκων εἰπεῖν,
εἰς τοῦτο κατέφυγε τετεχνασμένως, ἑτέρωθι πρὸς ἐπὶ τούτοις ἐπαγαγών·
"ἐγὼ δέ," φησίν, "οὐ δύναμαι διδόναι δαιμονίῳ τηλικαύτην δύναμιν, ἵνα
προφητεύῃ περὶ Σαοὺλ καὶ τοῦ λαοῦ τοῦ θεοῦ, καὶ προφητεύῃ περὶ βασιλείας Δαβὶδ ὅτι μέλλει βασιλεύειν." 2. εἶτα, φαίη τις ἄν, ὦ ἀνοητότατε
ἀνδρῶν, οὐ δίδως μὲν αὐτῷ προφητεύειν, ἐπιτρέπεις δὲ αὐτῷ προφήτας
ἀνάγειν ἐξ ᾅδου καὶ ἀγγελικοὺς ἄφνω μεταστέλλεσθαι χορούς, ὅπερ ἐστὶ

were not clearly established, which would be greater by comparison: to know that the kingdom was David's or to bring up from hell the souls of the prophets? 6. Moreover, the former has been demonstrated in the case of someone greater.[86] For the demons, when tortured in the presence of Christ, against their will cried out, shouting these very words, "What have you to do with us, Son of God? Have you come to destroy us before the time?" (cf. Matt 8:29). But to summon souls from hell and to call the choruses of angels that wing their way around heaven at the same moment—God alone and his most divine Son have the authority to do this. Absolutely no one else has this authority. 7. If, then, the demons recognized the kingdom of God, invisible and anointed by the Holy Spirit, how much more were they able to find out about David's kingdom, since it was publicly displayed by a perceptible anointing and a visible pouring of oil? But did the avenger not know the things accomplished and lying in store for David that are preserved in the scriptures? Indeed, he is the one who approached the Lord when he was clothed with a body and said audaciously, "If you are the Son of God, throw yourself down; for it is written, 'He will command his angels concerning you,' and 'on their hands they will bear you up, so that you will not dash your foot against a stone'" (Matt 4:6). 8. Surely, then, if he fashions his speech from the holy scriptures, he has a knowledge of what is written, even though he is poorly trained. And if he stood in knowledge of these words, surely he would not have been unaware of David's kingdom, which has been inscribed in the sacred writings. Therefore, the demon, by saying things that had already been written, did not prophesy a single thing at all.

24. 1. But the highly acclaimed Origen, because he could find nothing whatsoever to say, took refuge in a cunning artifice, introducing in addition to the words we have considered a further statement. He says, *For my part I cannot give such great power to a petty demon that he might prophesy concerning Saul and the people of God and prophesy concerning David's kingdom, that he was going to reign.*[87] 2. Someone then might say, "Most foolish of men, you do not grant it the power to prophesy, but you permit it to bring the prophets up from hell and summon the angelic choruses on a

---

[86] That is, the demons recognized Christ's kingdom.

[87] Cf. Origen, *Hom. 5 on 1 Kgdms* 8.3.

μεῖζον καὶ προῦχον καὶ θειοτέρας ἐχόμενον ἐξουσίας ; ἆρά γέ τις οὕτως ἐνόησεν ἀσθενῶς ἢ πτωχῶς ; ἀλλὰ μάλιστα μὲν ἔγωγε φαίην ἂν ἀνθυπενέγκας ὅτι μηδὲν ἐπροφήτευσεν ὁ δαίμων, ὥς γε καὶ πρόσθεν ἐδείξαμεν· 3. εἰ δ' ἄρα καὶ προφητείας ἄξια διαλεχθεὶς ἐτύγχανεν, οὐδ' οὕτως ἐχρῆν ὑπολαμβάνειν ὅτι πνεύματα καὶ ψυχὰς ὁ δαίμων ἀνήγαγεν ἐξ ᾅδου· καὶ γὰρ ὁ Καϊάφας ἐπὶ τῇ κατὰ τοῦ Χριστοῦ συστάσει προὐφήτευσεν, εἰρηκὼς ὅτι *συμφέρει ἡμῖν ἵνα εἷς ἄνθρωπος ἀποθάνῃ ὑπὲρ τοῦ λαοῦ καὶ μὴ ὅλον τὸ ἔθνος ἀπόληται.* 4. ταῦτα μὲν οὐκ εἶπεν *ἀφ' ἑαυτοῦ,* καθάπερ ὁ σοφώτατος ἐξέδωκεν Ἰωάννης, *ἀρχιερεὺς* δὲ τυγχάνων ἐκείνου τοῦ ἔτους *ἐπροφήτευσεν.* 5. εἰ δὲ οὗτος ὁ κατὰ τοῦ κυρίου βουλὰς ἀδίκους ἀράμενος ὅμως οὐκ ἀφ' ἑαυτοῦ προφητεύει, κινούμενος δὲ δήπουθεν ὑφ' ἑτέρου καθ' ἑαυτοῦ ποιεῖται τὸν ἔλεγχον, οὐδὲ εἴ τις ἄλλος ἄρα τοιοῦτό τι δρᾷ προσεκτέον ὅτι παρὰ τοῦτο θειοτέρας ἐξῆπται δυνάμεως, οὐδὲ ἀνασχετέον εἰ λέγοι τις ὅτι μαντεία δαιμονιώδει ψυχὰς ἀνάγειν ἔοικεν ἐξ ᾅδου καὶ στρατιὰς ἀγγέλων οἷα θεός. 6. ἐπακουστέον γὰρ οἷα περὶ τῶν τοιούτων ἐξαγορεύει προφητῶν ἐν τῷ Δευτερονομίῳ θεσπίζων ὁ Μωσῆς, *ἐὰν δὲ ἀναστῇ φάσκων ἐν σοὶ προφήτης ἢ ἐνυπνιαζόμενος ἐνύπνιον καὶ δῷ σοι σημεῖον ἢ τέρας, καὶ ἔλθῃ τὸ σημεῖον ἢ τὸ τέρας ὃ ἐλάλησεν πρὸς σὲ λέγων·* 7. *πορευθῶμεν καὶ λατρεύσωμεν θεοῖς ἑτέροις οὓς οὐκ οἴδατε, οὐκ ἀκούσεσθε τῶν λόγων ἐκείνου τοῦ προφήτου, φησίν, ἢ τοῦ ἐνυπνιαζομένου τὸ ἐνύπνιον ἐκεῖνο· ὅτι πειράζει κύριος ὁ θεὸς ὑμῶν ὑμᾶς, τοῦ ἰδεῖν εἰ ἀγαπᾶτε κύριον τὸν θεὸν ὑμῶν.* 8. ἀλλ' ἐνταῦθα μὲν τὴν δυάδα πατρός τε καὶ τοῦ μονογενοῦς υἱοῦ παριστῶν, ἄλλον μὲν τὸν ἐκπειράζοντα κύριον ὠνόμαζεν, ἄλλον δὲ παρὰ τοῦτον εἶναι τὸν ἀγαπώμενον κύριόν τε καὶ θεόν, ἵν' ἐκ δυάδος τὴν μίαν ἀποδείξοι θεότητα καὶ τὴν ἀληθῆ θεογονίαν. 9. εἰ δ' ὁ προφήτης ἐκεῖνος ὁ τὸ σημεῖον ὑποσχόμενος ἢ τὸ τέρας ὑποδεῖξαι παντάπασιν ἀποκριτέος ἐστὶ τῷ τὴν ἀθέμιτον εἰδωλολατρείαν εἰσηγεῖσθαι, κἂν ἡ τοῦ σημείου δύναμις ἐνεργοῦσα προτρέχῃ, πόσῳ δὴ μᾶλλον οὐ χρὴ δαίμονι πιστεύειν ἐπαγγελλομένῳ ψυχὰς ἐξ ᾅδου μεταπέμπεσθαι καὶ πνεύματα δικαίων ; 10. ἀλλ' οὐδὲ φαίη τις ἂν ἀσεβῶν

minute's notice, which is a greater and superior capacity and pertains to more divine authority? Who would reason in such a weak and impoverished way?" But I would especially emphasize in response that the demon prophesied nothing, as we have previously shown. 3. Yet even if he happened to have spoken words worthy of prophecy, not even then would it be necessary to suppose that the demon brought up spirits and souls from hell. For even Caiaphas at the meeting against Christ prophesied when he said, "It is better for us to have one man die on behalf of the people than to have the whole nation destroyed." 4. As John the wisest has explained, He did not say this "on his own," but being "high priest" that year he "prophesied" (John 11:50–51). 5. If this man who raised up wicked plots against the Lord all the same did not prophesy of his own accord but was doubtless moved by another to furnish condemnatory proof against himself, then if someone else did such a thing, neither should the connection be made that he was dependent upon a power more divine than this, nor should it be endured if someone says it befits demonic divination to bring up souls and armies of angels from hell such as God can do. 6. For what needs to be heard are the things Moses declares about such prophets, when he decrees in Deuteronomy, "If a prophet rises up among you or someone who divines by dreams, and gives you a sign or wonder, and the sign or wonder that he spoke to you of comes to pass, and he says, 7. 'Let us go and worship other gods whom you do not know,' you shall not heed the words of that prophet or the diviner of that dream, for the Lord your God is testing you to see if you love the Lord your God" (Deut 13:2–4). 8. Now Moses represents the duality of the Father and the only begotten Son. He calls the one who tests "Lord" and the other who exists beside him and is loved "Lord and God," so that from the duality he may demonstrate the single Godhead and the true divine generation.[88] 9. But if that prophet who promises to show a sign or wonder is to be absolutely rejected when he introduces lawless idolatry—even if the miracle associated with the sign should actively come forward—how much more necessary is it not to believe a demon who promises to summon souls and spirits of the righteous from hell? 10. Not even

---

[88] The LXX has κύριος ὁ θεός and κύριον τὸν θεόν, identical expressions. Eustathius obscures his point by omitting θεός from the first occurrence of the expression. What he must mean is that we have two instances of a single expression.

ὅτι μαντευομένων ἐκείνων ὁ θεὸς ἀνέστησε τὸν Σαμουὴλ ἐκπειράσαι τὸν ἄδικον ἐθέλων, ἵνα ἐπιγράψῃ τῇ τοῦ δαίμονος ἐπαγγελίᾳ τὸ δρᾶμα καὶ διὰ τῆσδε τῆς προφάσεως ἀπάτῃ φθείρῃ τινάς· ἀνάγκη γὰρ ἐξ ἅπαντος φυλάττεσθαι τὸ τῆς μαντείας ἄγος, ὡς ὁ νομοθέτης ἐθέσπισεν. 11. ἀλλ᾽ οὐ μυσερά τις ἡγεῖται τὰ τῆς οἰωνοσκοπίας αἴτια καὶ τὰ τῆς ἐγγαστριμύθου μαντεῖα καὶ σύμβολα κληδόνων ; ἀκουέτω πῶς ὀλίγῳ πρόσθεν ὑπερβὰς ἐδογμάτισε πάλιν· *ἐὰν δέ, φησίν, εἰσέλθῃς εἰς τὴν γῆν ἣν κύριος ὁ θεός σου δίδωσίν σοι, οὐ μαθήσῃ ποιεῖν κατὰ τὰ βδελύγματα τῶν ἐθνῶν ἐκείνων.* 12. *οὐχ εὑρεθήσεται ἐν σοὶ περικαθαίρων τὸν υἱὸν αὐτοῦ καὶ τὴν θυγατέρα αὐτοῦ ἐν πυρί, καὶ μαντευόμενος μαντείαν, καὶ κληδονιζόμενος καὶ οἰωνιζόμενος φαρμάκοις ἐπαοιδῶν ἐπαοιδήν, ἐγγαστρίμυθος καὶ τερατοσκόπος, ἐπερωτῶν τοὺς νεκρούς. ἔστι γὰρ βδέλυγμα κυρίῳ πᾶς ὁ ποιῶν ταῦτα.* 13. μετὰ δὲ τοῦτο μηνύων ὅτι καὶ τοῖς ἀλλογενέσι διὰ ταῦτα θανάτου γένεσιν ἀπειλεῖ καὶ φθοράν, ἐπήγαγεν εὐθέως· *ἕνεκα γὰρ τῶν βδελυγμάτων τούτων κύριος ἐξολοθρεύσει αὐτοὺς ἀπὸ σοῦ.* 14. φαίνεται τοίνυν ὡς ἡ μαντεία τῆς ἐγγαστριμύθου συνέζευκται μετὰ πάντων ὁμοῦ τῶν τῆς εἰδωλολατρείας αἰτιῶν, ὥσπερ ἂν εἰ πυρετῷ σκυβάλων ἔνδοθεν ὑποκειμένων, ἐγερτικῶν μὲν ἀρρωστίας, ὑπεκκαυμάτων δὲ μοχθηρῶν, οἰδήσει καὶ φθορᾷ τὴν λυμώδη νόσον ἀποκύειν εἰωθότων. 15. εἰ δὲ δὴ καὶ τερατοσκοπίας ὠνόμασε τὰς ἀμειδεῖς ὀπτασίας, ὅσαι διὰ τῶν ἐγγαστριμύθων ἱστοροῦνται, συνέστησεν ὅτι μηδέν ἐστιν ἀληθὲς ἐν αὐτοῖς· 16. ἐντεῦθεν, οἶμαι, πάλιν ἐν τῷ Λευϊτικῷ σκυθρωποτέραν ἀπόφασιν ἐξήνεγκε κατ᾽ αὐτῶν, ἐπαγαγὼν αὐτοῖς ῥήμασιν· *καὶ ἀνὴρ ἢ γυνή, φάμενος, <ὃς> ἂν γένηται ἐγγαστρίμυθος ἢ ἐπαοιδὸς ἐν ὑμῖν, θανάτῳ θανατούσθωσαν· λίθοις λιθοβολήσατε αὐτούς, ἔνοχοί εἰσιν.*

25. 1. Τί τοίνυν φασὶν οἱ τὰς Ὠριγένους ἀσπαστέας εἶναι τιθέμενοι δοξοκοπίας ; πότερον ὡς ἐχθίστων ἐπιτηδευμάτων αἰτίους ἀναιρεῖσθαι προστάττει τοὺς ἐγγαστριμύθους, ἢ τοὐναντίον ὡς ἀγαθῶν ὑποθήμονας ἔργων ; εἰ μὲν οὖν ἀσεβῶν εἰσὶ δραμάτων αὐτουργοί, δικαίως ὁ νομοθέτης ἀπελαύνει τοὺς ἐναγεῖς, οὐδὲν εἰσαγγέλλοντας ἀληθές. 2. εἰ δὲ καλλίστων

one of the impious would say that when demons were practicing divination God raised up Samuel because he wanted to test the wicked king, so that he might attribute the action to the promise of the demon and through this pretext would destroy some of them by deceit. For it is necessary to guard altogether against the pollution of divination, as the lawgiver has decreed. 11. Or would anyone think the taking of auguries, the divinations of the belly-myther, and the casting of lots are not loathsome things? Then let him hear how Moses a little later again taught. He says, "When you come into the land that the Lord your God is giving you, you shall not learn to act in accordance with the abominations of those nations. 12. No one shall be found among you who purifies his son and his daughter in fire, and who practices mantic divination, and who casts lots, and who takes omens with drugs by crafting a charm, a belly-myther and soothsayer, one who seeks oracles from the dead. For everyone who does these things is an abomination to the Lord" (Deut 18:9–12). 13. After this, indicating that because of these practices he is threatening even the foreign nations with forthcoming death and destruction, he immediately added, "It is because of these abominations that the Lord will utterly destroy them from your midst" (Deut 18:12). 14. Therefore, it is plain that the divinatory activity of the belly-myther is yoked together with all the other causes of idolatry as a group. It is just as in a fever when the excrement within exacerbates the illness and as a wretched fuel customarily gives birth to filthy disease with swelling and corruption. 15. And if Moses has given the name soothsayings to the gloomy visions such as are told through belly-mythers, he has established that there is nothing true in them. 16. It is for that reason, I suppose, that again in Leviticus Moses has pronounced a more severe judgment against them, which he introduced in these very words, "A man or a woman who becomes a belly-myther or a charmer among you shall be put to death. Stone them with stones, for they are guilty" (Lev 20:27).

25. 1. Therefore, what do those who think Origen's bids for popularity deserve a warm welcome say? Does Moses order the belly-mythers to be destroyed since they are the cause of the most hateful practices or, on the contrary, because they are counselors of good deeds? If, then, they are in themselves responsible for impious actions, then the lawgiver justly drives them away as accursed, since they have pronounced nothing true. 2. But if, on

εὑρεταὶ πράξεών εἰσι, περιττῶς ὁ νόμος ἐψηφίσατο κατ' αὐτῶν. εἰ γὰρ
ἀνάγουσι μὲν ἐξ ᾄδου ψυχάς, αἱ δὲ ἀφικνούμεναι δεῦρο κηρύττουσι τὸ
μέλλον, ἐφοδιάζουσι τοὺς δεομένους ἐπωφελῶς· οὐ δικαίως ἄρα λιθοβο-
λεῖσθαι τοὺς εὐεργέτας ἐθέσπισεν ὁ νομοθέτης. 3. ὥστε δυοῖν ἀνάγκη
θάτερον, ἢ ταύτας ἀχρειῶσαι τὰς φωνάς, ἢ τὰ τῆς ἐγγαστριμύθου ῥήματα διαβαλεῖν ὡς ἕωλα καὶ ψευδῆ. ἀλλὰ τί φῶμεν; ἀντιδοξοῦσιν ἑαυταῖς
αἱ θεῖαι γραφαί; ταῖς δὲ πολλαῖς ἡ μία μάχεται ψῆφος; εἰ δ' ἄρα καὶ
μάχη τίς ἐστιν, ἐπικρατοῦσιν αἱ πολλαί. 4. καὶ μὴν ἐκ τῶν ἐναντίων οὕτως ὁμοφώνῳ συνῳδίᾳ καταψηφίζονται τῶν ἐγγαστριμύθων ὡς ἀνόσια
δρώντων. οὐδὲν ἧττον ἔτι κἂν τῇ τετάρτῃ τῶν Βασιλειῶν ἀνειλημμένον
ἐστὶν ὅτι Μανασσῆς μὲν ἀσεβείας ὑπερβολῇ πρὸς οἷς ἐδικαιοκτόνει καὶ
παντοίας ἐθρήσκευεν εἰδωλομόρφους ὕλας *ἐποίησεν* ἑαυτῷ, φησίν, ἐγγαστριμύθους *καὶ γνώστας*. 5. ἀντιστρόφως δ' αὖ πάλιν ὁ δικαιοσύνης
ἀρετῇ διαπρέψας Ἰωσίας ὁ βασιλεὺς ἅπαντα μὲν ὁμοῦ τὰ χειρότευκτα
καθεῖλεν ἀφιδρύματα, πυρὶ δὲ τεφρώσας ἠφάνισεν· οὐ μὴν ἀλλά γε πρὸς
τούτοις ἀφεῖλεν ἔφη *τοὺς ἐγγαστριμύθους καὶ τοὺς γνώστας καὶ τὰ θερα-
φεὶμ καὶ τὰ εἴδωλα καὶ τὰ καρσαείν* εἶτα καὶ μετ' ὀλίγα φησὶν ὅτι καὶ
ἐνεπύρισεν, ὡς ἀθέμιτα δηλαδή. 6. τοιγαροῦν εἴπερ ὁ αὐτός ἐστιν συγγραφεὺς ἑκατέρου τοῦ γράμματος, ἐνταῦθα δὲ δύο πρόσωπα βιολογεῖ
βασιλέων, εἶτα τούτοιν τὸ μὲν ἄδικον εἰσάγει, τὸ δὲ δίκαιον—ἀλλὰ τὸ
μὲν ἀκράτῳ κεχορηγημένον ἀδικίᾳ μέμφεται, διὸ πρὸς τοῖς ἄλλοις εἴχετο
καὶ τῶν ἐγγαστριμύθων, τὸ δὲ ζήλῳ θείῳ διεγηγερμένον ἐπαινεῖ τῷ καὶ

the other hand, they are the inventors of the noblest deeds, the law has passed a strange verdict against them. For if they bring souls up from hell and the souls once they arrive here proclaim the future, then they are supplying a useful service for those who ask. Hence, the lawgiver has unjustly decreed that benefactors such as these should be stoned. 3. Therefore, one of two things is necessary: either invalidate these passages from scripture or discredit the words of the belly-myther as worthless and false. What shall we say? Do the divine scriptures contradict themselves? Does a single judgment contradict the many? Well then, if there is any contradiction, the passages in the majority prevail. 4. Indeed, to the contrary, in this way the scriptures with a single unanimous verdict cast judgment against the belly-mythers as practitioners of unholy deeds. No less is it included yet again in the fourth book of Kingdoms (21:16) that Manasseh in his excessive impiety against those whom he sentenced to death also worshiped idols of all kinds and shapes. The text says, "He made for himself belly-mythers and diviners" (4 Kgdms 21:6).[89] 5. But in a reversal of this policy King Josiah, who had earned distinction by his righteous virtue, at once tore down all the hand-made images that had been erected and obliterated them to dust by fire. Moreover, besides this it says, he removed "the belly-mythers and the diviners and the teraphim and the idols and the karsaein."[90] Then a little later it also says that "he burned them up," clearly because they were lawless (4 Kgdms 23:24). 6. Therefore, if the same author wrote each passage in which he told the lives of two characters, both kings, then of the two he describes the one as unjust and the other as just. He blames one for outfitting himself with unmitigated injustice because among other things he clung to belly-mythers, while he praises the other because he had roused himself with zeal to de-

[89] The word ἐγγαστρίμυθος does not occur in the LXX of 4 Kgdms 21:6, but it may be found in the parallel passage in 2 Chr 33:6. The word substituted for "belly-myther" in 4 Kgdms 21:6 is θελητής, usually translated "wizard," but quite possibly an attempt to render into Greek the Hebrew word for "necromancer" (אוב), misunderstanding the word as from the root "to will" (אבה). See LSJ, 788.

[90] This text comes from 2 Chr 35:19a, which is roughly parallel to 4 Kgdms 23:24 but is found only in the Greek of the LXX. Here we find τὰ καρασιμ. Simonetti (*La Maga di Endor*, 246) suggests that the word is related to the Hebrew root חרש and refers to the cultic practice of cutting oneself in idolatrous worship. We might possibly translate "those who cut themselves."

τοὺς ἐγγαστριμύθους ἐξᾶραι πρὸς ἅπασι τοῖς ἐχθροῖς—εἰ δὲ ταῦτα οὕτως ἔχει, συνέστηκεν ὡς οὐχ ἑαυτῷ μαχομένας ἐξεδίδου φωνάς. 7. οὐδ᾽ αὖ τὸ πνεῦμα τὸ ἅγιον ἔφασκεν ἀναβεβηκέναι τὸν Σαμουήλ, ἀλλὰ τοὺς τῆς ἐγγαστριμύθου διηγεῖτο λόγους, ὡς ᾤετο καὶ τῷ δοκεῖν ἐκόμπαζεν ἐκείνη, φαντασιοκοπίαις ἀναπτεροῦσα τὸν δυνάστην ἀδήλοις· οὐ γὰρ ἂν ἑαυτῷ καὶ ταῖς ἄλλαις ἁπάσαις ἐμάχετό πω γραφαῖς. 8. ἀλλ᾽ οὐχὶ μόνον αὗται ταῦτα διελέγχουσιν αἱ ῥήσεις, ἀλλ᾽ ἔτι γε τούτοις ἐπιψηφίζεται καὶ μάρτυς ἄλλος ἀξιοφανής, ὁ προφήτης Ἡσαΐας· πῇ μὲν ἀπαγορεύων τὰ τοιάδε μύση, πῇ δὲ παραινῶν ὀρθότατα τοῖς ὑπηκόοις αὐτῷ κελαδεῖ· *καὶ ἐὰν εἴπωσι πρὸς ὑμᾶς· ζητήσατε τοὺς ἐγγαστριμύθους, καὶ τοὺς ἀπὸ τῆς γῆς φωνοῦντας, τοὺς κενολογοῦντας οἳ ἐκ τῆς κοιλίας φωνοῦσιν, οὐχὶ ἔθνος πρὸς θεόν;* 9. εἶτα τί μετὰ ταῦτα προσθεὶς ἐπιφέρει; *τί ἐκζητοῦσιν*, ἔφη, *περὶ τῶν ζώντων τοὺς νεκρούς; νόμον γὰρ εἰς βοήθειαν ἔδωκεν, ἵνα εἴπωσιν οὐχ ὡς τὸ ῥῆμα τοῦτο, περὶ οὖ οὐκ ἔστι δῶρα δοῦναι.* 10. προδήλῳ μὲν ἱεροφωνίᾳ τὸ τῶν ἐγγαστριμύθων ἀπεκήρυξε γένος· εἰ δὲ κενολόγον ἀπέφηνε τὸ τοιοῦτο συνέδριον, ἀναμφιλόγως ἀπέδειξεν ὅτι τούτων οὐδὲν οὐδεὶς οὐδεπώποτε λέγει τὸ παράπαν ἀληθές, ἀλλὰ ψευδηγορίᾳ μὲν ὑποκένῳ πλάττουσι τὴν ἀπάτην, ἑώλῳ δὲ κενολογίᾳ φενακίζουσι τοὺς ἀμαθεῖς. 11. ὅθεν ἀκολούθως ἐπέσκωπτεν ἐκείνους ὅσοι περὶ τῶν ζώντων ἐρωτῶσι τοὺς νεκρούς· αὐτοὶ γὰρ ὅλοι νεκροὶ καὶ πηροὶ τυγχάνοντες οἱ κενολόγοι τὰς τῶν νεκρῶν ὑποτυποῦνται διακονεῖσθαι φωνάς. ὁ δὲ προφήτης ἐπεμαρτύρετο βοῶν ὅτι νόμος ἀρραγὴς ἔκκειται περὶ τούτων, ἵνα μὴ κατὰ τοὺς ἀποφθεγγομένους ὑπαχθῶσι κουφολογίαις ἑώλοις· 12. ἀκροτάτη γάρ, οἶμαι, φυλακὴ νόμου καθέστηκεν οὐρανόθεν ἐπικαλεῖσθαι τὴν βοήθειαν, ἀλλὰ μὴ ἐκ τῶν γηΐνων ἐρανίζεσθαι τὴν ἐπικουρίαν εἰς αὐτὰ τὰ καταχθόνια βλέποντας.

26. 1. Ἀλλ᾽ ὁ πάσας ἑρμηνεῦσαι τὰς γραφὰς οἰηθεὶς Ὠριγένης οὐ προσποιεῖται ταύτας εἰδέναι τὰς μαρτυρίας, οὐδὲ τίθησιν αὐτὰς ὡς δέον, ἀλλ᾽ ἐπεισκυκλεῖ μὲν ἐκείνας ὅσαι μηδὲν ἐν μηδενὶ τῷ ζητήματι δια

stroy the belly-mythers before all the other enemies. If this is so, then it is established that the author was not handing down contradictory statements. 7. Moreover, the Holy Spirit did not say that Samuel had come up but narrated the words spoken by the belly-myther—as she thought and appeared to boast, to raise the hopes of the ruler by vain murky illusions. In no way was the Holy Spirit contradicting itself or all the other scriptures. 8. Not only do these statements seal the conviction, but there is still another distinguished witness to add his vote to theirs, the prophet Isaiah. Sometimes forbidding such defilements, sometimes exhorting his hearers to what is most upright, he cries out, "And if they say to you, 'Consult the belly-mythers and the ones who give voice from the earth, those who speak empty things, those who give voice from the belly; should not a people be with God?'" (Isa 8:19). 9. Then he goes on to add something after this. He said, "Why do they consult the dead about the living? For he gave the law for a help so that they might not speak according to this word for which it is not right to give gifts" (Isa 8:20–21).[91] 10. By an overt, clear holy expression he has publicly outlawed the class of belly-mythers. If he denounced such an assembly of empty speakers, he has without doubt demonstrated that not a single one of them ever says anything at all that is in the slightest bit true. Rather, they fabricate deceit by empty, false speech and trick the unlearned with useless, empty talk. 11. This is why he quite logically used to mock those who ask the dead about the living. For such empty speakers, themselves as it were entirely dead and incapacitated, pretend to serve up the voices of the dead. The prophet continually bore witness, crying aloud that an unbreakable law is in place concerning them, lest people be subjected to those who speak useless nonsense. 12. For I think our highest guardian, the law, has established that help is to be called upon from heaven, but those who fix their sight on netherworldly things do not acquire assistance from earthly ones.

26. 1. But Origen, who supposed he had interpreted all the scriptures, pretends not to know these testimonies, nor does he cite them as he should have. Rather, while he piles up so many pas-

---

[91] Literally: "so that they might speak not as this word for which there are no gifts to give for it." The LXX text is difficult if not unintelligible, but the sense must be that the speech of the belly-mythers is against the law, and it is wrong to give them gifts for their speech.

φέρουσιν, ὑπερβαίνει δὲ τὰς αὐτῇ φύσει προσηκούσας· ἤτοι γὰρ ἀμαθίᾳ τοῦτο πράττειν ἔοικεν ἀφρόνως, ἢ κακοθελίᾳ πραγματεύεσθαι τολμηρῶς. 2. ἀλλὰ καὶ καθάπερ ἐπαμφοτερίζων εἰρηκὼς ὅτι "τί οὖν ποιεῖ ἐγγαστρίμυθος ἐνθάδε; τί ποιεῖ ἐγγαστρίμυθος περὶ τὴν ἀναγωγὴν τῆς ψυχῆς τοῦ δικαίου;" λόγου μὲν ἀπορίᾳ μετεώρως ἀπέφυγεν, ἄλλῳ τοῦτο ἐπιγράφων ὅπερ ἔδρασεν αὐτός· αὐτῇ δὲ τῇ γραφῇ τὸ πᾶν ἀναθείς, ἰσχυρίζεται μὲν ἀνῆχθαι τὸν Σαμουήλ, οὐκέτι δὲ τολμᾷ δευτερῶσαι τὸ τίς ἀνήγαγε αὐτόν. 3. οἶμαι δὲ ὅτι καὶ μετέπειτα διελεγχόμενος ὑπὸ τῶν ὀρθότατα φρονούντων ἀεί, δευτέρα πάλιν ἀπολογούμενος ἐξηγήσει, τετηρῆσθαι μὲν ἔφη τὸν τῆς ἐγγαστριμύθου τόπον· εἶτα λέγει καὶ ὅτι μὲν ἡ ἐγγαστρίμυθός τινα ἀνήγαγε γέγραπται, καὶ ὅτι Σαοὺλ εἶπεν τῷ Σαμουὴλ ἀναγέγραπται· 4. φλυαρίᾳ δὲ πολλῇ τοιαῦτα συχνά τινα ταυτολογήσας, ἐπιφέρει πάλιν· οὐκ εἴρηκεν δὲ φησὶν εἰ ἑκουσίως ἀναβέβηκεν· οὐ γὰρ ἔχεις ἔφη κείμενον εἰ ἀνήγαγεν αὐτὸν ἡ ἐγγαστρίμυθος· ἐπεὶ ἐλεγξάτω μέ τις ἀναγνοὺς τὴν γραφήν. 5. οὐκοῦν ἀντιπροσώπως ἐλεγχόμενος ἠρνήσατο λευκῶς ἅπερ ἀβουλίᾳ πρόσθεν ἐδόξασεν· ἐκεῖ γὰρ αὐτὴν ὡρίσατο τὴν γραφὴν εἰρηκέναι μᾶλλον, ἀλλ' οὐ τὴν γυναῖκα, τὸ **τίνα ἀναγάγω σοι;** δεῦρο δὲ καταφανῶς ἁλισκόμενος ἐκφυγεῖν ἐσπούδασε λήθῃ τὴν αἰτίαν. 6. οὕτως ἑκασταχοῦ μαχομένας ἑαυτῷ δόξας ἐκτίθεται γυμνῶς, ὥσπερ οὖν ἀμέλει κἀνταῦθα γνωσιμαχήσας ἑάλω, τὴν ἐγκληματικὴν ἀποδρᾶναι δίκην ἐπειχθείς. ἐπεὶ τοίνυν ἄκων ἑλκόμενος ὡμολόγησεν ὡς οὐκ ἀνήγαγεν ἡ γυνὴ τὴν τοῦ προφήτου ψυχήν, εἰπάτω

sages that are in no way whatsoever relevant to the inquiry at hand,
he passes over the passages that by their very nature are related.
For he seems either to act stupidly, due to poor training, or to be
trafficking with evil intent. 2. And even like a man hesitating between two opinions he said, *What, then, is the belly-myther doing
here? What is the belly-myther doing regarding the bringing up of the
righteous man's soul?*[92] At a loss for words, he has taken refuge in
the clouds, indicting someone else for what he has himself done.
Attributing the whole thing to scripture itself, he insists strongly
that Samuel was brought up, but he no longer dares to ask a second time who brought him up. 3. And I suppose that even after
he had been refuted by those who have had the right opinions all
along, still defending his view with a second exposition, he said
that the passage about the belly-myther is to be retained in a literal
sense.[93] Then he both says that "it is written that the belly-myther
brought someone up" and that "it is recorded that Saul spoke to
Samuel." 4. He repeated the same sort of ideas at length with great
nonsense and then continued, "It does not say if he had come up
willingly. For you do not have it literally saying whether the belly-
myther brought him up. Let someone try to refute me only after
he has read the scripture." 5. Therefore, when he was refuted
to his face, Origen clearly denied the opinion he had previously
inadvisably entertained. For there he determined that scripture
itself rather than the woman was the one who said, "Whom shall
I bring up for you?" Here, quite obviously caught out, he was eager to escape the accusation by a slip of memory.[94] 6. Thus, in
both places he nakedly set forth opinions that contradicted himself, just as here, too, he is caught actually fighting against his own
view, beating a hasty retreat from the writ of accusation against
him. Therefore, since when dragged against his will he admitted
that the woman did not bring up the prophet's soul, let him say

[92] Origen, *Hom. 5 on 1 Kgdms* 6.1.

[93] This reference and the citations from Origen that follow are thought
by the Nautins and others to come from a second homily, now lost, because the
words do not appear in the manuscript traditions of the first homily (see the
Nautins' attempted reconstruction in *Origène*, 210–12). This is quite plausible,
but we might allow also the possibility that Eustathius is engaging in more προσωποποιία here (see n. 11 in the Compositional Analysis).

[94] "There" and "here" refer either to the first and the second (lost)
homily or to the earlier "testimony" in 4.3–4 above.

τίς ὁ ταύτην ἀναγαγών ἐνέμεινε γὰρ ἀμεταστάτως ἀνῆχθαι μόνον αὐτὴν ὁρισάμενος. 7. αὐτὴ γοῦν ἡ πυθόμαντις ἐτύγχανε μόνη, καὶ Σαοὺλ ὁ δεόμενος ἐκείνης ἀνάξαι τὸν προφήτην. ἀλλ᾽ οὗτος μὲν οὐκ ἂν εἴη γε τοῦ δράματος αὐτουργός· οὐ γὰρ ἂν ἐδεῖτο τῆς ἐγγαστριμύθου νύκτωρ ἀφικνούμενος ὡς αὐτήν. εἰ δὲ γέγονεν ἡ πρᾶξις, οὐχ ἑτέρῳ τινὶ τὸ δραθὲν ἐπιγραπτέον. ὥστε δυοῖν ἀνάγκη θάτερον ἔστιν εἰπεῖν, ἢ τοῦτο μηδεπώποτε γεγονέναι μηδαμῶς ἢ διὰ τῆς ἐγγαστριμύθου καὶ τοῦ δαίμονος ἀνῆχθαι τὸν ἄνδρα τὸν ὄρθιον. 8. ἆρ᾽ οὖν ἀφοσιώσει τὰς ἑαυτοῦ φωνὰς ἀρνεῖσθαι δοκῶν ἄλλη μεθόδῳ τὴν αὐτὴν εἰσηγεῖται δοξοκοπίαν ἀπατηλῶς; ἀλλὰ δι᾽ ὧν μὲν ἔοικεν ἀπολογεῖσθαι, διὰ τούτων ὡς ἀλήθειαν εἰσηγεῖται τὸ ψεῦδος. 9. οὐ καταιδοῦσι δὲ αὐτὸν αἱ τοσαῦται καὶ τοιαῦται νομοθετικαὶ ψηφοφορίαι, οὐ σύμφωνοι προφητικαὶ μαρτυρίαι, οὐχ αἱ λοιπαὶ τῆς ἱστοριογραφίας ὁμόδοξοι συνῳδίαι· τὰ δὲ δὴ πανάγια παραλογισάμενος ἀποφθέγματα, προαιρέσει βεβαιοῖ τὰ τῆς ἐγγαστριμύθου ῥήματα, καινότερα μὲν εἰδωλολατρείας ὄργανα θεσπίζων, ἀσεβεῖ δὲ μαντείᾳ δαιμόνων ἐπεισκυκλῶν. 10. οὐ πείθει δὲ αὐτὸν οὐδὲ τὸ σύνθετον ὄνομα ποταπὴν ἔχει διαγωγήν· ἡ γὰρ ἐγγαστρίμυθος ἑρμηνεύεται παρὰ τὸ μῦθον ἐν γαστρὶ πεπλασμένον ἐμφαίνειν, ἡ δὲ τοῦ μύθου σύνθεσις ἐσχημάτισται σκηνοπηγουμένη πιθανῶς εἴσω γαστρός, οὐκ ἀλήθειαν ἀλλὰ τὸ ψεῦδος ἄντικρυς ἐκφωνεῖ. μακρῷ γοῦν ἄμεινον ἴσασιν οἱ ποικίλαις ὁμιλήσαντες λόγων ἀναφοραῖς ὁποῖόν ἐστι τὸ γένος αὐτοῦ.

27. 1. Κἂν τὰ μάλιστα δὲ δεισιδαιμονίαν πυρέττων Ἑλληνικὴν μαντείαν εἰσηγῆται λεληθότως, ἀλλ᾽ ὅμως οὐ παραιτητέον ἡγοῦμαι κἀντεῦθεν ἐλέγξαι τὴν ἀξυνεσίαν αὐτοῦ δι᾽ ὀλίγων, ὡς δέον. 2. αἱ γάρ τοι ῥητορικαὶ δηλοῦσι τεχνογραφίαι σαφῶς ὅτι μῦθός ἐστι πλάσμα συγκεί-

who is the one who brought it up. For he persisted without any change in his opinion, determining only that it was taken up. 7. Now the only people there were the Pythian prophetess and Saul, who asked her to bring up the prophet. But Saul would not have been able to carry out the deed on his own, for then he would not have come to the belly-myther at night and asked her to do it. If the act took place, we must ascribe what was done to no one else. Consequently, it is necessary to say one of two things: either this never happened at all, or the standing man was brought up by the belly-myther and the demon. 8. Consequently, then, by seeming to deny his own statements by this attempt at self-expiation, does Origen deceitfully bring in the same bid for popularity by another method? By the very words with which he seemed to defend himself, he introduced a lie as though it were the truth. 9. So abundant and pertinent decrees of the law do not shame him, nor do the prophetic testimonies, which are of one accord, nor do the rest of the like-minded voices of the scriptural narrative, which sing in complete concord. Fallaciously misrepresenting[95] the all-holy utterances, he chooses to confirm the words of the belly-myther, thereby decreeing still-newer instruments of idolatry and piling them up by the impious divination of demons. 10. But not even her compound name convinces Origen of what sort of bearing she had. For if[96] *"engastri-mythos"* ("belly-myther") is interpreted by derivation to indicate that "a myth is fabricated in the belly," and if the composition of a myth is given shape, sheltered persuasively within the belly, then the name does not broadcast the truth but the exact opposite—a lie. Indeed, those who are conversant with various forms of literary reference know much better to what genre[97] myth belongs.

27. 1. Even if Origen had introduced Greek mantic activity inadvertently, because he was seriously ill with the fever of superstition, nevertheless I do not think I should beg off from giving at this point a brief refutation of his lack of intelligence, since it is necessary. 2. In fact, the rhetorical handbooks clearly show

---

[95] παραλογίζεσθαι, the same word the woman uses in her accusation of pretence in Saul (1 Kgdms 28:12, cited by Eustathius in 3.6).

[96] Declerck, *Eustathii Antiocheni Opera*, who accepts Klostermann's emendation of ἤ to εἰ.

[97] The word is γένος. There may be a play on the γένος of the belly-myther; cf. 20.1 and 25.10 (where γένος is translated "class").

μενον μετὰ ψυχαγωγίας πρός τι τῶν ἐν τῷ βίῳ χρήσει διαφέρον· πλάσμα
δὲ δήπουθεν εἴρηται παρὰ τὸ πεπλάσθαι, φασίν, αὐτὸ συνωμολογημένως·
οὐ γὰρ ἂν ἔτι νομίζοιτο μῦθος, εἰ γεγονὼς εἴη κατὰ ἀλήθειαν. 3. εἰ δὲ
πλάσματος αὐτοσχεδίου σύνθεσίς ἐστιν ἡ μυθοποιία, πόρρω μὲν ἔργῳ
ἀληθείας ἐλήλεγκται, λόγῳ δὲ πραγμάτων ὕλας εἰκονίζει τῇ πράξει λει-
πομένη· τὰ γὰρ οὐκ ὄντα πιθανολογεῖν ἔοικεν ὡς ὄντα, καὶ διηγήσει
μίμησιν εἰσάγει πεπλασμένην· ἀνυπόστατα τοίνυν εἰδοποιεῖ πράγματα,
μηδεμιᾶς ὑποκειμένης ἕδρας ὡς οἷόν τε βεβαίας. 4. οὐδὲν δέ μοι δοκεῖ
διαφέρειν ἀψύχου σκιαγραφίας ἡ τοῦ μύθου πλαστουργία· καθ' ὁμοιό-
τητα γάρ, οἶμαι, τοῦ πίνακος αὐτῇ διαχαράττεται τῇ γραμμῇ· παρα-
πλησίῳ γέ τοι προσεμφερείᾳ προσωποποιεῖ μὲν ὑπόθεσιν, εἴς τι μέρος
ἀποβλέπουσα, αὐτὰ δὲ σχηματίζει τῇ μιμήσει τὰ πράγματα γραμμαῖς
ἐντεταμέναις. 5. ἀνομολογίαν μὲν οὖν ἐφ' ἑκάστων ἐς τὰ μάλιστα τη-
ρεῖ τῶν ῥυθμῶν, ἄκρα τε πολέμου γράφει καὶ τέλος, ἐοικότα βάσει, καὶ
χείλη φθεγγόμενα καὶ φωνῶν ἰδιώματα, καὶ γέλωτας καὶ κλαυθμούς,
ἢ δημηγορίας ἀρχοντικὰς ἢ συμπόσια καὶ κώμους ἢ βακχείας ἢ τελε-
τὰς ἢ μέθας ἀκολάστους ἢ παροινίας ἐρωτικὰς ἢ ληστρικὰς ἁρπαγὰς ἢ
φθορὰς ἀνηκέστους ἢ σφαγὰς ἀκρίτους ἢ πενίας ὑποκρίσεις ἢ πλούτων
ἐπιρροίας. 6. εἰκοτολογίᾳ μὲν οὖν ἅπαντα χαρακτηρίζει, προσωποποιΐᾳ
δὲ προσεμφερεῖ διαγορεύει πράξεις ἀδρανεῖς· οἱ γάρ τοι μυθοποιοὶ τὰς
ἀνθηρὰς ἀναλεγόμενοι λέξεις αὐτουργοῦσι ποικίλα χρωμάτων εἴδη καὶ
τῇ προσωποποιΐᾳ συμπλέκουσιν· εἶτα λόγοις ἐπιχρώσαντες ἡδέσι, πᾶσαν

that "a myth is a fabrication composed with persuasive attraction with an eye to some matter of vital importance and utility."[98] Doubtless, they say, it has been called a "fabrication," as derived from the verb "to have been fabricated"; this is commonly agreed upon, because it would no longer be considered a myth if it had truly happened. 3. And if it is an improvised composition or act of myth-making, it stands convicted of being far from the truth in deed, while it fashions in speech a likeness of concrete events, though it is bereft in fact. For it seems to use persuasive speech to show that what does not exist does exist, and it introduces in narrative form a fabricated copy. Therefore, it gives form to deeds without any substance, when there is no possible underlying ground for confirmation. 4. A fabricated myth seems to me no different from a lifeless scene-painting. For just like a painting, I think, it is given shape by its outlining letters.[99] Certainly by close verisimilitude it dramatizes its setting with a careful eye for each part, and by imitation it forms the actions with the outlining letters inscribed. 5. Thus, it preserves to the highest possible degree a purported correspondence with each of the movements. It depicts the beginning and ending of war, in a likely sequence, and of lips that speak and the particularities of speaking voices, and laughter and weeping, or rulers speaking in the assembly, or banquets and revels, or Bacchic frenzy, or mystery rites, or unbridled drunkenness, or love-sick drunken revels, or thievish robberies, or fatal disasters, or indiscriminate slaughters, or guises of poverty, or the influx of riches. 6. Thus, mythmaking depicts all these things with plausible speech and by like personification describes in detail deeds that were actually not done. For mythmakers gather flowery expressions and fashion them on their own with various kinds of colors and weave them together by person-

---

[98] This definition follows the standard ones found in the rhetorical handbooks. Compare, e.g., Theon, *Prog.* 1 [Spengel, *Rhetores Graeci*, 2:59, lines 21–22]; *Scholia in Theonem Rhet. Prog.* 1 [Walz, *Rhetores Graeci*, 1:259, lines 5–13]; Aphthonius (also at Antioch), *Prog.* 1 [Rabe, *Aphthonius, Progymnasmata*, 1, lines 4–5]; Grant, *Earliest Lives of Jesus*, 121–22; Anne Gangloff, "Myths, fables et rhétorique à l'époque impériale," *Rhetorica* 20 (2002): 25–56, and further discussion in Mitchell, "Rhetorical Handbooks in Service of Biblical Exegesis," and above, pp. cxv–cxvii.

[99] τῇ γραμμῇ, the stroke or line—of a pen for the myth, of a brush for the painting.

μὲν ἐπισυνάγουσι τὴν τοῦ μύθου διήγησιν, ὥσπερ δὲ ζῳδιογράφοι τὴν τῆς ὄψεως εἰκονίζουσιν ὥραν, ἐρυθροῖς ἠδ' ἀνθινοῖς χρώμασι κηρογραφοῦντες· 7. ῥήμασι δὲ καὶ σχήμασι μελοποιεῖν ἐπειγόμενοι χαρακτῆρας ὑλικούς, ἔργῳ τῆς ἀληθείας αὐτῆς ἀποδέουσιν. ἀλλ' οὗτοι μὲν τοιούτῳ ποικίλλουσι τρόπῳ τὰς τῶν μύθων εἰκόνας· ἐντεῦθεν δὲ μουσική τις ἁρμονία συνίσταται καὶ ποιητικῆς οἰησικοπίας εὕρεσις.

28. 1. Ἀμέλει γοῦν ἐρόμενος ὁ Πλάτων μουσικῆς μὲν εἶναι λόγους ὁρίζεται [λόγων]· "λόγων δὲ διττὸν εἶδος," ἔφη, "τὸ μὲν ἀληθές, ψεῦδος δὲ θάτερον· παιδευτέον δὲ ἐν ἀμφοτέροις, ἀλλά γε πρότερον ἐν τοῖς ψευδέσι." προηγουμένως γὰρ εἶπε τὰ παιδία καταθέλγεσθαι μύθων ἐπαοιδῇ. "τοῦτο δέ που ὡς τὸ ὅλον εἰπεῖν ψεῦδος, ἔνι δὲ καὶ ἀληθές. 2. οὐκοῦν ἀρχὴ παντὸς ἔργου μέγιστον, ἄλλως τε δὴ καὶ νέῳ καὶ ἁπαλῷ ὁτῳοῦν; μάλιστα γὰρ δὴ τότε πλάττεται καὶ ἐνδύεται τύπον, ὃν ἄν τις βούληται ἐνσημήνασθαι ἑκάστῳ." διὰ δὲ τῶν τοιούτων πειρᾶται ῥήσεων ἐκφαίνειν ὡς οὐ χρεὼν ἂν εἴη γε ψευδηγορίαις ἐπαντλεῖν ἀκράτοις τὰς τῶν νεηλύδων ἀκοάς, ἐπειδὴ τοῖς ἀρτίως ἐνσημαινόμενοι μείραξιν οἱ τύποι τῆς κακοδοξίας ἀμετάστατοι φιλοῦσι γίγνεσθαι καὶ δυσέκνιπτοι· 3. διόπερ ἀκολούθως ἐπιφέρει πάλιν· "ἆρ' οὖν ῥᾳδίως οὕτω παρήσομεν," ἔφη, "τοὺς ἐπιτυχόντας ὑπὸ τῶν ἐπιτυχόντων μύθους πλασθέντας ἀκούειν τοὺς παῖδας καὶ λαμβάνειν ἐν ταῖς ψυχαῖς ὡς ἐπὶ τὸ πολὺ ἐναντίας δόξας ἐκείναις ἃς ἐπειδὰν τελειωθῶσιν ἔχειν οἰησόμεθα δεῖν αὐτούς; οὐδ' ὁπωστιοῦν," εἴρηκεν ὅτι "παρήσομεν. 4. πρῶτον μὲν ἡμῖν, ὡς ἔοικεν, ἐπιστατητέον τοῖς μυθοποιοῖς, καὶ ὃν μὲν ἂν καλὸν μῦθον ποιήσωσιν ἐγκριτέον, ὃν δὲ μὴ ἀποκριτέον. τοὺς δὲ ἐγκριθέντας πείσωμεν τὰς τροφούς τε καὶ μητέρας λέγειν τοῖς παισίν, καὶ πλάττειν τὰς ψυχὰς αὐτῶν τοῖς μύθοις πολὺ μᾶλλον ἢ τὰ σώματα ταῖς χερσίν. ὧν δὲ νῦν λέγουσι τοὺς πολλοὺς ἐκβλητέον." 5. εἶτα ἐπειδή, περὶ τῆς ἑκάστων ἀναλόγου

ification. Then, employing pleasant words, they bring the whole narrative of their myth together, just as painters make a beautiful image of what they see and in encaustic painting color it with red and a palette of bright colors. 7. But in striving to give a melodious account of material characteristics by words and figures of speech, they in fact fall short of the truth itself. Yet they give varied expression to the portrayals of the myths in this way; from it a kind of music-inspired harmony and invention of poetic fancy are established.

28. 1. Indeed, Plato, when asked, defined literary works inspired by the muses by saying, "There are two forms of literature," he said, "one true and the other false. . . . one should be educated by both, but first by the false ones" (*Resp.* 376e–377a). For he said initially that children are enchanted by the spell of myths. "This type is, speaking generally, false, but there is also a true element. . . . 2. Consequently, is not the beginning of every endeavor the chief element, especially so when dealing with anything young and pliant? For it is especially then that it is fashioned and has pressed upon it the impression with which anyone wishes each to be marked" (*Resp.* 377ab). Through such statements he tries to show that it would by no means be necessary to flood the ears of newcomers with purely false tales, since the impressions of unorthodox opinions,[100] once they have made their mark on those who are barely boys, are wont to be unchangeable and hard to wash off. 3. For this reason he logically continues, "Hence shall we then so easily permit our children to hear any old myths fabricated by any old teachers and to receive in their souls opinions that are for the most part contradictory to those that we shall think it necessary for them to hold when they are grown up? In no way at all," he said, "will we permit it. 4. First, as it seems, it is necessary to superintend closely the mythmakers, and whatever myth they compose that is good is to be approved, and that which is not is to be rejected. And the myths that have been approved we shall persuade both the nurses and the mothers to tell to the children and to fashion their souls by the myths even more than they do their bodies by their hands. And the majority of those they now tell are to be thrown out" (*Resp.* 377bc). 5. Then, since he was asked about the proportional difference between the two, he said,

---

[100] κακοδοξία, as in 22.6 (cf. the adverb in 22.5).

διαφορᾶς ἐρωτώμενος, "ἐν τοῖς μείζοσιν," ἔφασκε, "μύθοις ἀναγνωρίζεσθαι καὶ τοὺς ἐλάττους," ὡς ἤρετο πάλιν ὁ Ἀδείμαντος, οὐδὲ τούτους εἰδέναι δηλῶν, αὖθις ἀνθυπενέγκας ἔφησεν· "οὓς Ἡσίοδός τε, εἶπον, καὶ Ὅμηρος ἡμῖν ἐλεγέτην· οὗτοι γάρ που μύθους τοῖς ἀνθρώποις ψευδεῖς συντιθέντες ἔλεγόν τε καὶ λέγουσιν."

29. 1. Εἰ τοίνυν Ὁμήρου τὰ ἔπη καὶ Ἡσιόδου μύθους ἀποφαίνει ψευδεῖς, ἃ δὴ μάλιστα καὶ παιδείας ἕνεκα ψυχαγωγεῖ τοὺς αὐτηκόους, οὐ μὴν ἀλλά γε καὶ καλλιλεξίᾳ διεγείρει τὸ φρόνημα πρὸς εὐγλωττίαν ἐντελῆ, πόσῳ δὴ μᾶλλον ὅσους ἡ δαιμονῶσα γραῦς ἀπεφθέγξατο λόγους οὐχὶ μυθοποιίας ὁριεῖταί τις εἶναι ψευδεῖς, ὁπηνίκα καὶ τοὔνομα τῆς ἐγγαστριμύθου τοῦτον ὑπαγορεύει τὸν νοῦν; **2.** εἰ γὰρ Ἑλλήνων παῖδες, οἳ καὶ τὰς ὀνοματοποιίας ἑκάστου πράγματος ἀκριβοῦντες, ἐν τῇ Ἑλλάδι φωνῇ πλάσματα ψευδῆ τοὺς μύθους ὀνομάζουσιν, ἀκόλουθον ἐκ τοῦ ὀνόματος ὑποπτεῦσαι τὸ πρᾶγμα καθ' οὗ τέτακται κυρίως. **3.** ἀλλ' αἱ μὲν Αἰσώπου λογοποιίαι τοιαῦτα μύθων ἴσασι πλάσματα, οἷα καὶ τὰ μειράκια πολλαχῶς ἐν ταῖς παιδιαῖς ἀσταϊζόμενα παίζει καὶ κορυβαντιῶσαι γραῖαι κωτίλοις ἐπᾴδουσι λόγοις ἔσθ' ὅτε ταῦτα δρῶσιν οἴνῳ μὲν ἐπιβρέχουσαι τὸν φάρυγγα συχνῷ, κύλικι δὲ προσέχουσαι καὶ ποτῷ φλυαροῦσιν ἀμέτρως. **4.** οἱ μέντοιγε φιλοσοφίας ἤθη πρεσβεύειν ἡγούμενοι καὶ τὰς ἐμμούσους ποιήσεις οἷα ψευδῆ μύθων εἴδη διέβαλλον, ὡς δέον.

30. 1. Εἰ οὖν αὐτὸ τοὔνομα κατὰ τοῦ πράγματός ἐστι τεταγμένον ὀρθῶς, ἐν γαστρὶ μῦθον ἔοικεν ἀναπλάττειν ἡ ἐγγαστρίμυθος· οὐ γὰρ ἐκ τοῦ φυσικοῦ φθέγγεται νοῦ σωφρόνως, ἀλλ' ἐν τοῖς ἐνδοτάτω μορίοις ἐμφωλεύων ὁ δαίμων αὐτὴν ἐπινέμεται καὶ βλάπτει τὴν φρόνησιν, ἐκ δὲ

"by the greater myths the lesser, too, will be recognized" (*Resp.* 377c). When Adeimantus asks again, showing he did not know what these were, Socrates responded in turn, stating, "As I said, those that both Hesiod and Homer ... told us. For these men, I suppose, having composed false myths, both told and still tell them" (*Resp.* 377d).[101]

29. 1. Therefore, if Plato declares the poems of Homer and Hesiod to be false myths—the very poems which most move the souls of their hearers because of their place in the school curriculum, not least because by the beauty of their language they rouse the mind to perfect eloquence—how much more will one designate the words the demon-colluding old crone uttered as false myth-making, when even the name belly-myther includes this meaning? 2. For if Greek school children, who can thoroughly recognize "name-coined"[102] expressions for each thing, call myths in Greek "false fabrications," it follows that we must regard the thing to which the name has been properly assigned as suspect. 3. But the tales of Aesop are acquainted with such mythic fabrications, just like the wordplays youths speciously make in their games or old crones do in their corybantic frenzy, as they release charms with babbling words (sometimes they do it when pouring a big gulp of wine down their throats; at other times they gaze intently into the cup and address their endless nonsense to the sauce!). 4. Indeed, those who consider ethics to outrank philosophy slander even the "inspired" poems as forms of false myths,[103] as they should.

30. 1. Therefore, if the name itself has been rightly assigned to the actual thing, the belly-myther in all likelihood fabricates a myth in her belly. For she does not speak from the natural mind in a sane fashion, but the demon lurking in her inner organs encroaches upon her and disables her thinking, and, composing

---

[101] In this last citation Eustathius omits "and the other poets" after "Homer."

[102] ὀνοματοποιία (cf. LSJ, 1233).

[103] Having appealed to the Platonic critique of the myths, Eustathius here alludes in passing to the debates, especially among the Stoics, about the value of myths for philosophical, especially cosmological and metaphysical, speculation, if read allegorically, and the problem of the significant ethical lapses on display in them, especially by the gods, if taken literally. See Grant, *Letter and Spirit*, 1–30, and the articles by Tate, Long, and Most in the bibliography.

τῆς γαστρὸς ἐξηχεῖ μυθώδη πλάσματα συγκροτῶν, εἰς ποικίλα δὲ μεταμορφούμενος εἴδη διαφόροις ἰνδάλμασιν ὑπάγει τὴν ψυχήν. 2. ἐπειδὴ δὲ παντοδαποῖς ἐξαλλάττεται σχήμασι πολυπρόσωπος ὤν, οὐδὲν ἧττον ἔτι καὶ ἐκ τῆς γῆς ἀναβαίνειν ὑποκρίνεται καὶ φωνεῖν· εἶτα παρ' ἑκάτερα τὰς διακονίας ἀμείβων ὁμοῦ ταῖς μορφαῖς, ἄλλον μὲν τὸν ἀναβαίνοντα παρὰ τὸν καλοῦντα δοκεῖ παριστᾶν, ὁ αὐτὸς δὲ τῇδε κἀκεῖσε περιτρέχων ἀλλάττει τὰς ἰδέας, ἵνα ἔργοις ἀποδεικνύῃ καὶ λόγοις ὅτι ψεύστης ἐστίν. 3. ὑποτυποῦται γοῦν αὐτὰ τὰ πρόσωπα νεκρῶν ἀνάγειν, ὡς εἰκός ἐστιν ἐκ τοῦ τοιοῦδε δράματος ὑπολαβεῖν, ἀμειδεῖς μὲν ὄψεις, σκυθρωπὰ δὲ φάσματα πεπλασμένως εἰσάγων, ὅλα δὲ κατηφῆ καὶ νεκρᾶς ὀδμῆς ἀνάπλεα παριστῶν ὡς ἐξ ᾅδου μετακεκλημένα δεινοποιεῖ, καὶ καθάπερ εἱρκτῆς ἢ δεσμῶν ἀνειμένα πρὸς ὀλίγον, εἶτα πάλιν ἐντεῦθεν ἐκεῖσε διαβαίνοντα. 4. τοιγάρτοι καὶ καταπλήττει τοῖς δείμασι τὴν ψυχὴν ἐκ τῶν ὄψεων, ὠχρὰ μὲν εἴδη πλάττων, ὄμμα δὲ βλοσυρὸν ἢ κατηφές, ἅτε δὴ νεκρῶν ἀρτίως ἐμπνεῖν καὶ πάλιν ἐκπνεῖν ὑπισχνουμένων· εἴωθε γὰρ ὑποκρίσει συσχηματίζεσθαι τοῖς δεινοῖς ὁ πλαστογράφος. 5. ἀλλ' ἔσθ' ὅτε μὲν αὐτὸς ἑαυτὸν εἰς πολλὰς ἀλλάττει μορφάς, ἔσθ' ὅτε δὲ συνεργοῖς ἀποκέχρηται τοῖς ὁμοήθεσιν αὐτῷ δαίμοσιν, οὔτε δὲ ψυχὰς ἐξ ᾅδου μεταπέμπεται προφητῶν οὔτε πνεύματα δικαίων οὔτε τὰς ἀγγελικὰς ἀξίας, ἀλλὰ τοὐναντίον ἐγένετο μὲν εἰς τὸ καταπαίζεσθαι πρὸς τῶν ἀγγέλων, ἐξεδόθη δὲ τοῖς ἀρίστοις ἀνδράσιν ὥστε πατεῖσθαι πρηνὴς εἰς τοὔδαφος ἀπορραγείς. 6. ἀλλ' οὗτος μὲν ἐκ τῶν ἀνωτάτω ῥοιζήματι βιαίῳ κατενεχθεὶς ὑπεστόρεσε τὰ νῶτα· μόνῳ δὲ τῷ παντοκράτορι πάρεστι θεῷ καὶ τῷ θειοτάτῳ τούτου παιδὶ ψυχὰς ἀνάγειν ἐξ ᾅδου καὶ χοροὺς ἀγγέλων ἐν τάξει παρεστῶτας ἔχειν, ὅπερ ἴδιον ἔκκριτον ὑπάρχει τῆς τοῦ θείου φύσεως.

mythic fictions, he makes them resound from her belly. Changing himself into diverse forms, he leads her soul[104] by various hallucinations. 2. And when he transforms himself into all sorts of different shapes, being a creature of many faces, no less does he pretend both to come up from the earth and to call out. Then in both ways, changing his ministrations at the same time as his forms, he seems to present himself coming up as someone different from the one who summons him. Yet though it is one and the same running about here and there, he changes his appearances so that he demonstrates in deeds and words that he is a liar (cf. John 8:44). 3. Then he gives the impression that he brings up the very persons of the dead, just as one is likely to suppose of such an act. Bringing up gloomy sights and sullen phantoms by sheer fabrication and presenting it all as dim and filled with the stench of death, he uses terrifying expressions to say that they have been summoned from hell and, as though freed for a short time from their prison or bonds, are going back there once again. 4. For that very reason he astounds the soul with terrors by these sights, fabricating pale shapes with grim or sunken eyes, as if the corpses just now respirated were on the verge of expiring once more. That forger of fictions customarily by pretense configures himself with terrifying features. 5. There are times when he changes himself into multiple forms and others when he has employed demons with a character like his as his co-workers. But he summons from hell neither the souls of prophets nor the spirits of the righteous nor the ranks of angels. On the contrary, he was with the angels only to be mocked (cf. Job 41:25) and was handed over to the best men with the result that he was trodden under foot, broken headlong on the ground. 6. Indeed, brought down from the highest places with a violent rushing noise, that beast has been laid low on his back.[105] But only to God who rules over all and to his most divine Son does it belong to bring souls up from hell and to have the choruses of angels standing by in rank. This belongs exclusively and above all to the divine nature.

---

[104] The text does not say whose soul, but the context indicates that it is the woman's. The wordplay is unmistakable: the devil ὑπάγει τὴν ψυχὴν (of the woman) but does not ἀνάγει τὴν ψυχὴν (of Samuel).

[105] Literally "he scattered his back" (ὑπεστόρεσε τὰ νῶτα). The translation is a bit of a guess, but sections 5–6 seem to allude to Luke 10:19; Acts 1:18; Wis 4:19.

(Ἀπολιναρίου)

Τὴν Χριστοῦ χάριν ἀγνοοῦντές τινες τὴν μετατιθεῖσαν ἐξ ᾅδου τὰς ψυχὰς διὰ τὸ καταλῦσαι τὴν βασιλείαν τοῦ θανάτου, οὐκ ἐπίστευσαν τῇ Γραφῇ τῇ περὶ τοῦ Σαμουήλ, ὡς ἐν ᾅδου κατεχομένης τῆς ψυχῆς αὐτοῦ καὶ διὰ δαίμονος ψυχαγωγηθείσης. ἔδει δὲ πιστεύοντας τῇ Γραφῇ μὴ πλάττειν αὐτοῖς δαίμονα ὡς φανέντα τῷ σχήματι τοῦ Σαμουὴλ — ὅπερ οὐκ ἐδίδαξεν ἡ Γραφή — ἀλλ᾽ ὁρᾶν ὅτι, εἰ καὶ δίκαιοι γεγόνασιν ἄνθρωποι πρὸ τῆς Χριστοῦ παρουσίας, *ἐβασίλευσεν ὁ θάνατος*, μέχρις οὗ κατήργησεν αὐτὸν ὁ Χριστὸς ἐλθὼν καὶ τὴν ἄνοδον ἔδωκε ταῖς ψυχαῖς καὶ τὴν εἰς τὰ οὐράνια μετάθεσιν· Θεοῦ γὰρ τὸ δῶρον, οὐ ψυχῶν δύναμις, οὐδὲ δικαιοσύνης ἀνθρωπίνης ἰσχύς. ἀναγκαίως οὖν ἀναγέγραπται τὰ κατὰ τὴν ψυχὴν τοῦ Σαμουήλ, ἵνα γνῶμεν τί νόμος καὶ τί Χριστός, ὅτι νόμος μὲν οὐκ ἔλυσεν τὴν ἀράν, Χριστὸς δὲ ἔλυσεν. καὶ νόμος μὲν οὐκ ἠλευθέρωσεν ἀπὸ διαβόλου, ὡς καὶ ἐξ ᾅδου μεταθεῖναι, ἀλλ᾽ ὅσον ἐν ᾅδου παραμυθίαν τινὰ παρέχειν ἐν ἐλπίδι Χριστοῦ. Χριστὸς δὲ *πύλας χαλκὰς συνέτριψε καὶ μοχλοὺς σιδηροῦς συνέκλασε*, διὰ τῆς ἀνόδου τῆς ἑαυτοῦ ταῖς κατεχομέναις ψυχαῖς ἀνοίγων τὴν ἀνάβασιν· *ἀνέβη γάρ, φησιν, εἰς ὕψος, ᾐχμαλώτευσεν αἰχμαλωσίαν, ἔδωκεν δόματα ἐν ἀνθρώποις.*

6. Apollinaris of Laodicea: A Fragment from the Catenae

There are some who fail to recognize the grace of Christ that has taken souls out of hell for the sake of the destruction of the kingdom of death. For this reason they have not believed the scripture concerning Samuel, how his soul was held fast in hell and was led up through a demon. But it was not necessary for those who believe the scripture to fashion in their minds a demon who appeared in the form of Samuel. Scripture has not taught this. Rather, they should have seen that even if there were righteous people before the coming of Christ, "death reigned" (Rom 5:14) until Christ came and destroyed it and gave souls an ascent and a way to change their abode to the heavenly places. For this takes place by the gift of God, not by the power of souls or the strength of human righteousness. Therefore, the accounts of the soul of Samuel have necessarily been recorded so that we may understand the difference between the law and Christ, since the law did not abolish the curse. It was Christ who abolished the curse (cf. Gal 3:10–14). The law did not give freedom from the devil so as to give release from hell, save insofar as it furnished some consolation in hell by the hope of Christ. But Christ "shattered the bronze gates and broke the iron bars" (Ps 106:16; Isa 45:2), opening through his own ascent a way up for the souls that were held fast. For it says, "he ascended on high; he made captivity itself a captive; he gave gifts among humans" (Eph 4:8; Ps 67:19).

(Διοδώρου)

Τινὲς οἴονται τὸν Σαμουὴλ ὑπὸ τῆς ἐγγαστριμύθου ἀνηνέχθαι, πολὺ τῆς ἀληθείας διαμαρτῶντες. οὐ γὰρ εἶπεν ἡ Γραφὴ ὅτι ἡ ἐγγαστρίμυθος ἀνήγαγεν, ἀλλ᾽ ἱστορεῖ ὡς αὐτὴ εἶπεν τῷ Σαοὺλ *τίνα ἀναγάγω σοι;* ὁ δὲ Σαοὺλ φησιν *τὸν Σαμουήλ.* οὐκ ἀνήγαγεν, ἀλλ᾽ *εἶδεν* παραγεγονότα· οὐχ ὡς ἔθος ἦν ἀνάγεσθαι τοὺς καλουμένους ὑπὸ τῶν ἐγγαστριμύθων, αὐτίκα *ἐβόησεν φωνῇ μεγάλῃ ἡ γυνή.* καὶ ὡς ἠρωτᾶτο τί θεασαμένη, ἐβόησεν *θεοὺς εἶδον ἐγώ,* φησίν, *ἀναβαίνοντας ἐκ τῆς γῆς.* καὶ εἶπεν αὐτῷ *ἄνδρα ὄρθιον ἀναβαίνοντα ὁρῶ ἀπὸ τῆς γῆς, ἀναβεβλημένον διπλοΐδα.* οὐ τέχνῃ δὲ τῆς γυναικός, ἢ δυνάμει τοῦ ἐνεργοῦντος ἐν αὐτῇ δαίμονος, ἀνῆλθεν ὁ Σαμουήλ· αὐτίκα ὁ μὲν Σαοὺλ τὸν Σαμουὴλ φησιν *ἀνάγεσθαί μοι,* ἡ δὲ πολλοὺς εἶδεν ἀνθ᾽ ἑνός, οὓς *θεοὺς* ὠνόμασεν. ὅθεν ξενίζεται πολλοὺς μὲν ἀνθ᾽ ἑνὸς ὁρᾶν οἰομένη, καὶ τοὺς *θεούς,* ἢ βουλομένη καλεῖν ἄνθρωπον ἢ ἀναγαγεῖν. οὐ γὰρ ἂν τοὺς ἑαυτῆς θεοὺς ἀναγαγεῖν ὡς νεκροὺς ἐπεχείρει, οὐδ᾽ ἂν εἶπεν *ἄνδρα* ὁρῶ *ὄρθιον,* εἴπερ ἦν συνήθεια ὀρθοὺς ἀνάγεσθαι τοὺς ὑπ᾽ αὐτῆς καλουμένους. ἐπείπερ τὸ καινὸν πρᾶγμα θαύματος καὶ κραυγῆς ἄξιον, ὃ δὴ καὶ πέπονθεν ἡ γυνή, διόπερ τινές φασιν ὅτι τῶν τετελευτηκότων, ὅσοι καλοῦνται ὑπὸ τῶν ἐγγαστριμύθων, οὕτως ἀνάγονται ὡς τὰ πολλὰ τίκτεται τῶν βρεφῶν ἄνω τοὺς πόδας ἔχοντα, τινὲς δὲ ὅτι ὑπτίως ὡς οἱ θαπτόμενοι νεκροί. ἐπειδὴ τοίνυν καὶ πολλοὶ ἐληλύθεισαν, ἐκείνης βουλομένης ἕνα καλέσαι, καὶ πρὸ τοῦ καλέσαι παραγεγόνασιν καὶ ὀρθοί (ὅπερ ξένον ἔδοξεν ὁρᾶν), ἡ γυνὴ *θεοὺς* εἶπεν *ὁρῶ ἐγὼ* — τουτέστιν οὐ τοιαύτης τέχνης τοῦτο τὸ ἔργον, ἀλλὰ ξένον καὶ θείας δυνάμεως.

Ἔδοξε δέ τισιν τὸν ἐνεργοῦντα διὰ τῆς γυναικὸς δαίμονα καὶ πολλοὺς ἐξαπατῶντα ἐν σχήματι τοῦ Σαμουὴλ ὦφθαι καὶ διειλέχθαι τῷ

7. Diodore of Tarsus: A Fragment from the Catenae

There are some, missing the truth entirely, who suppose that Samuel was brought up by the belly-myther. In fact, scripture did not say that the belly-myther brought him up but narrates that she said to Saul, "Whom shall I bring up for you?" and that Saul said, "Samuel" (1 Kgdms 28:11). She did not bring him up, but "saw" him when he appeared. Since this was not the usual way those summoned by belly-mythers were brought up, immediately "the woman cried out with a loud voice" (1 Kgdms 28:12). And when she was asked what she had seen, she said, "I have seen gods coming up from the earth." And she told him, "I see a man coming up from the earth standing, clothed in a double cloak" (1 Kgdms 28:13–14). It was not by the woman's craft or by the power of the demon operating in her that Samuel came up. The moment that Saul said that Samuel should be "brought up for me," the woman instead of one saw many, whom she called "gods." Therefore, she finds it strange when she supposes she sees many instead of one, and those "gods," since she wanted either to summon or to bring up a single man. For she would not have undertaken to bring up her own gods as though they were dead, nor would she have said "I see a man standing" if those she customarily summoned came up standing. What the woman experienced was worth her wonder and her crying out, since it was a novel event. This was because some people say of the dead—at least those who are summoned by belly-mythers—that they are brought up just the way many infants are born, feet first, while others say that they come up laid out flat, as corpses are buried. Therefore, since many had come, though that woman wanted to summon just one, and since they appeared both before her summons and standing (which seemed strange to see), the woman said, "I see gods." This means that this deed was not effected by a craft such as hers but was unusual and effected by divine power.

Some people have the opinion that it was the demon, who operated through the woman and deceived many, who actually ap-

Σαούλ, οὐ καλῶς οἶμαι· οὐ γὰρ συνεχώρει ὁ Θεὸς τὴν ἀπάτην ἐν σχήματι γενέσθαι τοῦ Σαμουήλ. ἀλλ᾿ ἔχουσί τι πρὸς ταῦτα λέγειν. δείκνυται
γάρ, φασιν, ὁ δαίμων ψευδόμενος δι᾿ ὧν λέγει τῷ Σαούλ *αὔριον σὺ καὶ*
Ἰωνάθαν μετ᾿ ἐμοῦ· οὐ γέγονεν δὲ τῇ ἑξῆς ὅπερ εἶπεν, ἀλλὰ τῇ τρίτῃ
ἡμέρᾳ. σφάλλονται δέ· οὐ γὰρ ἂν ἔχοιεν δεῖξαι ὅτι τῇ τρίτῃ ἡμέρᾳ μετὰ
τοὺς λόγους τοῦ Σαμουὴλ ἀπέθανεν ὁ Σαούλ, ἐπείπερ τὰ ἑξῆς τῆς ἱστορίας ἀνάληψίς ἐστιν τοῦ ὅλου πράγματος καὶ τοῦ πολέμου. οὐ γὰρ εἶπεν
ἡ θεῖα γραφὴ ὅτι μετὰ καὶ τὸ τὴν ἐγγαστρίμυθον εἰπεῖν *τῇ τρίτῃ ἡμέρᾳ*
ἀπέθανεν ὁ Σαούλ, ἀλλὰ διηγησαμένη τοῦ Σαοὺλ τὴν πλάνην καὶ τοῦ
Σαμουὴλ τὴν κατ᾿ αὐτοῦ ἀπόφασιν, αὖθις ἄνωθεν ἀναλαμβάνει τὸν λόγον. εἰ δὲ καὶ μὴ οὕτως ἔχοι ὅ φαμεν, οὐ συνίασιν ὅτι καὶ τὸ *αὔριον* οὐ
πάντως τὴν ἑξῆς δηλοῖ, ἀλλ᾿ ἔσθ᾿ ὅτε τὴν ἐγγύτητα τοῦ συμβησομένου,
ὡς καὶ τὸ *σήμερον, ἐὰν τῆς φωνῆς αὐτοῦ ἀκούσητε,* οὐ τὴν ἡμέραν δηλοῖ,
καθ᾿ ἢν ἐρρέθη, ἀλλὰ τὸν τῆς ἐπιστροφῆς τῶν Ἰσραηλιτῶν χρόνον.

Ἴδοι δ᾿ ἄν τις ὅ φημι καὶ ἑτέρως. πόθεν γὰρ τῷ δαίμονι, ὅτι οὐ
μόνος ὁ Σαοὺλ ἀναιρεθήσεται, ἀλλὰ καὶ Ἰωνάθαν; Ἐστοχάσατο, φασίν,
ὁ δαίμων· εἰδὼς γὰρ ὅτι ὁ Θεὸς ἐξέβαλε τὸν Σαοὺλ τῆς βασιλείας, δεδω-
κὼς αὐτὴν τῷ Δαυίδ, συνεῖδεν ὅτι καὶ τοὺς υἱοὺς ἀνάγκη συναπολέσθαι
τῷ πατρί. ἀλλὰ τὰ κατὰ στοχασμὸν φαίημεν ἂν οὐ πάντως ἐκβαίνειν
(ἐνδέχεται γὰρ καὶ μὴ γενέσθαι). πῶς δ᾿ ἂν ἠθέλησεν ὁ δαίμων ἀπὸ
στοχασμοῦ κινδυνεῦσαι αὐτῷ τὴν νομιζομένην ἀλήθειαν; ἀλλὰ τί ταῦτα
ἐπεξεργάζομαι, τῆς θείας γραφῆς ἄντικρυς λεγούσης ὅτι ὁ Σαμουὴλ τῷ
Σαοὺλ φησιν παραγεγονὼς *ἵνα τί παρηνώχλησάς μοι τοῦ ἀναβῆναί με;*
καὶ πάλιν *ἵνα τί ἐπερωτᾷς με; καὶ Κύριος ἀφέστηκεν ἀπὸ σοῦ καὶ γέγο-*
νεν μετὰ τοῦ πλησίον σου;

Μετασχηματίζεταί, φασιν, *ὁ σατανᾶς εἰς ἄγγελον φωτός,* ὡς εἶπεν
ὁ Παῦλος· ἀλλὰ φειδόμενος τοῦ Ἰσραὴλ ὁ Θεὸς (ᾔδει γὰρ αὐτοῦ τὰς
ἀσθενείας καὶ τὸ πρὸς ἀσέβειαν ἐπιρρεπὲς) οὐκ ἂν συνεχώρησεν δαίμονι ἐν σχήματι τοῦ Σαμουὴλ παραγενέσθαι. τοὐναντίον μὲν δὴ ἔπληττεν

peared in the form of Samuel and conversed with Saul. I do not think this is right. For God would not have permitted the deception to take place in the form of Samuel. Nevertheless, they do have something by way of a counter-argument. For they say it is proved that the demon is lying by what it says to Saul, "Tomorrow you and Jonathan will be with me" (1 Kgdms 28:19), since what he said did not happen the next day but on the third day. But they have stumbled far from the truth. For it would not be possible to prove that Saul died on the third day after Samuel's words, since what follows in the narrative is a resumption of the entire course of events and of the war. For divine scripture did not say that Saul died "on the third day" after the belly-myther spoke.[1] Rather, after telling the story of Saul's error and of Samuel's pronouncement against him, it takes up the account again from the beginning. But even if what we say were not the case, they fail to understand that even the word "tomorrow" would not in every case indicate the next day. Instead, there are times when it refers to the proximity of a coming event. For example, "today if you will hear his voice" (Ps 94:7; Heb 3:7) would not indicate the day on which the verse was spoken but rather the time of the Israelites' conversion.

One might see what I am saying also in another way. Where did the demon get the idea that not only Saul would be killed but also Jonathan? The demon, they say, conjectured, for since he knew that God had removed Saul from the kingdom and given it to David, he was aware that it was necessary that the sons also be destroyed with the father. On the contrary, we should say that what is conjectured does not in every case come to pass, for something can be expected and yet not happen. And how is it that the demon would have been willing by his guess to risk what he only supposed to be true? But why do I elaborate my investigation, since the divine scripture says quite plainly that Samuel, when he had appeared, said to Saul, "Why have you disturbed me by bringing me up?" and again, "Why do you ask me? Has the Lord turned from you and sided with your neighbor" (1 Kgdms 28:15–16)?

They say, as Paul said, "Satan disguises himself as an angel of light" (2 Cor 11:14). But God, sparing Israel (for he knew their weaknesses and their inclination to impiety), would not have permitted a demon to appear in the form of Samuel. On the con-

---

[1] "The third day" is possibly an allusion to 2 Kgdms 1:2.

τοὺς Ἰουδαίους, φασίν, τὸ νομίζειν αὐτοὺς τῇ δυνάμει τῆς ἐγγαστριμύθου ἀνηνέχθαι τὸν Σαμουήλ. τί δήποτε οὖν εἴποι τις πρὸς αὐτούς;
οὐκ εἴρηκεν ἡ Γραφὴ ὅτι ὁ δαίμων τῆς γυναικὸς μετεσχηματίσατο εἰς
τὸν Σαμουήλ, τὸ δὲ ἐναντίον ὅτι ὁ Σαμουὴλ παραγέγονε — ὃ μᾶλλον
ἔπληττεν τοὺς Ἰουδαίους, οἰομένους ὑπὸ γυναικὸς δαιμονώσης παράγω-
γον γενέσθαι τὸν Σαμουήλ. πλὴν εἰ μὴ λέγοι τις τὸ μὴ καλεσάσης τῆς
ἐγγαστριμύθου παραγενέσθαι τὸν Σαμουήλ, τό τε εἰπεῖν τὴν ἐγγαστρίμυθον **θεοὺς ἀναβαίνοντας ἐγὼ ὁρῶ ἐκ τῆς γῆς**, ἐδόξασε τὸν Θεὸν τὸν
οὕτω μέγαν καὶ δυνατόν, ὡς τὸν Σαμουὴλ καὶ τοὺς σὺν αὐτῷ φανέντας
θεοὺς νομίσαι αὐτήν — συνᾴδων οἷς ἡμεῖς νοοῦμεν.

Ἔχει δὲ οὕτως. ἐπειδή, ζῶντος τοῦ Σαμουήλ, ἐδίωκε τὰς ἐγγαστριμύθους ὁ Σαούλ, ὑπὲρ οὗ πολλάκις τὸν Θεὸν ἱκετεύων ὁ Σαμουὴλ
οὐκ εἰσηκούετο, ἡνίκα ἀναγαγεῖν αὐτὸν ὁ Σαοὺλ διὰ τῆς ἐγγαστριμύθου
οὐκ ὤκνησεν, ἀνάγει τὸν Σαμουὴλ ὁ Θεὸς καὶ μετ᾽ αὐτοῦ δυνάμεις ἁγίας
καὶ οὐρανίους, πρῶτον μὲν διὰ τῶν συνόντων αὐτῷ δοξάζων τὸν ἑαυτοῦ
προφήτην, ἔπειτα δὲ δεικνὺς αὐτῷ, καὶ μονονουχὶ λέγων ὅπερ ἐδείκνυ,
ὅτι οὗτός ἐστιν ὁ Σαμουήλ· Ὁ ἡνίκα μὲν ἐν σαρκὶ ἦσθα τὰς ἐγγαστριμύθους καὶ τοὺς μάντεις καὶ τοὺς γνώστας διώκων· νῦν δὲ αὐτόν σε
δι᾽ αὐτῶν ἀναγαγεῖν ἐλπίσας, καὶ τοσοῦτον ἀνομίσας ὡς δι᾽ ὧν ἀσεβεῖ
κρατεῖν, αὐτὸν οἰηθῆναι τὸν ἐχθρόν — οὗτός ἐστιν, ὑπὲρ οὗ προσηύχου.
ταῦτα προειδώς, καὶ τὰ μὲν ὁρῶν ὑπὸ σοῦ γινόμενα κακῶς, τὰ δὲ προγι-
νώσκων οὐκ ἤκουσά σου. μὴ τοίνυν ἀθύμει ὡς τότε παρακουσθείς, ἀλλὰ
γίνωσκε ὅτι τὰ ὑπὸ τοῦ Θεοῦ γινόμενα μετὰ σοφίας γίνεται.

Ταῦτα παρ᾽ ἡμῶν, κρατείτω δὲ ὅπερ ἂν φανείη κρεῖττον ἔχειν.

trary, they say, "God struck the Jews with amazement so that they supposed Samuel had been brought up by the power of the belly-myther." What, then, should one say to them? Scripture has not said that the woman's demon disguised himself as Samuel. On the contrary, it said that Samuel was present—which struck the Jews all the more with amazement, because they supposed that Samuel had been brought forward by the demon-possessed woman. If, however, someone were to say that Samuel appeared without the belly-myther summoning him and that the belly-myther said, "I see gods coming up from the ground," he has glorified God, who is so great and mighty (since she had thought Samuel and those who appeared with him were gods!). This person would be in agreement with what we think.

My view is as follows. Since Saul persecuted the belly-mythers while Samuel was alive, and since Samuel was not heard when he often interceded with God for Saul, when Saul did not hesitate to try to bring him up through the belly-myther, God brought up Samuel and with him holy and heavenly powers. God did this, first, to glorify his own prophet through those who were present with him and, second, because this was Samuel, to make clear to the prophet[2] what he all but said to him: "When you, Samuel, were in the flesh, Saul persecuted the belly-mythers, the prophets, and the diviners. But now Saul has invested hope in bringing you up through them, because he has become so lawless that he has supposed he can prevail over the enemy by his impious action. This is the man for whom you prayed. I knew this beforehand and saw that what he would do would be evil.[3] And since I foreknew it, I did not listen to you. Therefore, do not be discouraged thinking you were not heard at that time, but know that what happens by God's agency takes place with wisdom."

These are our opinions, but let whatever view may seem to be the stronger prevail.

---

[2] The pronoun in Greek does not have a clear referent. Devreesse takes it to refer to Saul rather than Samuel, presumably because he supposes in what follows that God is addressing Saul (Robert Devreesse, *Les anciens commentateurs grecs de l'Octateuque et des Rois* [Studi e Testi 201; Vatican City: Biblioteca apostolica vaticana, 1959], line 67).

[3] Devreesse in *Les anciens commentateurs* emends the manuscript to read ὑπὸ σοῦ instead of ὑπ' αὐτοῦ. The MS reading implies that God is addressing Samuel, and such a view accords with what Gregory of Nyssa says in 2.2.

Γρηγορίου ἐπισκόπου Νύσσης ἐπιστολὴ διὰ τὴν ἐγγαστρίμυθον πρὸς Θεοδόσιον ἐπίσκοπον

101.* Ὁ εἰπὼν τοῖς ἑαυτοῦ μαθηταῖς *ζητεῖτε καὶ εὑρήσετε*, δώσει πάντως καὶ τὴν πρὸς τὸ εὑρεῖν δύναμιν τοῖς φιλομαθῶς κατὰ τὴν ἐντολὴν τοῦ κυρίου διερευνωμένοις καὶ ἀναζητοῦσι τὰ κεκρυμμένα μυστήρια· ἀψευδὴς γὰρ ὁ ἐπαγγειλάμενος, ὑπὲρ τὴν αἴτησιν ἐπιδαψιλευόμενος τῇ μεγαλοδωρεᾷ τῶν χαρισμάτων. οὐκοῦν *πρόσεχε τῇ ἀναγνώσει, τέκνον Τιμόθεε·* πρέπειν γὰρ οἶμαι τῇ τοῦ μεγάλου Παύλου φωνῇ πρὸς τὴν σὴν ἀγαθότητα χρήσασθαι καὶ *δώῃ σοι κύριος σύνεσιν ἐν πᾶσιν*, ὥστε σε πλουτισθῆναι *ἐν παντὶ λόγῳ καὶ πάσῃ γνώσει*. νῦν δὲ περὶ ὧν ἐπέταξας· ὅσαπερ ἂν ὁ κύριος ὑποβάλῃ, δι' ὀλίγων ὑπηρετήσασθαί σου τῇ προθυμίᾳ καλῶς ἔχειν ἐδοκίμασα, ὡς ἂν διὰ τούτων μάθοις ὅτι χρὴ δι' ἀγάπης ἀλλήλοις δουλεύειν ἡμᾶς ἐν τῷ ποιεῖν τὰ ἀλλήλων θελήματα.

Πρῶτον τοίνυν ἐπειδὴ καὶ τῶν λοιπῶν ἦν κεφαλαίων προτεταγμένον τὸ περὶ τοῦ Σαμουὴλ ἐπιζητούμενον νόημα, διὰ **102.** βραχέων ὡς ἔστι δυνατὸν θεοῦ διδόντος ἐκθήσομαι. ἤρεσέ τισι τῶν πρὸ ἡμῶν ἀληθῆ νομίσαι τῆς γοητίδος ἐκείνης τὴν ἐπὶ τοῦ Σαμουὴλ ψυχαγωγίαν καί τινα λόγον τοιοῦτον εἰς συνηγορίαν τῆς ὑπολήψεως αὐτῶν ταύτης παρέσχοντο, ὅτι λυπουμένου τοῦ Σαμουὴλ ἐπὶ τῇ ἀποβολῇ τοῦ Σαοὺλ καὶ πάντοτε τοῦτο τῷ κυρίῳ προσφέροντος τὸ ὅ τι θέλεις, τὴν ἐκ τῶν ἐγγαστριμύθων γινομένην γοητείαν ἐπὶ ἀπάτῃ τῶν ἀνθρώπων ἐξεκάθαρεν ἐκ τοῦ λαοῦ Σαούλ, καὶ διὰ τοῦτο δυσανασχετοῦντος τοῦ προφήτου ἐπὶ τῷ μὴ θελῆσαι τὸν κύριον διαλλαγῆναι τῷ ἀποβλήτῳ, συγχωρῆσαί φασι

---

* These numbers correspond to page numbers in GNO 3 (see p. xxii).

8. Gregory of Nyssa, *Letter to Theodosius concerning the Belly-Myther*

101. He who said to his own disciples, "search, and you will find" (Matt 7:7), will certainly also give the power of finding to those who, with a desire to learn according to the Lord's command, interpret and search out the mysteries that have been hidden. For he who promised does not lie (cf. Titus 1:2), since he freely bestows the munificence of his gifts beyond what is asked. Therefore, "give attention to the reading of scripture, Timothy, my child" (cf. 1 Tim 4:13; 1:18). Indeed, I think it is fitting to employ the voice of the great Paul for the sake of your goodness, and "may the Lord give you understanding in everything" (cf. 2 Tim 2:7), so that "you may be enriched in speech and knowledge of every kind" (1 Cor 1:5). Now concerning the things that you enjoined, I have judged it good to submit briefly to your eager request, inasmuch as the Lord has set down, so that you may learn through this that we must serve one another in love (cf. Gal 5:13) by carrying out one another's wishes.

First, then, since the disputed question about Samuel (1 Kgdms 28:3–25) has had a more important place than the other topics **102.**, I shall briefly give my opinion, so far as I can with God's help. It has pleased some before us to suppose that the bringing up of Samuel's soul by that sorceress is true. They offer this type of argument to support their assumption about this: that when Samuel was grieved because of Saul's rejection (1 Kgdms 15:35; 16:1) he constantly addressed the Lord, saying, "Saul has done what you will[1] and has cleared away from the people the sorcery done by the belly-mythers to deceive the people." And because the prophet was greatly vexed that the Lord did not want to be reconciled to the rejected king, they say that God permit-

---

[1] The text appears corrupt. M reads ὅ τι θέλει. Simonetti in *La Maga di Endor* reads ὅτι θέλει rather than ὅ τι θέλεις. It is necessary to supply a verb before the phrase.

τὸν θεὸν ἀναχθῆναι τὴν τοῦ προφήτου ψυχὴν διὰ τῆς τοιαύτης μαγγα-
νείας, ἵνα ἴδη ὁ Σαμουήλ, ὅτι ψευδῆ ὑπὲρ αὐτοῦ τῷ θεῷ προετείνετο,
λέγων αὐτὸν πολέμιον εἶναι ταῖς ἐγγαστριμύθοις τὸν τηνικαῦτα διὰ τῆς
αὐτῶν γοητείας τὴν ἄνοδον τῆς ψυχῆς αὐτοῦ μαντεύσαντα. ἐγὼ δὲ πρὸς
τὸ εὐαγγελικὸν χάσμα βλέπων, ὃ διὰ μέσου τῶν κακῶν τε καὶ ἀγαθῶν
ἐστηρίχθαι φησὶν ὁ πατριάρχης, μᾶλλον δὲ ὁ τοῦ πατριάρχου κύριος,
ὡς ἀμήχανον εἶναι τοῖς τε κατακρίτοις ἐπὶ **103.** τὴν τῶν δικαίων ἄνεσιν
διαβῆναι καὶ τοῖς ἁγίοις πρὸς τὸν τῶν πονηρῶν χορὸν διαπεράσαι, οὐ
δέχομαι ἀληθεῖς εἶναι τὰς τοιαύτας ὑπολήψεις, διδαχθεὶς μόνον ἀληθὲς
εἶναι πιστεύειν τὸ εὐαγγέλιον. ἐπειδὴ τοίνυν μέγας ἐν ἁγίοις ὁ Σαμουήλ,
πονηρὸν δὲ κτῆμα ἡ γοητεία, οὐ πείθομαι, ὅτι ἐν τοσούτῳ τῆς ἰδίας ἀνα-
παύσεως ὁ Σαμουὴλ καταστὰς τὸ ἀδιόδευτον ἐκεῖνο χάσμα πρὸς τοὺς
ἀσεβοῦντας διήρχετο οὔτε ἑκὼν οὔτε ἄκων. ἄκων μὲν οὖν οὐκ ἂν ἔτι
ὑπέμεινε τῷ μὴ δύνασθαι τὸ δαιμόνιον διαβῆναι τὸ χάσμα καὶ ἐν τῷ
χορῷ τῶν ὁσίων γενόμενον μετακινῆσαι τὸν ἅγιον, ἑκὼν δὲ οὐκ ἂν τοῦτο
ἐποίησε τῷ μήτε βούλεσθαι ἐπιμιχθῆναι τοῖς κακοῖς μήτε δύνασθαι· τῷ
γὰρ ἐν ἀγαθοῖς ὄντι ἀβούλητον ἀπὸ τῶν ἐν οἷς ἐστιν ἡ πρὸς τὰ ἐναντία
μετάστασις· εἰ δέ τις καὶ βούλεσθαι δοίη, ἀλλ' ἡ τοῦ χάσματος φύσις
οὐκ ἐπιτρέπει τὴν πάροδον.

Τί οὖν ἐστίν, ὃ περὶ τούτων ἡμεῖς λογιζόμεθα; ἐχθρὸς τῆς ἀνθρωπίνης φύσεώς ἐστιν ὁ κοινὸς πάντων πολέμιος, ᾧ πᾶσά ἐστιν ἐπίνοια καὶ
σπουδὴ εἰς αὐτὰ τὰ καίρια βλάπτειν τὸν ἄνθρωπον. τίς δὲ τοιαύτη και-
ρία κατὰ τῶν ἀνθρώπων ἄλλη πληγὴ ὡς τὸ ἀποβληθῆναι ἀπὸ τοῦ θεοῦ
τοῦ ζωοποιοῦντος καὶ πρὸς τὴν ἀπώλειαν τοῦ θανάτου ἑκουσίως αὐτομο-
λῆσαι; ἐπειδὴ τοίνυν σπουδή τίς ἐστι κατὰ τὸν βίον τοῖς φιλοσωμάτοις
γνῶσίν τινα τῶν μελλόντων ἔχειν, δι' ἧς ἐλπίζουσιν ἢ τῶν κακῶν ἀποφυ-
γὴν ἢ πρὸς τὰ καταθύμια χειραγωγίαν, τούτου χάριν, ὡς ἂν μὴ πρὸς τὸν
θεὸν οἱ ἄνθρωποι βλέποιεν, πολλοὺς τρόπους τῆς τοῦ μέλλοντος γνώσεως
ἡ ἀπατηλὴ τῶν δαιμόνων ἐτεχνάσατο φύσις, οἰωνοσκοπίας, συμβολομαν-
τείας, χρηστήρια, ἡπατοσκοπίας, νεκυίας, ἐνθουσιασμούς, κατοκωχάς,
ἐμπνεύσεις καὶ ἄλλα τοιαῦτα **104.** πολλά. καὶ ὅπερ ἄν τις εἶδος προγνώσεως ἔκ τινος ἀπάτης ἀληθὲς εἶναι νομίση, ἐν ἐκείνῳ τὸ ἀπατηλὸν
δαιμόνιον παραφαίνεται εἰς δικαίωσιν τῆς ἡπατημένης ὑπολήψεως τοῦ

ted the prophet's soul to be brought up by magical arts of this kind. This was so that Samuel might see that he was proposing lies to God on behalf of Saul by saying that he was hostile to the belly-mythers when at that very time Saul was using divination through their sorcery to bring up his soul. For my part, when I consider the chasm mentioned in the Gospel (Luke 16:26), which the patriarch—or rather the patriarch's Lord—says has been fixed between the wicked and the good and how impossible it is for the condemned **103.** to pass over to the repose of the righteous and for the saints to cross to the chorus of evil ones, I do not accept such assumptions as true, since I have been taught to believe that only the Gospel is true. Therefore, since Samuel is great among the saints but sorcery is an evil attainment, I am not persuaded that Samuel, established as he was in so great a place of his own rest, would have passed over that trackless chasm to the impious, either willingly or unwillingly. If he had been unwilling, he would not, then, have submitted at all because the demon would have been unable to pass over the chasm and remove the saint who was in the chorus of the holy ones. And if willing, he would not have done this, because he would neither have wished nor been able to be mingled with the wicked. For no one who is among the good would want to be switched from being with them to the opposite. And even if someone were to grant him such a wish, nevertheless, the nature of the chasm does not permit his passage.

What account, then, do we give about these matters? The enemy of human nature is the common adversary of all. His entire thought and effort is to disable humanity in its vital parts. And what other blow is so aimed at the vital parts of humans as to be cast away from God who gives life and to be a willing deserter to death's destruction? Since, therefore, those who love bodily things are eager in this life to have some knowledge of the future, by which they hope either to escape evils or to be guided to what they desire, because of this and so that humans might not look to God, the deceitful nature of demons has devised many artful ways of knowing the future: the observation of birds' flights, divination by tokens, oracles, the inspection of livers, necromancy, frenzies, possessions, inspirations, and many other such things. **104.** And whatever method of procuring foreknowledge—based on whatever deceit—a person supposes to be true is the one the deceitful demon displays in order to justify the deceived assump-

πεπλανημένου. οὕτως καὶ τὴν τοῦ ἀετοῦ πτῆσιν πρὸς τὴν τοῦ παρατετη-
ρηκότος ἐλπίδα συνδραμεῖν παρασκευάζει ὁ δαίμων καὶ τοῦ ἥπατος τὸν
παλμὸν καὶ τὴν ἐκ τοῦ φυσώδους γινομένην τῶν μηνίγγων παραφορὰν
καὶ τῶν ὀμμάτων παραστροφήν· καὶ ἕκαστον κατὰ τὴν σημειωθεῖσαν
ἐκ τῆς ἀπάτης παρατήρησιν ἡ τοῦ δαίμονος πανουργία προδείκνυσι τοῖς
ἀπατωμένοις, ὥστε ἀποστάντας τοὺς ἀνθρώπους τοῦ θεοῦ προσέχειν τῇ
θεραπείᾳ τῶν δαιμόνων, δι' ὧν ἐνεργεῖσθαι τὰ τοιαῦτα πιστεύουσιν.

Ἓν τοίνυν ἀπάτης εἶδος ἦν καὶ τὸ τῶν ἐγγαστριμύθων, ὧν ἡ μαγ-
γανεία ἐπιστεύετο δύνασθαι τὰς τῶν κατοιχομένων ψυχὰς πάλιν πρὸς τὸν
ἄνω βίον ἐφέλκεσθαι. τοῦ τοίνυν Σαοὺλ ἐν ἀπογνώσει τῆς σωτηρίας γε-
γονότος διὰ τὸ πανστρατιᾷ συγκεκινῆσθαι κατ' αὐτοῦ πᾶν τὸ ἀλλόφυλον
καὶ ἐπὶ ταύτην ἐλθόντος τὴν ἐπίνοιαν, ὥστε τὸν Σαμουὴλ αὐτῷ τρόπον
ὑποθέσθαι τινὰ σωτηρίας, τὸ παραμένον τῇ ἐγγαστριμύθῳ δαιμόνιον, δι'
οὗ ἠπατᾶτο ἐκ συνηθείας τὸ γύναιον, εἰς διαφόρους μορφὰς σκιοειδῶς ἐν
τοῖς ὀφθαλμοῖς τοῦ γυναίου ἐσχηματίζετο, οὐδενὸς τῷ Σαοὺλ προφαινο-
μένου ὧν καθεώρα τὸ γύναιον. ὡς γὰρ ἥψατο τῆς γοητείας καὶ ἤδη τῷ
γυναίῳ ἦν ἐν ὀφθαλμοῖς τὰ φαντάσματα, πίστιν τοῦ ἀληθῆ τὰ φαινόμενα
εἶναι ταύτην ὁ δαίμων ἐμηχανήσατο τὸ πρῶτον αὐτὸν **105.** κεκρυμμένον ἐν τῷ εἴδει τοῦ προσχήματος διασαφῆσαι, δι' οὗ μᾶλλον ὁ Σαοὺλ
κατεπλάγη, ὡς οὐδὲν ἔτι τῆς γυναικὸς σφαλησομένης τῷ τὸ ἰδιωτικὸν
σχῆμα τὴν γοητικὴν δύναμιν μὴ ἀγνοῆσαι. εἰπούσης τοίνυν αὐτῆς **θεοὺς**
ἑωρακέναι **ἀναβαίνοντας** καὶ ἄνθρωπον **ὄρθιον** ἐν διπλοΐδι, πῶς στήσουσι
τὸ καθ' ἱστορίαν οἱ δοῦλοι τοῦ γράμματος; εἰ γὰρ ἀληθῶς ὁ Σαμουὴλ
ἐστιν ὁ ὀφθείς, οὐκοῦν κατ' ἀλήθειαν καὶ θεοί εἰσιν οἱ ὀφθέντες παρὰ
τῆς φαρμακίδος· **θεοὺς** δὲ ἡ γραφὴ τὰ δαιμόνια λέγει· **πάντες** γὰρ **οἱ
θεοὶ τῶν ἐθνῶν δαιμόνια.** ἆρ' οὖν μετὰ τῶν δαιμόνων καὶ ἡ ψυχὴ τοῦ
Σαμουήλ; μὴ γένοιτο. ἀλλὰ τὸ πάντοτε ὑπακοῦον τῇ φαρμακίδι δαιμόνιον παρέλαβε καὶ ἄλλα πνεύματα πρὸς ἀπάτην αὐτῆς τε τῆς γυναικὸς
καὶ τοῦ δι' ἐκείνης ἀπατωμένου Σαοὺλ καὶ τὰ μὲν δαιμόνια θεοὺς νομίζε-

tion of the person who has been misled. In this way the demon contrives it so that even the flight of the eagle accords with the hope of the one who is keenly observing it. And it does the same thing with the throbbing of the liver, the derangement that comes from the swelling of cerebral membranes, and the distortion of the eyes. The demon's cunning displays to those who are deceived each method in accordance with the type of close observation deceitfully signified there, so that people desert God and cleave to the worship of the demons by which they believe such things are effected.

So then, one form of deceit was that of the belly-mythers, whose sorcery was believed capable of dragging the souls of those who dwell below back to life above ground. Thus, when Saul despaired of being saved because the entire foreign nation had mobilized their entire army against him, and when he came to the idea that Samuel would suggest to him some way of being saved, the demon abiding in the belly-myther and by whom the foolish woman was customarily deceived disguised himself in a shadowy way into different forms before the foolish woman's eyes, even though nothing that the foolish woman saw appeared to Saul. For when she had undertaken the sorcery, and the apparitions were already before the foolish woman's eyes, the demon, so that what appeared would be believed true, contrived to make the one who at first **105.** had been hidden[2] plainly visible in a disguised form. Saul was all the more dumbfounded by this, as though it meant that the woman would yet in no way be led astray, since her magical power did not fail to recognize the form of an individual. Therefore, since she said she had seen "gods" coming up, as well as a man "standing" and in a double cloak, how will those who serve the letter establish the narrative meaning? For if the one who appeared was truly Samuel, then also in truth those who appeared because of the sorceress are gods. Now scripture calls the demons "gods," for "all the gods of the nations are demons" (Ps 95:5). Was, then, Samuel's soul also with the demons? Certainly not. Rather, the demon that always answered the sorceress took to itself other spirits to deceive both the woman herself and the man who was deceived through her, Saul. It made the demons be thought gods in

---

[2] πρῶτον αὐτὸν κεκρυμμένον. Simonetti's emendation is πρόσωπον τοῦ κεκρυμμένου. The reading of M is πρῶτον αὐτοῦ κεκρυμμένου.

σθαι παρὰ τῆς ἐγγαστριμύθου ἐποίησεν, αὐτὸ δὲ πρὸς τὸ ἐπιζητούμενον εἶδος ἐσχηματίσθη καὶ τὰς ἐκείνου φωνὰς ὑπεκρίνατο καί, ὅπερ εἰκὸς ἦν ἐκ τῶν φαινομένων λογίσασθαι, τὴν ἐκ τοῦ ἀκολούθου ἐκβήσεσθαι προσδοκηθεῖσαν ἀπόφασιν ὡς ἐν εἴδει προφητείας ἐφθέγξατο. ἤλεγξε δὲ καὶ ὡς οὐκ ἠβούλετο ἑαυτὸν ὁ δαίμων εἰπὼν τὴν ἀλήθειαν ὅτι *αὔριον σὺ καὶ Ἰωνάθαν μετ᾽ ἐμοῦ·* εἰ γὰρ ἀληθῶς ἦν Σαμουήλ, πῶς ἐνεδέχετο τὸν ἐν πάσῃ κακίᾳ κατεγνωσμένον μετ᾽ ἐκείνου γενέσθαι; ἀλλὰ δῆλον, ὅτι ἀντὶ τοῦ Σαμουὴλ ὀφθὲν τὸ πονηρὸν ἐκεῖνο δαιμόνιον μεθ᾽ ἑαυτοῦ ἔσεσθαι τὸν Σαοὺλ εἰπὸν οὐκ ἐψεύσατο. εἰ δὲ λέγει ἡ γραφὴ **106.** *ὅτι καὶ εἶπεν ὁ Σαμουήλ,* μὴ ταρασσέτω τὸν ἐπιστήμονα ὁ τοιοῦτος λόγος, ἀλλὰ προσκεῖσθαι νομιζέτω, ὅτι ὁ νομισθεὶς εἶναι Σαμουήλ. εὑρίσκομεν γὰρ τὴν γραφικὴν συνήθειαν πολλαχοῦ τὸ δοκοῦν ἀντὶ τοῦ ὄντος διεξιοῦσαν, ὡς ἐπὶ τοῦ Βαλαάμ, νῦν μὲν λέγοντος αὐτοῦ ὅτι *ἀκούσομαι τί λαλήσει ἐν ἐμοὶ ὁ θεός,* μετὰ ταῦτα δὲ ὅτι γνοὺς [δὲ] ὁ Βαλαάμ, ὅτι ἀρεστὸν ἦν τῷ θεῷ μὴ καταρᾶσθαι τοὺς Ἰσραηλίτας, οὐκέτι *κατὰ τὸ εἰωθὸς* ἀπῆλθεν *εἰς συνάντησιν τοῖς οἰωνοῖς·* ὁ γὰρ ἀνεπίσκεπτος κἀκεῖ τὸν ἀληθινὸν θεὸν νομίσει διαλέγεσθαι τῷ Βαλαάμ, ἡ μέντοι ἐπαγωγὴ δείκνυσιν, ὅτι τὸν ὑπὸ τοῦ Βαλαὰμ νομιζόμενον θεὸν οὕτως ὠνόμασεν ἡ γραφή, οὐχὶ τὸν ὄντως ὄντα θεόν. οὐκοῦν καὶ ἐνταῦθα ὁ δόξας εἶναι Σαμουὴλ τοὺς τοῦ ἀληθινοῦ Σαμουὴλ ὑπεκρίνατο λόγους, εὐφυῶς τοῦ δαίμονος ἐκ τῶν εἰκότων μιμουμένου τὴν προφητείαν.

Τὸ δὲ κατὰ τὸν Ἠλίαν πλείονος μὲν χρῄζει τῆς θεωρίας, οὐ μὴν ἐν τῷ προτεθέντι ζητήματι. καὶ γὰρ *ἐκ τοῦ χειμάρρου ὕδωρ πίνειν* προσταχθεὶς κατὰ τὸ λεληθὸς παρὰ τοῦ θεοῦ συνεβουλεύετο, ὥστε τὴν παρὰ τοῦ προφήτου ἐκφωνηθεῖσαν κατὰ τῶν Ἰσραηλιτῶν τῆς ἀνομβρίας ἀπό-

the eyes of the belly-myther, as it disguised itself in the form being sought. It feigned Samuel's words and uttered a likely deduction from what was apparent as a pronouncement of what would be expected to happen in what followed, as though it were a form of prophecy. Without wishing to, the demon convicted itself, since it spoke the truth when it said, "Tomorrow you and Jonathan will be with me" (1 Kgdms 28:19). For if it had truly been Samuel, how would he allow the man charged with every wickedness to be with himself? Nevertheless, quite clearly that evil demon that appeared instead of[3] Samuel did not lie when it said that Saul would be with it. If the words in scripture are **106.**, "And Samuel said" (1 Kgdms 28:15), let such a statement not trouble someone intelligent. Rather, let him think that it is placed here to refer to the one thought to be Samuel. For we find it characteristic of scripture often to relate what seems to be instead of what is. Take the example of Balaam. First he said, "I shall hear what God will speak to me" (cf. Num 22:8). But afterwards, when Balaam learned that it was God's pleasure not to curse the Israelites, he no longer went off "as was his custom to consult the flight of birds" (cf. Num 24:1). The careless reader will suppose that even in the first passage it was the true God who conversed with Balaam, but what follows demonstrates that scripture used the term "god" to refer to the one Balaam supposed to be god and not to the one who is really God. Therefore, here, too, the one who seemed to be Samuel feigned the words of the true Samuel, since the demon cleverly imitated prophecy on the basis of verisimilitudes.

The story about Elijah (3 Kgdms 17:1–7) needs a good deal more by way of spiritual interpretation,[4] but not with reference to the question you have proposed.[5] Indeed, when he was commanded "to drink water from the stream," he was being secretly advised by God that his decree shutting up the rain, which had been announced by the prophet against the Israelites, had been

---

[3] The preposition ἀντί, translated here and subsequently as "instead of," can also mean "as," i.e., "in the place of."

[4] On θεωρία (again in 6.1, with the verb θεωρεῖν) as "spiritual interpretation," see *PGL*, 647–49.

[5] Here Gregory turns to the other questions Theodosius has asked. For the traditions about Elijah, see Louis Ginzberg, *The Legends of the Jews* (7 vols.; Philadelphia: Jewish Publication Society of America, 1909–38; repr., Baltimore: Johns Hopkins University Press, 1998), 4:196–97.

φασὶν δι' αὐτοῦ πάλιν ἀναλυθῆναι· ᾧ γὰρ ἐδόθη ἐκ μόνου τοῦ χειμάρρου πίνειν, τοῦ δὴ κατὰ τὸ εἰκὸς ἐν τοῖς αὐχμοῖς ἀποξηραινομένου, ἄλλης τῷ προφήτῃ μὴ εὑρισκομένης πρὸς τὴν δίψαν παραμυθίας, διὰ τὸ ἀπειρῆσθαι αὐτῷ ἀλλαχόθεν πιεῖν ἐπάναγκες ἦν αἰτῆσαι τὸν ὄμβρον, ἵνα μὴ ἐπιλείπῃ τὸ ὕδωρ τὸν χείμαρρον. γίνεται δὲ τῷ προφήτῃ παρὰ τῶν κοράκων ἡ τῶν πρὸς τὴν ζωὴν ἀναγκαίων διακονία, δεικνύντος διὰ τούτων τοῦ θεοῦ τῷ προφήτῃ, ὅτι πολλοί εἰσιν οἱ **107.** παραμεμενηκότες τῇ τοῦ ἀληθινοῦ θεοῦ λατρείᾳ, ὅθεν ἐχορηγεῖτο διὰ τῶν κοράκων ἡ τροφὴ τῷ προφήτῃ· οὐ γὰρ ἂν τῶν μεμιασμένων αὐτῷ προσῆγεν ἄρτων ἢ τὸ εἰδωλόθυτον κρέας, ὥστε καὶ διὰ τούτων ἐναχθῆναι τὸν Ἡλίαν καθυφεῖναί τι τοῦ κατὰ τῶν ἠσεβηκότων θυμοῦ, μαθόντα διὰ τῶν γινομένων, ὅτι πολλοί εἰσιν οἱ πρὸς τὸν θεὸν ὁρῶντες, οὓς οὐκ ἔστι δίκαιον συγκαταδικασθῆναι τοῖς ὑπαιτίοις. εἰ δὲ πρωῒ μὲν ὁ ἄρτος, ἐν δὲ τῇ ἑσπέρᾳ τὸ κρέας αὐτῷ διακονεῖται, ἴσως δι' αἰνίγματος πρὸς τὸν ἐνάρετον βίον σπουδὴν τὸ γινόμενον ἔχει, ὅτι χρὴ ἀρχομένοις μὲν τῆς κατ' ἀρετὴν ζωῆς, ἧς σύμβολόν ἐστιν ἡ πρωΐα, τὸν εὔληπτον παρέχειν λόγον, τοῖς <δὲ> τελειουμένοις τὸν τελειότερον κατὰ τὴν τοῦ Παύλου φωνήν, ὅς φησιν ὅτι *τελείων δέ ἐστιν ἡ στερεὰ τροφή, τῶν διὰ τὴν ἕξιν τὰ αἰσθητήρια γεγυμνασμένα ἐχόντων.*

Τὸ δὲ κάλυμμα τοῦ Μωυσέως οὐκ ἀγνοήσεις, πρὸς ὅ τι βλέπει, τῇ πρὸς Κορινθίους ἐπιστολῇ τοῦ Παύλου καθομιλήσας. Ὅσα δὲ περὶ τῶν θυσιῶν ἐπεζήτησας, καλῶς ποιήσεις ὅλον τὸ Λευϊτικὸν φιλοπονώτερον ἐξετάσας καὶ μετὰ πλείονος τῆς προσεδρίας καθολικῶς τὸν ἐν τούτοις θεωρήσεις νόμον· οὕτω γὰρ συγκατανοηθήσεται τῷ ὅλῳ τὸ μέρος· ἐφ' ἑαυτοῦ γὰρ τοῦτο μόνον οὐκ ἂν διευκρινηθείη πρὸ τῆς τοῦ παντὸς θεωρίας. Ἐν δὲ τοῖς περὶ τῆς ἀντικειμένης δυνάμεως ἐπηπορημένοις πρόδηλός ἐστιν ἡ λύσις, ὅτι οὐχ ἁπλῶς ἄγγελος, ἀλλ' ἐν ἀρχαγγέλοις ἦν τεταγμένος ὁ ἀποστάτης γενόμενος. δῆλον οὖν, **108.** ὅτι τῇ ἀρχῇ συν-

cancelled by him. For it was granted him to drink only from the stream, and when it dried up, as was to be expected in the drought, and when there was no other relief to be found for the prophet's thirst, because he was not allowed to drink anywhere else, he was compelled to pray for rain so that the water in the stream would not run dry. And the ministration of the necessities of life came to the prophet from the ravens. Through them God showed the prophet that there were many who **107.** had remained loyal to the worship of the true God. It was from them that food was supplied to the prophet through the ravens. For they would not have set before him[6] polluted bread or meat sacrificed to idols. As a result, by this experience Elijah was led to moderate somewhat his anger against those who had committed sacrilege, since he learned from what happened that there were many who were looking to God whom it would not be right to condemn along with those who were guilty. And if bread was served to him in the morning and meat at evening, perhaps this is an enigmatic reference to having zeal for the virtuous life. This is because it is necessary to supply those who are just beginning the virtuous life—which is symbolized by early morning—with an easily apprehended word, but those who are moving toward perfection require a more perfect word. This agrees with the statement of Paul, who says, "Solid food is for the perfect, for those whose faculties have been trained by practice" (Heb 5:14).

You will not fail to understand Moses' veil—what it some-how looks toward—if you have become familiar with Paul's letter to the Corinthians (2 Cor 3:13–18; Exod 34:33–35). So far as what concerns your question about sacrifices, you will do well to exam-ine all of Leviticus with great care, and with still closer attention you will understand in a general way the spiritual meaning of the law in them. In this way the part will be conceived in the mind in its relation to the whole, for the part taken by itself alone should not be interpreted before the spiritual meaning of the entire book. As to the doubts you have raised concerning the opposing power, the solution is obvious. The one who became an apostate was not simply an angel but had been ranked among the archangels. Therefore, it is clear **108.** that the order subject to him is indi-

---

[6] M and GNO read προσῆγεν. In *La Maga di Endor*, Simonetti, whom we follow, accepts Klostermann's emendation, προσῆγον.

ενδείκνυται καὶ τὸ ὑποχείριον τάγμα, ὥστε λελύσθαι τὴν ζήτησιν περὶ τοῦ πῶς εἷς ἦν καὶ μετὰ πλήθους ἐστίν· τῆς γὰρ ὑποχειρίου στρατιᾶς αὐτῷ συναποστάσης σεσαφήνισται τὸ ζητούμενον. Τὸ δὲ τελευταῖον τῶν ἐπιζητηθέντων κεφάλαιον (λέγω δὴ τὸ πῶς παραγίνεται τὸ πνεῦμα πρὸ τοῦ βαπτίσματος) πλατυτέρας ἐξετάσεώς τε καὶ θεωρίας δεόμενον ἰδίῳ περιγράψαντες λόγῳ, θεοῦ διδόντος, ἀποστελοῦμέν σου τῇ τιμιότητι.

cated in conjunction with his rule, so that the question about how he could be one and yet be accompanied by a multitude is solved.[7] Now the final topic among the questions you have asked (I mean how the Spirit could be present before baptism) requires a longer investigation and spiritual interpretation. God willing, we shall write a separate treatise and send it to your excellence.

---

[7] As in Origen, *Hom. 5 on 1 Kgdms* 6.2–3, we have here the characteristic form of question (ζήτημα) and solution (λύσις).

Bibliography

PRIMARY TEXTS OF PATRISTIC INTERPRETATIONS
OF I KINGDOMS 28

Archambault, Georges. *Justin: Dialogue avec Tryphon*. Paris: Picard et fils, 1909.

Declerck, José H. *Eustathii Antiocheni Opera*. CCSG 51. Turnhout: Brepols; Leuven: Leuven University Press, 2002.

Devreesse, Robert. *Les anciens commentateurs grecs de l'Octateuque et des Rois*. Studi e Testi 201. Vatican City: Biblioteca apostolica vaticana, 1959.

Hörner, Hadwiga. *De pythonissa ad Theodosium episcopum*. Pages 99–108 in vol. 2 of *Opera dogmatica minora*. Edited by J. Kenneth Downing, Jacobus A. McDonough, and Hadwiga Hörner. GNO 3. Leiden: Brill, 1987.

Musurillo, Herbert. *Acts of the Christian Martyrs*. Oxford: Clarendon, 1972.

Nautin, Pierre, and Marie-Thérèse Nautin. *Origène: Homélies sur Samuel*. SC 328. Paris: Cerf, 1986.

Simonetti, Manlio. *La Maga di Endor: Origene, Eustazio, Gregorio di Nissa*. Biblioteca Patristica 15. Florence: Nardini, 1989.

Waszink, Jan Hendrik. *Tertullian: De anima*. 2nd ed. Amsterdam: Meulenhoff, 1947.

OTHER PRIMARY TEXTS AND TRANSLATIONS

Brooke, A. E. *The Commentary of Origen on S. John's Gospel*. 2 vols. Cambridge: Cambridge University Press, 1896.

Butterworth, G. W. *Origen: On First Principles*. London: SPCK, 1936. Repr., Gloucester, Mass.: Smith, 1973.

Chadwick, Henry. *Origen: Contra Celsum*. Cambridge: Cambridge University Press, 1953.

Corrigan, Kevin. *The Life of Saint Macrina by Gregory, Bishop of Nyssa*. Peregrina Translations Series 10. Toronto: Peregrina, 1987.

Dilts, Merwin R., and George A. Kennedy, eds. and trans. *Two Greek Rhetorical Treatises from the Roman Empire*. Mnemosyne Supplements 168. Leiden: Brill, 1997.

Doutreleau, Louis, ed. *Origène, Homélies sur la Genèse*. SC 7 bis. Paris: Cerf, 1976.

Evans, Ernest. *Tertullian: Adversus Marcionem*. Oxford Early Christian Texts. 2 vols. Oxford: Clarendon, 1972.

Felten, Josephus. *Nicolaus: Progymnasmata*. Leipzig: Teubner, 1913.

Foerster, Richard. *Libanii Opera*. 12 vols. Leipzig: Teubner, 1903–23. Repr., Hildesheim: Olms, 1963.

Froehlich, Karlfried. *Biblical Interpretation in the Early Church*. Sources of Early Christian Thought. Philadelphia: Fortress, 1984.

Hock, Ronald F., and Edward H. O'Neill. *The Chreia in Ancient Rhetoric*, vol. 1: *The Progymnasmata*. SBLTT 27. Atlanta: Scholars Press, 1986.

Holl, Karl. *Fragmente vornicänischer Kirchenväter aus den Sacra Parallela*. TU 20/2. Leipzig: Hinrichs, 1899.

Kennedy, George A. *Progymnasmata: Greek Textbooks of Prose Composition and Rhetoric*. SBLWGRW 10. Atlanta: Society of Biblical Literature, 2003.

Malherbe, Abraham J., and Everett Ferguson, trans. *Gregory of Nyssa: The Life of Moses*. CWS. New York: Paulist, 1978.

Rabe, Hugo. *Aphthonius, Progymnasmata*. Leipzig: Teubner, 1926.

———. *Hermogenes, Opera*. Leipzig: Teubner, 1913.

Smith, John Clark. *Origen: Homilies on Jeremiah, Homily on 1 Kings 28*. FC 97. Washington, D.C.: Catholic University of America Press, 1998.

Spengel, Leonard. *Rhetores Graeci*. 3 vols. Leipzig: Teubner, 1854–56.

Spira, Andreas, and Christoph Klock, eds. *The Easter Sermons of Gregory of Nyssa*. Patristic Monograph Series 9. Cambridge, Mass.: Philadelphia Patristic Foundation, 1981.

Trigg, Joseph W. *Biblical Interpretation*. Message of the Fathers of the Church 9. Wilmington, Del.: Glazier, 1988.

———. *Origen*. The Early Church Fathers. London: Routledge, 1998.

Walz, Christian. *Rhetores Graeci*. 9 vols. Stuttgart: Cottae, 1932–36.

SECONDARY WORKS

Alexandre, Monique. "L'interprétation de Luc 16, 19–31, chez Grégoire de Nysse." Pages 425–41 in *Epektasis: Mélanges patristiques offerts au Cardinal Jean Daniélou*. Edited by Jacques Fontaine and Charles Kannengiesser. Paris: Beauchesne, 1972.

Bardy, Gustav. "Origène et la magie." *RSR* 18 (1928): 126–42.

Barnard, L. W. "Justin Martyr's Eschatology." *VC* 19 (1965): 86–98.

Barnes, Timothy David. *Tertullian: A Historical and Literary Study*. Oxford: Clarendon Press, 1971.

Brockmeier, Wilhelmine. *De Sancti Eustathii episcopi Antiocheni dicendi ratione*. Klassische Philologie. Bonn: Noske, 1932.

Brown, Peter. *Power and Persuasion in Late Antiquity: Towards a Christian Empire*. Madison: University of Wisconsin Press, 1992.

Cameron, Averil. *Christianity and the Rhetoric of Empire: The Development of Christian Discourse*. Sather Classical Lectures 55. Berkeley and Los Angeles: University of California Press, 1991.

Chadwick, Henry. "Origen, Celsus, and the Resurrection of the Body." *HTR* 41 (1948): 83–102.

Clark, Elizabeth A. *Reading Renunciation: Asceticism and Scripture in Early Christianity*. Princeton, N.J.: Princeton University Press, 1999.

Connor, Steven. *Dumbstruck: A Cultural History of Ventriloquism*. Oxford: Oxford University Press, 2000.

Cox, Patricia. "Origen and the Witch of Endor: Toward an Iconoclastic Typology." *AThR* 66 (1984): 137–47.

Crouzel, Henri. "L'exégèse origénienne de I Cor. 3, 11–15 et la purification eschatologique." Pages 273–83 in *Epektasis: Mélanges patristiques offerts au Cardinal Jean Daniélou*. Edited by Jacques Fontaine and Charles Kannengiesser. Paris: Beauchesne, 1972.

———. "L'Hadès et la Géhenne selon Origène." *Greg* 59 (1978): 291–329.

———. *Origen*. Translated by A.S. Worrall. Edinburgh: T&T Clark, 1989.

———. "Le thème platonicien du 'véhicule de l'âme' chez Origène." *Did* 7 (1977): 225–37.

Daley, Brian E. *The Hope of the Early Church: A Handbook of Patristic Eschatology*. Cambridge: Cambridge University Press, 1991.

Daniélou, Jean. *L'Être et le temps chez Grégoire de Nysse*. Leiden: Brill, 1970.

———. *Origen*. Translated by Walter Mitchell. London: Sheed & Ward, 1955.

———. *Platonisme et théologie mystique: Doctrine spirituelle de saint Grégoire de Nysse*. Paris: Aubier, 1944.

Dawson, John David. *Allegorical Readers and Cultural Revision in Ancient Alexandria*. Berkeley and Los Angeles: University of California Press, 1992.

———. *Christian Figural Reading and the Fashioning of Identity*. Berkeley and Los Angeles: University of California Press, 2002.

Dennis, T. J. "Gregory on the Resurrection of the Body." Pages 55–80 in *The Easter Sermons of Gregory of Nyssa*. Edited by Andreas Spira

and Christoph Klock. Patristic Monograph Series 9. Cambridge, Mass.: Philadelphia Patristic Foundation, 1981.

Dodds, E. R. *The Greeks and the Irrational*. Boston: Beacon, 1957.

Drobner, H. "Three Days and Three Nights in the Heart of the Earth: The Calculation of the Triduum Mortis according to Gregory of Nyssa." Pages 263–78 in *The Easter Sermons of Gregory of Nyssa*. Edited by Andreas Spira and Christoph Klock. Patristic Monograph Series 9. Cambridge, Mass.: Philadelphia Patristic Foundation, 1981.

Gangloff, Anne. "Mythes, fables et rhétorique à l'époque impériale." *Rhetorica* 20 (2002): 25–56.

Ginzberg, Louis. *The Legends of the Jews*. 7 vols. Philadelphia: Jewish Publication Society of America, 1909–38. Repr., Baltimore: Johns Hopkins University Press, 1998.

Goodenough, Erwin R. *The Theology of Justin Martyr*. Jena: Frommann, 1923. Repr., Amsterdam: Philo, 1968.

Grant, Robert M. *The Earliest Lives of Jesus*. New York: Harper & Brothers, 1961.

———. *Irenaeus of Lyons*. London: Routledge, 1997.

———. *The Letter and the Spirit*. London: SPCK, 1957.

———. *A Short History of the Interpretation of the Bible*. 2nd ed. with David Tracy. Philadelphia: Fortress, 1984.

Grillmeier, Aloys. "Der Gottessohn im Totenreich: Soteriologische und christologische Motivierung der Descensuslehre in der älteren christlichen Überlieferung." *ZKT* 71 (1949): 1–53, 184–203.

Hanson, R. P. C. *The Search for the Christian Doctrine of God*. Edinburgh: T&T Clark, 1988.

Kaster, Robert A. *Guardians of Language: The Grammarian and Society in Late Antiquity*. Berkeley and Los Angeles: University of California Press, 1988.

Kelly, J. N. D. *Early Christian Doctrines*. New York: Harper, 1958.

Kennedy, George A. *Classical Rhetoric and Its Christian and Secular Tradition from Ancient to Modern Times*. Chapel Hill: University of North Carolina Press, 1980.

Long, Anthony A. "Stoic Readings of Homer." Pages 41–66 in *Homer's Ancient Readers: The Hermeneutics of Greek Epic's Earliest Exegetes*. Edited by Robert Lamberton and John J. Keaney. Princeton, N.J.: Princeton University Press, 1992.

Mitchell, Margaret M. *The Heavenly Trumpet: John Chrysostom and the Art of Pauline Interpretation*. HUT 40. Tübingen: Mohr Siebeck, 2000; Louisville: Westminster John Knox, 2001.

———. "Reading Rhetoric with Patristic Exegetes: John Chrysostom on Galatians." Pages 333–56 in *Antiquity and Humanity: Essays on*

Ancient Religion and Philosophy Presented to Hans Dieter Betz on His Seventieth Birthday. Edited by Adela Yarbro Collins and Margaret M. Mitchell. Tübingen: Mohr Siebeck, 2001.

———. "Rhetorical Handbooks in Service of Biblical Exegesis: Eustathius of Antioch Takes Origen Back to School." Pages 349–67 in *The New Testament and Early Christian Literature in Greco-Roman Context: Studies in Honor of David E. Aune*. Edited by John Fotopoulos. NovTSup 122. Leiden: Brill, 2006.

Most, Glenn W. "Cornutus and Stoic Allegoresis: A Preliminary Report." *ANRW* 36.3:2014–65.

Nautin, Pierre. *Hippolyte et Josipe*. Paris: Cerf, 1947.

Neuschäfer, Bernhard. *Origenes als Philologe*. Schweizerische Beiträge zur Altertumswissenschaft 18/1–2. Basel: Reinhardt, 1987.

Norris, Richard A., Jr. *Manhood and Christ: A Study in the Christology of Theodore of Mopsuestia*. Oxford: Clarendon, 1963.

Ogden, Daniel. *Greek and Roman Necromancy*. Princeton, N.J.: Princeton University Press, 2001.

———. *Magic, Witchcraft and Ghosts in the Greek and Roman Worlds: A Sourcebook*. Oxford: Oxford University Press, 2002.

Patterson, Lloyd G. *Methodius of Olympus: Divine Sovereignty, Human Freedom, and Life in Christ*. Washington, D.C.: Catholic University of America Press, 1997.

Schäublin, Christoph. *Untersuchungen zu Methode und Herkunft der antiochenischen Exegese*. Theophania 23. Cologne-Bonn: Hanstein, 1974.

Schmidt, Brian B. *Israel's Beneficent Dead: Ancestor Cult and Necromancy in Ancient Israelite Religion and Tradition*. FAT 11. Tübingen: Mohr Siebeck, 1994.

———. "The 'Witch' of En-Dor, 1 Samuel 28, and Ancient Near Eastern Necromancy." Pages 111–29 in *Ancient Magic and Ritual Power*. Edited by Marvin W. Meyer and Paul A. Mirecki. Religions in the Greco-Roman World 129. Leiden: Brill, 1995.

Scott, Alan. *Origen and the Life of the Stars: A History of an Idea*. Oxford Early Christian Studies. Oxford: Clarendon, 1991.

Sellers, Robert V. *Eustathius of Antioch*. Cambridge: Cambridge University Press, 1928.

Sheerin, Daniel. "St. John the Baptist in the Lower World." *VC* 30 (1976): 1–22.

Simonetti, Manlio. *Biblical Interpretation in the Early Church: An Historical Introduction to Patristic Exegesis*. Translated by John A. Hughes. Edinburgh: T&T Clark, 1994.

Smelik, K. A. D. "The Witch of Endor: 1 Samuel 28 in Rabbinic and Christian Exegesis till 800 A.D." *VC* 33 (1979): 160–79.

Smith, Jonathan Z. "Towards Interpreting Demonic Powers in Hel-
    lenistic and Roman Antiquity." *ANRW* 16.1:425–39.
Spanneut, Michel. *Recherches sur les écrits d'Eustathe d'Antioche avec une
    édition nouvelle des fragments dogmatiques et exégétiques.* Lille: Fa-
    cultés Catholiques, 1948.
Spira, Andreas. "Der Descensus ad Inferos in der Osterpredigt Gre-
    gors von Nyssa *De Tridui Spatio*." Pages 195–261 in *The Easter
    Sermons of Gregory of Nyssa.* Edited by Andreas Spira and
    Christoph Klock. Patristic Monograph Series 9. Cambridge,
    Mass.: Philadelphia Patristic Foundation, 1981.
Tate, J. "The Beginnings of Greek Allegory." *Classical Review* 41 (1927):
    214–15.
———. "Cornutus and the Poets." *CQ* 23 (1929): 41–45.
———. "On the History of Allegorism." *CQ* 24 (1930): 1–10.
Trencsényi-Waldapfel, Imre. "Die Hexe von Endor und die griechisch-
    römische Welt." *Acta orientalia academiae scientiarum Hungaricae*
    11 (1960): 201–22.
Trigg, Joseph W. "Eustathius of Antioch's Attack on Origen." *JR* 75
    (1995): 219–38.
———. *Origen: The Bible and Philosophy in the Third-Century Church.*
    Atlanta: John Knox Press, 1983.
Tropper, Josef. *Nekromantie: Totenbefragung im Alten Orient und Alten
    Testament.* AOAT 223. Neukirchen-Vlyn: Neukirchener, 1989.
Vogels, Heinz-Jürgen. *Christi Abstieg ins Totenreich und das Läuterungs-
    gericht an den Toten.* Freiburg: Herder, 1976.
Wilken, Robert L. *John Chrysostom and the Jews: Rhetoric and Reality in
    the Late Fourth Century.* The Transformation of the Classical Her-
    itage 4. Berkeley and Los Angeles: University of California Press,
    1983.
Winden, J. C. M. van. *An Early Christian Philosopher: Justin Martyr's
    Dialogue with Trypho, Chapters One to Nine.* Philosophia patrum
    1. Leiden: Brill, 1971.
Young, Frances. *The Art of Performance: Towards a Theology of Holy
    Scripture.* London: Darton, Longman, & Todd, 1990.
———. *Biblical Exegesis and the Formation of Christian Culture.* Cam-
    bridge: Cambridge University Press, 1997. Repr., Peabody, Mass.:
    Hendrikson, 2002.
———. "The Rhetorical Schools and Their Influence on Patristic Ex-
    egesis." Pages 182–99 in *The Making of Orthodoxy: Essays in
    Honour of Henry Chadwick.* Edited by Rowan Williams. Cam-
    bridge: Cambridge University Press, 1989.

Index of Biblical References

Note that the references to the Old Testament and the Apocrypha are to the Septuagint and that the arabic page numbers refer to the English translations of the primary texts.

APOCRYPHAL / DEUTEROCANONICAL BOOKS

NEW TESTAMENT

Printed in the United States
83102LV00003B/28-78/A

9 781589 831209